Taking to the Streets

The Transformation of Arab Activism

EDITED BY LINA KHATIB *and* ELLEN LUST

Johns Hopkins University Press

Baltimore

Johns Hopkins University Press
2715 North Charles Street
Baltimore, Maryland 21218-4363
www.press.jhu.edu

Library of Congress Cataloging-in-Publication Data
Taking to the streets : the transformation of Arab activism / edited by Lina Khatib and Ellen Lust.
    pages cm
  Includes bibliographical references and index.
  ISBN-13: 978-1-4214-1311-2 (hardcover : alk. paper)
  ISBN-13: 978-1-4214-1312-9 (pbk. : alk. paper)
  ISBN-13: 978-1-4214-1313-6 (electronic)
  ISBN-10: 1-4214-1311-6 (hardcover : alk. paper)
  ISBN-10: 1-4214-1312-4 (pbk. : alk. paper)
  ISBN-10: 1-4214-1313-2 (electronic)
  1. Arab countries—Politics and government—21st century.   2. Arab Spring, 2010–
3. Protest movements—Arab countries.   4. Social movements—Arab countries.
5. Revolution—Arab countries.   6. Democratization—Arab countries.   I. Khatib, Lina
(Lina H.), editor of compilation.   II. Lust, Ellen, editor of compilation.
  JQ1850.A91T343 2014
  322.40917'4927—dc23   2013027752

A catalog record for this book is available from the British Library.

Special discounts are available for bulk purchases of this book. For more information, please contact Special Sales at 410-516-6936 or specialsales@press.jhu.edu.

CONTENTS

FOREWORD

HICHAM BEN ABDALLAH EL ALAOUI

T HE PRESENT VOLUME'S genesis was a conference held at Stanford University in the spring of 2011 under the auspices of the Arab Reform and Democracy (ARD) program housed in the Center on Democracy, Development, and Rule of Law, a constituent element of the Freeman Spogli Institute for International Studies. Since its inception in the fall of 2009, ARD's community of scholars has taken particular pride in the program's forward-looking perspective. Whereas many social scientists were accustomed to studying the singular question of the persistent authoritarianism in the Arab world, our intellectual inclination was tilted toward studying the more ineluctable advent of pluralism across the region, as symbolized by the very name of the program.

This conference was the second annual meeting held by the ARD program. What began as an adventurous path proved to be premonitory with the crystallization of the Arab Spring. Consistent with the underlying philosophy of the program, the conference generated a rich set of papers that combined different perspectives—scholars and activists, Westerners and Arabs, regional analysts and country specialists—which combined to propel an ongoing debate. The present volume unifies a careful selection of those presented papers and others, which, taken together, span the diversity of a region now being reshaped by the Arab Spring. In some countries, political change was abrupt and unexpected; in others, it has been subtle and ongoing; in still others, gradual pressures are building for a sudden breakthrough.

The volume demonstrates articulately how Tunisia was undergoing considerable political contestation behind an autocratic facade that projected institutional stability, economic growth, and middle-class affluence. It was a great irony that the Arab Spring ignited in this county, where many expected it the least. The roots of the revolt can be traced to different labor protest movements culminating in the Gafsa riots; concurrently, students and civil society activists protested in the capital of Tunis. Though initially isolated and partial, these episodes eventually converged into a revolutionary dynamic that ultimately toppled the regime.

Farther east, in Egypt, a similar pattern of contentious politics emerged. There, an unprecedented wave of labor unrest collided with the resurgent demands of Egyptian youth. While all had grown tired of the false promises for reform, in this case the youth movements became the apparent face of this national revolt. Liberation technology—that is, social networks—served as vital tools of mobilization. Whereas in Tunisia the hermetically sealed character of the authoritarian regime gave these tools the power to propagate bold ideas, in Egypt it was the decay of the old dictatorship that fueled these new forms of activism.

Libya's political moment revealed distinctive differences but also common denominators with other contexts of change. As in Tunisia and Egypt, the nepotism and brutality of the regime had become a source of much anger within the populace. Yet unlike in the other cases, the autocratic regime's weakly institutionalized nature permitted it to respond with blunt violence. The disorganization of the coercive apparatus and the absence of a professional standing army revealed a leadership solely reliant upon foreign militias and marauding thugs. This situation precipitated another novelty—the military intervention of the outside world at the request of the Arab League. Such external intervention facilitated the overthrow of the Qaddafi regime; whether this would have been possible without it remains an open question, and at the very least the conflict would have been protracted.

The Yemeni case provides yet another variation of national political change. As in Egypt, the youth spearheaded the opposition against the regime, but several local dynamics also contributed to this political churning prior to the moment of rupture: the enduring saliency of the north-south divide, the conflict with the Houthis, and the low-intensity insurgency by Al-Qaeda in the Arabian Peninsula. The latter two factors created an open pathway for geopolitical interference into the internal dynamics of the country, which led to a shallow resolution between the opposition and the state that resulted in the replacement of the old autocratic symbols with more acceptable political figureheads. Whether this will generate a real political transformation remains to be seen.

Elsewhere in the region, preexisting ethnic cleavages transformed movements for change into bloody showdowns between stubborn autocrats and the popular opposition. In Bahrain, a historically aggrieved Shia majority found itself emboldened to call for economic and political parity with the ruling elite. Such demands reflected a deeper desire to convert the existing authoritarian dynasty into a constitutional monarchy, one that allowed for equal participation and meaningful competition for all. The opposition also mimicked mobilization strategies elsewhere by occupying the largest public spaces endowed by Manama's city planners. Fearing the reproduction of another Tahrir Square, the government dispersed the protesters with force, but the ensuing cascade of antiregime demonstrations provoked military intervention by Gulf Cooperation Council forces. This is yet another eloquent expression that, unlike the iconic Third Wave of Democracy, the 1974–1999 period in which more than sixty autocratic regimes around the world democratized, the Arab Spring has been heavily influenced by a variety of external factors.

Reinforcing this argument is the tragic case of Syria, where again a nonviolent protest against the regime turned into a violent confrontation with a sectarian dimension. Here, the opposition directed longstanding demands for change at an ossified Arab nationalist regime, which used the facade of the Baath Party as a legitimizing force to perpetuate dictatorship by the Assad clan embedded within a larger clique of cronies. Lacking any framework for cooptation and integration and frightened by the Libyan precedent, the regime clumsily deployed disproportionate force against its unarmed protesters. Like the preceding cases, the opposition reflected vibrant youth movements, but unlike their counterparts elsewhere in the Arab world, most hailed from the provincial hinterlands rather than the metropolitan urban center. The regime initially gained the upper hand but was unable to extirpate the protests. Village defense committees evolved into armed rebel insurgencies, a process facilitated by defections from the regular army. This domestic conflict in turn fed a regional geopolitical drama that pitted the so-called radical Shiite camp of Syria, Iran, and Hezbollah against the moderate pro-Sunni side of Saudi Arabia, the Gulf, and their Western allies. What began as a local problem has strengthened divisive geopolitical considerations that have now become hegemonic.

Nowhere do these geopolitical fears dampen indigenous demands for political reform more strongly than in Saudi Arabia, where the specter of regional competition with Iran exerts a palpable shadow on political discussion. A supplementary factor in this equation is the enormous oil resources injected into the economy by the state to finance new development projects, generous welfare programs, and various social subsidies designed to quell public demands for change—but for how long remains the operative question.

This is clearly not the case with the tiny neighboring emirate of Kuwait, where the Arab Spring has accelerated and amplified preexisting patterns of social opposition and political uncertainty that have put the ruling Al-Sabah family at odds with many sectors of society. For decades, Kuwait has nurtured a genuine, if limited, brand of parliamentary politics that has given voice to many contentious elements in society. The present conjuncture has given organized opposition forces inroads into the political system. Though diverse, the demands boil down to a single issue: whether the emir will relinquish his management of government to somebody outside the royal family who can exercise real authority and stand accountable to parliament. Given the historical nature of such contention, more than in any other Gulf state a meaningful breakthrough in Kuwait seems within reach. In turn, the possibility of democratic change here can shape the trajectory of the other Gulf states, although they share common characteristics—tiny native populations, large expatriate worker communities, and vast hydrocarbon riches—that mitigate pressures to democratize.

While the possibility for the status quo to be sustained may be prevalent in these Gulf monarchies, their larger royal counterparts face a different situation. In Jordan, a regime that lacks access to either oil or water and has long depended on Western support now faces its moment of truth. The longstanding Islamist opposition wishes to maintain the monarchy because its collapse would give instant credence to the alternative homeland project long fronted by the Israeli Right. Yet their ambition to implement their vision of reform confronts the absolutist reality of the monarchy. In a sense, this has been the more predictable element influencing Jordanian politics. The real surprise emanates from the monarchy's social bedrock, the Bedouin and tribal community. For various economic and social reasons, tribal Jordanians have also joined the panoply of voices desiring reform within the kingdom. The regime's response to such demands has been timid and lukewarm, characterized more by frantic cabinet shuffles and superficial constitutional amendments than an authentic process to build a new political order.

Analogous circumstances are unfolding in Morocco. There, the process of contestation was initiated by the February 20 youth movement, which vocally articulated the demands for accountable governance and an end to corruption. The protests mobilized large sectors of Moroccan society. Unlike Jordan, however, the Moroccan regime has been able to preempt the popular challenge by announcing constitutional reforms and then holding early elections. The reforms, which did not divert real power from the monarchy to parliament, were welcomed by most political actors as a step forward. The ensuing government has been led by a parliamentary coalition headlined by the moderate

Islamist PJD Party, but its lack of real power has allowed old patterns of autocracy to reassert themselves, heralding a return to the status quo. Impatience with the monarchy and exploding social demands are giving birth to routinized general protests. It is unrealistic to believe that these will not ultimately coalesce into a united national movement for change. Although the Moroccan political system has shown an aptitude for managing specific and limited challenges thanks to the depth of state institutions and the capacity of the monarchy to coopt opponents, it remains to be seen whether it can withstand the pressure of a sustained popular challenge from below.

The initial phases of the Arab Spring offer tentative conclusions worth pondering. First, most of the movements that led to political breakthroughs have not heralded social revolutions, have not completely transformed state and society; in this sense, they are better considered "successful political insurrections." As a result, large segments of the old authoritarian orders have escaped unscathed, and their attempts to reconstitute themselves in a coherent and countervailing way have become apparent in many of these instances. They are nonetheless kept in check by the persistence of contentious politics; Tunisia and Egypt furnish the best examples.

Second, the youth groups that triggered these rebellious episodes have been unable to reap the dividends of their success. The principal reason for this irony is their preference for remaining informal, leaderless movements. The absence of organizational structure, strategic planning, and coalition building has made it possible for competing forces to occupy the political void left by the abdicating regimes. Their reification of liberation technology underlines the same strength and weakness. Social media and online networks have proven extremely useful in confronting autocrats at the moment of confrontation but are ineffective at sustaining long-term political commitment after the exit of the old regime. This reinforces a universal reality that runs throughout the history of social movements: internal organization, territorial reach, and strategic preparation are indispensable elements for the construction of a viable alternative political system.

Third, the geopolitical dimension is playing a far larger role in shaping the outcomes of the Arab Spring than in previous waves of regional transformation in other geographic settings. To this effect, the range of external interventions into domestic political struggles has varied greatly. In the most benign instances, institutional actors, such as the monarchies of Morocco and Jordan, leveraged their support from Western powers like the United States and

France to bolster their perceived standing. At the other end of the spectrum, one finds outright military involvement by outside forces, of which the most representative examples are Bahrain, Libya, and Syria.

In sum, the Arab Spring encompasses a complex process of regional change involving multiple actors in different national contexts. The interplay between political forces—domestic and international, authoritarian and democratic, religious and secular, young and old—will be dynamic and unpredictable and contingent on the structural conditions facing each country. Yet one thing is sure: the status quo has been ruptured. The era of the old authoritarian model is decisively over.

ACKNOWLEDGMENTS

THIS BOOK IS the first edited collection produced by the Program on Arab Reform and Democracy at Stanford University. The program launched one year before the Arab Spring, and the study of how political activism could lead to democratic change has been a key concern for the program from the start. It was the theme of the program's second annual conference, which took place in May 2011, and that, in turn, sparked the creation of this book. The conference was conceptualized and planned before the Arab Spring, and the uprisings of 2011 simply affirmed the importance of its research focus—the transformation of activism in the Arab world—in the context not just of countries in transition but also of those countries that appear to witness little political activism and are therefore perceived as more "stable."

The editors thank all of the authors who have contributed to this book, especially the Arab activists who have shared their firsthand experiences and analyses. We also thank the Moulay Hicham Foundation under the leadership of Prince Hicham Ben Abdallah al-Alaoui for its vision and generous support of the Program on Arab Reform and Democracy. We are also grateful to Larry Diamond for his enthusiasm, insights, and assistance and to Suzanne Flinchbaugh at Johns Hopkins University Press for her belief in this book.

We would also like to extend our gratitude to Tabitha Decker, Stephan Okar, Fatima Malik, Danny Buerkli, Klara Chlupata, Nura Suleiman, Fadi El Khatib, and Miriam Wakim for their research assistance; Annette Mullaney for her excellent conference notes; and Sean Yom and Dina Matar for their help and support.

Taking to the Streets

Reconsidering Activism in the Arab World

Arab Uprisings and Beyond

LINA KHATIB *and* ELLEN LUST

THE STORYLINE OF THE Arab Spring is by now well known. On December 17, 2010, in Tunisia's underprivileged interior city of Sidi Bouzid, a downtrodden fruit-seller, Mohamed Bouazizi, having been fundamentally offended by a policewoman in the city's marketplace, set himself ablaze in response. This sparked the outrage of fellow Tunisians, many—like him—youth who remained un- or underemployed while the lucky few who ran the country's sluggish economy enriched themselves. Angry mobs took to the streets; protests escalated across the country; and on January 14, Tunisia's president Zine El Abidine Ben Ali fled to Saudi Arabia. The abrupt end to more than two decades of rule in a seemingly unshakable regime sparked the imagination of Arabs across the region. If change was possible in Tunisia, could it happen at home as well?

The uprisings spread across the region to varying degrees and with diverse effects, leading to speculation about why an apparently dormant region seemed to erupt overnight. The narrative was based on a number of assumptions. First, the uprisings were seen as unprecedented, not only in scale and effect but also in the willingness of citizens to engage in public protest to repress brutal regimes.[1] Some students of Arab politics recognized increasing mobilization as early warning signs to the regimes,[2] but to many observers, political activism in the region had gone from zero to a hundred nearly overnight.[3] Second, the

I

uprisings were perceived as having been made possible because disgruntled, unemployed youth used Facebook, Twitter, text messages, and other social networking tools to take to the streets. It was the combination of unemployed youth and technology—the narrative went—that mobilized and sustained the protests.[4] Third, the uprisings appeared to be a spontaneous outpouring of angry people fed up with brutal dictatorships. They lacked leadership and strategy but were unified in their demands to end the regime.[5]

Yet, to what extent does this storyline match reality? Did the Arab Spring truly emerge from nowhere? Was it driven by tech-savvy, disgruntled youth? And what was the nature of activism in the Arab world, before, during, and after the year that shook the Arab world? How did the uprisings that spread in 2011 affect activism in the region, shaping activist goals and strategies?

This book explores these questions with three tasks in mind. First, bringing together scholars and activists, it presents an in-depth look at the uprisings as they were experienced in ten Arab countries, spanning from Morocco to Saudi Arabia. It provides insight into the unprecedented outpourings that have intrigued scholars, policymakers, and observers across the world. Second, it critically examines the conventional narrative, determining the extent to which the common assumptions hold true. Third, it seeks to understand how the massive outpourings in 2011 shaped political activism, both by changing the political landscape and providing a valuable template that activists elsewhere could use.

Exploring this not only helps us make sense of the road ahead, it also sheds light on activism and social mobilization more generally. First, it clearly demonstrates the importance of focusing on the full range of activism in both the formal and informal structures. The conventional focus of scholars and policymakers on civil society organizations and social movements has tended to overlook the importance of activism taking place far outside these formal institutions in the informal—and often transnational—sphere.[6] So, too, a focus only on the informal or everyday resistance is only half-satisfying; it misses the important intersection of activism in the formal and informal spheres, which became strikingly salient in the 2011 uprisings. This interaction had been taking place since well before the Arab revolutions of 2011, forming part of what can be termed a "revolutionary infrastructure."[7] Second, the studies that follow in this volume remind us of the fluid, constantly changing nature of activism. Activists' relations with each other and the state constantly evolve; they innovate new strategies and change their demands. This is true even in authoritarian regimes, which may on the surface appear stagnant.[8] It is even more true after the Arab uprisings, for the uprisings themselves—and the political changes that result from them—create both new opportunities and new challenges for activists. Indeed, even as scholars and policymakers seek to make sense of the conditions that led to the uprisings in 2011, they also need to recognize that the political ruptures of that year have had a profound effect on the nature and level of activism in the years that followed.

Origins of the Arab Spring

Political activism in the Arab world reached unprecedented heights in 2011, with sometimes dramatic results, but in contrast to conventional wisdom, it was not entirely new. Citizens ruled by even the most repressive dictatorships engaged in activities that challenged the regime and, as the chapters in this volume point out, had been doing so with increasing frequency and intensity in the decade leading up to 2011. Far from passively accepting their economic and political conditions, many persistently pushed boundaries—often focusing on what Pippa Norris has termed "cause-oriented" activism related to specific issues or interests.[9] That these activities were largely overlooked was due to the failure to consider the importance of both formal and informal activism and to the stereotypes of the region as stagnant and repressive that blinded scholars and policymakers to the important changes taking place. Michelle Pace and Francesco Cavatorta rightly point out that before the Arab Spring, the scholarly community was too focused on analyses of the state and of elites to pay proper attention to the changes occurring within the broader society.[10]

The chapters in this book demonstrate a wide range of activism before the uprisings of 2011.[11] In Tunisia, miners had been taking to the streets of Gafsa since 2003 to demand better working conditions, while in Egypt, the Youth for Change movement—Kifaya—formed in 2005 to push the boundaries of electoral politics, and the April 6 movement put unprecedented pressure on the regime for labor reform.[12] Activism was not limited to those countries that ultimately pushed leaders from power. In countries like Jordan, Morocco, and Syria, activists also mobilized to make their demands known.

Where and how they mobilized varied, partly in response to different political environments (or political opportunity structures) and social organizations.[13] Scholars have increasingly pointed out that what constitutes the political space for mobilization may vary widely; as Joel Beinin has convincingly argued, the salient factors of what are often viewed as institutional structures are the *perceptions* of opportunities and threats.[14] Such perceptions are related to the existence of underlying social networks that can be used to mitigate costs and sustain collective activity.[15] As some of the contributions in this volume show, in countries where political mobilization was particularly restricted, activists turned to the social milieu to make demands. For example, in Bahrain, where political parties are banned, Shia religious organizations became a space where scholars gathered and formed the nuclei of "political societies." In Syria, where the regime tightly controlled political activity, activists mobilized around social issues in lieu of direct political action. In Tunisia, activists took up scattered, localized protests, mainly in rural areas, as the regime clamped down on more organized activities. In Yemen, on the other hand, which was more politically open, activists used civil society and opposition political parties to press for demands.

Diasporas also played a key role in political activism, particularly in the most repressive political regimes. In Tunisia, Libya, and Syria, organized activism was relegated to groups that established themselves in Paris, London, or Washington.[16] The groups played an important role in highlighting the political repression within the country and providing some activists an exit option when their condition inside the country became unsustainable.

That domestic activism frequently played out in unexpected places and that the linkages between diaspora groups and domestic activists were often weak and unstable led many to overlook the increasing mobilization taking place across the region. In Syria, the seemingly nonpolitical nature of the activism within cultural circles and civil society masked a move toward outright politicization, while in Tunisia, the remoteness and the informality of rural protests blinded onlookers to the growing patterns of cooperation among different segments of society as well as to the existence of expressions of political dissent. It is precisely because of the informal nature of the activism that countries like Tunisia, Syria, and Libya appeared to be politically inert.

The Evolution of Activism

Political activism was not only evident across the Arab world, it was also constantly evolving. The notion that politics in the region was stagnant (or that political participation is absent or stagnant in authoritarian regimes in general) is highly misleading. Particularly in the decade leading up to the Arab Spring, the actors and their demands and strategies took new forms, depending in part on changing political opportunity structures that allowed activists to capitalize on external factors to empower their work. So, too, the Arab uprisings themselves influenced activism, bringing new actors into the fray, changing the relationships among activists as well as between these actors and the state, creating new demands.

Actors and Venues of Activism

In the decade before the Arab Spring, the locus of activism began to shift from the formal venues of "old" opposition parties and civil society groups to more amorphous, often transnationally linked social movements and organizations.[17] The concern that civil society organizations were counterproductive to political engagement was only partly borne out.[18] It was true that in countries like Syria, where political parties were effectively banned, civil society organizations came to fill the gap. Often, however, rather than turn to formal civil society organizations to play this role, activists increasingly established new, less formal groups through which they expressed their views and made demands, while other citizens mobilized outside of formal institutions altogether.

In countries like Egypt, Yemen, and Bahrain, social movements began to arise, playing a critical role in mobilization. The April 6 movement in Egypt is perhaps the best known of such movements. As Rabab El-Mahdi explains in chapter 2 of this book, the movement was formed in 2008 by an activist from Youth for Change—itself one of the first groups to organize along demographic lines (rather than class-based, ideological, or regional ones)—in commemoration of the April 6 textile strikes in Mahalla, and it played a major role in mobilizing prodemocracy demonstrations.

Social movements were not alone. Beyond institutionalized politics and the politics of "groups," the Arab world was rich in informal political activity on the level of individual citizens, what Asef Bayat calls "non-movements."[19] Non-movements resisted state oppression quietly, creating support networks for citizens that eventually formed an activist infrastructure that played a key role in the Arab Spring.

Youth played an increasingly important role in these new movements, coming to the fore particularly after the Arab Spring.[20] Through online activity as well as offline networks, youth had long formed a significant proportion of members of "non-movements," but much like these phenomena, they were often ignored or not taken seriously as political actors and agents in their societies.[21] One of the major changes in the Arab world during the Arab Spring was the emergence of the youth as prominent activists across the region.

In some cases, youth previously seen as "apolitical" eventually became leading forces. This was the case in Syria, for example, where leftist parties and groups had led the opposition under the Assad regime; in 2011, such groups gave way to new, younger voices emerging from civil society and intellectual circles previously unaffiliated with the "old opposition." Similarly, in Morocco, the February 20 movement that emerged in 2011 was born out of informal networks of secular youth who had engaged in online activism calling for individual freedoms. In Egypt, the youth football fans known as "Ultras" played a critical role in the January 25 Revolution demonstrations, even though their affiliation was not political but social. Their unity during the Revolution was firmly based on their sense of identity and their organizational hierarchy and rules—qualities that proved useful during the regime crackdowns on the protesters in Tahrir Square.

In other cases, the youth that played leading roles in the 2011 uprisings had more political experience going in. Youth had long been in the ranks of Yemeni opposition parties, but during the 2011 uprising they came to play an independent role, no longer directed by party leaders in their action against the Ali Abdallah Saleh regime. In Egypt, the youth behind the April 6 movement and the "We are all Khaled Said" Facebook group were the primary catalysts of the January 25 Revolution. Those youth had found a voice and presence with the start of the Kifaya movement in 2005, which saw the creation of loose activist networks outside of the remit of the old opposition parties like al-Wafd that had negotiated with the regime, and who merged social activism with political demands.

Women also became increasingly prominent. As Intissar Rajabany and Lihi Ben Shitrit discuss in their chapter in this book, authoritarian regimes have often seen women as less threatening and thus granted them more room to mobilize politically. In Libya, the Abu Salim prison protests that sparked the February 17 Revolution were coordinated and led by women—mothers and relatives of Libyans who had been detained in the prison and killed—and were only the latest in a series of similar women-led protests that had been gaining in momentum over the years. In Kuwait, women's groups have been pioneers in coordinating activist strategies like sit-ins, marches, petitions, conferences, and media dissemination that inspired other activist groups in the country. In Yemen, women have been active in civil society for a number of years and have also engaged in political debates in religious discussion groups. During the 2011 uprising, not only did women participate in the demonstrations, they led them as well. Perhaps most notable was Tawakkol Karman, a journalist, activist, and member of the Al-Islah Party who led several demonstrations against the Saleh regime prior to 2011 and continued to lead calls for political reform in Yemen. She won the Nobel Peace Prize in 2011.

Finally, in several countries, the role of diaspora communities became even more important in the ongoing struggle. This is not entirely surprising, as diasporas have long been recognized for playing a number of political roles aimed at changing politics in their homelands, from providing material support to pressuring the foreign policies of their host countries.[22] From Tunisia and Libya to Syria and Bahrain, activists abroad engaged in a number of activities: lobbying the international community, providing logistical aid to local activists, and spreading information about opposition actions and regime responses through the international media. As discussed earlier, diaspora activities took place well before the 2011 uprisings, but during the Arab uprisings, the community often took on new roles, providing critical support to the on-the-ground action. After the fall of the authoritarian regimes in Tunisia, Egypt, and Libya, some activists in the diaspora community also moved back to their countries to play a more direct role in rebuilding their nations and participating in politics, with several such activists running for elections or establishing new political parties and civil society organizations.

In contrast to the youth, women, and diaspora communities, the old opposition groups were left behind, highlighting the importance of activists outside the easily identifiable formal civil society and political parties that traditionally receive attention. Many joined the uprisings late; Islamist groups in Tunisia, Egypt, and Syria initially sat on the sidelines, choosing to hedge their bets before finally taking part. In Bahrain, the main opposition political society, al-Wefaq, had been so thoroughly coopted by the regime that it never participated in the 2011 uprising. In Yemen, opposition parties had been well established, and their members did take to the streets, but they did not lead the protests. A similar dynamic occurred in Morocco. There, the Moroccan Association for Human Rights (AMDH) and the Democratic Alliance for the Left (DAL) issued a joint communiqué supporting the planned February 20 protest on the day that lent the movement its name, but they chose not to lead the protest and later halted their cooperation with the February 20 youth altogether.

Importantly, it was not the ascendance of any particular actor or group but rather the coming together of different members of society, whether consciously or not, that explains the success of the 2011 uprisings. Tunisia, Egypt, Libya, and Yemen were notable in this regard. In Tunisia, the engagement of broad sections of society was partly a legacy inherited from earlier rights-based protests in rural areas that youth online activists in cities had chosen to support, but it was also somewhat accidental. Different socioeconomic classes in Tunisia poured into the streets with their own grievances, ranging from calls for bread to calls for dignity, but in the process of mobilization, their diffuse goals fused into one common demand: the fall of the regime. In Egypt, the January 25 demonstrations saw participation by citizens from different classes, social backgrounds, and political leanings. In Libya, too, the Revolution involved both a wide range of citizens as well as activists in the diaspora, and it began to succeed only when cooperation between the eastern and western areas in the country took place, and in Yemen, the street protests saw the formation of coalitions among youth from different parties and backgrounds.

Activist Methods

Such coordination was not entirely new, nor was it entirely accidental. Activists' methods of mobilization had evolved over time and across the region, and in the process, they had increasingly built bridges across political groups that had previously been divided. This was in part the result of an evolution in the tactics used and organizational structures employed.[23]

Activists made a number of tactical innovations in the decade leading up to 2011. The most notable was the increasing use of online and offline activism in countries such as Tunisia, Egypt, and Yemen, where activists used these forms of mobilization simultaneously or used one form to support the other. There was also the expansion of subtle methods of criticism, as in Syria, where artists, intellectuals, and other members of the country's cultural sphere used humor to air their grievances. Such tools eventually played a key role in the nonviolent protests in the Syrian uprising of 2011.

The emergence of new, loosely connected, amorphous organizational structures, such as in Egypt, also spurred the uprisings. Mobilization against social, economic, and political grievances (from the U.S. invasion of Iraq to the Israeli attack on Gaza in 2008/2009 to the torture of political detainees to strikes for workers' rights) created new activist groups that became the basis for the mobilized citizens of the January 25 Revolution. Similarly, in Morocco, civil society activity had been decentralized since the 1990s, when local coordinating committees were established in different regions to allow activists to demand economic and social reform. This decentralization provided the infrastructure for the different February 20 groups that emerged across the country in 2011.[24]

Such affinities also helped to bridge divides that often characterized the traditional political parties and their associated civil society organizations. For example, in Egypt, the youth movement that catalyzed the revolution took deliberate steps to mobilize diverse segments of society. Since 2008, the April 6 movement had supported worker strikes, using online and offline methods to mobilize people. After years of trial and error, these youth realized that successful street mobilization required reaching out beyond their familiar circles. Their efforts were strengthened by increasing cooperation between Islamist and secular groups before the January 25 Revolution, from a joint campaign to release political prisoners after the rise of Kifaya in 2005 to efforts in late 2010 to boycott the second round of Egyptian parliamentary elections and then form a shadow government. Those experiences strengthened social ties across diverse groups and provided momentum for the January 25 Revolution.

A commitment to nonviolence, which had also emerged in the years leading up to 2011, played an important role in the uprisings.[25] The roots of this approach could be clearly seen in Egypt through the cultural sphere as well as youth activism and in Yemen through the nonviolent actions of the southern al-Hirak movement. But it became even more apparent in the 2011 uprisings, when activists self-consciously and publicly declared a commitment to peace, proclaiming calls of *silmiyya* (peaceful). This was the case in Syria, even as regime forces fired at protesters. Many believed the only way to gain the moral upper hand (and national and international support) was to maintain a nonviolent approach. Such commitment to nonviolence and demonstrated self-sacrifice are an important part of what Sidney Tarrow and Charles Tilly call "public self-representation," in which contenders (particularly the opposition) try to garner public support by presenting a sense of worthiness, unity, support, and commitment.[26]

At times, the opposition took advantage of the regime's own desire to secure a clean image to press its demands. For example, in Tunisia, before the Jasmine Revolution, activists learned to play on the regime's "modern" image by organizing public protests in which women participated prominently, knowing that any crackdown on those protests would tarnish the regime's carefully constructed pro-women image aimed at the West.

Many of the actions that activists engaged in—or, what social movement theorists call the "repertoires of collective action"—were not new.[27] Some had been firmly established for generations. Civil disobedience, mainly in the form of strikes, was an established method used by activists well before the uprisings.

Traditional cultural practices also had come to play a role in mobilization and continued to do so in the uprisings, with qat chew circles in Yemen and *diwaniyyas* (salons, or gatherings) in Kuwait having been venues for political debate for several decades.[28]

Yet, during the Arab Spring, activists in different countries also quickly innovated new methods in response to the changing circumstances. Syria saw the establishment of "*tanseeqiat,*" local coordination committees, during the 2011–12 revolution as well as the emergence of a cadre of video activists who used amateur videos posted to YouTube as a way to call attention to their cause and challenge the regime. In Libya, even looser citizen committees coordinated activist actions in individual areas, distributing aid and protecting neighborhoods from regime violence. And in Egypt, activists used the newscasts of satellite TV stations such as Al Jazeera to announce upcoming demonstrations, thereby broadcasting messages to supporters across the country.

New tactics often spread across the region, whether via active communication across regional networks or the demonstration effect.[29] Perhaps the signature tactic became the turnout of large demonstrations in public squares, with shouts of "*ashaab yurid isqat an-nitham*" ("the people want the fall of the regime") echoing across the region. This slogan, and variations on it, came to represent the people's determination to emulate the change that had first occurred in Tunisia.

Of course, opposition activists were not always united in their efforts. Divisions among activists were a major weakness for opposition members both before and during the uprisings. In Syria, not only were different opposition groups divided on the subject of international intervention, but they were also divided over the wisdom of negotiating with the regime, over strategies, and over the question of who actually represented the Syrian population. The two main opposition groups that emerged during the revolution, the SNC and the NCC, also failed to reach out to all Syrians and thus did not succeed in carving wide credibility on the ground. In Jordan, the division between Palestinians and Transjordanians meant that public action could not reach the necessary critical mass to force the demands to be consolidated and escalated. Regime strategies contributed to these divisions. In Bahrain, al-Wefaq's cooptation meant that it never took part in the 2011 uprising, while monetary handouts to citizens—a strategy used in Saudi Arabia as well—succeeded in quelling a good number of grievances.

Activist Demands

Indeed, activists' demands were not uniform across the region; however, in the period leading up to and including 2011 they did change in predictable ways. Before 2011, the main change in activism was the rise of issue-based demands, which increasingly replaced demands based on ideological differences.[30] The vast majority of these demands were economic, with strikes and demonstrations for better wages and working conditions becoming increasingly common. Anger at foreign policy positions also played a role. Demonstrations against the U.S. invasion of Iraq in 2003—and before it the Palestinian intifada in 2000—not only voiced popular opposition but also domestic discontent; such events provided activists with a "legitimate" pretext to organize pro-Iraq/Palestine demonstrations that were then used to voice antiregime sentiments. Perhaps most important, these occasions gave activists from different political factions a chance to practice collaboration, paving the way for the creation of movements like Kifaya.

After 2011, the demands became increasingly pointed. The demands differed across the region—ranging from equal rights for Shiite groups in Saudi Arabia and Bahrain to political and economic reform in Morocco and Jordan and finally to regime change in Tunisia, Egypt, Libya, Yemen, and Syria. Yet in each case the calls for change had become more strident and all-encompassing than ever before. Those calling for economic equality stood side by side with those advocating a broader notion of "dignity" (*karama*) or, even more brazenly, an end to the regime.

Political Opportunity Structures and Mobilization

Changes in the sociopolitical environment—or what is called "political opportunity structures"—partly fostered the emergence of new movements and the change in demands.[31] As noted above, regional events such as the U.S. invasion of Iraq in 2003 provided activists with an opportunity to mobilize. So too in Kuwait, the invasion by Iraq catalyzed the formation of organized human rights and civil society groups that later protested government corruption. As discussed earlier, mobilization around regional events allowed people to explore their commonalities and differences in a "non-explosive" environment, as Rabab El-Mahdi argues in chapter 2 in this book. The nature of regime repression also affected mobilization, although not in predictable ways. Eitan

Alimi argues that threat is an important factor spurring collective action.[32] The classic argument is that inconsistent repression can increase dissent, while consistent repression is more successful at quelling dissent.[33] However, the variety of reactions to regime responses during the Arab Spring (for example, consistent repression in Syria did not quell the rebellion there, while it largely did in Bahrain) complicates this argument.

One factor behind this complication is the international dimension. International forces influenced activists' mobilization and the outcomes they achieved more directly as well.[34] The international community's action against the Qaddafi regime in 2011 only strengthened the protests on the ground and contributed to the downfall of the regime. The intervention also influenced unrest in Syria, although with more ambiguous effect. Many Syrian activists argue that the lack of strong international intervention there hindered their progress, while other Syrian activists vehemently opposed any form of foreign military intervention. In Yemen, the Gulf Cooperation Council Initiative that ended the 2011 uprising through offering a deal to former president Saleh had a mixed reaction, with some activists welcoming it and others seeing it as halting the progress of the revolution. Perhaps most notably, the GCC's intervention in Bahrain (under Saudi leadership and with the apparent acquiescence of the United States) brutally repressed protesters and shored up the regime. There is little question that in this case international intervention succeeded in quashing mobilization, at least in the short run. This suggests the need for rethinking the relationship between linkage with the West and democratization, as increased linkage in the case of Bahrain did not translate into further pressure from the West on the authoritarian regime there to democratize.[35]

Activism after the 2011 Arab Uprisings

The Arab Spring had an enormous impact on activism across the region. Whether or not they succeeded in tearing down their regime, activists made significant gains during the Arab uprisings. However, they also continued to face enormous challenges. Some of these challenges were part of the continued evolution of activism in the region. Others, however, were driven by the shock of the Arab Spring itself.

It is first worth considering the key achievements that activists made during the Arab Spring. Street protest became the norm across the Arab world, as people broke the wall of fear and were increasingly vocal in expressing their demands directly, without mediation by organizations or other intermediaries.

The youth still largely lack the political skills that would allow them to play a more decisive role in democratic transition, but they rose in prominence, emerging as new political actors whose opinions matter—a great departure from the taken-for-granted status they had endured under authoritarian rule.

Activists in several Arab countries also departed from rallying around ideologies and instead began working together to push for issues, further consolidating the issue-based activism that first took root in Egypt and Bahrain. This consolidation is both a result of and a catalyst for the formation of coalitions among different activist groups. Despite the divisions among the opposition in Syria, Egypt, and Tunisia, those countries have also witnessed the establishment of coalitions that cross party, sectarian, and ideological lines. Coalitions were a product of the rise of a number of new political parties in the region, particularly in countries where the existence of independent parties had been restricted, as in Egypt and Tunisia, or not allowed, as in Libya. Despite the lack of political experience among many such parties, transitioning countries have embarked on the first step toward creating avenues for activists who were operating in the informal political sphere to form and work within political institutions for the first time.

A major achievement for activists across the Arab world has been the rise of civil society.[36] As presented earlier, civil society had been active in several countries in the region, despite regime suppression and cooptation. The post–Arab Spring era has seen the creation of new nongovernmental organizations, and it has also witnessed an increased viability for groups that had been active before the uprisings. In Tunisia, the most successful and credible civil society action after the Jasmine Revolution has been by local organizations that had learned from the experience of negotiating regularly with the Ben Ali regime. In Yemen as well, the civil society organizations that established credibility through criticizing the regime before the uprising have played a more prominent role after the uprising, too. In Libya, where civil society was practically nonexistent under Qaddafi, the post-revolution era has seen the creation of civil society for the first time, with new local organizations working on human rights, freedom of expression, and transitional justice. In Syria, as the uprising continued, the line between civil society and political activism became increasingly blurred, as several civil society groups found themselves forced to perform political roles.

However, activists face major difficulties. Divisions among activists persisted, not only in terms of tactics and demands but also in terms of identity and longstanding social cleavages, as seen in Jordan, where divisions between

Palestinians and Transjordanians as well as between Islamists and other groups persisted. In Kuwait, the main cleavages were between the tribes and the urbanites, who, with their different agendas and visions, mistrusted one another. In Saudi Arabia, divisions between Sunni and Shia groups not only have continued, but there are also divisions between radical Sunni Islamists and other more "liberal" Sunni groups. Sunni-Shia sectarianism also continued in Bahrain and Syria; in the latter country, this was complicated by the existence of tensions and divisions among and within the country's other sects, such as the Christians and the Kurds. In Libya, divisions among activist groups were not sectarian but were sparked by the persistence of old social dynamics inherited from the Qaddafi era, like a widespread mistrust of strangers, which presented a challenge to the formation of new political coalitions. The country also witnessed renewed cleavages between the East and the West after a brief unity of purpose during the revolution. Such regional divisions also persist in Saudi Arabia, namely between central areas and peripheral areas like the Eastern Province, which is mostly Shia. In Tunisia and Egypt, ideological divisions and clashes increased between Islamists and secular groups.

With different groups making different demands and with a lack of cooperation among different social sectors, activists in Bahrain, Saudi Arabia, and Yemen failed to transcend their regimes' "divide and rule" strategies. Some also failed to transcend cooptation. In Morocco, particularly, Islamist groups broke off their cooperation with the February 20 movement after the 2011 parliamentary elections that saw Justice and Development Party leader Abdelilah Benkirane become the country's first Islamist prime minister.

Even where protesters deposed their rulers, the path forward is difficult. In several countries, like Tunisia, Egypt, and Yemen, activists in general and youth in particular lack organization or common political agendas. The horizontal structure adopted by the youth-led February 20 movement in Morocco and the lack of opposition solidarity in Kuwait have led to the youth eventually playing a less influential role in national politics than organizations with hierarchical structures, like Islamist groups. After the revolutions, youth rarely formed new political parties, meaning that the youth who sparked the revolutions in places like Egypt and Yemen were not involved in the transition; rather, older political entities like the Muslim Brotherhood and the Joint Meeting Parties have performed this role. In Egypt and Tunisia, the cooperation between Islamist and secular groups witnessed during the revolutions was overtaken by intense competition both between those groups as well as among secular groups. In Syria, as the uprising continued, the opposition became consumed by internal competition among different groups, who lacked a unified strategy.

Moreover, the Arab Spring itself—and in general, the major political ruptures that followed the Arab Spring, including the color revolutions and revolutionary change in sub-Saharan Africa—presents unique challenges for activists. Post-revolutionary periods see the "normal" demobilization of the population, most of whom want to return to their work and families to carry on "life as usual."[37] While such demobilization is expected, it is also difficult.

In addition, the greater political opportunities—and the ability to shape the political sphere—that follow major political ruptures tend to fragment activist groups. As James DeNardo noted long ago, political possibilities lead to the fragmentation of radicals from moderates; activists who previously worked together to achieve the common goal of tearing down the regime suddenly find themselves wanting very different futures.[38] This is particularly true when elections are added to the mix. Previous days of unity quickly give way to infighting and fragmentation as well as demobilization.[39]

Indeed, from Latin America to the Far East, the experience of democratization has proven both a source of opportunities and new challenges for activists in civil society and political parties.[40] This is no less true for those engaged in the continuing struggles that followed the Arab uprisings of 2011. The contributors in this volume turn their attention not only to understanding the emergence of these uprisings but also their implications for activism.

Conclusion

As the chapters in this book make clear, much of the conventional wisdom about the Arab uprisings of 2011 is misleading. The uprisings did not emerge out of nowhere but were part of a longer evolution in the landscape of activism persistently challenging the regime. The uprisings were also not simply driven by tech-savvy youth; rather, they were the outcome of various groups that came together, each making varied demands. Nor were they entirely spontaneous; activists simultaneously capitalized on a changing set of skills and tactics they had developed in the previous decades and continued to adapt to new realities as the uprisings continued.

The voices of activists and observers not only call on us to revise our understanding of activism in the Arab Spring, but they also focus our attention on longstanding misconceptions about activism more generally. First, they remind us that activism takes place far outside the formal political parties, civil society organizations, and social movements that typically command our attention. Activism can develop in overlooked spaces—among soccer fans in Egypt or artists in Syria—with dramatic effects. Second, they turn our attention to the ever-changing nature of activism. Even in apparently stagnant authoritarian regimes, activism consistently evolved and renewed itself, even in the harshest of situations. Finally, they explore the relationship between the changing spaces for mobilization, the entrance and exit of social and political actors, and the evolving relationship between them.

In this view, the Arab uprisings of 2011 are not just a result of the evolution of activism but also a major turning point in the continuing process. The Arab Spring creates many advantages but also significant challenges for activists. On the one hand, it opens up new space for activism, allowing the emergence of political parties and civil society organizations. At the same time, however, the uprisings are followed by enormous challenges: the massive demobilization of the vast majority of citizens seeking to return to everyday life; the fragmentation of movements as members come to focus on their very different visions of the future, now that the unifying goal of regime change is achieved; and a need to develop organizations capable of mobilizing support and achieving demands in increasingly open, transparent regimes.

To some extent, it is the very project many of these activists sought to achieve that creates these challenges. Success depends on the ability of activists to transform into the kind of actors that many of them (especially newly mobilized youth) despise. The year 2011 led to major accomplishments across much of the region, yet it is just the beginning of the struggle, not its end.

Notes

1. Cedric Dupont and Florence Passy, "The Arab Spring or How to Explain Those Revolutionary Episodes," *Swiss Political Science Review* 17(4) (2011): 447–451, p. 447; F. Gregory Gause III, "Why Middle East Studies Missed the Arab Spring: The Myth of Authoritarian Stability," *Foreign Affairs* 90(4) (2011): 81–90, p. 81; Michelle Pace and Francesco Cavatorta, "The Arab Uprisings in Theoretical Perspective—An Introduction," *Mediterranean Politics* 17(2) (2012): 125–138, p. 125; Volker Perthes, "Europe and the Arab Spring," *Survival* 53(6) (2011): 73–84, p. 84.

2. See Philip Marfleet and Rabab El-Mahdi (eds.), *Egypt: The Moment of Change* (London: Zed Books, 2009); Joel Beinin and Frédéric Vairel (eds.), *Social Movements, Mobilization, and Contestation in the Middle East and North Africa* (Stanford, CA: Stanford University Press, 2011).

3. Fouad Ajami, "The Arab Spring at One: A Year of Living Dangerously," *Foreign Affairs* 91(2) (2012): 56–65, p. 56; Eva Bellin, "Reconsidering the Robustness of Authoritarianism in the Middle East," *Comparative Politics* 44(2) (2012): 127–149, p. 127.

4. For a range of conclusions on the role of social media, see Philip N. Howard and Muzammil M. Hussain, "The Role of Digital Media," *Journal of Democracy* 22(3) (2011): 35–48; Bruce Etling, Robert Faris, and John Palfrey, "Political Change in the Digital Age: The Fragility and Promise of Online Organizing," *SAIS Review* 30(2) (2010): 37–49; Marc Lynch, "Media, Old and New," in *The Arab Uprisings in Comparative Perspective,* ed. Marc Lynch (New York: Columbia University Press, forthcoming). For a careful analysis of Twitter feeds during the revolution, see Gilad Lotan et al., "The Revolutions Were Tweeted: Information Flows during the 2011 Tunisian and Egyptian Revolutions," *International Journal of Communication* 5 (2011): 1375–1405.

5. See, for example, Sheheryar Sardar and Adeel Shah, *Sandstorm: A Leaderless Revolution in the Digital Age* (Global Executive Board, 2011); Charles P. Ries, "The Year of the Arab Spring," The RAND Blog, December 20, 2011, available at www.rand.org/blog/2011/12/the-year-of-the-arab-spring.html, accessed July 10, 2013; Yousri Marzouki and Olivier Oullier, "Revolutionizing Revolutions: Virtual Collective Consciousness and the Arab Spring," *Huffington Post,* July 17, 2012, available at www.huffingtonpost.com/yousri-marzouki/revolutionizing-revolutio_b_1679181.html, accessed July 10, 2013; and Wael Ghonim, *Revolution 2.0: A Memoir from the Heart of the Arab Spring* (New York: Houghton Mifflin Harcourt, 2012).

6. Historically, much literature on political mobilization focuses on organized protest movements. See, for example, John D. McCarthy and Mayer N. Zald, "Resource Mobilization and Social Movements: A Partial Theory," *American Journal of Sociology* 82(6) (1977): 1212–1241; Charles Tilly, *From Mobilization to Revolution* (Reading, MA: Addison-Wesley, 1978). New social movement theory adds nuance to the analysis of protest movements and is thus useful in understanding mobilization in the Arab world in a number of ways, through its focus on the importance of symbolic action, its emphasis on issue-driven activism, and its propagation of the important role of temporary networks in mobilization. For more on these aspects, see Steven M. Buechler, "New Social Movement Theories," *Sociological Quarterly* 36(3) (Summer 1995): 441–464; Ronald Inglehart, "Values, Ideology, and Cognitive Mobilization New Social Movements," in *Challenging the Political Order,* ed. Russell Dalton and Manfred Kuechler (Oxford: Polity Press, 1990), 43–66; Carol McClurg Mueller, "Conflict Networks and the Origins of Women's Movements," in *New Social Movement,* ed. Enrique Larana, Hank Johnston, and Joseph R. Gusfield (Philadelphia: Temple University Press, 1994), 234–263. However, social movement theory is constrained by largely limiting those three dimensions to the context of

organized collective action that overlooks what Asef Bayat calls "nonmovements," in reference to actions by people who are not in organized groups. Bayat, *Life as Politics: How Ordinary People Change the Middle East* (Stanford, CA: Stanford University Press, 2009). More recently, attention has focused productively as well on the role of transnational linkages. See, for example, Stefaan Walgrave et al., "Transnational Collective Identification: May Day and Climate Change Protesters' Identification with Similar Protest Events in Other Countries," *Mobilization* 17(3) (2012): 301–317; Maha Abdelrahman, "The Transnational and the Local: Egyptian Activists and Transnational Protest Networks," *British Journal of Middle Eastern Studies* 38(3) (2011): 407–424.

7. Lina Khatib, *Image Politics in the Middle East: The Role of the Visual in Political Struggle* (London: I.B. Tauris, 2013), 135.

8. Marta Fuentes and Andre Gunder Frank, "Ten Theses on Social Movements," *World Development* 17(2) (1989): 179–191.

9. Pippa Norris, "Political Activism: New Challenges, New Opportunities," in *Oxford Handbook of Political Science*, ed. Carles Boix and Susan C. Stokes (Oxford: Oxford University Press, 2009), 628–652, p. 639.

10. Cf. Michelle Pace and Francesco Cavatorta, "The Arab Uprisings in Theoretical Perspective—An Introduction," *Mediterranean Politics* 17(2) (2012): 125–138.

11. A limited number of other academic literature written or published before 2011 also pointed to this phenomena. For instance, see Marfleet and El-Mahdi (eds.), *Egypt*; Beinin and Vairel (eds.), *Social Movements, Mobilization, and Contestation*; Laryssa Chomiak, *Confronting Authoritarianism: Order, Dissent, and Everyday Politics in Modern Tunisia,* PhD dissertation, University of Maryland, 2011.

12. On Gafsa, see Amin Allal, "'Ici, si ça ne 'bouge' pas ça n'avance pas!' Les mobilisations protestataires de l'année 2008 dans la région minière de Gafsa. Réformes néo libérales, clientélismes et contestation," in *L'État face aux débordements du social au Maghreb,* ed. Myriam Catusse, Blandine Destremau, and Éric Verdier (Paris: Karthala, 2010).

13. On the difficulties of conceptualizing and measuring political opportunity structures, see David S. Meyer, "Conceptualizing Political Opportunity," *Social Forces* 82(4) (2004): 1457–1492; Eitan Alimi, "Mobilizing under the Gun: Theorizing Political Opportunity Structure in a Highly Repressive Setting," *Mobilization* 14(2) (2009): 219–238.

14. See Beinen and Vairel, *Social Movements, Mobilization, and Contestation*; Joel Beinin, "Egyptian Workers and January 25th: A Social Movement in Historical Context," *Social Research* 79(2) (2012): 323–348.

15. On the role of social networks in overcoming collective action problems, see Chaeyoon Lim, "Social Networks and Political Participation: How Do Networks Matter?" *Social Forces* 87(2) (2008): 961–982. With regard to the Arab uprisings, see Eitan Y. Alimi and David S. Meyer, "Seasons of Change: Arab Spring and Politi-

cal Opportunities," *Swiss Political Science Review* 17(4) (2011): 475–479; Reinoud Leenders and Steven Heydemann, "Popular Mobilization in Syria: Opportunity and Threat, and the Social Networks of Early Risers," *Mediterranean Politics* 17(2) (2012): 139–159.

16. Such political parties in exile, for example, the Tunisian October 18 Collectif, can be important actors.

17. See contributions in Hendrik Kraetzschmar (ed.), *The Dynamics of Opposition Cooperation in the Arab World* (London: Routledge, 2012).

18. Vickie Langohr, "Too Much Civil Society, Too Little Politics? Egypt and Other Liberalizing Arab Regimes," in *Authoritarianism in the Middle East*, ed. Marsha Pripstein Posusney and Michele Penner Angrist (Boulder, CO: Lynne Rienner, 2005), 193–220.

19. Bayat, *Life as Politics*.

20. For additional analyses focused on the role of youth in the Arab uprisings, see Mohammad Al-Momani, "The Arab 'Youth Quake': Implications on Democratization and Stability," *Middle East Law and Governance* 3(1–2) (2011): 159–170; Constance A. Flanagan et al., "Youth Civic Development: Theorizing a Domain with Evidence from Different Cultural Contexts," *New Directions for Child and Adolescent Development* 2011(134) (2011): 95–109; Leila Austin, "The Politics of Youth Bulge: From Islamic Activism to Democratic Reform in the Middle East and North Africa," *SAIS Review* 31(2) (2011): 81–96; Emma C. Murphy, "Problematizing Arab Youth: Generational Narratives of Systemic Failure," *Mediterranean Politics* 17(1) (2012): 5–22; Michael Hoffman and Amaney Jamal, "The Youth and the Arab Spring: Cohort Differences and Similarities," *Middle East Law and Governance* 4(1) (2012): 168–188; and Tina Rosenberg, "Revolution U: What Egypt Learned from the Students Who Overthrew Milosevic," *Foreign Policy,* February 16, 2011.

21. See, for example, the contributions in Noel Meijer (ed.), *Alienation or Integration of Arab Youth: Between Family, State, and Street* (Richmond, U.K.: Curzon, 2000).

22. See Paul Collier and Nicholas Sambanis (eds.), *Understanding Civil War: Evidence and Analysis, Volume 1: Africa* (Washington, DC: World Bank, 2005); Daniel Byman et al., "Trends in Outside Support for Insurgent Movements," *RAND*, 2001; Kristian Gleditsch, "Transnational Dimensions of Civil War," *Journal of Peace Research* 44(3) (2007): 293–309.

23. Arab activists also learned from peers outside the Arab world. For example, the Green Movement of 2009 inspired Egyptian activists to hone their visual communication skills, particularly when reaching out to the outside world. See Maryam Ishani, "The Hopeful Network," *Foreign Policy,* February 7, 2011, available at www .foreignpolicy.com/articles/2011/02/07/the_hopeful_network, accessed July 11, 2013.

24. In the beginning, Feb20 was helped by the participation of Islamist group al-Adl wal-Ihsan, which had been engaging in activism against the regime for a long time.

25. Many theorists argue that nonviolent struggle is particularly effective. See, for instance, Maria J. Stephan and Erica Chenoweth, "Why Civil Resistance Works: The Strategic Logic of Nonviolent Conflict," *International Security* 33(1) (2008): 7–44; Stephen Zunes, "Nonviolent Revolution in the Middle East," *Peace Review* 23(3) (2011): 396–403; Peter Ackerman and Berel Rodal, "The Strategic Dimensions of Civil Resistance," *Survival* 50(3) (2008): 111–126. On nonviolent struggle preceding the uprisings, see Maria J. Stephan (ed.), *Civilian Jihad: Nonviolent Struggle, Democratization, and Governance in the Middle East* (New York: Palgrave Macmillan, 2009).

26. Sidney Tarrow and Charles Tilly, "Contentious Politics and Social Movements," in *Oxford Handbook of Political Science,* ed. Boix and Stokes, 435–460.

27. For a classic discussion, see contributions in Mark Traugott (ed.), *Repertoires and Cycles of Collective Action* (Durham, NC: Duke University Press, 1969).

28. Amaney Jamal and Lina Khatib, "Actors, Public Opinion, and Participation," in *The Middle East,* ed. Ellen Lust (Washington, DC: CQ Press, 2013), 246–286; Lisa Wedeen, *Peripheral Visions: Publics, Power, and Performance in Yemen* (Chicago: University of Chicago Press, 2008); David Weir, "Cultural Theory and the Diwan," *Innovation: The European Journal of Social Sciences* 21(3) (2008): 253–265.

29. See David Patel, Valerie Bunce, and Sharon Wolchik, "Diffusion and Demonstration," in *Arab Uprisings,* ed. Lynch.

30. Jillian Schwedler and Janine A. Clark, "Islamist-Leftist Cooperation in the Arab World," *ISIM Review* 18(1) (2006): 10–11; Janine A. Clark, "The Conditions of Islamist Moderation: Unpacking Cross-Ideological Cooperation in Jordan," *International Journal of Middle Eastern Studies* 38(4) (2006): 539–560; Janine A. Clark, "Threats, Structures, and Resources: Cross-Ideological Coalition Building in Jordan," *Comparative Politics* 43(1) (2010): 101–120.

31. More specifically, political opportunity structures are considered to include the degree of regime openness, stability of political alignments, presence of allies, divisions among allies, and tolerance of protest. Sydney Tarrow, *Power in Movement* (New York: Cambridge University Press, 1994).

32. Alimi, "Mobilizing under the Gun."

33. Mark Lichbach, "Deterrence or Escalation? The Puzzle of Aggregate Studies of Repression and Dissent," *Journal of Conflict Resolution* 31(2) (1987): 266–297; Karen Rasler, "Concessions, Repression, and Political Protest in the Iranian Revolution," *American Sociological Review* 61(1) (1996): 132–152.

34. Cf. Laurence Whitehead (ed.), *The International Dimension of Democratization: Europe and the Americas* (Oxford: Oxford University Press, 1996); Thomas Risse, Stephen C. Ropp, and Kathryn Sikkink (eds.), *The Power of Human Rights: International Norms and Domestic Change* (New York: Cambridge University Press, 1999).

35. Steven Levitsky and Lucan A. Way, "Linkage versus Leverage: Rethinking the International Dimension of Regime Change," *Comparative Politics* 38(4) (2006): 379–400.

36. Guillermo O'Donnell and Philippe C. Schmitter, *Transitions from Authoritarian Rule: Tentative Conclusions about Uncertain Democracies* (Baltimore: Johns Hopkins University Press, 1986).

37. Ulrich K. Preuß, "The Rule-Making and Policy Actors in the Transition and the Issue of the Strategy of Transformation," *Studies in East European Thought* 53(3) (2001): 183–195.

38. James DeNardo, *Power in Numbers: The Political Strategy of Protest and Rebellion* (Princeton: Princeton University Press, 2005).

39. Julia Paley, *Marketing Democracy: Power and Social Movements in Post-Dictatorship Chile* (Berkeley: University of California Press, 2001).

40. Alberto J. Olvera, "The Elusive Democracy: Political Parties, Democratic Institutions, and Civil Society in Mexico," *Latin American Research Review* 45(4) (2010): 78–107; Lorenzo Fioramonti, "Civil Societies and Democratization: Assumptions, Dilemmas and the South African Experience," *Theoria: A Journal of Social and Political Theory* 107 (2005): 65–88; Lorenzo Fioramonti and Antonio Fiori, "Civil Society after Democracy: The Evolution of Civic Activism in South Africa and Korea," *Journal of Civil Society* 6(1) (2010): 23–38; Muthia Alagappa (ed.), *Civil Society and Political Change in Asia: Expanding and Contracting Democratic Space* (Stanford, CA: Stanford University Press, 2004); Patricia L. Hipsher, "Democratization and the Decline of Urban Social Movements in Chile and Spain," *Comparative Politics* 28(3) (1996): 273–297; Peter P. Houtzager, "Social Movements amidst Democratic Transitions: Lessons from the Brazilian Countryside," *Journal of Development Studies* 36(5) (1996): 59–88.

CHAPTER 1

Architecture of Resistance in Tunisia

LARYSSA CHOMIAK

Mapping Activism in Tunisia

The January 14, 2011, Revolution that unfolded rapidly in Tunisia and resonated across the Arab world prompted academic and policy circles to try to
pinpoint the origins of a movement that toppled ousted dictator Zine El Abidine Ben Ali. The most popular story approximating a creation myth has been
that of the young produce seller Mohamed Bouazizi setting himself on fire in the
south-central town of Sidi Bouzid in order to protest local corruption, indig-
nity, and economic frustration. The dramatic self-immolation, according to
popular recounting, unchained years of political obedience and pushed thousands to take to the street for the first time and protest—then illegally—against
the ancient authoritarian regime. Or so it seemed.

As the Bouazizi story began to lose purchase among Tunisians, foreign observers started searching for new stories that might explain the astonishing
events of 2010 and 2011 in Tunisia.[1] Origin stories have since become notorious in Tunisia's public discourse, with radically divergent accounts identifying
the first signs of transgression against the Ben Ali regime: from the Tunisia in
White e-mobilization protest campaign in May 2010 to a melee at a spring
2010 soccer game at the Stade El Menzah around the same time as the
Monastir self-immolation by Abdesslem Trimesh, to the 2008 rebellion in the
southern mining towns of Redeyef and Métlaoui as well as the city of Gafsa,
and the 2005 World Internet Freedom conference, among others.[2] None-

"Finally Free," graffiti in Tunis in the wake of the revolution. Photo by the Centre d'Etudes Maghrébines à Tunis / CEMAT. Laryssa Chomiak.

theless, Bouazizi's self-immolation sparked a nationwide protest movement insofar as his grievances occurred at the height of Tunisia's most recent economic crisis and were quickly captured by Al Jazeera and disseminated widely via social media networking sites.[3] Yet the "spark" also relied on a thick history of political contention and activist mobilization that had matured over time; already in 2008, a rebellion in a southern mining town was covered by French television, and leftist Tunisian activists began using social media to mobilize more broadly and effectively.

Origin stories have contributed little analytical value in explaining the January 2011 toppling of Ben Ali. Quite simply, there was no single point of origin. Rather, as this chapter will show, the revolution emerged from seemingly scattered activism in pre-revolutionary Tunisia and certain moments of resistance under dictatorship that were closely interconnected. Beginning in the early 2000s, when Ben Ali's reversion to authoritarian rule was confirmed and street-based protests in support of Palestinian solidarity across the region abounded, Tunisian activists too were carving out spaces for domestic dissent.

Contrary to the grim pictures of quiescence under dictatorship, Tunisians under Ben Ali in the 1990s did protest the dominance of the state, but the everyday dissidence that later grew into activism was often pushed into informal, often seemingly nonpolitical spaces such as soccer stadiums, cafes, and urban beer halls, while faint rumblings of transgression could be detected in the press, especially in online publications and political cartoons.[4] Over the next decade, from 2002 to 2011, Tunisian activism under the constraints of dictatorship converged from scattered and isolated moments of political transgression by activists pushing for freedom of expression, political liberties, and the release of unlawfully detained political prisoners to what by 2008 had morphed into broader grievance-based movements spanning the entire nation. During this period, instances of transgression against the police, which had become synonymous with the Ben Ali regime, expanded to more politicized spaces such as street-based protests and e-mobilization campaigns. Activism evolved from localized and isolated moments of transgression to nationwide campaigns, with closer cooperation among individual activists and more sophisticated and efficient mobilization tactics, and it was organized around various issues, from unfair hiring processes in southern mining towns to regime-led PR efforts in hosting conferences on internet freedom to broader issues of human rights and freedom of expression locally as well as internationally. The Tunisian Revolution of January 14, 2011, then, marks a political moment on a continuum of activism that had been building over time and across space. It is also a political moment that fundamentally transformed public debate and opened new spaces of expression and opportunities for a new political order.

Scattered Activism and Early Instances of Transgression, 2001–2006

Political activism in post-revolutionary Tunisia cannot easily be divorced from previous efforts to engage with the Ben Ali regime—however informal or unorganized—to ameliorate the everyday political, economic, and social conditions that plagued Tunisians living under the dictatorship. In the early 2000s, scattered activism clustered around political opportunities, and it mainly took place at government-sanctioned protests and international conferences. Activism was largely concentrated in Tunis, though at moments, activists from other regions, including the underdeveloped South, began mobilizing against increased government repression. While grievances primarily pivoted around restrictions of political freedoms, different actors used a variety of mobilization techniques. Activists and members of the opposition would often critique and subvert the Ben Ali government during pro-Palestinian/anti-Israel or pro-Iraq/anti–United States protests, which constituted the few instances of government-sanctioned protests. Domestic grievances focused on police violence, liberty of expression, jailing of Parti Communiste des Ouvriers de Tunisie (PCOT) and an-Nahda supporters, and harassment of oppositional journalists. Pushed out of public space, Tunisian activists began exploring alternative spaces of expression, including cyber-activism, a form of resistance that became more sophisticated and widespread in the decade leading up to the January 14, 2011, Revolution.

While Tunisia's history since the late colonial period has been defined by activism in the form of a young nationalist movement led by the country's first president, Habib Bourguiba, as well as contentious union activity in the late 1950s to the 1970s,[5] the country's youth in the 2000s had experienced political life only under Ben Ali, who severely restricted oppositional political activism.[6] While Ben Ali flirted with political liberalism between 1987—when he came to power in a bloodless coup d'état ousting Bourguiba, who had ruled the country since independence—and 1989, by the turn of the century he had successfully consolidated authoritarian rule.[7] During the short moment of political openness between 1987 and 1989, Ben Ali expanded multi-party politics, allowed members of the Islamist party an-Nahda, formerly the Mouvement de Tendance Islamique to run as independents in the 1989 legislative elections,[8] and scheduled pluralistic legislative and presidential elections for 1994. Within a year, however, an-Nahda was banned, with its leadership escaping into exile, while opposition parties, associations, and activists were increasingly harassed and their activity severely repressed. By 1994, Tunisia's reversion to authoritarian rule had been confirmed—Ben Ali's ruling Constitutional Democratic Rally (RCD) political party won just short of 98 percent of the legislative vote, while the president himself claimed 100 percent of the popular vote in a landslide "victory."

From the early 1990s, Ben Ali's politics were thus defined by two dominant trends: consolidation of political dictatorship and growing economic corruption.[9] The obliteration of formal oppositional space in the form of political parties and independent associations forced Tunisian activists to be creative in their search for spaces and opportunities to push back against the Ben Ali regime. Already in 2001, Tunisian activists had begun engaging in cyber-activism to dodge government censorship. In July 2001, for instance, economist Zoubir Yahyaoui, nephew of oppositional Judge Mokhtar Yahyaoui, created TUNe-Zine, an online portal critiquing the Ben Ali regime.[10] TUNeZine primarily published articles about the regime's human rights abuses as well as Judge Ya-hyahoui's infamous open letter to President Ben Ali criticizing the absence of an independent judiciary. Both Zoubir and Mokhtar Yahyahoui were subjected to regular harassment, detention and arbitrary prison sentences. Zoubir died of a heart attack in 2005 following an eighteen-month prison sentence, after which TUNeZine shut down, yet Judge Yahyaoui continued fighting for the release of arbitrarily held political prisoners, freedom of expression, respect for human rights, and an independent judiciary. As I will demonstrate, Tunisian activists, oppositional journalists, and bloggers—such as the widely known regime critic and author Taoufik Ben Brik—later supplemented by a new generation of ac-tivists, have consistently used the internet to publish critiques of the Ben Ali regime and eventually to mobilize Tunisians to take to the streets.[11]

Early transgressions against the Ben Ali regime also occurred during street-based protests aimed at regional political conflicts, primarily sparked by the region-wide Palestinian solidarity movement of 2002.[12] On April 6, 2002, left-wing student activists in Tunis, mainly supporters of the Progressive Demo-cratic Party (PDP) and the then-outlawed Communist PCOT, organized an unauthorized march in support of Palestine. That march followed a similar pro-Palestinian protest on April 3, 2002, called for by the ruling RCD Party, in which state-created women's organizations, unions, as well as student and youth groups linked to the RCD took part. Despite the inability of the leftist opposition to attain a protest permit, hundreds of protesters turned out on Avenue 9 Avril in downtown Tunis, near the Kasbah area—the seat of govern-ment and the Tunisian Parliament as well as a major university campus. Within minutes, the police started dispersing the protesters, resulting in clashes between the police and protesters. As the police crackdown began, protesters in turn began collectively chanting against the Tunisian police, which had al-ready become synonymous with the illegitimate state. The April 6, 2002, pro-Palestinian march in Tunis would become the first instance in which a protest for an international cause organized by a political party (PDP), a number of associations, and student activists would turn to domestic grievances once the police suppressed collective mobilization.

The year 2002 turned out to be especially difficult for the Ben Ali regime. Within a week of the April 6 crackdown in downtown Tunis, members of al-Qaeda attacked the El-Ghriba Synagogue in Djerba on April 11, leaving a total of nineteen European tourists and Tunisian bystanders dead. The Tunisian security services subsequently conducted waves of arrests of suspected terrorists. Many of those arbitrarily arrested were supporters of the outlawed an-Nahda movement who had nothing to do with the attacks. The Tunisian regime's violent response opened new arenas of criticism from international and human rights activists related to unfair detention and arrest, atrocious prison conditions, and torture. These critiques were followed by Judge Yahyaoui's open letter to Ben Ali and an outpouring of condemnatory reports by international human rights associations. It is unclear whether or not the next RCD-sanctioned street-based protest in Tunis was a government response to the poor reputation Tunisia had garnered in 2002, but an interesting dynamic unfolded nonetheless.

On March 11, 2003, the ruling RCD, a group of regime-authorized oppositional parties, and some state-controlled associations organized a pro-Iraq march in downtown Tunis on Place 7 Novembre.[13] According to international news sources, approximately five thousand protesters participated calmly, and no clashes with the police were reported. On March 25, 2003, the Tunisian General Labor Union (UGTT), with the support of regime-compliant oppositional parties and the Tunisian Commission for Human Rights (also coopted by the regime) organized a similar pro-Iraq march in downtown Tunis, again with no reports of clashes. Within weeks, young members of PCOT from the mining region of Gafsa had organized an unauthorized protest in support of Iraq in the small mining town of Redeyef on the Algerian border. The youth activists in Gafsa and Redeyef were supported by student adherents of the illegal PCOT in Tunis, and they took the opportunity of the demonstrations in Tunis to take to the streets in support of an international issue elsewhere. The loosely organized protest by activists in Gafsa and Redeyef as well as Marxist-Leninist students in Tunis represented one of the first instances of nationwide mobilization of radical leftists under Ben Ali. As with the unauthorized pro-Palestinian march in 2002, the police quickly turned against protesters who again began collectively chanting against the police for restricting their freedom of assembly and expression.

Activism more than a decade after the start of Ben Ali's rule remained scattered across Tunisia, and mobilization techniques varied from online regime critiques to street-based protests that had not been intended as antiregime or antipolice events. By 2005, however, activism against internet censorship and for freedom of expression had become more organized through linkages with international activist groups and domestic oppositional actors. The spark was the Tunisian government's decision to host the UN World Summit on the

Information Society (WSIS) in November 2005, unleashing critiques from oppositional journalists and bloggers, including Slim Amamou, who became known as blogger and activist "Slim 404" for his longstanding internet freedom activism.[14] The summit in Tunis was part of a larger PR effort on the part of Ben Ali to solidify Tunisia's international image as a liberal and progressive Arab state.[15] The meeting aroused much criticism among local and international internet freedom activists, especially given that Tunisia had succeeded in heavily restricting internet traffic while harassing, detaining, and jailing internet activists and bloggers. A group of seven Tunisian oppositional actors, including Ahmed Nejib Chebbi, the president of the PDP; Judge Mokhtar Yahyaoui; and an attorney named Samir Dilou who would become interim minister for transitional justice and human rights after the Tunisian Revolution, planned a parallel citizen summit. As part of the parallel summit, the group of oppositional actors agreed to engage in a month-long hunger strike to draw international attention in order to pressure the Tunisian government to release arbitrarily held political prisoners and to lift its restrictions on freedom of expression for Tunisian citizens. While the hunger strike did take place, the parallel citizen summit during the official WSIS summit never occurred because the Tunisian government refused to grant authorization for an organized and public meeting.

As in 2003, the attempt to organize oppositional meetings in Tunis in 2005 signaled to activists in other regions that collective action was indeed possible, albeit difficult and heavily censored. Prior to the 2008 rebellion in Tunisia's mining region, which today is often viewed as a precursor to, if not the root of, the 2011 revolution, a young activist from Redeyef, Hassen Ben Abdellah, organized the first public meeting of the then-illegal and unauthorized Union for Unemployed Graduates (UDC) in 2006.

After a visit by PCOT leader Hamma Hammami, Ben Abdellah was inspired to build a local institutional base from which he could negotiate with state elites in Tunis. The move to establish a parallel union resulted from local residents' belief that their demands and needs would not be addressed by the UGTT's local chapter and that new channels of communication were necessary to negotiate with state elites in Tunis. Ben Abdellah's decision to establish the UDC was a response to local concerns about the cooptation of the main workers' union, the UGTT, under Ben Ali not only at the national level but also at the municipal level in Gafsa. Local residents believed not only that the UGTT had been coopted by the ruling RCD political party but also that it engaged in corrupt dealings with the state-run Gafsa Phosphate Company

(CPG) as well as the small clan of families that controlled the majority of economic resources and investments in Gafsa. Ben Ali had nurtured the coalition uniting these powerful families, the local RCD office, the UGTT, and the CPG; it was his contention that they were best positioned to invest in their local communities and thus would not conspire against the regime in Tunis. This coalition also became the main site of contention for local residents, especially the unemployed, who increasingly began organizing with every political opportunity.

When Hassen Ben Abdellah organized the first unauthorized congress of the newly established UDC in 2006, he was promptly arrested and jailed for three years, two of which he spent in solitary confinement. The charges against him were membership in an illegal political organization, the PCOT, and the unauthorized establishment of a union. That same year, state-sanctioned protests in solidarity with Palestine were organized in Tunis, as in 2002, and reached Gafsa and Redeyef. Local residents mobilized by PCOT activists and de facto members of the UDC took to the streets in support of Palestinians but also used the moment to organize publicly and collectively against Ben Ali. During the heavily policed protests, residents tried to convince the police to march in solidarity with them—both with Palestine and against Ben Ali. When the police refused, protesters, questioning the police's loyalty to citizens versus the state, began chanting, "Police, you too are victims of the state, join us and participate in our cause!"[16] In October 2006, a few months after the Palestine solidarity march, PCOT activists in Redeyef organized the town's first widespread sit-in against the state's ineffective anti-unemployment policies as well as unfair hiring practices on part of the CPG. Even though protest organizers were promptly arrested and jailed, residents of Redeyef, Métlaoui, Melares, and Gafsa did not hesitate to engage in a subsequent rebellion in 2008, protesting the same conditions that had earlier led to sit-ins and protests.

Scattered activism, such as that chronicled above, is frequently overlooked because it does not constitute a clearly defined social movement.[17] Studies of social movements as well as of the repression-dissent nexus often do not systematically consider the type of sporadic and dispersed activism that occurs under closed political systems.[18] Some studies do consider symbolic resistance and other "mundane" forms of political transgressions, but the effect of these moments of resistance and the coping strategies of the state remain unclear.[19] Moreover, rarely are sporadic activist moments connected because of the seemingly different demands made by activists and those taking to the streets, despite the overlap in identifying political opportunities and sharing strategies.

Most recently, sociologists have written about "social non-movements" rooted within the "quiet encroachment of the ordinary" or the mundane daily activities of countless individuals.[20] These activities, Asef Bayat writes, form the lived circumstances that can easily and swiftly snowball into grievance-based protests, as witnessed in the 2008 Gafsa/Redeyet/Métlaoui events as well as the Facebook mobilization preceding the Tunisia in White campaign.

Tunisian Activism Converges, 2008–2010

During the last three years of Ben Ali's rule, activism in Tunisia became significantly more sophisticated, as activists, bloggers, and oppositional journalists began seizing on any political opportunity to transgress regime-imposed boundaries. Unlike the scattered moments of activism that had occurred previously, the period from 2008 to the ouster of Ben Ali in 2011 was marked by an overlap of activists and mobilization strategies. Activists more confidently evaded government censorship, linking cyber-activism with traditional strikes and street-based protests. The convergence of activism in this period was the result of activists increasingly exploiting any issue, from unemployment to internet freedom, that could be used to push against the Ben Ali state. This momentum clearly defined the trajectory of the protests in 2010 and 2011, initially marked by a myriad of grievances, which eventually coalesced under the banner of *Dégage!*

On January 5, 2008, a series of protests broke out in the country's fifth-largest city, Gafsa, in the southern mining region, an area that has historically been a site of contention and consistent antiregime activism.[21] The protests in early 2008 were initially directed against the Gafsa Phosphate Company, the local branch of the UGTT, and a small network of privileged families.[22] Characterized by high unemployment rates and underdevelopment, residents of the area have depended largely on employment by the CPG or the surrounding mines. In January 2008, protests broke out in the mining towns of Redeyef and Métlaoui against unfair hiring practices by the CPG as well as corruption within the company and the local branch of the UGTT. Residents of the towns, led by local left-wing activists, protested the results of a yearly entry exam for recruitment into the CPG workforce. The protesters believed that the UGTT and the CPG had struck an unfair deal in their hiring preferences, unevenly distributing jobs to union members and their families. Furthermore, while the CPG needed to recruit four hundred miners in 2008, a 1986 directive introduced by Mohamed Mzali, Bourguiba's prime minister until 1986, limited the

UGTT to select only 20 percent, rather than the previous 80 percent, of any given workforce. Thus, in 2008, 20 percent of the mining workforce, or eighty positions, was directly selected by the UGTT, with jobs distributed exclusively among the UGTT families. The majority of the remaining positions were negotiated between the UGTT and the CPG, trumping merit with nepotism and unleashing waves of street-based protests. In an interview with this author, a member of the executive bureau of the UGTT who served under Ben Ali and was reelected during the December 2011 UGTT National Congress stated openly that "the real roots of the January 14, 2011, Revolution were the 2008 events in Gafsa."[23] His statement echoes the many diverse origin stories circulating in Tunisia, but he nonetheless recognized that resistance had built up over time, that activists continuously attempted to engage with the Ben Ali regime, and that activism had become more organized and sophisticated by 2008.

In late January, after protesters in Gafsa and the surrounding mining towns made multiple unsuccessful attempts to demand the public release of CPG exam results for comparison with the hiring decisions, they decided to take their cause to the streets. They directed their grievances against the municipality of Gafsa, which symbolized the control of the region's financial resources. In February 2008, unemployed miners from Redeyef staged a sit-in, a hunger strike, and a protest, all of which were unauthorized and thus illegal. According to an activist from Redeyef, the protesters were trying desperately to negotiate with any agent of the state, yet as police forces were increasing in the area, it became clear that the state was unlikely to respond to the protesters' demands and had chosen instead to resort to crackdowns.[24]

The protests continued on a weekly basis and swiftly culminated in a larger protest movement that was supported by other activists across the nation, mainly left-wing students—both members of the General Union of Tunisian Students (UGET) and followers of PCOT. According to a member of the UGTT executive bureau, the 2008 protests were initially weak and scarcely organized and only grew into a regular and organized movement when the extreme left, led by Hamma Hammami, secretary general of PCOT, and Mohamed Kilani from the Parti Socialiste de Gauche (PSG) used the waves of protests as a political opportunity to mobilize others with broader political goals. At the same time, the police arrested activists as well as members of the UGTT who appeared to have defected and joined the protest movement. In response, large protests broke out in the mining town of Redeyef, clashing regularly with the police. The wives and mothers of jailed husbands and sons planned a "women's protest" in the hopes that the police forces would be more lenient with only women taking to the streets.[25] Within months, wives of unemployed miners, school teachers, and local union members joined the protest movement, resulting in Ben Ali's move to send in police forces to curb the protests, arresting and jailing hundreds, and eventually fatally shooting two protesters.

A number of crucial developments occurred during this period that lend insight into the larger activist mobilization just prior to the January 2011 Revolution as well as into the gradual convergence of previous activism tools. In spring 2008, leftist student activists from Tunis formed national solidarity groups across Tunisia to support the protesters in Redeyef and Métlaoui and organized a national day of solidarity on April 4, 2008, on which family members of imprisoned workers and unemployed miners organized a march. As the state-controlled Tunisian press was not covering the protest activity and journalists from oppositional newspapers[26]—including *al-Mawkif* ("The Point of View"), *al-Tariq al-Jadid* ("The New Way"), and *al-Mouatin* ("The Citizen")—covering the events, such as Fahem Boukadous, were routinely harassed and imprisoned, activists across the country began relying on social networking sites, including Facebook, to spread information about the protests and police violence directed against ordinary citizens taking to the streets.[27] The French television channel France 24 picked up a number of online videos of police violence and, responding to pressure from the Tunisian diaspora community in Toulouse (mainly from Redeyef), ran a documentary on the growing rebellion in Tunisia. Ben Ali decided to bolster security by sending twelve thousand additional police forces to the area to help quell the protests.[28] Rumors circulate to this day that Ben Ali sought advice from Serbian war experts, who warned him that the recurrent and escalating street-based protest activity almost certainly constituted "the beginning of the end."

Following the national day of solidarity on April 4, 2008, the protest movement slowed down significantly. In response, Ben Ali authorized the release of some political prisoners if they would sign a pledge never to engage in organized collective action against the state. On May 6, 2008, the illegal PCOT and members of the unlicensed and heavily censored UDC led by activist and PCOT member Hassen Ben Abdellah helped organize a sit-in outside the offices of the Tunisian Electricity and Gas Company (STEG) in Tabdit, a village approximately twelve miles from Redeyef, to protest rampant electricity and gas outages. The police immediately attempted to break up the sit-in and arrest all participants, including the UDC leadership; as Ben Abdellah put it, "2008 was the year in which all of Redeyef was imprisoned."[29] However, one protester,

Hisham A'alemi, refused to leave and held onto a power cable where the electricity currents had been cut. The police threatened to increase the voltage should he not leave. A'alemi refused and was subsequently publicly electrocuted and killed.[30]

Police repression against the protests and sit-ins in the area only fueled widespread public anger and expanded regular protest activity. As with his response during the protests in December 2010, Ben Ali hastily labeled the nonviolent and peaceful protests as an organized coup attempt and a terrorist strategy to destabilize Tunisia. Just a month later, on June 6, 2008, the police shot two protesters, ending waves of protest and legitimate attempts by activists to negotiate with the state. As unemployed workers and residents continued to take to the streets in Redeyef despite increased state repression, the police shot Hafnoui Maghzaoui, who died immediately, and Abdelkalik Amedi, who died on September 3 from complications. Several protesters who tried to help Amedi on June 6 by removing him from the street suffered gunshot wounds. What started as a targeted and small-scale protest against unfair hiring practices on the part of a local phosphate company and the UGTT only six months earlier had culminated into a broader movement with clear political demands. As in 2010, protesters took to the streets in an attempt to negotiate with the Ben Ali regime and plead for more jobs, expanded social justice, reduced corruption, and more political liberties.

The street-based movement itself was suppressed after the police shooting in June 2008, but left-wing activists in the southern mining region as well as across university campuses continued to spread the message, under increased police surveillance and censorship, using various online tools, especially Facebook, Twitter, and Vimeo. Like in 2010, Ben Ali propagated a concise narrative of terrorism and national security, justifying continuous random arrests, harassment, and censorship. As part of his repressive strategy, Ben Ali finally ordered for Facebook to be shut down on August 18, 2008, citing national security violations by terrorists, who were purportedly pouring in through the Algerian border.[31] Tunisian activists using external servers such as Hotspot Shield and supported by Tunisian diaspora communities in France, Canada, and the United States immediately organized a Facebook campaign against the growing censorship in Tunisia. On September 3, 2008, Ben Ali reluctantly lifted the Facebook ban, thus reopening alternative venues for activists to continue pushing against the state.

As resentment against the regime brewed, the next large-scale mobilization effort occurred on May 22, 2010, against internet censorship. Six young activists

Memories from the Underground
KERIM BOUZOUITA

Kerim Bouzouita is a Tunisian journalist, producer, advocacy expert for the United Nations, and academic (associate professor at the Higher e-Business School of Tunis, visiting professor at Loyola University Chicago). He is also known as a human rights activist and blogger who uses humor and satire in his political critiques. His productions and publications include papers about soft power, hacktivism, and new forms of e-citizenship and an investigative documentary on the Tunisian political police. Bouzouita is committed to open movement, promoting the sharing and participating of culture in art, technology, and governance.

I am often asked questions about Tunisian and international cyber-activism. Did bloggers really produce revolutions? Can we change the world from behind a keyboard and a laptop screen? Though often relevant, these questions hide the most important questions: How does cyber-dissidence work, and what is its potential for local and global change? Let me share some memories from the Tunisian underground, a firsthand experience of my activism.

Under Ben Ali's Tunisia, *citizenship* was but a phony word in the political discourse of the dictator. In this context, public space was like a pool swarming with sharks. Tunisians could not create nongovernmental organizations (NGOs) or political parties. We were not allowed to speak, and we were discouraged from thinking about politics. The regime was a system of tentacles, each with thousands of informants. Under such oppressive political conditions, the internet and social media became natural spaces of dissent. In many ways, these media created a new public space, one that was more complicated for the regime to police.

At the end of December 2010, I changed my Facebook profile picture to a black Tunisian flag, subverting the official flag, which is red. Searching for an easy and efficient way to involve more people into the opposition, I drew my inspiration from Umberto Eco's "semiotic guerilla."

Shortly after I changed my profile picture, I began receiving messages and phone calls from my Facebook friends, warning me that the photo "could put me and my family in danger." In contrast, other Facebook friends rallied around this new standard of the opposition, adopting the black Tunisian flag as their own profile picture. "I loved your flag on Facebook, in fact I just adopted it as my profile picture.... When people walk to Carthage Palace, I will be among them." Small commitments such as changing one's Facebook profile picture were soon followed by others that were increasingly risky. For example, the same person who made the above comment filmed himself virulently protesting the regime at the Carthage Palace demonstration and posted the video on Facebook. The same individual also posted videos of the January 14 protests on Avenue Habib Bourguiba in which he fearlessly challenged the police while wrapped in the Tunisian flag.

The concept of mimesis helps to explain the spread of symbolic weapons, such as the black Tunisian flag, employed as a method of self and group identification. Nowhere was mimesis more present than in the Tunisian social media web under Ben Ali, where millions of users processed the symbolism of images and appropriated and propagated them. In the Tunisian context, cyber-activism had a real, subversive dimension. Hitherto confined to the world of hacktivists and cyber-utopians, mimesis was one of the most remarkable mechanisms of dissent during the initial stages of the Tunisian uprising. Facebook was the vector of antiregime symbols, which were spread and replicated at exponential speed by everyday users. Peer-to-peer philosophy, the powerful viral potential of the social "weak links" (in contrast with strong links like those we develop with our family members or close friends); the adoption and propagation of these symbols of dissent were one of the most important phenomena of the Tunisian revolution.

Indeed, during the Tunisian Revolution, 812 of my 867 Facebook contacts—close to 94 percent—changed their Facebook profile picture to my subversive black Tunisian flag. The ordinarily silent masses often give the impression of stability and lethargy, hiding underground movements, which are themselves led by children, not academics or policy activists. The speed by which these underground movements were able to channel and direct opposition to the regime underscores the unpredictability of revolutions.

In short, the Tunisian Revolution did not surprise Tunisian citizens or cybercitizens. In fact, the pioneers of Tunisian cyber-dissent, www.TuneZine.com, prophetically wrote on November 16, 2005: "We hug, cry: We kiss, cry, howl: it is an explosion of joy that invades the streets of Tunis. President Zine El Abedine Ben Ali has resigned under pressure from the people. The 'Jasmine Revolution' lasted two days, and no blood was spilled."

The Tunisian Revolution is not just a revolution. Rather, it revolutionized the way of making revolution.

---

in Tunis who had been involved in the 2008 Gafsa/Redeyef national support campaign, including the blogger Slim Amamou ("Slim 404"), organized a protest event on Facebook entitled Tunisie en Blanc (Tunisia in White).[32] The event was creative: the activists called on those Tunisians who had been affected by the deepening internet censorship to dress in white and simply have a coffee in one of the many cafes on Avenue Habib Bourguiba, the main avenue traversing Tunis that would later become the principal site of the January 14, 2011, Revolution. The flash mob in white would be the pinnacle of nonviolent protest, as organizers stressed that there was nothing illegal in dressing in white and meeting for a coffee in downtown Tunis. "An entire avenue in white," they wrote on the Facebook event wall, "is much more effective than a traditional protest confronting the police." The organizing activists, especially Slim Amamou and Yassine Ayari, attempted to complement the Tunisia in White flash mob with a more traditional protest in front of the Ministry of Communication and Technology, a few streets away from Avenue Habib Bourguiba.

It remains unclear whether the Ministry of Interior's refusal to grant them a protest permit caused the shutdown of the Tunisia in White Facebook page, the subsequent dispersal of those dressed in white and sipping coffee on May 22, and the detention of activists involved in organizing the events. Some pessimistic observers regarded the quick protest shutdown by the government as yet another activist defeat, a less violent version of the police intervention in 2008. However, some of the strategies and conversations occurring during the May 2010 e-mobilization effort give us crucial insights to the January 14, 2011, puzzle.

First, an important debate among activists and supporters of the Tunisia in White initiative ensued on the Facebook event page immediately after the event was publicized. As the number of supporters for the campaign mushroomed daily with the number of invited participants "liking" the page (a public political statement in itself) reaching approximately one thousand, so did the Facebook wall discussion. Interested individuals engaged in a virtual yet anonymous debate about political participation, freedom of expression, the freedom to protest nonviolently, the limits of government censorship, and the meaning and duties of citizenship. The vibrant debate was moderated by the event organizers, who continuously stressed the right to nonviolent citizen mobilization and encouraged supporters to discuss taboo topics. The strategy to support street-based protests and clashes between citizens and the police with cyber-activism mirrors the strategies of the Gafsa/Redeyef support groups in 2008. Only seven months later, the same mobilization strategies appeared on activists' Facebook walls, this time contributing to the ouster of Ben Ali.

Second, supporters from all over Tunisia as well as the Tunisian diaspora across the world publicly pledged their support. In Tunisia particularly, supporters from other large cities including Sfax, Sousse, Gafsa, and Nabeul attempted to organize similar nonviolent flash mobs, by committing to dress in white and consume a coffee in public on May 22. In 2011, a similar synergy occurred between activists inside and outside Tunisia.

Third, the public Facebook debate during the week preceding Tunisia in White signaled the increased willingness of ordinary Tunisians to debate resistance politics publicly as well as take to the streets. While those analysts writing of a "Tunisian paradox" questioned the inability or unwillingness of the urban middle class to press for political liberties, contentious moments such as Tunisia in White show that urban Tunisians were indeed willing to resist if given the opportunity. Unlike the 2008 waves of protest in the southern mining towns, Tunisia in White was clearly about a middle-class issue, about free and uncensored access to information and liberty of expression, both in Tunisia and abroad. This regional variation in grievances directed against the state once again became pronounced in the months following the January 14, 2011, Revolution, as different catalysts drove different social sectors to take to the streets under the umbrella of a common call for the fall of the regime.

On May 22, 2010, the small groups of courageous Tunisians who flocked to Avenue Habib Bourguiba to have a coffee in public were met by the police, who dispersed any group dressed in white. While neither the flash mob in white nor the protest in front of the Ministry of Communication and Technology occurred as planned, by then activism in Tunisia had taken on a radically different character. Activists, bloggers, and oppositional journalists were supporting and covering any attempt to transgress and contest the Ben Ali regime. Their mobilization became more sophisticated, linking cyber-activism with street-based protest or supporting street-based rebellions with online activism. The catalyst was not only the increase in internet usage from 6 percent in 2003 to 36 percent in 2010 but also the anonymity of online profiles. Activists were generally under police surveillance, but Tunisian youth, students, and those growing increasingly disgruntled with the regime became the consumers of mounting critiques and new forms of activism. Nowhere is this clearer than in the linkages between the 2008 rebellion in the mining region and the 2010 planned flash mob in Tunis—the overlap in activists, mobilization strategies, and outreach techniques. What remains distinctive in these moments as well as during the buildup to the 2011 Revolution is that Tunisian activists were willing to absorb any issue, from the plight of unemployed miners to internet freedom, that challenged the dominance of the Ben Ali regime.

T.Unis: A Nation United, 2011

A number of structural conditions in late 2010 help explain why scattered clashes with the police and the ensuing protests transformed into large-scale mobilization that would snowball into a nationwide movement aimed at ousting a dictator. First, the combination of inflation, rising unemployment, Qaddafi's expulsion of Tunisian workers from Libya, the lingering effects of the 2008 global financial meltdown, and the November 2010 release of U.S. State Department diplomatic "cables" by WikiLeaks distinguishes the months leading up to the December 2010 rebellion. The WikiLeaks information dump in particular contributed to public grievances, as it confirmed the rumors about the corruption and extravagant lifestyle of the Ben Ali clan that for many years had circulated quietly among ordinary Tunisians. The endorsement of these previously unconfirmed popular stories juxtaposed with the reality of deteriorating socioeconomic conditions, not only in Tunisia's impoverished South but also in poor urban neighborhoods, may have constituted the final straw. After all, Ben Ali incessantly touted the story of the "Tunisian miracle," whether on the front pages of every government-sponsored newspaper, in the infrequent speeches given by him and his appointed cabinet and diplomats, or in the output of the international public relations firms he employed.

Second, any explanation of activism during the revolution has to be positioned within the scattered and later converged forms of activism that allowed Tunisians to learn how to escape the chains of censorship and repression. Those activists and students who were involved in organizing Tunisia in White, supporting the 2008 Gafsa/Redeyef rebellion, and participating in previous protests, including criticizing the 2005 WSIS event, had refined their techniques to call for citizens to take their grievances to the streets.

Third, the architecture of resistance chronicled in the previous two sections provides a glimpse of the accumulation of different grievances among Tunisian citizens over a decade, which catalyzed a variety of groups to take to the streets simultaneously. In following the flow of protests in 2010 and 2011, one can see that grievances developed from basic economic demands in Sidi Bouzid, Thala, Kasserine, and the mining region in the South, along the Algerian border toward the north of the country and also to Jendouba in the northwest, to overt demands for increased political liberties. By the time the popular protests reached Tunis on January 8, 2011, Tunisians had united in demanding the departure of Ben Ali as well as his family and cronies. The regional variation in grievances mattered less in the days before the revolution, when Tunisians felt united in their collective grievance towards the Ben Ali regime, than it did in the subsequent vulnerable period of democratic consolidation. In early 2011, opposition parties, lawyers, professional organizations, and the UGTT broke with the regime late in the game to join the flourishing movement. It was only on January 13, 2011, that the UGTT called for a nationwide strike, encouraging thousands to take to the streets the next morning to call for Ben Ali's departure. By then, activists all over Tunisia had become united behind this single cause.

From Activism to Civil Society: A Promising Micro-Model

After the three-year anniversary of the Tunisian Revolution and over two years after the National Constituent Assembly (NCA) elections that brought the Islamist an-Nahda Party to power, widespread dissatisfaction with the new leadership and the inability of political elites to achieve the "objectives of the revolution" dominated the public discourse, including opinion-based journalism and the daily conversations at the workplace, at home, in cafes, and even among many of the smaller oppositional political parties. These public sentiments have been exacerbated following the assassinations of leftist political opposition leaders Chokri Belaid and Mohamed Brahmi in 2013 and a growing protest movement demanding the dissolution of the Nahda-led government first amid a suspended NCA. The conditions that primarily pushed Tunisians to take to the streets—widespread unemployment, lack of economic opportunities, the delayed effects of the global financial meltdown—had not been quickly ameliorated, or at least that is what Tunisians felt. In fact, unemployment rates were higher than many expected, with international firms steadily pulling out of Tunisia and no significant reforms of investment laws or the tax code that would have eased business transactions and attracted more investment. The deteriorating security situation, political assassinations, and activity of Al-Qaeda in the Islamic Maghreb in the Chaambi mountain region further weakened citizen trust and confidence in the government, pushing Tunisians yet again to the streets to demand radical government restructuring.

Within this seemingly bleak picture, three positive developments occurred, especially among activist communities. The first was that the arena of activism had changed. With a dizzying multitude of voices pushing the transitional and later newly elected government to respond to issues of unemployment, economic development, freedom of expression and association, Islam and politics, martyrdom and reparations, the rights of women, and national security, the forms of activism seen in the previous few years suddenly become the prevailing modus operandi in Tunisia. The second development was that the means of activism had also transformed. For the first time in Tunisia's modern history, an unprecedented array of voices entered the previously obliterated political space, with thousands of new civil society organizations and 113 political parties competing in the Constituent Assembly elections on October 23, 2011. The third development was that, although overshadowed by protests, strikes, violent confrontations, and sit-ins, micro-level civil society initiatives rooted in decades of antidictatorial activism evolved, creating a successful activism-to–civil society model. Part of the explanation for their success was their previous experience in negotiating with state elites in Tunis, something that many of the nascent civil society organizations that registered immediately after the revolution did not possess. Another explanation is the legitimacy these initiatives have gained among their respective communities over time, especially as they represent some of the most pressing and basic needs among Tunisians, mainly unemployment and wage negotiations.

An illustration of this model can be found in the case of Redeyef, located in the governorate of Gafsa, the contentious inland mining region. This was the principal site of the 2008 uprising in a region that has suffered from some of the highest unemployment rates in the country, similar to other areas such as Le Kef, a northern mountain town close to the Algerian border, and Jendouba, an impoverished northwestern city. Statistics show that the unemployment rate for college graduates in the governorate of Gafsa is 37.5 percent. According to local residents, however, unemployment in the area is well over 50 percent. The Redeyef case indicates a crucial variation in activism in post-revolutionary Tunisia: whereas initiatives in areas most affected by dire economic conditions with deep histories of activism have been more successful in pushing against the state and garnering local support, the more lucrative, internationally financed initiatives dealing with high-level institutional transformations and political liberties in the larger cities, especially the capital Tunis, have been heavily criticized by Tunisian citizens.

The southern mining region remained relatively quiet since the 2008 violent crackdown until the December 2010 protests that commenced in Sidi Bouzid. A spatial trajectory of the protests preceding the January 14 Revolution shows that the first towns to engage in ongoing protests were Thala, Kasserine, Gafsa, Redeyef, and Métlaoui, before heading north along the Algerian border, through Jendouba, and finally reaching Tunis in early January. While the earliest protests suffered from the most brutal police crackdowns, those areas were also among the first to organize collectively with new associations and unions. Hassen Ben Abdellah immediately helped register the UDC and began holding regular meetings with local residents as well as the UGTT and the CPG in Gafsa in order to preempt the same conditions that had previously led to protests and violent police reactions in the region. Ten

December 17, 2010: Mohamed Bouazizi sets himself on fire after Fedia Hamdi, a municipal inspector from Sidi Bouzid, slaps the informal produce vendor and seizes his produce cart. Bouazizi's self-immolation sparks a series of local protests.

December 18, 2010: Protests immediately spread to Gafsa, Redeyef, Kasserine, and Thala.

December 24, 2010: Rapper El Général is detained and questioned for publishing "Rais El Bled," the first anthem of the revolutionary movement, on his Facebook page.

December 29, 2010: Ben Ali appears on television with a twofold promise: to create jobs and to punish rioters dubbed "terrorists," just as he had labeled striking phosphate workers from the Gafsa Basin in 2008 to invoke the 2003 Anti-Terrorism Law and justify heavy repression. The military is deployed to quell protests.

December 31, 2010: Protests reach Tunisia's north, including Le Kef and Ben Arous.

January 8, 2011: Protests reach the capital of Tunis. Deadly clashes break out between protesters and the police in Gafsa and Kasserine. This day later becomes known as "the slaughter of Kasserine."

January 9, 2011: Violence escalates across Tunisia, with more than fifty deaths after a week of clashes between security forces and protesters in Meknassy, Kasserine, Gafsa, Regueb, Thala, Seliana, Maktar, Mdenine, and Le Kef.

January 11, 2011: General Rachid Ammar refuses orders to shoot at protesters. Ben Ali deploys military to Tunis and surrounding areas. Leader of the Communist Party PCOT Hamma Hammami is arrested.

January 12, 2011: Ben Ali pledges not to run in the 2015 elections and removes internet censors.

January 13, 2011: Amid protests in Sfax, Tunis, Nabeul, and other large cities, the military is deployed nationwide into towns and cities and to protect headquarters of major banks and companies.

January 13, 2011: The largest labor union, UGTT, calls for a general strike.

January 14, 2011: After thousands of Tunisians storm Avenue Habib Bourguiba demanding Ben Ali's ouster, Ben Ali flees to Saudi Arabia. The Ben Ali regime under the political party RCD collapses, marking the Tunisian Revolution. A curfew of 7 p.m. is immediately imposed.

January 15, 2011: Head of the Constitutional Council declares the presidency vacant, and appoints speaker of the National Assembly, Fouad Mbazza, interim president. Prime Minister Mohammed Ghannouchi is confirmed as prime minister in the transitional government.

January 17, 2011: Yadh Ben Achour is appointed to preside over the High Political Reform Commission (Ben Achour Commission), overseeing constitutional reform in Tunisia.

January 19, 2011: Switzerland's federal council freezes Ben Ali's assets.

February 27, 2011: As a result of the Casbah-1 sit-in demanding the resignation of the prime minister and the dismantling of the RCD, Mohamed Ghannouchi resigns. Interim president Fouad Mebazaa names Beji Caid-Essebsi, a former minister under Habib Bourguiba and Ben Ali, interim prime minister.

March 9, 2011: Street celebrations abound after a Tunisian court instructs that Ben Ali's former party, the Constitutional Democratic Rally (RDC) be dismantled.

April 23, 2011: After 111 days of incarceration, a Sidi Bouzid tribunal releases Fedia Hamdi, the municipal inspector jailed for slapping street vendor Mohamed Bouazizi.

May 8, 2011: Tunisia restores an emergency nighttime curfew to run from 9 p.m. until 5 a.m. after four days of clashes between police and protesters.

May 10, 2011: Tunisian authorities arrest 197 people on charges of committing vandalism, theft, and violating curfew hours.

May 27, 2011: G8 leaders pledge US$20 billion of loans and aid to Tunisia and Egypt over the next two years, contingent upon their continued path to democracy. The transitional government confirms July 24, 2011, as the date for national constituent assembly elections.

May 31, 2011: Following a disagreement on election dates, Islamist party an-Nahda suspends its membership in the transition government.

June 6, 2011: Security forces are deployed as clashes between youth in the southern mining town of Métlaoui result in eleven deaths and more than one hundred injured.

June 8, 2011: Elections are postponed until October 23, 2011, to rectify the almost four hundred thousand unregistered voters and numerous incorrect mailing addresses.

June 21, 2011: A Tunisian court sentences Ben Ali and wife, Leila Trabelsi, to thirty-five years in jail in absentia on charges of theft and unlawful possession of cash and jewelry and fines the couple 91 million Tunisian dinars.

June 23, 2011: Rached al-Ghannouchi, leader of Tunisia's Islamist party an-Nahda, cautions against the further delay of elections, claiming that elites are trying to "escape the ballot box."

June 27, 2011: Tunisia becomes the 116th signatory, and first North African country, to the Rome Statute that established the International Criminal Court.

July 5, 2011: Moncef Marzouki, chairman of the Congress Party for the Republic (CPR), briefly suspends his party's participation in the transition government because of its inability to settle important issues.

July 18, 2011: Protests continue throughout the country as police kill a fourteen-year old in Sidi Bouzid, four are wounded in protests in Menzel Bourguiba, and two hundred angry protesters set fire to a police station in the Intilaka district of the Tunis suburb of Ariana.

July 21, 2011: The Progressive Democratic Party (PDP) withdraws from the transition government in protest of the political party draft-decree law, which prohibits any foreign funding for political parties.

July 27, 2011: An interim presidential decree extends a state of emergency until August 1.

August 23, 2011: The European Union announces 110 million Euros in aid to help Tunisia's fledgling economy, following a similar pledge by the United States in March 2011.

September 19, 2011: Election figures are announced: 11,333 candidates will compete on 1,570 lists in 33 constituencies for the 217-seat National Constituent Assembly.

September 22, 2011: Former Libyan prime minister Al-Baghdadi Ali al-Mahmoudi is arrested in Tunisia. Tunisia will later extradite him to Libya on June 25, 2012.

October 11, 2011: Following the release of controversial French-Iranian film *Persepolis,* Salafist protesters attack Tunisian TV station Nessma and the University of Sousse.

October 23, 2011: 4.1 million Tunisians register to determine the new 217-seat government in the country's first free and fair election; only 3.7 million Tunisians turn out to vote for a National Constituent Assembly tasked with drafting the Constitution and overseeing the work of the government.

October 25–26, 2011: An-Nahda receives the majority of votes, as final election results are determined: an-Nahda takes 90 seats, centrist secularists CPR win 30 seats, center-left party Ettakatol wins 21, Sidi Bouzid popular party Aridha Chabia 19, and liberal secularist party PDP win 17.

October 28, 2011: Protests break out in Sidi Bouzid after local party favorite, Aridha Chabia, has eight invalidated seats reassigned to competing parties.

November 22, 2011: Tunisia's newly elected 217-member National Constituent Assembly meets for the first time.

December 13, 2011: Moncef Marzouki is sworn in as Tunisia's new president in front of the National Constituent Assembly. Hamadi Jebali, secretary general of an-Nahda, is appointed prime minister.

months after the Tunisian Revolution and only weeks after the elections on October 23, 2011, the CPG once again refused to release entrance exam results, which prompted residents to take to the streets, organize sit-ins, even self-immolations. The police responded with a series of imposed curfews.

In the meantime, the UDC, in coalition with UGTT activist Adnan Hajji, a spokesperson for the 2008 Gafsa rebellion, began negotiations with the ministries in Tunis. The institutionalization of the previous waves of protests, in coalition with UGTT activists like Hajji, shifted the balance between protesters, residents, and the state in Tunisia. At the same time, since the beginning of 2011, a vibrant and new civil society arena instigated by the UDC has emerged in the country's phosphate region and has since spread throughout the country. For instance, on January 21, 2012, the UDC held a town hall meeting in Redeyef, in which residents directly voiced their grievances to the local UDC leadership. During the meeting, the UDC elected a number of representatives who would negotiate reparations for families of martyrs and deceased miners, unemployment, and minimum salaries with ministries in Tunis. That same afternoon the UDC organized a public meeting in Gafsa with representatives of the Gafsa Phosphate Company, the Bank of Mines, political parties, and local civil society organizations that began operating in the region after the October 23, 2011, elections. The public meeting was organized after the January 5, 2012, visit of Khalid Zaoui, the minister of social affairs, to Redeyef and Gafsa, marking the four-year anniversary of the 2008 rebellion. Accompanied by Houssein Abassi, the newly elected secretary general of the UGTT, Zaoui promised to make the development of the phosphate region a national priority. The three hundred attendees engaged in a lively and often contentious debate with the invited representatives about local distress, including prospects for employment, availability of microcredit funding, and potential areas for sustainable foreign investment. In response, the CPG suggested three new areas of development to increase employment opportunities: cement and glass production as well as IT training for local students to make them more marketable. Local civil society organizations pushed for cultural projects, including cinemas, music concerts, and theater events that would serve to stimulate the region's hitherto absent "civic culture." During the public meeting, the UDC was selected as the primary regional representative and main negotiating body with state institutions in Tunis, especially the Ministry of Social Affairs.

After the January 21 public meeting, the elected regional representatives of the UDC attempted to negotiate with Zaoui, Abassi, and other ministers on a regular basis, but to no avail. In response, the UDC organized a series of demonstrations in Tunis and called for multiple general strikes and sit-ins in the mining area. Once again, the mining region's activism made national headlines at the same time that the transitional government was beset by a growing security problem, an increasing schism between political Islam and secularist opposition, unemployment, daily protests and strikes, and increased organized violence and petty crime. Yet the unyielding commitment by local activists from Redeyef and Gafsa finally commenced a sustainable and promising negotiation with the national government in Tunis. On April 14, 2012, a number of ministers, major Tunisian economic players, and a group of foreign investors from Spain, Slovakia, and Austria signed an agreement to implement ten new projects ranging from agro-business, cement production, and floriculture to recycling industries across the mining region.[33] The Gafsa Regional Development Plan went into effect immediately, slowly weakening reliance on the economic and political monopoly of the Gafsa Phosphate Company.

The case of Tunisia's mining region, one of the most contentious and economically disadvantaged regions of the country, exemplifies the transformation of the scattered and later organized activism prior to the January 14, 2011, Revolution into a nascent civil society. Unlike in other regions, this localized civil society has been able to establish new channels of negotiation with state elites, indicating that despite an increasingly complicated transitional political field, activism has found a space in new political institutions.

Conclusion

Activism in Tunisia underwent tremendous changes in the periods leading up to and after the 2011 Revolution. First, those young activists who pushed the boundaries of the permissible under Ben Ali over the last decade of his rule assumed new roles as civil society leaders, prominent bloggers, political commentators, writers, and elected politicians. Some, especially those in the southern regions, continued to fight for the amelioration of their communities. Second, while activism before the revolution was mostly directed against a dictator and illiberal politics, after the revolution activists from a wide political spectrum openly and freely critiqued the work of an elected government and its opposition. The regional variation of grievances that united a nation in 2010 and 2011 later contributed to a fragmented political landscape, as residents of areas with high unemployment and economic underdevelopment felt once again alienated from the political developments in the capital and the wealthier coastal regions. Third, a trend emerged among the political opposition, civil society, and longstanding activists to organize around issues—such as unemployment and economic development, transitional justice, judiciary reform, human rights, women's rights, and freedom of expression—rather than adhere to rigid and outdated ideologies. Fourth, a new area of Islamist activism, whether related to an-Nahda, Salafism, or other political Islamist trends, expanded rapidly.

Since the assassinations of Chokri Belaid and Mohamed Brahmi and a deteriorating security situation starting in 2012, pro- and antigovernment activists have shoehorned Tunisia's political landscape into a superficial Islamist vs. secularist playing field. But activists representing the many shades of Tunisia's political spectrum have not clearly aligned with either political parties or civil society organizations. The challenge for activism in Tunisia after the revolution remained primarily in linking new issues with the appropriate political and social organizations, beyond the anti- or progovernment protests that have caused a dangerous political standoff. Without a doubt, activists no longer needed to carve out spaces to channel divergent grievances into a nationwide movement, but rather to help establish effective channels for communicating grievances without threatening the reversal of Tunisia's democratic transition.

Notes

1. In March 2010, Abdessalam Trimesh, a street vendor from Monastir, also set himself on fire, protesting corruption. See Yasmine Ryan, "How Tunisia's Revolution Began," Al Jazeera, January 26, 2011.

2. At an April 2010 soccer game between Club Sportif de Hammam-Lif and Espérance, a fight broke out between hundreds of spectators and the police. Hammam-Lif was leading 3-0 when a supporter of Espérance stormed the field to attack the referee. In response, the police switched off the stadium's electricity and began indiscriminately assaulting soccer fans. The event was never covered in the news.

3. Joel Beinin and Frédéric Vairel (eds.), *Social Movements, Mobilization, and Contention in the Middle East and North Africa* (Stanford, CA: Stanford University Press, 2011), 237–238.

4. For a discussion of such forms of expression focusing on Syria as a case study, see Lisa Wedeen, *Ambiguities of Domination: Politics, Rhetoric, and Symbols in Contemporary Syria* (Chicago: University of Chicago Press, 1999).

5. Charles Micaud, Leon Carl Brown, and Clement H. Moore, *Tunisia: The Politics of Modernization* (New York: Fredrick A. Praeger, 1964); Clement H. Moore, *Tunisia since Independence: The Dynamics of One-Party Government* (Berkeley: University of California Press, 1965); Lars Rudebeck, *Party and People: A Study of Political Change in Tunisia* (New York: Fredrick A. Praeger, 1969); Leon Carl Brown, *The Tunisia of Ahmad Bey, 1837–1855* (Princeton: Princeton University Press, 1974); Lisa Anderson, *The State and Social Transformation in Tunisia and Libya, 1830–1980* (Princeton: Princeton University Press, 1986); Julia Clancy-Smith,

Rebel and Saint: Muslim Notables, Populist Protest, Colonial Encounters (Algeria and Tunisia, 1800–1904) (Berkeley: University of California Press, 1994); John P. Entelis, "The Unchanging Politics of North Africa," *Middle East Policy* 14(4) (2007): 23–41; Kenneth J. Perkins, *A History of Modern Tunisia* (Cambridge, U.K.: Cambridge University Press, 2008).

6. During this period, academic work on Tunisian politics since the "medical coup" of Ben Ali in 1987 focused almost exclusively on the gradual cooptation of civil society and political institutions, including unions, associations, leagues, political parties, elections, and the rule of law. See Eva Bellin, *Stalled Democracy: Capital, Labor, and the Paradox of State-Sponsored Development* (Ithaca: Cornell University Press, 2002); Stephen J. King, *Liberalization against Democracy: The Local Politics of Economic Reform in Tunisia* (Bloomington: Indiana University Press, 2003); Melani Claire Cammett, *Globalization and Business Politics in Arab North Africa: A Comparative Perspective* (Cambridge, U.K.: Cambridge University Press, 2007); Béatrice Hibou, *The Force of Obedience* (Cambridge, U.K.: Polity, 2011); Clement Henry and Robert Springborg, *Globalization and the Politics of Development in the Middle East* (Cambridge, U.K.: Cambridge University Press, 2001); Christopher Alexander, *Tunisia: Stability and Reform in the Modern Maghreb* (New York: Routledge, 2010); John P. Entelis, "The Democratic Imperative vs. the Authoritarian Impulse: The Maghrib State Between Transition and Terrorism," *Middle East Journal* 59(4) (2004): 537–558; Michel Camau and Vincent Geisser, *Le Syndrome Autoritaire: Politique en Tunisie de Bourguiba à Ben Ali* (Paris: Presses de Sciences Po, 2003); Hamadi Redissi, "État Fort, Société Civile Faible en Tunisie," *Maghreb Machrek* 192(2007): 89–117; Larbi Sadiki, Heiko Wimmen, and Layla al-Zubaidi (eds.), *Democratic Transition in the Middle East: Unmaking Power* (London: Routledge, 2012); Greg White, *A Comparative Political Economy of Tunisia and Morocco: On the Outside of Europe Looking In* (Albany: State University of New York Press, 2001). Scholarly attention to the consolidation of the authoritarian state, coupled with the policy and development world's focus on Tunisia's socioeconomic success story, diverted attention from ongoing and interconnected activist activity since Ben Ali's rise to power. Part of the explanation for the absence of studies of resistance and political activism under Ben Ali was the attention directed to the frameworks of civil society and democratization, with a predominant focus on the transformation of political institutions. Analysts thus examined the cooptation of oppositional political parties as well as the state's expanding control over independent civil society activity and concluded that Tunisia is plagued by a so-called development paradox: a country with comparatively high levels of socioeconomic development, an expansive middle class, yet little pressure for political liberalization. Oppositional politics, according to work on Tunisia since the 1990s, were therefore severely restricted or simply nonexistent. However, studies of highly

repressive regimes in the Middle East and North Africa have shown that resistance is not necessarily absent under dictatorship—rather it occurs outside of the institutional and formal realm of politics. See Lisa Anderson, "Political Pacts, Liberalism, and Democracy: The Tunisian National Pact of 1988," *Government and Opposition* 26(2) (1991): 245–260; Michael J. Willis, "Political Parties in the Maghrib: The Illusion of Significance?" *Journal of North African Studies* 7(2) (2002): 1–22; Michele Penner-Angrist, *Party Building in the Modern Middle East* (Seattle: University of Washington Press, 2006); Bellin, "Stalled Democracy"; Redissi, "État Fort"; James C. Scott, *Domination and the Arts of Resistance: Hidden Transcripts* (New Haven: Yale University Press, 1990); Diane Singerman, *Avenues of Participation: Family, Politics, and Networks in Urban Quarters of Cairo* (Princeton: Princeton University Press, 1993); Wedeen, *Ambiguities of Domination*; Lisa Wedeen, *Peripheral Visions: Publics, Power, and Performance in Yemen* (Chicago: University of Chicago Press, 2008); Asef Bayat, *Life as Politics: How Ordinary People Change the Middle East* (Stanford, CA: Stanford University Press, 2009).

7. Dirk Vandewalle, "From the New State to the New Era: Toward a Second Republic in Tunisia," *Middle East Journal* 42(4) (1988): 602–620.

8. An-Nahda was outlawed entirely after the 1989 elections, when an-Nahda members running on independent tickets came in second after the RCD. Their strongest performance was in Bizerte, Tozeur, Ben Arous, and Kelibia. See Michel Camau and Vincent Geisser, *Le Syndrome Autoritaire: Politique en Tunisie de Bourguiba à Ben Ali* (Paris: Presses de Sciences Po, 2003), p. 301.

9. King, *Liberalization against Democracy*; Emma Murphy, *Economic and Political Change in Tunisia: From Bourguiba to Ben Ali* (New York: St. Martin's Press, 2001).

10. The "Zine" of TUNeZine refers to Ben Ali's first name, Zine El Abedine.

11. The popular and independent blogging community Nawaat (www.nawaat .tn) was created in 2004 amidst heavy censorship; it played a critical role in information dissemination before, during, and after the Tunisian Revolution. Nawaat, for instance, published a subset of the November 2010 WikiLeaks data dump under the name TuniLeaks, as well as videos and commentaries about protest activity and police violence in Sidi Bouzid, Kasserine, Thala, and Gafsa in December 2010.

12. Asef Bayat, "Activism and Social Development in the Middle East," *International Journal of Middle East Studies* 34(1) (2003): 1–28.

13. Place 7 November, now Place 14 Janvier, links the two major avenues in Tunis—Avenue Bourguiba and Avenue Mohamed V—and is located between the former RCD headquarters and the Ministry of the Interior. The march was organized on the opposite side of town as the location of the 2002 pro-Palestinian protest, in an area that could be easily controlled and patrolled by the police. See Agence France Press, "Quelque 5.000 personnes manifestent pour l'irak et contre Bush à Tunis," March 22, 2003.

14. 404 is the error message given when a website is not available or, more pertinently, has been censored. Slim Ammamou/"Slim 404" was arrested on January 6, 2011, along with the rapper El Général before the January 14 Revolution. During the protest that led to the ouster of Ben Ali, some people held up signs calling for the release of Slim 404. Ammamou was later appointed minister of youth and sports, a post he held for only a few months.

15. Laryssa Chomiak and Shana Marshall, "Polishing the Police State: PR Campaigns in Tunisia and Syria," paper presented at the Middle East Studies Association Annual Meeting, San Diego, California, November 18–21, 2010.

16. Protesters chanted the same slogan in 2003 during a state-sanctioned protest in support of Iraq. In an interview, an activist from Redeyef confirmed that throughout the last decade, broader international issues such as the violence in Iraq and Palestine allowed an opportunity for individuals to take to the streets and to express frustration collectively. In these moments, protesters used the opportunity to articulate collectively anti–Ben Ali and antipolice grievances, using international causes to protest local conditions. Interview with the author, Tunis, Tunisia, January 19, 2011.

17. Exceptions are Beinin and Vairel, *Social Movements, Mobilization, and Contention*; and Jillian Schwedler, "Cop Rock: Protest, Identity and Dancing Riot Police in Jordan," *Social Movement Studies* 4(2) (2005): 155–175. The literature on social movements and studies of the nexus between repression and dissent provide useful analytical tools for research on mobilization, contestation, and political activism. Studies of social movements in particular have evolved from the linking of moments of political opportunity and mobilization efforts to more sophisticated frameworks in which social movements are dissected and micro-processes within movements are compared across time and cases to investigate macro-political outcomes, such as democracy, nationalism, revolution, or protest. See Doug McAdam, Sidney G. Tarrow, and Charles Tilly, *Dynamics of Contention* (Cambridge, U.K.: Cambridge University Press, 2001); Charles Tilly, *Social Movements, 1768–2004* (Boulder, CO: Paradigm, 2004); Charles Tilly, *Democracy* (Cambridge, U.K.: Cambridge University Press, 2007); Charles Tilly and Signey G. Tarrow, *Contentious Politics* (Boulder, CO: Paradigm, 2007). Social movements are now more directly linked to broader questions of political contention or collective claim-making but nonetheless remain empirically tied to the contours of a clearly demarcated social movement. See Tilly, *Social Movements*; Kevin J. O'Brian and Li Lianjiang, *Rightful Resistance in China* (Cambridge, U.K.: Cambridge University Press, 2007). In a similar vein, scholarly work on the nexus between repression and dissent examines how state repression destructs social movements yet does not always consider that state repression also gives rise to other forms of mobilization and contentious activity that do not necessarily fall into the identifiable contours of social movement. See, for instance, Mark Irving Lichbach, "Deterrence of Escalation? The Puzzle of Aggregate Studies of

Repression and Dissent," *Journal of Conflict Resolution* 31(2) (1987): 266–297; William H. Moore, "Repression and Dissent: Substitution, Context, and Timing," *American Journal of Political Science* 42(3) (1998): 851–873; Christian Davenport, Hank Johnston, and Carol McClurg Mueller, *Repression and Mobilization* (Minneapolis: University of Minnesota Press, 2005). An exception is Jillian Schwedler's recent work on the spatial and legal dimension of protest and policing in Jordan, where she examines parallel policing as well as protesting efforts despite or because of repressive state strategies.

18. The reasons for this omission are certainly not linked solely to analytical commitments. A significant hindrance to studies of activism and resistance under authoritarianism is the unavailability of information, especially in cases where the press and the internet are tightly controlled by the state. An interesting exception in the Arab world is the case of Algeria, where thousands of protests occur annually with regular reporting in the national and international press. In 2012, for instance, there were 10,910 interventions by the riot police. See Robert P. Parks, "Algeria at Fifty: Weak Society, Weak State, Resistant Regime," paper presented at the Middle East Studies Association Annual Meeting, Washington, D.C., December 1–4, 2011; Robert P. Parks, "Algeria and the Arab Uprisings," in *The Arab Spring: Will It Lead to Democratic Transitions?*, ed. Clement Henry and Jang Ji-Hyang (Seoul: Asan Institute for Policy Studies, 2012), 102–125.

19. See Wedeen, *Ambiguities of Domination*; Diane, *Avenues of Participation*; Scott, *Domination and the Arts of Resistance*. Work within the "everyday forms of resistance school" does not necessarily seek to reveal hidden channels of communication between resistant actors and the state; rather, it shows that widespread forms of resistance exist even under the most dictatorial conditions and, more important, that actors *do* engage in oppositional activities. Political engagement, however, occurs in hidden spaces, including subversion in media, widespread jokes, soccer games, and so on. Mundane coping mechanisms both widen the gap between citizen and state and fulfill the welfare role the state cannot perform. Asef Bayat writes that for this very reason, states tolerate informal economic and political activity.

20. Bayat, *Life as Politics*, 43–46.

21. P. R. Baduel, "Emigration et transformation des rapports sociaux dans le sud tunisien," *Peuples Méditerranéens* 17 (1982): 3–22.

22. Noaman Ben Ammar, activist from Redeyef and active member of the UDC, interview with the author, Tunis, Tunisia, January 19, 2012.

23. Interview with the author, Tunis, Tunisia, November 9, 2011.

24. Noaman Ben Ammar interview.

25. In interviews, activists in Redeyef explained that in February 2008, the police began making random arrests in order to spread fear in the mining region. Activists responded with a new strategy to organize protests with women only so that the

police would be less likely to crack down on the protests. Reacting violently to women in the streets would not gel with the women's rights propaganda narrative of Ben Ali.

26. Some journalists likewise attempted to push boundaries in private media, especially after Ben Ali announced the diversification of the media landscape in 2003, which led to the creation of such local media entities as Radio Mosaique, Radio Zaituna, Shems FM, and Hannibal TV. See Rikke Hostrup Haugbølle and Francesco Cavatorta, "'Vive la grande famille des medias tunisiens': Media Reform, Authoritarian Resilience, and Societal Responses in Tunisia," *Journal of North African Studies* 17(1) (2012): 1–16. For subversion in private print media, see Laryssa Chomiak, "Confronting Authoritarianism: Order, Dissent and Everyday Politics in Modern Tunisia," PhD dissertation, University of Maryland (2011), ch. 4.

27. Lamjed Jerli, interview with the author, Tunis, Tunisia, November 9, 2011. Jerli covered the events for *al-Mouatin* and was imprisoned in 2008 and 2009, despite writing under the penname "Protagoras."

28. Civil society activist, interview with the author, Gafsa, Tunisia, January 22, 2012. See also "Tunisia to Jail Sick Journalist Fahem Boukadous," BBC News, July 7, 2010, available at www.bbc.co.uk/news/10535282, accessed July 11, 2013.

29. Hassen Ben Abdellah, interview with the author, Redeyef, Tunisia, January 21, 2012.

30. Noaman Ben Ammar interview. Those who died as a result of police violence in the 2008 uprisings have not yet officially received martyr status, as Mohamed Bouazizi and those killed following the December 2011 protests have. Origin stories are thus politically charged, as any official recognition of martyrdom requires the state to pay reparation to families of martyrs. For a discussion of the political dimension of martyrdom in Tunisia, see Thomas DeGeorges's forthcoming historical analysis of martyrdom in Tunisia.

31. Saloua Charfi, "Tunisie: Terreur Intégriste sur Facebook," *Realités*, no. 1269, April 22–28, 2010, pp. 26–29.

32. Laryssa Chomiak, "The Making of a Revolution in Tunisia," *Middle East Law and Governance* 3(1) (2011): 68–83; Laryssa Chomiak and John P. Entelis, "The Making of North Africa's Intifadas," *Middle East Report* 41(259) (2011); Laryssa Chomiak and John P. Entelis, "Contesting Order in Tunisia: Crafting Political Identity," in *Civil Society Activism Under Authoritarian Rule: A Comparative Perspective,* ed. Francesco Cavatorta (London: Routledge, 2012).

33. Hassan Ghediri, "Un accord, dix projets. . . ." *Le Quotidien,* April 15, 2012.

CHAPTER 2

Egypt

A Decade of Ruptures

RABAB EL-MAHDI

Since the beginning of the Egyptian uprising on January 25, 2011, much analysis has conceptualized this "revolution" as a sudden "awakening" of middle-class "youth" using internet social networks, especially Facebook, to mobilize for "democracy." This narrative frame ignores the decade of contentious politics and mobilization in Egypt that paved the way for the January 25 uprising. This chapter looks at the changing landscape of political activism over the past decade and what it means for changing politics in Egypt post–January 25. By focusing on the different forms of activism that preceded it, the chapter aims to demonstrate that the Egyptian revolution was not simply a momentary explosion but the outcome of a historical process.

The first section focuses on three cycles of protest preceding January 25 and the contribution of each to political activism in Egypt, specifically the Palestinian Second Intifada and the movement against the war on Iraq (2000–2003), the prodemocracy movement (2004–2006), and the labor and youth protests (2006–2011). This section highlights the cross-ideological bridges, the marginalization of traditional political parties, and the rise of fluid networks of activists as significant outcomes of this decade, ones upon which activists capitalized during the 2011 uprisings. The second section examines the activism of previously nonpoliticized actors who became mobilized during the events of January, specifically the football fan clubs known as ultras. It looks at how and why they have become entangled in politics and the impact they have. The chapter then delves into the complex relationship that has unfolded between the different forms of non-institutionalized political activism and the shift to institutional politics brought on by the first parliamentary elections. It examines the continuity of challenges such as the secular-Islamist divide, persistent dynamics of cooptation, and the lack of political projects among contenders as well as the rise of established players (particularly the Muslim Brotherhood) and the entry of new ones (such as the Islamist Salafis) in a new, open, and competitive landscape.

Despite the fall of Hosni Mubarak and the presence of different dissenting actors at the fore, the chapter concludes that Egypt might not yet be on the road to democratic transition, let alone more structural changes. Hence, this chapter calls into question the assumption that there is a sharp discontinuity between politics and activism before and after January 25, 2011. It also suggests that the changing landscape might not favor the earlier forms of dissent or the actors who played exceedingly important roles in the anti-Mubarak cycles.

The Activism Landscape

For decades nonviolent, public political activism seemed to be entirely absent in Egypt. The print media were closely controlled, rallies and lobbies were banned, and those who dared to organize demonstrations or marches risked assault, arrest, imprisonment, and worse. But between the Palestinian Second Intifada in 2000 and the January 25 Revolution, voices of dissent have been heard, and a series of movements, groups, and initiatives have managed to break the stalemate of the 1990s. What has happened in Egypt since January 25, 2011, was a culmination of a number of different forms of mobilization over the past several years: the cumulative effect of protest movements against the wars in Iraq in 2003 and Gaza in 2008; the rise of the prodemocracy movement with Kifaya in 2004 and 2005 and, later on, the "youth movements" that have appeared since 2008; the labor protests that started in Mahalla in 2006 and spread throughout the country to eventually include more than 1.7 million people; and finally, the antisectarian protests that peaked after the church bombing in Alexandria in early 2011. Each of these movements created the fertile conditions for January 25. They politicized different groups of society over specific issues that they cared most about and reinstated the dynamics of collective resistance and active expression against different forms of abuse, be they social, political, or economic. Those different movements and processes exposed the regime's exploitative policies on all of those fronts and enriched new formations of activists and patterns of activism that later played out in the revolution.

It is not an overstatement to say that the Palestinian Second Intifada in the autumn of 2000 marked a new era of Egyptian street politics. As Nicola Pratt correctly notes, "The second intifada triggered perhaps the largest and most radical spontaneous demonstrations in the Arab world since the first Gulf war."[1] In Egypt thousands of students took to the streets from different campuses, including the more elite and highly secluded American University in Cairo; even high school students participated. The intifada assumed "a spiritual importance in the eyes of the millions of Arabs, epitomizing hope that people-power resistance might one day enable disaffected Arabs to achieve their objectives of justice, equality, and emancipation," and the Egyptians were no exception.[2] It provided an opportunity for broad sectors of the Egyptian masses, especially students, to practice expression of disenchantment toward the regime through demonstrations, on-campus student activities, and boycott campaigns against companies alleged to be supporting Israel.

Not only did the intifada bring back collective political action to the streets of Egypt, it also pushed actors into establishing new forums of collaboration. Moved by the new mood for action in the region in general and on the Egyptian streets in particular, a collection of twenty NGOs and independent activists of diverse backgrounds established the Popular Committee to Support the Intifada (PCSI) in 2000.[3] For the first time in modern Egyptian history, a committee brought together members from rival political factions (the Muslim Brotherhood, Socialist-Leftists, Nasserites, and so on) as well as activists from professional syndicates and NGOs. In a span of two years, the committee managed to collect the equivalent of US$400,000 in cash, food, and medical supplies for convoys to Palestine and to gather more than one hundred thousand signatures on its petition calling for cutting diplomatic relations with Israel.[4] The committee was a breakthrough within Egyptian political society, both in terms of its membership's ability to overcome ideological differences and historical grievances (even if among a limited number of individuals) and in its ability to capitalize on the moment and translate popular sympathy into mass campaigns. This new pattern continued and was further strengthened in the antiwar movement, to the point that for six years starting in 2002, the Revolutionary Socialists, the Nasserites, and the Muslim Brotherhood organized a yearly international conference and social forum against American and Israeli occupation. The Cairo Conference against Zionism and Imperialism, which included a student forum, was the incubator of positive interaction between young Islamists, leftists, and liberal activists.[5] Regional issues were an excellent starting point for traditional archenemies to find a common dominator that would allow them to collaborate for the first time.

Following the model of the Popular Committee to Support the Intifada and the Cairo Conference against Imperialism and Zionism, a number of embryonic groups also emerged from 2001 to 2003. The most visible of these was the Anti-Globalization Egyptian Group (AGEG), the 20 March Movement for Change, and the Defense Committee for Labor Rights. These groups provided forums for engagement of activists outside the long-discredited political party platforms as well as being spaces for continued cooperation and interaction among activists with different ideological backgrounds, which further developed in the prodemocracy movement that started in 2004. Such forums, especially the Cairo Conference against Zionism and Imperialism and the AGEG also fertilized cross-ideological and transnational connections between local and international actors working on similar issues.[6]

Almost a year before the presidential referendum scheduled for September 2005 that would mark Mubarak's fifth six-year term in office, Egypt started witnessing a relatively new phenomenon of collective action demanding political liberalization and directly attacking the President and his family. Starting with the Popular Campaign for Change (Freedom Now) and the Egyptian Movement for Change rallying under the slogan *Kifaya* (Enough), there was a burgeoning of groups "calling on President Mubarak not to seek a fifth term and . . . rejecting the prospect that Gamal Mubarak, the president's younger son, would 'inherit' power."[7] This included groups under the names Women for Democracy (The Street is Ours), Youth for Change, Journalists for Change, and Workers for Change, to name just a few. Despite their differences, the underlying principle for all of these groups was "No to a New Mandate. . . . No to Inheritance of the Presidency," an explicit call for ending Mubarak's rule and establishing a legal and political framework for electoral democracy in Egypt. Between December 2004 and September 2005, Kifaya's name and activities were closely followed by both local and international media. Thus, as Joel Beinin has observed, "While Kifaya's national organizational capacity was limited, the slogan caught on in Egypt and abroad."[8] A few months after its first demonstration, which was attended by a few hundred political activists, Kifaya demonstrations started attracting young people—for whom Kifaya was their first collective political action.

A horizontally structured network, Kifaya's decisions were made by consensus in a steering committee composed of the different political forces it included, namely the Nasserites (Al-Karama Party), the Marxist-Socialists (the Revolutionary Socialist Organization), liberals (al-Ghad Party), Islamists (al-Wasat Party and the Egyptian Islamic Labor Party), and some independent figures.[9] Except for the al-Ghad Party, none of these political organizations were legal political parties officially licensed by the state.[10] And even al-Ghad was a new offshoot of the historic Wafd Party (liberal), whose leader, Ayman Nour, was prosecuted by the state under allegations of forging the party's establishment documents. There was no formal coordination between Kifaya and the established political parties, which were seen by the movement as complacent and lacking popular support. As a consortium of new political contenders, Kifaya breathed new life into the Egyptian political landscape.

The rise of these groups and their activities (rallies, demonstrations, and statements) signified a drastic change within Egyptian political society in a number of ways. As Maha Abdelrahman put it: "Any observer of political life in Egypt in recent years could not have failed to notice the growing forms of cooperation between various political forces, mainly the nationalist Nasserists, Leftists and Islamists, and the debate to which this new process has given rise within circles of political activists as well as in independent media. This cooperation has blossomed as part of a growing wave of political activism that is sweeping the extra-parliamentary political scene in Egypt which currently counts some 14 'movements' and 'initiatives.' Among these are Kefaya (Enough)."[11] Before the rise of Kifaya and its offshoots, a majority of scholars and large sections of Egyptian society could agree that "Mubarak has subdued Egypt's Islamists, leftists, and human rights community to the point where little domestic impetus for reform remains."[12] So the Kifaya movement can claim the rise of an oppositional call directly attacking the presidency as a significant achievement. Second, it was the first time in fifty years that political liberalization became the sole cause for which groups formed and mobilized. During previous decades, the few cases of demonstration were directly linked to either economic or regional concerns.

Third, Kifaya and its offshoot, *Shabaab min agl al-taghyeer* (Youth for Change), also represented the first time that generational politics had ever appeared at the forefront. Youth for Change was the first attempt in Egypt to organize along demographic lines (age) and not ideology, class, or geographic location. While the earlier generational divide manifested itself in the distinction of the student movement and organization within university campuses,

Youth for Change was the first group that set a dividing line according to age alone. It included students, unemployed graduates, and young professionals. Despite being predominantly middle-class, it did not identify itself either with a specific class or political ideology but instead stressed the fact that it was for people under the age of thirty years. The group elected its own coordination committee according to its own by-laws and managed itself independently of Kifaya. It had its own listserv, depended on blogging to spread the news of its activities, used text messaging to mobilize for its otherwise unannounced protests (to surprise the security services), and organized separate activities as well as joining Kifaya's events and protests. It marked the rise of increased use of telecommunications and the internet in activism in Egypt.

Later on, the more famous April 6 group—formed in 2008 by one of the activists from Youth for Change—followed this model, identifying itself away from ideology and around broad demands for regime change. It also identified itself according to age, stressed the fact that it is a group for youth, and depended heavily on the internet for mobilization. And after the revolution, an umbrella group called the Coalition of the Youth of the Revolution—which for a while was seen by the media and the state authorities as the "leading authority" of the revolution—was created by key figures in Youth for Change and younger members of the Muslim Brotherhood.

Consequently, the fourth feature of the wave of prodemocracy activism was its inclusion of the biggest political organization in Egypt: the Muslim Brotherhood. As Michaelle Browers correctly points out, it was "not only the existence of this ideologically diverse grouping, but the links it has created with the country's largest opposition group, the Muslim Brotherhood, that reveals the most about the changing landscape of Egyptian politics."[13] While the Brotherhood participation in Kifaya was only symbolic, they entered into an alliance with the extreme-left Revolutionary Socialists; together they organized the biggest prodemocracy demonstrations during that period. Finally, the rise of the prodemocracy movement with its formation of actors attested to the crisis of "action" and to a great extent the complacency of legal older political parties (al-Wafd, al-Tagammu, al-Nassery), thus confirming that any challenge for the regime, if not the political system at large, would come from outside the classical matrix of political parties.

All of those features continued to grow over the years following the prodemocracy movement, which only lasted for a short period (2004–2006), and became characterizing features of activism both before and after January 25, 2011.

The Revolution as Evolution
Ahmed Salah

Ahmed Salah is an Egyptian activist and a member of the April 6 Youth Movement. This passage comes from his presentation at the second annual conference of the Program on Arab Reform and Democracy at Stanford University, on May 12, 2011.

Egyptian activists had been trying for years to fight corruption. For a long time we felt that there was a common enemy above us all. In 2003, people protested against the U.S. invasion of Iraq. This led to the establishment of the Kifaya movement, in September 2004. Kifaya protests were repressed by the state, but Kifaya grew in 2005. I joined Kifaya from the beginning. Through mobilizing people in the street, we thought, we are getting there, we are liberating our country. We all spent time in jail. We were tortured. Some went on seventeen days of hunger strike. We came out of jail but were under siege, unable to do much. Youth for Change (the youth arm of Kifaya) disappeared in 2006 after fractures and disputes took over because there was nothing else to do.

In 2008, there was a call for a workers' strike in El-Mahalla El-Kubra, which was part of a labor struggle that started in the city since December 2006. The earlier strike ended with one condition: either the government meets workers' demands by March 2008 or a new strike would start. The demands were not met, naturally. In parallel to the workers' strike in El-Mahalla, we discussed—Should we organize demonstrations? How can we demonstrate? Some people found a way to do so through establishing a Facebook group. The news went viral, and the group membership quickly reached 70,000 members. This led to a mistake by the regime, which was not used to how the internet worked: They made a strong statement against the group on television. This gave us the best propaganda ever. We saw it was our chance, so we tried to create another youth movement (the April 6 Youth Movement), but our next call for a general strike failed, maybe because the government did not give us propaganda like before. Since then, we kept trying, but nothing was working.

Then came Tunisia, and with it hope. Thanks for the slogan! But Egypt is different from Tunisia—there were some self-immolations in the beginning, but nothing was happening. There was a call for demonstrations on the 25th of January calling for the ousting of Interior Minister Habeeb El-Adly by the "We are all Khaled Said" Facebook group as well as the rest of the internet community and youth groups including April 6, Leftists, and others.

One cannot make a revolution without planning, but we had been planning forever! About three dozen activists had a few meetings, tried to plan a bit, probing different ideas. I was thinking that it would be another failure. But the next day, we went around the streets talking to ordinary people, in order to find out: What would bring people out? We found out that news of the planned January 25th demonstration had not reached the street. Only one student out of many we talked to said yes, he had heard about it and would participate. Most people we asked about Mubarak said they did not like him.

"So you hate him—there will be protests, would you want to participate?" The answers were often, "No! They are too strong, nothing will ever shake them!" "I could be tortured," "If I stop working for one day, I cannot feed my family." "What would get you out there?" we asked. "If everybody else goes out, we will." So we thought we should work on creating the illusion that everyone else was out. On January 25, we started rallying small numbers of protesters in small alleys, so that the streets looked full, and then steered them into the central areas of each small neighborhood. And the pool of protesters accumulated until we reached Tahrir Square. The January 25 events were very surprising to everyone, including myself.

In December 2006—a few months after the decline of the prodemocracy movement—the workers at the Misr Textile Factory in the city of El-Mahalla in the Nile Delta started a strike that initiated the biggest wave of labor protests since the 1940s. It was quantitatively significant, with more than 1.7 million workers estimated to have participated in actions in the 2006–2009 period. It also marked a qualitative leap from earlier labor action in Egypt. Worker-leaders outside official union committees organized the overwhelming majority of these strikes and actions, in many cases rendering the official unions redundant as, in many of the places where the struggles emerged, workers and employees elected their own strike committees responsible for managing ongoing action, representing workers in negotiations with the authorities, and organizing future action. They developed a whole new repertoire of tools to fight employers and the state, ranging from street protests and strikes to extended sit-ins in front of official buildings (Parliament and cabinet headquarters) and factory occupations, all of which were adopted by the protesters during and after January 25.

This new and independent form of organization reached its apogee when the real estate tax collectors formed an independent union in April 2009—the first autonomous nonstate union since the 1940s. In contrast to the hierarchies and bureaucratic structures of the state-controlled trade unions, labor protests after 2005 created new mechanisms from below that slowly challenged the institutional basis of state corporatism. Sidelining the official union workers committee, the strike committee had to operate democratically. This novel form of organization contradicted the internal logic of state corporatism, set a useful precedent, and sowed the seeds for independent organization away from the state-manipulated union elections that had been so closely associated with organized labor since 1957. New sites of contention and activism were being created outside the circle of political activists and their foothold within downtown Cairo.

Thus, it is not a coincidence that what can be called a "rehearsal" for the January 25 Revolution took place in the city of El-Mahalla on April 6, 2008. During that day the workers of the textile industrial complex had called for a strike within the factory. Activists from the prodemocracy movement as well as journalists and bloggers started to circulate the news, and some called for a general strike that day. With more than twenty-seven thousand workers in the factory having been on strike months earlier, there was a feeling among the Cairene activists that this might be their chance to break away from the protests of a few hundred into mass mobilization. The Facebook group created for that call, from which the famous April 6 Youth Movement later evolved, managed to get more than seventy thousand members in less than a week. But there were no organic links between the workers in El-Mahalla and those activists, some of whom had never been to the city before. However, it was the myth of virtual reality at its best; there seemed to be a growing belief that you can change the world from behind the comfort of your computer screen. Interestingly, when the security forces stopped the workers from entering the factory to strike, the whole city was agitated, and thousands flooded the streets in protest. Protesters tore down a huge poster of Mubarak, an image that captured the imagination of Egyptians in the years to follow. Due to the magnitude of the protests, the security forces used extreme violence, in which at least two were reported dead; for the first time in decades, the authorities announced a curfew. The call for protests in Cairo and the general strike were not successful, but the intensity of the protests and confrontations in El-Mahalla, where there was no strong presence of any of the political movements, was a testimony to the missing links between the Cairene political activists and disenchanted Egyptians elsewhere. This shortcoming continued to stall new forms of activism in Egypt even after the revolution.

The Domestic and Regional Environment

Three main factors seem to have fostered the new forms and patterns of activism in Egypt over the course of a decade. The first is the successive regional crises including the Palestinian Intifada, the American invasion of Iraq in 2003, and the Israeli attacks on Lebanon (2006) and Gaza (2008). These regional crises not only prompted a reaction among activists and attempts at harnessing more solidarity toward each other whenever they faced state repression, but they also provided continued pressure for activists from different backgrounds to work together in joint campaigns for these regional causes. The subject of regional issues was one over which the political forces were united, making it an excellent opportunity for them to collaborate and investigate their differences and common positions on other issues in a non-explosive environment.

The second development was the hastened pace of neoliberal changes, which limited the regime's ability to appease and coopt its traditional social bases, prompting the possibility of the rise of labor activism. For precisely the same reason, the regime became more dependent on coercion and repression in governance, and that gave rise to activism directed against the security apparatus (the "We are all Khaled Said" Facebook group and the ultras groups), as discussed in the next section. The government of Prime Minister Ahmed Nazif, who took office in 2004—the last prime minister in Mubarak's reign, with a cabinet composed of unabashedly neoliberal technocrats and businessmen—"promoted a second wave of privatization and enacted other measures to encourage foreign direct investment," raising unprecedented and quite justified fears about layoffs and accelerating the move away from the labor-state alliance established in 1952.[14] Unlike earlier prime ministers, Nazif speeded up the move towards neoliberalization. Not only was the cabinet composition telling, with its technocrats and businessmen, but privatization under Nazif was more extensive than anything since the start of the economic reform program in 1991.[15] Prices, especially of food and transportation, experienced sharp and unprecedented increases, leading to heightened inflation despite a proclaimed increase in GNP.[16] The Nazif government was quickly moving away from the earlier model of state-guaranteed socioeconomic privileges.

The enforcement of neoliberalism increased daily coercion and repression of Egyptians. It was not directed at or limited to political opposition and dissent, as in the earlier reigns of Nasser and Sadat. Rather, it was systematically extended toward the popular classes who were now seen as a threat to the evolving socioeconomic model. Hence, the mushrooming of shantytowns went hand in hand with the appearance of gated communities and the privatization of public space.[17] There was a shift away from coopting important sectors of society through material handouts to state-controlled collective bodies like state unions, farmers' cooperatives, and student bodies. Even though

A mural celebrating the January 25 Revolution, freedom, and religious harmony in Egypt. Photo by Ben Rowswell.

these organizations were antidemocratic and not very inclusive, they did give out material benefits such as small, redistributed land holdings to farmers, subsidies, permanent employment to workers and employees, and free social services. Moreover, they guaranteed at least the minimal response of the state to these important sectors of society. Due to neoliberal changes, the regime could not afford to appease its population economically, as it used to do in earlier phases; because the growth model depended on concentration of wealth, the regime had to shift more toward the use of coercion to keep the "losers" in check. However, it is from within this search for stability and increased monopoly over wealth and power that a rising tide of resistance emerged that led to the demise of Mubarak in 2011.

The third development was the crisis of succession and the presumptive ascendancy of Gamal Mubarak, who had been groomed to succeed his father. Since 2000, Mubarak's son Gamal was gradually becoming the main figure in the ruling National Democratic Party (NDP)—there seemed to be signs that the then-novel Syrian scenario of father-son succession was very plausible, especially with Gamal heading a newly established body in the NDP called the Policy Secretariat.[18] By 2004, with the 2005 presidential referendum and parliamentary elections not far off, more and more people began to suspect that "a leadership succession will take place within the next few years—President Hosni Mubarak is seventy-six and was hospitalized in Germany this summer." These fears "energized politics and led to fresh efforts at cooperation among opposition groups."[19]

Over the next few years the arrangements for succession moved ahead despite the opposition. Not only was Mubarak reelected, but a number of constitutional amendments were passed in 2007 to ease Gamal's takeover. Similarly, the NDP and the Nazif cabinet of 2004 were structured to replace the regime's old guard with members of Gamal's entourage (for instance, businessmen such as Ahmed Ezz, Ahmed El Maghrabi, and Rasheed M. Rasheed and younger technocrats such as Youssef Boutros Ghali, Mahmoud Mohi Eddin, and Mohamed Kamal). Such changes were necessary prerequisites for the succession, but they further fueled activism in two ways: The new elite managed not only to alienate the upper echelons of the regime but also represented a new generation of politicians (rich, foreign-educated, and detached) that most Egyptians could not relate to. This made them an easy target for different activist groups and movements, from prodemocracy to labor, who focused on the "corruption" of this elite and their odious combination of wealth, political clout, and foreign assumptions. Unlike older generations of politicians, who were more subtle and populist, Gamal's entourage showed off their wealth and alienated even the mid-level brokers of power within the NDP and different ministries. Their obliviousness provided activists with the needed ammunition to attack them. Such divisions and rivalry were a necessary condition for the deposing of Mubarak's family and their entourage of politicians in the January 25 Revolution.

Rise of New Actors

As 2010 approached, Egyptian activism had become clearly antiregime not just in terms of how groups identified themselves but also in the demands they made. Yet the final months of 2010 witnessed a significant change with the rise of two groups that did not define themselves as political or clearly anti-Mubarak and yet became an important part of the political scene, specifically "We are all Khaled Said" and the ultras football fan clubs. They represented a new form of activism, similar to "new social movements" in the sense that their focus was on quality-of-life issues rather than finding identity in ideology, geography, or class. Each targeted different audiences, but they were predominantly young (under the age of thirty), used different tools of mobilization, and in different ways continue to play a huge role in post-Mubarak Egypt.

The brutal death of Khaled Said at the hands of Alexandria's plainclothes policemen in June 2010 was a turning point. Said's infraction was supposedly posting a YouTube video showing police officers dividing seized drugs among themselves. The picture of Khaled Said's deformed face after his death was widely circulated on the internet alongside with a picture of his face prior to the beating. The brutality used against Said, who was neither a militant nor an activist nor a criminal, caused a stir among middle-class youth, who were able to identify with him. A group of anonymous activists who were later identified as members of the Mohamed ElBaradei campaign (including Google executive Wael Ghoneim) created a group on Facebook to protest the incident and called it "We are all Khaled Said."[20] The group organized a number of peaceful protests in which they called on its members to wear black and carry the picture of Khaled Said. According to Shehata, "We are all Khaled Said Campaign organized a series of protest activities, which attracted a large number of young people most of whom were not associated with any political party or movement."[21] Unlike Kifaya and the earlier prodemocracy demonstrations, they did not attack Mubarak or call for the end of the regime and accordingly did not identify themselves as political, even though their calls against the police state were in every sense political. But what seemed a demotion in terms of political demands obviously constituted much of the appeal of this group, as it managed to attract a huge following and to steer the attention of its audience to politics. Within a short time the group grew to become the largest Egyptian political group on Facebook, with hundreds of thousands of subscribers. And while the group's protests were very small and only attracted a few hundred at most, the Facebook page attracted hundreds of thousands and was widely used to circulate news to an audience that otherwise had little interest in politics. The Khaled Said page marked a new form of activism in Egypt, one in which individuals were not asked to be bound by ideological or partisan constraints even as they could feel relatively safe in not being labeled as "political opposition." In post-Mubarak Egypt, the page grew to host millions of subscribers, and one of its administrators, Wael Ghoneim, became an icon of the revolution and of this newly politicized generation. He represented the new form of activism: middle-class, not belonging to a political party, anti-ideological, technologically savvy, and with no organizational backing.

The second group, significantly different in terms of its organizational capabilities but equally new to politics, is the football support groups known in Egypt as ultras. Appearing as late as 2007, the groups started with the Ultras Ahlawy, Zamalek's Ultras White Knights, Ismaily's Ultras Yellow Dragons, and a smaller regional club called Port Said's Ultras Masry, each group supporting a different football team. The ultras groups came to the limelight after a series of clashes with security authorities both in football stadiums and on the streets. Having been known for confronting the police only in football-related matters, their first visible political engagement was on January 25, 2011. While they participated in the protests individually and not as a group, they were visible not only because they identified themselves to other protesters as "ultras" but also because that night, when security clamped down on Tahrir Square, they were the ones who were clearly able to navigate through the mayhem and save many protesters. On September 9, 2011, during what was known as a "Correcting the Path" demonstration, the Ultras Ahlawy and the Ultras White Knights, the fan groups for the two biggest football clubs, made their first appearance in Tahrir Square as a collective.

Predominantly young and possessing a strict code of conduct that does not allow them to accept media appearances, the ultras are known for their extreme bravery in confronting the police. "We defend what is right, we don't brag, and we don't accept credit for what we do," declared one ultras leader.[22] A cross-class network organized by neighborhood, their signature chant summarizes what they stand for: freedom and a strong animosity toward the regime's repressive apparatus. "Hey government, tomorrow you will be cleansed by the people's hands. Hey stupid regime, when will you understand that what I demand is freedom, freedom, freedom?" goes the chant. As Ashraf El-Sherif explains, "The key to understanding the Ultras phenomenon is to imagine it as a way of life for these youth—for them, becoming a football fan became a symbolic action that was both joyful and a means of self-expression. But the broader social, psychological, and cultural contexts were unable to adapt to the groups' activities, by virtue of their rebellious nature and their defiance of norms."[23] While the groups use social media in communication, they differ from "We are all Khaled Said" in having strict membership rules (including membership dues), in holding regular meetings, and in organizing collectively before each match. Their now-famous chant, their fondness for fireworks, and their flags have been decisive in many protests and confrontations ever since.

On the surface, both "We are all Khaled Said" and the ultras stressed that they were apolitical and not antiregime, but in reality both were striking at the very heart of the regime—its security apparatus—and doing it in very different ways. The new pattern of activism that both the ultras and the Khaled Said group represent is predominantly youthful, tends to have a creative repertoire of protest tools (from protesting in black to the use of fireworks), and is not fond of political labels.

A third group that was not only apolitical in how it identified itself but also in terms of its activities and slogans—unlike the two groups discussed above— was the Salafis, who became a key political player after the ouster of Mubarak. Starting in university campuses during the 1970s, the Salafis gained momentum during the last decade of Mubarak's rule. Having established "an array of social services in neighborhoods, mirroring the activities of the Muslim Brotherhood," the Salafis had the backing of the regime for consciously declaring and avowing to stay out of politics.[24] Moreover, since the start of the new millennium the regime allowed the Salafis to launch TV channels in order to cater to the rising religiosity in society but also to counter the appeal of the more politicized Muslim Brotherhood, which "allowed the group to establish strong ties with ordinary Egyptians."[25] The Salafis remained apolitical until well into the start of the revolution. By and large, they were initially opposed to the revolution, and many of their prominent sheikhs, including their leader, Yasser Burhami, publicly called on their followers not to join the demonstrations. They declared their support for "Tahrir Square" just a few days before Mubarak stepped down.[26]

Yet, unlike the Ultras and the youth movements of April 6, "We are all Khaled Said" and the El-Baradei Campaign, the Salafis managed to establish three political parties since the revolution (the biggest being El-Nour) and garnered 28 percent in the People's Assembly (lower house) in the first elections in 2011. Despite the fact that they were late-comers to politics, and even in joining the revolution, their longstanding social networks paid off politically more than the virtual links established by youth movements and used in mobilization.

The Move from Informal to Party Politics

Despite the developments that discredited the existing political parties and rendered them redundant for years, the new forms of activism that evolved over a decade and the enthusiasm for "youth" that came with the revolution were not enough to reinvent institutional politics in post-Mubarak Egypt. The new formations suffered from many of the classical political syndromes in addition to their own novel shortcomings. Three main challenges seem to be undermining the possibility of structural change within the political system: (1) the hegemonic superstructure remains widely intact—the dividing line within the political sphere being Islamist vs. non-Islamist (or secular); (2) the activist formations have been and continue to be based on loose networks rather than solid organizational structures; (3) consequently, except for the Islamists, none of the groups or movements have enough *organized* grassroots support.

The hegemonic superstructure in which the media, the political elite, and public figures set the public discussions and discourse agendas remains intact. Not only has there been a very limited reshuffling of individuals but, more importantly, there is also a continuity of patterns. Soon after the euphoria of the eighteen days in Tahrir Square faded and the first formal political battle around the constitutional amendments began in March 2011, the new political forces succumbed to old patterns and old tools. Highly dependent on managing the battle through media outlets and social networking systems, the new political actors reverted to the traditional division along Islamist-secular lines. While these divisions were partially overcome during the few years preceding the revolution (as discussed earlier), identity-based politics reminiscent of the 1990s became the supreme issue leading to convergence and attempts to appease the ruling military junta. During the 1990s, with the increasing occurrence of militant Islamist groups bombing public places and assassinating officials and public figures, the magnified conflict between Islamist and seculars was the main dividing line in Egyptian politics, and after the March 2011 referendum this divide reasserted itself. With the approach of the parliamentary elections in November 2011, which resulted in an overwhelming majority for Islamists (almost 70% of the lower house), the rivalry was set.

As most activist groups fell into this trap of identity politics, they moved away from identifying political projects that reflected the clear demands of many of the people who participated and supported the revolution, namely "social justice" and "dignity." That is, while Islamists and non-Islamists engaged in debates about the nature of the political system, the Islamists had a social network they could use, as opposed to the other political forces, which needed to engage on policy issues that the majority of Egyptians could relate to, such as education, employment, health care. Hence, the representation of non-Islamists was meager in the Parliament (less than 25%), and only three activist-candidates managed to win seats in the parliament.

With the move to electoral politics, another shortcoming became visibly clear: The political activists who were in the leadership after the revolution proved to be closer to icons than real leaders. With most groups being loose networks rather than having a solid organizational structure, the ability of these groups to mobilize beyond general calls for protests was very limited. Not only did they fail to lead successful campaigns or establish strong parties but compared to the Muslim Brotherhood, none of these groups even had the idea to sustain street mobilization beyond one-off calls for demonstrations. Over the months that followed Mubarak's deposal, none of the activists' parties such as al-Adl, al-Wa'ee, al-Tayyar al-Masry, or Misr al-Huriyaa were able to establish themselves as real contenders to power. The loose network structure that seemed to be an advantage under the Mubarak regime, minimizing the potential of repression and providing individuals with enough space and freedom, seemed to be a shortcoming within formal politics.

Another important challenge confronted by the activist groups after February 11, 2011, was the inadequacy of their mobilization tools for the post-Mubarak era. Whereas the use of social media and direct political action proved to be necessary tools for bypassing the constraints imposed by the Mubarak regime on political parties and movements, in the post-Mubarak era these tools of youth activists proved to be insufficient. Being predominantly of the middle class, the different groups and movements could not identify the necessary tools for reaching out beyond the direct circle of large cities. While the social media networks were excellent tools for spreading information, they came up short as a means for mobilization without a direct relationship between the groups and their potential audience. Moreover, none of these movements could provide a clear political alternative for people to rally around. Beyond their long-held calls against Mubarak's regime and his security apparatus and the ruling party, they could not formulate a positive political model that would provide enough structure and a clear pathway for grassroots participation or even as a choice for voters.

The Way Forward

The first decade of the new millennium marked a breakthrough in activism in Egypt. While the Palestinian Intifada brought back street politics, student

January 1, 2011: A bomb detonates in a Coptic church in Alexandria, leaving twenty-one dead and seventy injured. Three days of protests by Christians throughout the country follow the attack.

January 11, 2011: Amer Ashour Abdel Zaher, an off-duty police officer, kills one Christian and wounds five others after opening fire on a train bound for Cairo. Protests by Christians follow the incident.

January 17, 2011: In protest of dismal economic conditions, fifty-year-old Abdu Abdel-Monaim Kamal attempts self-immolation in Cairo.

January 18, 2011: Twenty-five-year-old Ahmed Hashem El-Sayed, an unemployed man from Alexandria, self-immolates, dying shortly thereafter. As the number of self-immolations and protests grow, dissident Mohamed ElBaradei warns of a "Tunisian-style explosion."

January 25, 2011: Thousands of antigovernment protesters clash with riot police to demand the end of Hosni Mubarak's reign. The government disables mobile networks in Cairo's Tahrir Square, which has the biggest demonstrations. During clashes in Suez governorate, the first protester is killed.

January 26, 2011: Defying the ban on protests, thousands of Egyptians return to the streets calling for the end of Mubarak. Hundreds are detained and six die as police use tear gas and beatings to scatter protesters.

January 27, 2011: Mohamed ElBaradei returns to join demonstrators for their third day of protests. Protesters torch a police post in Suez and clash with police in two eastern Egyptian cities. Egypt suspends its stock exchange.

January 28, 2011: The "Friday of Rage," the biggest demonstration in more than three decades, ends in police clashes with tens of thousands of protesters. Around nine hundred people die, and more than four thousand are injured. Mobile and internet services are suspended in most areas of the country. President Mubarak makes his first TV address, promising to promote democracy and dismissing his government. Police stations and NDP offices are attacked and torched while the police forces withdraw. Military forces are deployed throughout the country.

January 29, 2011: Mubarak names intelligence chief Omar Suleiman the first vice president in his thirty-year tenure. As protests continue in Cairo, a mob kills three police officers in Rafah. The military does not block demonstrations.

January 30, 2011: Fighter jets fly over Cairo in an attempt to maintain control of the city. Gangs attack at least four jails, freeing hundreds of militants and thousands of other inmates. Al Jazeera is ordered to close its Cairo office. For the first time in three decades, Israel allows Egypt to move several hundred troops into the Sinai Peninsula.

January 31, 2011: Mubarak names a new government composed largely of cronies from the old regime. The military makes its first statement, promising not to fire on Egyptian civilians.

February 1, 2011: More than 250,000 people fill Tahrir Square. Meanwhile, on television Mubarak insists that he will stay in power through the transition but will not run in the next election scheduled in September 2012.

February 2, 2011: Mubarak supporters attack antigovernment protesters in Tahrir Square in what came to be known the "Battle of the Camel" because the attackers rode on horses and camels; many people are killed, nearly a thousand are wounded.

February 4, 2011: In the largest day of protests yet, Egyptians stage a "day of departure" protest to oust Mubarak.

February 5, 2011: Heads of the ruling National Democratic Party (NDP), including Mubarak's son Gamal, resign. Secretary-General Safwat el-Sharif is replaced by Hossam Badrawi as a peace offering to protesters on the twelfth day of demonstrations. Vandals attack an Egyptian pipeline supplying gas to Jordan, and authorities are forced to switch off a twin pipeline to Israel.

February 6, 2011: Newly elected vice president Omar Suleiman meets with opposition groups, including the Muslim Brotherhood, for the first time.

February 7, 2011: Struggling to maintain control, the regime offers a 15 percent increase in salaries and pensions in an attempt to appease antigovernment protesters.

February 8, 2011: Wael Ghonim, thirty-year-old administrator of the "We are all Khaled Said" Facebook page and one of the key organizers of the first protests, is released after twelve days of detention.

February 10, 2011: In a late-night address to Egyptians, Mubarak nominally hands over most of his power to Omar Suleiman. Demonstrations escalate as enraged protesters vow not to leave the square until Mubarak steps down.

February 11, 2011: Mubarak flees to a beach resort and officially relinquishes control over the army after three decades of rule. The Supreme Council of the Armed Forces, headed by Defense Minister Hussein Tantawi, takes over. Protesters celebrate across the country and particularly in Tahrir Square.

February 13, 2011: To appease protesters, the Supreme Council of the Armed Forces dissolves the parliament and suspends the constitution. It promises to hand power to elected civilians by June 2011.

February 14, 2011: Military forces of 470,000 troops issue an ultimatum to the protesters in Tahrir Square: Go home or face arrest. A day later they form a committee to issue a constitutional declaration intended to be a road map for the transition.

February 19, 2011: For the first time since its first attempt in court in 1996, al-Wasat al-Jadid (Islamist party) receives a court license and is accordingly officially established.

March 3, 2011: Mubarak-appointed prime minister Ahmed Shafiq resigns and is replaced by former transport minister Essam Sharaf.

March 5, 2011: About a thousand people storm the headquarters of the state security forces in Cairo and Alexandria and call for an end to the state security apparatus and an end to the emergency laws.

March 8, 2011: Thirteen people are killed and 140 wounded as clashes break out in Cairo over the burning of a church on March 4. Also in Cairo, an international women's day protest turns violent as female protesters are attacked.

March 9, 2011: Military detain eighteen women in Tahrir Square, forcing them to undergo "virginity tests."

March 15, 2011: The infamous state security agency is dissolved.

March 19, 2011: Nearly 41 percent of eligible voters—more than 14 million Egyptians—vote in favor of changing the constitution by a 77 percent majority, ushering in a constitutional declaration that outlines a new wave of parliamentary and presidential elections.

March 22, 2011: During protests by police officers demanding better working conditions, the Interior Ministry is set on fire.

March 30, 2011: The Supreme Council of the Armed Forces issues an interim constitutional declaration based on the March 19 referendum stating that the country's first presidential elections will be held in November.

April 8, 2011: One hundred thousand protesters gather in Tahrir Square to demand the resignations of former regime officials and trials for Mubarak's family. The military forcefully disperses protesters, fatally wounding one and injuring seventy-one others.

April 9, 2011: For the first time since his removal, Mubarak makes a public appearance in which he denies charges of corruption.

April 13, 2011: Despite a purported heart attack, Mubarak is put under detention in his hospital room on accusations of corruption.

April 19, 2011: A government-sponsored fact-finding mission reports that during the eighteen days (January 25–February 11) 846 people were killed and over 4,600 were injured.

May 8, 2011: Twelve people die in clashes between Christians and Muslims near a church in northern Cairo's Imbaba neighborhood. The government enacts a ban on gatherings outside places of worship and arrests twenty-three people connected to the riots.

May 13, 2011: Mubarak's wife Suzanne is investigated on corruption charges. Tens of thousands of Egyptians return to the streets to show nonsectarian solidarity and to encourage the government to do more for Palestinians.

May 27, 2011: Egypt opens the Rafah crossing to Gaza as thousands of protesters return to Tahrir Square to call for a "second revolution."

June 28, 2011: Furthering the end of Mubarak's dynasty, a court order closes more than 1,750 municipal councils.

June 29, 2011: Security forces clash with youth for the second day of protests in Cairo, leaving about one thousand injured.

July 5, 2011: Protesters clash with security forces after ten police officers charged with killing protesters are released.

July 13, 2011: To meet protesters' demands, nearly six hundred top police officers are dismissed.

July 17, 2011: To appease protesters, Prime Minister Essam Sharaf fires several senior cabinet ministers.

July 23, 2011: In Cairo, at least 143 people are injured and one dies in clashes between protesters and a pro-army mob during a march from Tahrir Square to the headquarters of the Supreme Council of the Armed Forces.

July 29, 2011: In a show of force against the military and other political factions, hundreds of thousands of Islamists demonstrate in Tahrir Square for the "Friday of Popular Will."

August 5, 2011: The Egyptian Trade Union Federation, the infamous controller of strikes and labor activities, is dismantled.

September 9, 2011: Protesters return to Tahrir Square led by ultras groups. Before day's end, some protesters a few miles away storm the Israeli Embassy; it is the first time such a thing has occurred since the establishment of diplomatic relations between Egypt and Israel in 1979.

October 9, 2011: Twenty-six die and more than two hundred are injured after an attack by military forces on protesters marching toward the state TV building in Cairo's Maspero neighborhood against an attack on a church in Aswan governorate.

November 2, 2011: Egyptian ruling generals pardon 334 civilians who have imprisoned since February 2011.

November 13, 2011: Protests in Aswan and Damietta leave two dead and scores injured.

November 18, 2011: Tens of thousands, including members of the Muslim Brotherhood, return to Tahrir Square to protest the military rule. The Muslim Brotherhood withdraws later in the day; over the next few days, police clash with protesters, leaving thirty-three dead and more than two thousand injured.

November 25, 2011: Crowds in Tahrir Square grow to an estimated one hundred thousand, demanding the end to military rule. A counterprotest of about ten thousand people takes place just two miles away.

November 28–29, 2011: Egyptians vote in the first parliamentary elections since Mubarak's ouster. Over the next six weeks, voting takes place in all twenty-seven governorates.

December 4, 2011: Initial election results show Islamist parties receiving 65 percent of all votes in the first round of the parliamentary elections. Secular liberals bring in just 13.4 percent of the vote. By the end of the three rounds, Islamists will end up with a comfortable majority of 70 percent.

December 16, 2011: Egyptian troops clash with protesters staging a sit-in in front of the cabinet headquarters. In the four days of violence that follow, fourteen protesters are killed and over 441 are injured.

December 20, 2011: More than twenty thousand angry women march in central Cairo to denounce the violence inflicted on the protesters and an infamous attack on a veiled female protester.

December 24, 2011: The Muslim Brotherhood reports that it has won 86 of the estimated 180 seats open for election.

December 29, 2011: Soldiers and police storm at least eighteen nongovernmental organization offices throughout Egypt.

activism, and cross-ideological networks, the prodemocracy movement represented the start of heavy use of social media and the internet, organization along generational lines, extroverted antipartisan stances, and increased internal democracy within movements. Following those two waves, a cycle of labor protests and activism seemed to expose the regime and erode its long-held repressive capacity.

These waves enriched each other in terms of tactics and tools, and they, along with a split in the ruling elite, led to the fall of Mubarak, but they did not create a different strategy. That is, the new forms of activism did not evolve strategically to provide a clear alternative that can change the political choices in Egypt. A lot of the patterns that have governed politics in Egypt under Mubarak remain intact despite the huge changes, including a lack of strong and varied contenders and electoral choices. Similarly, the experience in formal politics with flexible alliances, different tools for mobilization, and electoral politics has not materialized. Paradoxically, the biggest organized force is not any of the ones that mushroomed during the past decade but the oldest of all present formations: the Muslim Brotherhood.

As it stands, the biggest challenge facing democratic transition in Egypt is the difficulty for activist groups and movements to organize in a novel and sustainable way that makes them not just a temporary phenomenon but a recognizable and persistent force. This seems to be the case with the rise of some new Islamist political forces like the Salafis who, in less than a year, made the transition from an apolitical social force to Egypt's second-largest political party. This evolution has not happened in the more politicized activist movements that have been engaged in politics over the last decade. The activism of the last decade was characterized by a lot of street politics and innovation in mobilization and repertoires of protest and contention, but it later suffered from a huge deficit in organizational structures. It is this deficit that has so far left its negative mark on Egypt's incomplete revolution.

Notes

1. Nicola Pratt, *Democracy and Authoritarianism in the Arab World* (Boulder, CO: Lynne Rienner, 2007), 170.

2. Sadiki Larbi, "Popular Uprisings and Arab Democratization," *International Journal of Middle East Studies* 32(1) (2000): 71–95, 83.

3. Pratt, *Democracy and Authoritarianism.*

4. Rabab El-Mahdi, "The Democracy Movement: Cycles of Protest," in *Egypt: The Moment of Change,* ed. Philip Marfleet and Rabab El-Mahdi (London: Zed Books, 2009), 87–103.

5. Michaelle Browers, "The Egyptian Movement for Change: Intellectual Antecedents and Generational Conflicts," *Contemporary Islam: Dynamics of Muslim Life* 1(1) (2007): 69–88.

6. For more on this, see Maha Abdelrahman, "The Transnational and the Local: Egyptian Activists and Transnational Protest Networks," *British Journal of Middle Eastern Studies* 38(3) (2011): 407–424.

7. Dina Shehata, "Opposition Politics in Egypt: A Fleeting Moment of Opportunity?" *Arab Reform Bulletin* 2(9) (2004): 3–5, 4.

8. Joel Beinin, "Neo-Liberal Structural Adjustment, Political Demobilization, and Neo-Authoritarianism in Egypt," in *The Arab State and Neo-Liberal Globalization: The Restructuring of State Power in the Middle East,* ed. Laura Guazzone and Daniela Pioppi (Reading, U.K: Ithaca, 2009), 11.

9. The Revolutionary Socialist Organization is an underground radical leftist group that has been among the founding members of all of these movements and is the only common faction in all of them. It stirred an uproar in June 2005 after it formed a united front with the Muslim Brotherhood.

10. According to the Egyptian law of the time, all parties should be licensed and approved by a state-appointed body called the Parties' Affairs Committee.

11. Maha Abdelrahman, "'With the Islamists?—Sometimes. With the State?—Never!' Cooperation between the Left and Islamists in Egypt," *British Journal of Middle Eastern Studies* 36(1) (2009): 37–54, 38.

12. Jason Brownlee, "The Decline of Pluralism in Mubarak's Egypt," *Journal of Democracy* 13(4) (2002): 6–14, 11.

13. Michaelle Browers, "The Egyptian Movement for Change: Intellectual Antecedents and Generational Conflicts," *Contemporary Islam: Dynamics of Muslim Life* 1(1) (2007): 69–88, 71.

14. Joel Beinin, "Workers Struggles under 'Socialism' and 'Neoliberalism,'" in *Egypt: The Moment of Change,* ed. Philip Marfleet and Rabab El-Mahdi (London: Zed Books 2009), 68–86, 77.

15. Heba Khalil, "Ganzouri and Privitization," Egyptian Center for Economic and Social Rights, December 7, 2011, available at http://ecesr.com/report/5022, accessed July 11, 2013.

16. "Food Prices Spur Egypt Inflation to 16-Year High," Egyptnews.com, August 11, 2008, available at http://news.egypt.com/en/200808113474/news/-egypt-news /food-prices-spur-egypt-inflation-to-16-year-high.html, accessed July 11, 2013.

17. Philip Marfleet, "State and Society," in *Egypt: The Moment of Change,* ed. Philip Marfleet and Rabab El-Mahdi (London: Zed Books 2009), 14–33; Hazem Kandil, "Revolt in Egypt," *New Left Review* 68, March–April 2011, available at http:// newleftreview.org/II/68/hazem-kandil-revolt-in-egypt, accessed July 11, 2013.

18. The idea of grooming Gamal—who did not have a public profile until the late 1990s and did not even live in Egypt—for the presidency first became a live possibility at the NDP First National Conference in 2000, in which the policy secretariat and Gamal personally played the main role in setting the party's agenda and determining governmental policies.

19. Shehata, "Opposition Politics in Egypt," 3.

20. Dina Shehata, "Youth Movements and the January 25th Revolution," in *Arab Spring in Egypt: Revolution and Beyond,* ed. Bahgat Korany and Rabab El-Mahdi (Cairo: AUC Press, 2012).

21. Ibid.

22. Hamza Hendawi, "Egypt Ultras Grow Increasingly Political," *Huffington Post,* February 9, 2012, available www.huffingtonpost.com/2012/02/10/egypts-ultras-_n _1267697.html, accessed July 11, 2013.

23. Ashraf El-Sherif, "The Ultras' Politics of Fun Confront Tyranny," *Egypt Independent,* February 3, 2012, available at www.egyptindependent.com/opinion/ultras -politics-fun-confront-tyranny, accessed July 11, 2013; Tarek El-Sherif, "Egypt's Ultras: Politically Involved but Not Politically Driven, Yet," *Ahram Online,* January 12, 2012, available at http://english.ahram.org.eg/NewsContent/1/0/31904/Egypt/0/Egypt%E2 %80%99s-Ultras-Politically-involved-but-not-politi.aspx, accessed July 11, 2013.

24. Stéphane Lacroix, "Sheikhs and Politicians: Inside the New Egyptian Salafism," *Brookings Policy Briefing* (June 2012), 1–9, 2.

25. Ibid.

26. Husam Tammam and Patrick Haenni, "Egypt: Islam in the Insurrection," *Religioscope,* February 22, 2011, available at http://religion.info/english/articles/article _519.shtml, accessed July 11, 2013.

CHAPTER 3

Activism and Civil War in Libya

INTISSAR K. RAJABANY *and* LIHI BEN SHITRIT

Repression, oppression, exploitation, and violent bloodshed
cannot stop the victory of the people

MUAMMAR QADDAFI, MARCH 3, 1979

O N FEBRUARY 15, 2011, Libyans in the country's second largest city,
Benghazi, staged a demonstration demanding justice for the victims of
the infamous Abu Salim prison. In the past years, Libyans had become familiar with the solidarity campaigns for these political prisoners, estimated at
1,270 and rumored to have been executed in 1996 after a prison uprising.[1] In
2011, however, the demonstration took place only two days before Libya's
planned "Day of Rage." Given recent events in Tunisia and Egypt, the demonstration signaled a potential threat to the Qaddafi regime, which consequently
reacted by attacking and arresting the protesters. Although the Qaddafi regime was not unusual in using violence to quash rebellion, the success of
the revolutions in Tunisia and Egypt had empowered the Libyan protesters.
Instead of halting public action, the violent quelling of the protest sparked an
armed uprising across the country and the invocation of the Responsibility to
Protect (R2P) article by the United Nations Security Council (UNSC). The ten-
month conflict in Libya ended in October 2011, when the opposition, under
the leadership of the National Transitional Council (NTC), declared the
liberation of Libya.

Given the decades of heavy repression, many outside observers have perceived
Libyan activism during the 2011 uprising to have come out of nowhere. But
this was not the case. Despite the extraordinarily difficult conditions under

Qaddafi's iron rule, Libya has seen episodes of political engagement. These were highly risky and limited efforts, but they nevertheless merit discussion in any account of political activism in Libya.

This chapter explores activism in Libya before, during, and after the 2011 uprising and highlights continuity as well as change in the forms of activism in each period. The first section of the chapter discusses activism during the decades of Qaddafi's rule. Activism was made difficult by regime persecution and the tremendous barriers to communication and coordination across the vast geographical breadth of the county. Consequently, oppositional activities were isolated and short-lived, and the most organized opposition groups operated mainly in exile with little coordination between them and potential supporters in Libya. The second section focuses on the 2011 uprising, exploring how activism shifted to more coordinated grassroots movements across Libya, paying particular attention to how new communications technology and regional circumstances shaped the types of action activists could undertake. The final section considers the capacity of activists to translate the experience and skills they have acquired during the uprising into democratic activism in the post-Qaddafi period. The section focuses on civil society, which has come to represent the heart of newly organized activism in the transitional period.

Activism prior to 2011: Repression and Isolation

To foreign observers, the Libyan uprising of 2011 seemed entirely unprecedented. For decades any open political activism or criticism of the regime had little place in the Libyan public sphere. Heavy penalties on dissent deterred the vast majority of Libyans from political involvement. Many viewed the highly manipulated spaces for political participation crafted by the regime as a mockery of democracy and therefore shunned these as well. The 2011 uprising, however, was not the first iteration of dissent. Several groups and individuals had organized to challenge unjust rulers in Libya long before the dramatic events of 2011.

These struggles by Libyan society in fact predate the country's independence. When Italy invaded the country in 1911, Libya's eastern and southern regions put up a fight until 1931, while in 1918 the western regions organized themselves into the Tripolitanian Republic, which defeated Mussolini's army in 1922.[2] From colonization to independence, a rich mosaic of resistance movements emerged. It is not surprising, then, that during the 2011 uprising protesters brandished the pictures of the anticolonial national heroes of their cities, invoking the legacy of Libya's history of resistance.[3]

From independence to the Qaddafi coup in 1969, Libyans were discontented with the rule of King Idris due to the widespread corruption of his government, regional favoritism, and the perceived preference of foreign interests over those of Libyans. The monarchy did little to foster national unity and managed the internal affairs of the country poorly.[4] As a result, most Libyans initially supported Colonel Muammar Qaddafi's bloodless coup on September 1, 1969, also known as al-Fateh Revolution. Many saw the regime change as a step toward redressing the various ills plaguing the country.

Soon, however, Qaddafi's repressive methods and his eccentric experimental policies led to deteriorating political, social, and economic conditions and quickly moved the country toward autocracy. Qaddafi held on to power by carefully engineering Libya's political structure and culture in a number of stages.[5] He first saw to the consolidation of his regime (1969–1973), then initiated his Cultural Revolution (1973–1976), followed by the establishment of the *Jamahiriya* or "state of the masses" (1976 onward). Finally, in the latter period of his rule, Qaddafi relinquished the armed struggle against the West and pursued rapprochement (1999–2011).

Qaddafi pursued a policy of depoliticization and atomization of Libyan society, effectively dismantling all existing and potential pillars of power, including the Libyan army, traditional and religious social structures, professional unions, and political organizing frameworks.[6] Political parties had been banned since 1952 under King Idris, a policy the Qaddafi government continued. In his *Green Book,* which outlined his political philosophy, Qaddafi argued that political representation is an anathema to a true "people's democracy." He instituted several laws meant to prevent oppositional activity, including Law 71 (1972), which declared group organization around oppositional agendas as tantamount to treason and punishable by execution; Law 75 (1973), which forbade dissent and made advocacy and activism extremely risky; and the Law of Collective Punishment (1997), which in effect punished the entire family, tribe, or city of an individual found to have engaged in illegal activity.[7]

The Jamahiriya form of governance, based on the *Green Book* and implemented systematically since 1977, stipulated a unique form of carefully controlled and limited participation.[8] The system was made up of a number of Basic People's Congresses, open to all citizens, which theoretically would be able to influence higher level decision-making. Members of the Basic Congresses elected representatives to the higher body of governance, the General People's Congress (GPC). A parallel system of Revolutionary Committees was also established to monitor the population, mobilize revolutionary zeal, and motivate attendance in the Congresses.[9] These began as enforcers but grew to pervade every aspect of the life of Libyans, exceeding their mandate and becoming too powerful even for Qaddafi's own comfort. Because religion was and is an important component of Libyan social life, Qaddafi sought to bring it under his control as well. His attack on mosques began in 1978; it was later extended to all types of religious activism. Qaddafi labeled anyone who did not subscribe to his eccentric interpretation of religion as a heretic, or *zindīq*. A *zindīq* could be a Sufi, a Muslim Brother, a Salafist, or even a person who simply prayed regularly in the mosque.[10]

Within this context, activism in Libya faced severe challenges, but it was not completely erased. Libyans employed a repertoire of subtle resistance, of the kind James Scott has termed "weapons of the weak," which included evasion, foot-dragging, and understated noncompliance.[11] Most significant of these was the passive resistance of many Libyans enacted through nonparticipation in the People's Congresses. Another widespread practice, similar to a phenomenon that Lisa Wedeen has identified in Assad's Syria, was the telling of subversive popular jokes that implicitly criticized the political state of affairs in the country.[12] The student demonstrations of April 1976 marked perhaps the first significant expression of dissent.[13] Students at Tripoli and Benghazi universities elected their own student unions in defiance of the government's attempt to establish government-backed unions.[14] The regime responded by arresting and then releasing a large number of students. The same students were arrested again on the anniversary of the event in 1977. They were courtmartialed and given long prison sentences. A number of them were publicly executed at both universities, and the executions were broadcast live on television.[15] This tragic and macabre ending set a chilling precedent, which deterred the expression of dissent on campuses and in the public sphere for years to come. Similarly harsh punishments for military dissenters and others who dared to challenge Qaddafi also sent a strong message to all activists.

Alongside the severe repression, another challenge facing opposition actors in Libya was the immense territory of the country and the absence of any communications infrastructure. This made coordinating collective action across Libya logistically difficult. The dearth of communications channels also meant that news of uprisings and army mutinies spread very slowly and often only after their suppression by Qaddafi's forces. Such was the case with the 1980 military uprising in Tobruk and the rebellions in Misrata, Bani-Walid, Tarhuna, and other cities on October 11, 1993, by almost two thousand soldiers, according to some accounts.[16]

Regional rivalry between the western and eastern parts of Libya presented an additional obstacle to collective action. The Qaddafi regime was astute in exploiting regional tensions and stirring up conflict between tribes. For example, while Qaddafi developed his native town, Sirte, staple food was not consistently available in Benghazi. Another example was the installation of the headquarters of international oil companies in Tripoli, even though most of the drilling took place in the eastern part of the country. Qaddafi also tried to win the support of the largest tribe in Libya, the Warfalla tribe, by bestowing favors on its members, a practice that caused resentment among other tribes.

Because of the barriers to coordination outlined above, opposition actors present during that period did not create a uniform strategy and could not cultivate a unified support base inside Libya. Unable to close ranks within the country, many Libyans, especially students, launched their activism abroad. Student oppositional activism outside of Libya, however, was mainly limited to a number of universities in the United States in the 1980s.[17]

Political Islam was another opposition force in Libya as the Muslim Brotherhood predated even the Kingdom. In 1974, Qaddafi ordered some of the leadership to leave the country and imprisoned others.[18] The most prominent organized group in the diaspora was the National Front for the Salvation of Libya (NFSL), a collection of opposition movements based in the United States and the United Kingdom. Established in 1981, the NFSL was one of the oldest and largest movements in exile broadly affiliated with the Muslim Brotherhood; it boasted several thousand followers.[19] Another organization that rose to prominence in the 1990s was the Libyan Islamic Fighting Group (LIFG), which started as a response to the Afghan campaign against the Soviet Union. The group was active in Libya, but following extensive repression, it began to operate mainly in exile. Other Islamist and non-Islamist opposition organizations also operated abroad but had only a limited impact inside Libya.

Due to Libyan political activism abroad, Libyan students returning home after graduation were subjected to interrogation and abuse. The most well-known and tragic example was the case of Al-Sadek Hamed al-Shuwehdy, who had taken part in the 1976 demonstrations in Benghazi.[20] When he returned from his studies in the United States in 1984, he immediately started campaigning against the Qaddafi regime.[21] Al-Shuwehdy was apprehended on the heels of a failed NFSL assassination attempt against Qaddafi at the Bab al-Azizia Barracks in Tripoli in May 1984. He was summarily executed, and his execution was aired on live television at the time of *iftar* (breaking the fast) in the holy month of Ramadan on June 25, 1984. The gruesome execution, which took place in a basketball stadium full of children and families bused in for the occasion, came as a shock to Libyans. During the sacred month of Ramadan Muslims are required to refrain from waging war, and the timing of the act made it clear that the regime was willing to transgress even the most sacred of traditions in order to suppress dissent.[22] While al-Shuwehdy served as a public example, many other activists and suspected activists were imprisoned or executed quietly. The activists of the 1970s, 1980s, and 1990s, as we have seen, consisted mostly of students, intellectuals, Islamists, members of the military, or the opposition movements in exile. The fragmented nature of the opposition and the regime's zero-tolerance policy on dissent meant that space for action was extremely constrained.

Qaddafi's anti-Western stance also had consequences for Libyans in general and for political activism in particular. The various acts of terror that Qaddafi sponsored—the burning of the U.S. embassy in 1979, the 1986 bombing of the Berlin disco, the 1988 Lockerbie bombing, the 1989 bombing of UTA flight 772, ongoing support for the IRA, and others—led to sanctions against Libya by the United States and the UN from 1981 through 2003.[23] Qaddafi attempted, with some limited success, to use the sanctions and tensions with the West to bolster his anti-imperialist credentials and thus his legitimacy in the eyes of Libyans as well as in the Arab and Muslim world.

The sanctions brought with them deteriorating economic conditions. Libyans old enough to remember will recall the difficult years between 1982 and 1985, when graffiti drawings of bananas, apples, and chocolate appeared on walls in Tripoli, accompanied by the sentence "Lest we forget." These messages tacitly targeted Qaddafi, alluding to the unavailability of these food items in the Libyan markets due to his economic and foreign policies and the UN and U.S. sanctions.[24] In the absence of formal avenues for dissent, the graffiti voiced many people's sentiments without explicitly naming Qaddafi. Nevertheless, even this form of action could entail imprisonment in the notorious Abu Salim jail.[25]

Libya's isolation and internal repression made communication with the outside world extremely difficult before the advent of the internet. Calling internationally from one's home was dangerous, public phones were not available, and international calls made at post offices required the registration of the caller's identity card. Incoming and outgoing mail was heavily censored. The American and British governments closed their embassies, leaving Libyans with very few opportunities to interact with Westerners. In 1985, the regime stopped teaching English in schools, adding another obstacle to communication with the rest of the world.

The barriers to communication impeded relations between Libyans inside Libya and members of opposition groups in exile. Libyans within the country had come to view Libyans abroad with suspicion. They saw them as operating from the safety of their exile and thus not exposed to the same risks and challenges as Libyans inside the country. Many felt that the opposition abroad did not represent them. An LIFG attempt on Qaddafi's life in 1996, which was allegedly supported by the British security agency MI6, further discredited the exiled opposition.[26] As much as Libyans wanted Qaddafi out, they had always been skeptical of foreign interference due to Libya's recent colonial past.

Rapprochement with the West and the lifting of sanctions following the 2003 relinquishing of Libya's program of Weapons of Mass Destruction (WMD) improved the economic prospects of Libyans only slightly. It opened some new avenues for employment and education as Libya tried to adjust its workforce to the international economy. However, rapprochement did not change much in terms of political freedom. Dissidents were still persecuted, while the West, eager to normalize ties with Libya and profit from Libyan oil, did little to stop these infractions.[27] At the same time, the more relaxed attitude toward the West did increase the number of students who traveled to the Great Britain and the United States to study. Embassies reopened in Libya and reinstituted cultural exchange programs. Travel visas, now available locally, meant that more people were permitted to travel. Most important of all, English was reintroduced into the school curriculum. The rapprochement enabled the consolidation of cross-border social networks, which, after the uprising began, provided an instrumental mobilization resource for activists to draw on.

Another crucial development was the communications revolution. Libya introduced mobile phones to the public in 1998, and by 2006 it was the country with the highest mobile phone penetration in Africa—at 100 percent. The internet was introduced in 1998 through the state operator General Posts and Telecommunications Company and then to the wider public in 2000. At first internet use was uncensored, as penetration was miniscule; furthermore, before the lifting of the sanctions, the regime had limited access to modern surveillance technology. However, by 2010 14 percent of the population was online according to the International Telecom Union.[28] This opened up avenues for communication with Libyans abroad and with opposition groups in exile. The exiled opposition's online activities became more organized in the

The Birth of Libyan Civil Society
RIHAB ELHAJ

Rihab Elhaj is the president and cofounder of the New Libya Foundation (NLF). The NLF runs civil society organization capacity-building centers in Tripoli and Misrata in Libya and is engaged in developing and promoting civil society organization advocacy networks.

Can you tell us a little about your experiences during the revolution?
In some ways, the Libyan revolution began before we took to the streets. I remember sitting on the couch next to my father, watching a scene from Tahrir Square. It was midnight, and Egyptian flags were waving in natural synchronicity. A crowd of millions roared as the statement was read: "Hosni Mubarak is stepping down." My eyes got itchy and wet; my head was dizzy. I looked over at my father. His head was laid back on the couch, tears streaming down his face. It was the first time I had seen him cry. For the next ten minutes, we cried in silence, both trying to believe what we were witnessing.

That evening, we experienced a painful flood of emotions one can only describe as an awakening. These foreign feelings were intense, but they also were the fuel we Libyans each invested in the Libyan revolution.

What was Libya like under Qaddafi?
Libyan society under Qaddafi is difficult to grasp for those who live in normal social and public settings. There is a peculiar duality: On one hand, there is a home life that is rich, colorful, full of life and peace. On the other hand, there is a public life, stark and bleak. This part of life is something women rarely engaged in and men engaged in begrudgingly.

With the exception of family and people from known families, Libyans rarely engaged with strangers. The fear was, of course, that one was speaking to one of Qaddafi's tens of thousands of spies, spies who were able to capture people on very little evidence and condemn them to life in prison or execution.

The public space was also tainted with the regime's ideology. Once you stepped out of your home, the "Brother Leaders" image was peppered on every building side, shop, billboard, and even in our pockets, gracing the currency with Qaddafi in a pair of designer shades. The infiltration went further, with the regime's color green occupying every storefront, shutter, light pole, city square, and public piece of property.

Libyan civil society was nonexistent. All that existed outside the realm of our homes was Qaddafi's backyard, and all in it were an accessory to his ideology and threat of persecution.

How has civil society changed since the revolution?

The revolution gave birth to Libyan civil society. With the emergence of a common goal to be free, people began to see allies in the faces of others. On February 16, in the East of the country, Libyans left their homes to bravely face guns and tanks in order to announce that risking their life was worth our freedom. This sacrifice was witnessed by millions in their homes, and it moved them to respond in kind. People rose simultaneously to reclaim their neighborhoods, their streets, their schools, their hospitals, their country, and themselves. Two days after Benghazi rose, Libyans in fourteen cities protested to the tune of a now-famous slogan: "With our blood and with our spirit, we stand with you, Benghazi." And so began a budding trust and regard between Libyans around the world.

During the revolution, Libyan civil society responded to meet virtually every need of the people when government operations came to a halt. It was Libyan civil society that brought in hospital equipment, medication, and specialized doctors to treat the wounded. They imported and distributed food, housed our refugees in Tunisia, paid the tuition of students cut off from state funds, and supported the families of martyred rebels. Abroad, they lobbied governments for NATO intervention, protested the countries that withheld their vote for intervention, held hundreds of protests and fundraisers for humanitarian aid, and launched makeshift media outlets and television stations when media was not permitted in Libya.

The birth of Libyan civil society was a historic event. A longing to connect and belong so deep that it manifested in a passionate expression of love and life. The revolution created a new and special bond between Libyans. This bond is the rare currency that will ultimately build the New Libya.

Can you tell us a little about your own experience in cofounding the New Libya Foundation?

The New Libya Foundation's humanitarian aid mission first took me to Malta, where I befriended Libyan strangers for the first time. I was taken in as a younger sister by a dozen businessmen who had escaped Libya to turn profits from their shipping, construction, and retail businesses into humanitarian aid operations. They had once been fierce rivals, but for the moment they turned into a humanitarian aid team, each chipping in a vessel, delivery trucks, and mobile hospitals for the sake of their new country. At night, we would eat dinner by the seaside and exchange stories about our backgrounds and why we came to Malta. When international aid organizations could not operate due to the UN sanctions on Libya, it was these newly born civic initiatives that provided food and medical needs during war.

I then went to Tunisia, where working in a refugee aid mission in the remote desert town of Tataouine brought me into a community of conservative male activists. After we shared a hotel for several weeks, our mutual suspicion finally broke down when a doctor from among them treated me for food poisoning. He was a founding member of a Libyan charity run by the Muslim Brotherhood. The quiet group of bearded men that I first held in contempt soon became my greatest allies. We ate dinner together nightly, saving spaces for one another and not eating until everyone was there or was accounted for. During the day, we made the rounds to the local hospitals, greeting injured rebels, receiving their news, and meeting their needs. The psychosocial center for refugees we launched attracted strangers from all over the world, mostly Libyan women looking to do something for their countrymen. For two months, I worked closely with eight women who were strangers to me in a foreign land. Together, we ran the center, fed our community, fasted, prayed, shopped for *jalabiyas* [traditional Middle Eastern garments—Ed.], swam after midnight in our pajamas—and, of course, had the best laughs and cries of my life. It was the first time I understood that Libyan strangers could become like family.

What are the most important challenges facing Libyan civil society today?
Today, civil society is still viewed primarily as a charitable body. We are still learning about democracy and how to create and protect it. It is necessary to raise awareness regarding the role of civil society as a body for advocacy. We need to engage our newly formed civil society organizations in the next phase of their life, particularly as we prepare to draft our constitution. In this fluid environment, my experience taught me to keep going and keep positive. Things that have never happened before seem to happen pretty often.

---

mid-2000s, and it began engaging more effectively with Libyans inside the country by posting the latter's messages, letters, and comments, giving them a platform for free expression without revealing their identities.[29] Inside Libya, blogging became popular in 2003, but, as fear and self-censorship prevailed, political criticism was often veiled. Those who expressed dissent more explicitly faced prison time and even death. Still, even when not used explicitly to demand reform and democratization, the internet can generate new citizen subjectivities under authoritarian regimes by helping users overcome the distrust, atomization, and isolation that authoritarian conditions often generate. Evidence from Syria suggests that internet penetration in that country produced such an effect.[30] In Libya similar processes were taking place, helping to solidify the cross-border social networks that the rapprochement with the West gave rise to.

The 2011 Uprising

 The event that ignited the 2011 Libyan uprising was a demonstration by the mothers of prisoners of the Abu Salim prison, who had in previous years formed an unofficial organization and held periodical peaceful demonstrations in Benghazi to demand information about the fates of their sons.[31] In 1996 prisoners in Abu Salim demonstrated for better treatment, food, and visitation rights. The prison authorities first agreed to review their demands on the condition that they return to their cells. After the prisoners conceded, they were rounded up in the courtyard and allegedly executed by the guards under orders from Abdullah Senussi, Qaddafi's chief of intelligence who at the time of writing was in Libyan custody and wanted by the International Criminal Court for crimes against humanity. Estimates indicate that 1,270 prisoners were killed. The bodies are believed to have been buried in a mass grave on the prison grounds.[32] The authorities did not inform the families that their relatives were dead, yet kept accepting parcels, money, and food that families sent to the prisoners for twenty years. A prison break allowed an ex-convict who witnessed the incident to bring it to light. International pressure and pressure from families, in addition to support by Qaddafi's son Saif Al Islam Qaddafi—in his attempt to represent a reformist side of the regime—led the authorities to issue death certificates for some of the prisoners.

Like the Madres de Plaza de Mayo in Argentina who have protested the disappearance of their children, the mothers of the Abu Salim prisoners became a public fixture in Benghazi.[33] As was the case under authoritarian rule in Latin America and elsewhere, such action by women, especially in their capacity as mothers, was somewhat tolerated by the regime because it was understood to express a "private" maternal concern, one that is less threatening than explicitly political and "public" dissent.[34] Over the years, however, tensions had escalated between the government and the families, for whom silent protest in front of the courthouse had become a routine. On January 24, 2010, YouTube access was blocked in Libya after it featured videos of families of the Abu Salim detainees demonstrating in Benghazi. This was a preview of events to come. The new availability of online means of communication meant that incidents of this kind could be shared throughout the country. In April 2010, the families' regular event in front of the courthouse was disrupted by a government-sponsored counterprotest that turned violent and led the Secretariat of Justice to prohibit demonstrations.[35]

The February 15, 2011, demonstration that sparked the uprising unsurprisingly resulted in the imprisonment of Fathi Terbil, the lawyer representing the Abu Salim families. What was unusual, however, was that the demonstrators did not disperse after the arrest but rather continued to demand his release in front of the police station. Even more extraordinarily, Terbil was in fact quickly released. Possibly, the recent uprisings in Tunisia and Egypt led the authorities to seek to diffuse the situation quickly. This was starkly different from the prior encounter between demonstrators and the authorities in Benghazi on February 17, 2006. What started as protests against the Prophet Mohammed Danish cartoons in front of the Italian consulate turned into an anti-government demonstration—and ended with security forces shooting at the protesters.

This time, however, the demonstrators were emboldened by the accession to their demands. The events in Tunisia and Egypt perhaps also played a role in inspiring the protesters. The uprisings in those countries signaled a change in the existing political opportunity structure under Middle Eastern authoritarian regimes. It marked a new possibility for regime change that was largely inconceivable before the onset of the Arab Spring.[36] Instead of dispersing, the protesters continued demonstrating in the streets of Benghazi, specifically calling for the end of Qaddafi's rule. Their ranks quickly swelled with other citizens who proceeded to burn government buildings. These protesters were not members of the old opposition groups located abroad or the LIFG. They were ordinary Libyan citizens expressing their grievances publicly, many for the first time. The protesters were soon met with a hail of bullets followed by the use of high-caliber firearms, allegedly by Libyan police forces, which injured and killed many. Insight from social movement theory teaches that it is not only "political opportunity" but also "threat perception" that can contribute to the fueling and persistence of social mobilization.[37] As in the Syrian case, as Reinoud Leenders and Steven Heydemann show, severe regime violence can generate a condition of "threat" that makes the cost of inaction outweigh the risk of mobilization.[38] In response to the escalation of regime violence, the protesters in Benghazi regrouped and fought back with improvised weapons such as the famous *gelatina,* or fishing bomb—a type of homemade gelignite bomb used by fishermen in Libya. They also raided police stations and munitions depots. Their actions inspired Libyans, and soon the uprising turned into an armed insurgency against the regime, albeit on unequal terms.

Unlike in previous uprisings, when the government was able to control the situation before word reached the rest of the country, the events of February

2011 were quickly relayed online, on satellite television, and by word of mouth as Libyans tuned in to Al Jazeera to see the footage coming in from Benghazi, Derna, Tobruk, and Bayda. In a daring move, Libyans used mobile phones to share the news during the first few days, before the government clamped down.[39] Cities and regions in the west, such as the Nafusa Mountains, Tripoli, Zawiya, and Misrata, joined in the uprising on February 16 with peaceful protests against the regime's violence in Benghazi. The government responded by firing on the protesters.

The flames in Benghazi were still settling on February 20 when lawyers and jurists in Tripoli were joined by other residents in front of the courthouse to protest the arrest of Abdul Hafiz Ghoga, president of the Bar Association. Saif Al Islam Qaddafi sent his top aides to negotiate with the protesters, who agreed to disperse when the negotiators promised his release. Shortly after his release, Ghoga went on to become a prominent member of the National Transitional Council (NTC) in Benghazi. Tripolitanians had hoped that this conciliatory attitude would continue, but on that same day Saif Al Islam gave a speech in which he threatened that the uprising would lead to separatism, Islamic extremism, poverty, and a foreign takeover of Libya, adding that his family would fight until the bitter end.[40]

On that evening Tripolitanians carried out their largest-ever peaceful night protest in the Green Square, estimated at three thousand protesters.[41] The sounds of the heavy artillery targeting the protesters that night continued into the early morning hours. The survivors speak of chaos and fear, as do the limited number of YouTube videos uploaded after the liberation of Tripoli.[42] On February 22 Libyan activists staged more protests in the city, burning the People's Hall and other government buildings. In response to this act and to the attack on Qaddafi's Katiba forces in Benghazi, Qaddafi made a chilling speech in which he likened protesters to "rats" and pledged to "cleanse" the country "house by house and alley by alley." In the aftermath of these events, military checkpoints spread both inside and outside the city where authorities, among other things, began to search mobile phones for incriminating information. The regime also used closed-circuit footage of demonstrations to identify and then round up protesters caught on camera. As the conflict continued, many activists disappeared. Hundreds are still missing.

Due to the violent repression of demonstrations, Libyans resorted to a new tactic of civil disobedience. Staying home instead of going to work or school served as a peaceful means for citizens to express their discontent.[43] However, a week after the start of the civil disobedience, authorities forced civil servants

A rebel parade celebrating the Libyan revolution. Photo by Intissar K. Rajabany.

back to work by threatening them with salary cuts and layoffs. Private businesses were threatened with confiscation if they did not reopen.[44] A few weeks later the government declared Saturday a working day, hence shortening the weekend in the hopes of curtailing further action.

Activists in western Libya decided to emulate the Friday protests that had been so successful in Tunisia and Egypt. The Friday of February 25 was chosen as D-Day to challenge the authorities again in Tripoli and in other cities in western Libya in which protests had been put down violently earlier in the week. As activists came out into the streets after the Friday prayer, they found paramilitary forces and riot police stationed near mosques in areas known for their opposition activities, such as Souk Juma and Fashloom, and also near some of the popular mosques in downtown Tripoli that lead to the Green Square. These forces opened fire at people coming out of mosques, making no effort to distinguish between protesters and non-protesters.[45] The crackdown effectively ended public Friday protests in Tripoli.[46] Still, clandestine protests continued and were videotaped and uploaded to YouTube.

The Dynamics of the Escalating Conflict

As the dynamics of protest and crackdown transformed into an armed insurgency, the youth remained at the forefront of the struggle. They were joined by a cross-section of Libyan society—doctors, teachers, taxi drivers, engineers, students, unemployed laborers, waiters, managers, housewives, pensioners, and others—all united around the goal of regime change in the country.[47] Very early, military deserters also joined the uprising. They were quickly followed by many highly visible individuals from the top echelons of leadership in Libya. The earliest desertions were those of the military in the eastern cities. Even soldiers who did not join the rebel forces assisted the uprising by leaving their posts as rebels overtook Katiba Al-Fadil in Benghazi, liberating the city from the remaining Qaddafi loyalists. Had the soldiers chosen to put up a strong resistance, the liberation of the city would have been much more difficult. The defection of Major General Abdul Fatah Younis, minister of the interior and "number two" in the Libyan regime (who was originally from the east) together with his Special Forces contingent was also pivotal to the success of the uprising.[48] Abdul Fatah Younis was from the Al Obeidi tribe, which is a major tribe in the eastern region of Libya and he could therefore count on many to rally round him. With Benghazi liberated from Qaddafi forces on February 20, 2011, and followed by other cities in the east, the rebels marched in convoys to liberate other areas of the country on their way to Tripoli.

The leadership that defected from the Qaddafi regime formed the National Transitional Council (NTC) as a representative of the Libyan people, establishing its headquarters in Benghazi, which served as the de facto rebel capital. This gave the uprising a semblance of organized leadership. Defection by high-profile leaders continued, as ministers, government officials, diplomats, military officers, business leaders, and influential clerics resigned from their positions. The defection of Libya's permanent representative to the UN and his aide was perhaps the most influential move in terms of drawing international attention to the gravity of the situation in Libya. The level of defection in Libya was greatly helped by support from the West as well as international condemnation, but money from Qatar also allegedly played an important role, as a large number of defectors had fled to that country since the start of the uprising.[49] Defection numbers also rose exponentially after the UN approved a no-fly zone in Libya on March 17 and NATO began air strikes two days later. Qaddafi's defeat increasingly came to appear inevitable.

The efforts of activists in eastern Libya now focused on overcoming their dependence on the western part of the country, which was still under Qaddafi's control—a consequence of Qaddafi's centralization of power and resources there. Circumventing this dependence was required in order to return normalcy to life in eastern Libya, to attend to the new needs brought about by the conflict, and to continue the armed struggle against Qaddafi. In this regard, activists concentrated on three areas: securing material resources and humanitarian assistance, acquiring arms, and maintaining channels of communication.

First, activists had to attend to the rising scarcity of resources. Conditions deteriorated as international sanctions descended on Tripoli, affecting banks and making cash flow in western Libya limited as money withdrawal was rationed. Rebel enclaves outside of Tripoli were affected due to the centralization of the banking system. Citizens and rebels sought to overcome this challenge by establishing their own central bank in Benghazi, independent of the Central Bank of Libya. They then restored services like Western Union that could supply money to Benghazi. Though Tripoli had cut off connections with bank branches in eastern Libya, some activists in these banks in western Libya had kept a clandestine link active in order to allow Benghazi residents to withdraw funds.

The central warehouses for medical resources and essential subsidized food staples were also located in Tripoli. When eastern Libya broke off contact with the rest of the country, the regime stopped the delivery of medical supplies and food to the region. The need for these, however, only increased with the rising number of people wounded in the fighting, internally displaced Libyans, and illegal immigrants and their families fleeing conflict zones. With outside help, Libyans organized the delivery of humanitarian aid and food through the Benghazi port and the Egyptian border. Medical staff was scarce in all cities, and the medical infrastructure in the country could not attend to the swelling number of casualties. Medical students volunteered in hospitals, and military medical equipment captured from army brigades and Qaddafi's forces was used to supplement the scant medical resources that were available.

Weapons and ammunition were in short supply, further disadvantaging the rebel forces. Libyan fighters "learned to weld captured rocket launchers guns [sic] to wheelbarrows and beds of their Toyota pickups. Clad in flip-flops and t-shirts, they crafted weapons out of sewage pipes and, lacking an air force, hoisted artillery to rooftops with cranes."[50] Rebels also smuggled ammunition to the front lines until help started coming in from abroad. Ammunition was also smuggled to cities under siege, such as Misrata and Tripoli, to prepare for the final showdown with Qaddafi's forces.

The centralization of communications in Libya meant that Tripoli could switch off internet and mobile telephone systems. The internet had flickered on and off since the start of the conflict but was shut down by the authorities on March 3, 2011. IT engineers in eastern Libya took control of the Libyana mobile operator, disconnected it from the main system, and reconnected it to operate independently of the rest of the country. Other activists did the same for Libya Telecom & Technology internet, reconnecting it via Etisalat in Egypt. The ability to spread information quickly and widely was a key resource not available in previous Libyan uprising attempts. For the first time, Libyans could overcome geographical distance and isolation, share information, and plan and execute actions in real time across the entire span of the country, and Libyans abroad could also partake in this effort. Earlier in the uprising, many used social media to spread the word about the February 17 "Day of Rage." Libyans inside the country showed their support by changing their surname to "Libya" on Facebook.[51]

As the uprising evolved, an army of virtual freedom fighters on websites, blogs, and social networks amplified the voices of those inside the country—in areas where internet access was available—to the outside world.[52] People uploaded videos and tweeted updates. Even in the areas where the internet was down, a few individuals had sophisticated equipment and got their message across with the help of Libyans who risked their lives in land journeys across the border to Tunisia to carry audio and video content out of the country physically.[53]

Mohammed Nabbous, a citizen journalist, set up Libya Alhurra TV online to counter Qaddafi's internet blackout. He broadcast updates about the situation in Libya to the world. His messages reached the parts of the country still under Qaddafi's control through satellite channels and anyone who still had a working internet connection. In March, Nabbous was killed by a sniper. His efforts were continued by his wife and many others, and Libya Alhurra TV, the first independent channel since 1969, continued to broadcast over Nilesat.[54]

A key lesson that the rebels learned from other uprisings in the region was the importance of international recognition for their cause. Thus, in addition to humanitarian and military action on the ground, individual Libyans, to the best of their abilities and resources, engaged in a multilevel lobbying effort, targeting neighboring Arab countries, the Arab League, the UN, and the leaders of Western countries. The NTC began to exert tremendous effort to convince the international community to support their cause. For this purpose, they partnered with the opposition factions in the diaspora and with Libyan expatriates who were experienced with lobbying in the West. With their contacts and experience, diaspora Libyans kept the Libyan cause in the spotlight, ensuring that information coming out of the country reached audiences and decision-makers in the West. They advocated for legal intervention and for the international community to address the situation in Libya. This relentless work, which involved Libyans abroad and in the country, culminated in UN Security Council Resolutions 1973 and 1970 stipulating the responsibility to protect Libyan citizens and the installation of a no-fly zone just as the forces of Qaddafi was entering the outskirts of Benghazi.

Qaddafi had underestimated the united power of the opposition. Following Libya's involvement in the war in Chad, he had intentionally weakened the Libyan army in order to prevent it from becoming a threat to his regime. Instead, he relied on special elite brigades that were charged primarily with protecting him. It was reported that during the uprising Qaddafi resorted to foreign mercenaries for additional support. In addition to his limited military means, Qaddafi also miscalculated the reaction of the West. Due to his rapprochement policy he mistakenly believed that the world would not intervene in the Libyan conflict.

Qaddafi compensated for these weaknesses in several ways. He attempted to buy loyalists off with money, cars, drugs, alcohol, and bank loans. He also used the threat of violence. His forces held female relatives of loyalists and opposition members captive, placed families under house arrest, increased the presence of militias on the streets, and resorted to collective punishment, torture, killing, and forced disappearances. His media machine also produced frightening propaganda to intimidate Libyans into submission. On talk shows he reached out to the citizenry, manipulating news by parading on television people who "confessed" that they had been bribed by al-Qaeda to destroy Libya. He made flamboyant speeches and called the NATO raids "Christian imperialist crusades." He brought in international media to Tripoli and kept them at the luxurious Rixos hotel. His teams orchestrated regular press conferences with "everyday Libyans" who parroted the regime's position. In an attempt to sabotage communication, he shut down the internet and deployed his massive surveillance capacities to monitor Libyans online or over the phone. An army of virtual electronic trolls descended on blogs, news sites, and social network sites and hacked the accounts of Libyans who were still active online.

Realizing his disadvantage, Qaddafi went so far as to offer a truce and negotiate with the rebels. He suggested that rebels might be granted amnesty. When these approaches failed, he resorted to cutting off water and electricity to cities, planting landmines, and attempting to resurrect the old tribal rivalries to divide the opposition, a tactic he had used for decades. In an effort to win back the support of Libyans, the Qaddafi regime also raised salaries by 150 percent, created a minimum social assistance wage of 150 Libyan dinars to the unemployed, and distributed a US$400 social aid package to families. Despite these multipronged efforts, Qaddafi's support bases in Libya shrank, until only Bani Walid and Sirte and some of the more impoverished areas of Tripoli were left.

The relative unity of the Libyan opposition during the uprising is noteworthy, especially given regional and political differences and the experience of the other major armed uprising of the Arab Spring—the rebellion in Syria. The Syrian opposition was divided between old and new leaderships and at times splintered along sectarian lines (see chapter 5). The relatively homogeneous ethnic and religious composition of Libya, on the other hand, meant that sectarian factionalism, a factor that often contributes to the prolonging of civil wars, was not a decisive feature in the Libyan conflict.[55] Assad could also draw on the rhetoric of Syrian exceptionalism, grounding the legitimacy of his regime—compared with the illegitimacy of the regimes in Egypt or Tunisia—in its leadership of the anti-Western, anti-Israel resistance front in the Middle East.[56] Qaddafi's one-man rule, on the other hand, lacked any real base of support or ideological legitimacy, which Assad's regime did enjoy. The common hatred and contempt felt for Qaddafi and his relatives acted as a rallying point for the opposition. For these reasons, Qaddafi was not able to divide the Libyan people once the uprising started, as Assad was able to do in Syria.

Another significant difference between the Libyan and Syrian uprisings was the position of the international community. The literature on civil wars has argued that an intervention by external parties tends to increase the duration of the war significantly.[57] However, in the Libyan case, external intervention on the side of the rebel forces facilitated a fairly swift and decisive rebel victory. The most devastating blow for Qaddafi was the unanimity of the world against him, represented in the UN Security Council resolutions. In comparison, the international community was not as vocal on Syria and, unlike the friendless Qaddafi, Assad could rely on support from Russia, China, and Iran, at least initially.

Activism in the Libyan West and Coordination across the Regions

During the uprising, activism depended on one's location in the country and would change over time depending on the circumstances of one's city, village, or region. The onset of the uprising in Benghazi emerged not only due to the new structure of political opportunity created by the events of the Arab Spring in other Arab countries and the threat that presented itself in the violent response of the regime, it was also made possible by the presence of thicker and overlapping social networks in the eastern part of the country as compared with the western part of the country.[58] In the east, extended families and community and tribal networks facilitated effective mobilization of resources, dissemination of information, and coordination among activists.[59]

The east was liberated early on in the uprising, so protesting at the Benghazi courthouse became more symbolic than defiant. The images of the residents rallying at the courthouse and praying and making speeches were seen daily by Libyans throughout the country and lent hope to residents of other regions. Activism in the east after the rebel takeover consisted of cleaning the cities, treating and helping the wounded, setting up media centers, cooking and sending food to the front lines, volunteering at hospitals, carrying out charity work, and attempting to restore normal life as much as possible. In this short period, hundreds of NGOs were formed, and Libyans learned the ropes of civil society organizing, activism, and advocacy.

The situation for activists in the West was very different. Qaddafi's military machine was concentrated in the western part of the country, and Tripoli and its suburbs were heavily fortified. Furthermore, because Tripoli is an urban city and not a tribal region, blood relations could not be as easily exploited as in a place like Benghazi. In Tripoli, it was difficult to know and trust the loyalties of the individuals in one's social network, and networks were infiltrated by regime informants. Activists had to create new networks to overcome this challenge. The difficulty was to identify like-minded individuals and form trusting relationships, both inside and outside of Libya. Elham Saudi from Lawyers for Justice in Libya, who was working abroad, recounts, "We were seven people, most of whom did not know each other, compelled to come together to do something, anything to contribute to the incredible events unfolding in Libya . . . . We had to shed the paranoia instilled in us by the previous regime and trust each other fully."[60] The extent of the stranglehold in Tripoli was exemplified in the questioning of school students about the type of TV channels their families watched and about the behavior of their parents.[61] Regime informants were everywhere, even checking TV sets in shops to see if they were tuned in to a prohibited channel.[62]

Citizens-turned-activists found ways to conceal and coordinate their efforts. If someone was caught, the others would go into hiding; if hiding was no longer an option, they would attempt to flee the country and continue their work from abroad. Many activist networks were on a "need-to-know" basis, and many did not even know each others' names in order to protect trusted allies in the event of capture. Activists in the non-liberated areas only spoke to each other face to face or briefly in code over the phone.

In Tripoli and in a number of other cities in the west, Libyans engaged in improvised activism of various kinds, but they were limited by the constraints of their situation. Some activists documented the uprising by video to collect evidence, while others contacted the international media. Those who had medical knowledge set up field clinics in their houses and smuggled supplies from government hospitals. Others organized mini-demonstrations at universities or covert protests.[63] Many small networks of family and friends were formed to smuggle ammunition to the front lines and to Tripoli. Women used their handbags to hide bullets and deliver them to secret sites.[64] Some turned their hobbies into activism, such as shipping weapons into Tripoli by dinghy.[65] One IT expert used his satellite connection to pass information to NATO.[66] Libyans also began to take up some of the labor usually carried out by foreign workers and took turns guarding their neighborhoods.

The collective effort of activists culminated in "Operation Mermaid Dawn"— the code name for the final battle for Tripoli. For months, activists in Tripoli, Benghazi, the Nafusa Mountains, Misrata, Zawiya, Sebha, and abroad coordinated the training of fighters from the city; provided NATO with coordinates for ammunition and command and control centers; ensured that there would be water, food and fuel to relieve the city; smuggled in weapons; identified sympathizers of the uprising in the military, police, and the security and information services and clandestinely recruited them to the war effort. They also prepared messages for the media and the hashtags for the army of Twitter users, and reached out to doctors in anticipation of a large number of casualties. Coordination between activists in Tripoli and those in the areas under the NTC was done via Skype in safe houses or by satellite phones, which would then quickly be switched off to avoid detection. Operating clandestinely, the activists were able to hide this enormous planning effort from the regime.[67]

As the preceding sections have shown, the 2011 uprising was not the first act of oppositional activism against the Qaddafi regime. The decades leading up to the uprising saw aborted coups, mutinies, attempts on Qaddafi's life, and limited protest and student activism. Nevertheless, there were some crucial differences between Libyan political activism in the decades before the uprising and the activism during the 2011 events. In the years of Qaddafi's iron rule, opposition groups operated mainly abroad. These were institutionally organized bodies in the West that had limited impact on the ground in Libya. Their sporadic actions against Qaddafi never succeeded in mobilizing the Libyan population. Protests, mutinies, and other oppositional activity from within Libya remained isolated and short-lived. The Qaddafi regime was quick to suppress dissent, and spreading information or coordinating action across regions in Libya was extremely difficult. The 2011 uprising, on the other hand, was characterized by the spontaneous mobilization of youth, students, and loosely organized citizens. Like the other uprisings of the Arab Spring, the Libyan revolution was not initially orchestrated by an established, institutionalized organization. The availability of new means of communication made effective cross-regional, as well as international, coordination possible for the first time.

Activism after the Uprising

The 2011 uprising mobilized large segments of the Libyan population—military and regime deserters, the old opposition groups in Libya and abroad, and eventually the international community through the NATO intervention all joined in the effort. However, in the transitional period, the activism entered a new phase. With the end of the fighting, activists have largely turned their attention to formalizing and institutionalizing their work in civil society organizations and political parties. All faced significant obstacles, yet even during the first year of transition, they made significant steps in overcoming them.

Activists faced a decline in enthusiasm, with diminished levels of volunteerism and commitment following the transitional period. During the uprising, Libyans put aside divisive issues and cooperated to achieve a common goal. In the transitional stage, however, mistakes by the transitional government, the resurfacing of regional and tribal divisions, and difficult security conditions contributed to waning enthusiasm.

Decades of indoctrination also made Libyans suspicious of one another and of political and civic organizations. Under Qaddafi, Libyans learned to become suspicious of others, having internalized the regime's constant monitoring of their lives and its infiltration of their social networks. Qaddafi also cultivated a zero-sum culture in which gains to one group came at the expense of another. Before the uprising, regime propaganda labeled the idea of political parties divisive and antidemocratic, and the only NGOs working on "advocacy" were the regime-sponsored enterprises of Qaddafi's children—the Qaddafi International Foundation for Charity Associations headed by

Saif al-Islam and Waatasemu Charity Association headed by Aisha Qaddafi. Their monopoly over advocacy did a great deal to discredit the term, and decades of restrictions and repression prevented the formation of strong movements and networks, which impeded the effectiveness of new parties after the uprising.

Activists faced a funding problem as well. The uprising saw an outpouring of support from Libyans around the world and in the country who donated funds and aid. Libyans also contributed to a number of efforts to help displaced communities. With the end of the fighting, funding became more limited. In June 2012 the transitional government adopted a new law to control the activities of international organizations supporting civil society in Libya that had the practical effect of banning "domestic NGOs from receiving money from foreign counterparts and partners" unless they have registered in Libya with the Ministry of Culture and Civil Society.[68] The law alleges to counter misunderstandings that may result from the activities of foreign organizations in Libya. Naturally, this move severely handicaps the independent work of civil society organizations and political parties. To address the scarcity of funding, some organizations met to coordinate a response, exploring the possibilities of cultivating a culture of giving in Libya that would build on the value of Islamic zakāt (charity) as well as encourage collaborative efforts to lobby the government for funding for civil society activity as a line item in the annual budget.

Activism remained subject to the political environment. Although the transitional government was more accepting of activism and civil society organizations than the Qaddafi regime, it remained to be seen how much latitude the regime would grant activists. Early on, the transitional government created the Ministry of Culture and Civil Society, which, together with the Ministry of Planning, the office of the United Nations Development Program (UNDP) in Libya, and the International Center for Not-for-Profit Law (ICNL), organized consultation workshops in February 2012 on the new legal framework for associations in Libya. The main themes tackled during the workshop were (1) the formation and internal governance of associations; (2) the funding of associations; and (3) government supervision over associations and applicable sanctions.

These themes were essential to institutionalizing activism in Libya and to replacing repressive attitudes and practices of the previous regime, such as registration procedures to monitor and limit organizations critical of the government or the selective regulation of funding for NGOs. Yet there was no immediate follow-up on this effort, and surprisingly, the government has imposed the aforementioned NGO funding restrictions.

The transition also saw a more open playing field for political parties. In January 2012 the interim government legalized political parties in Libya.[69] In April 2012, in a move to further regulate political parties, the NTC issued a law that aimed to prevent tribalism and religious or political extremism in campaigning and party platforms.[70] Hundreds of parties formed prior to the election, but the ones that did well in the election were those affiliated with prominent figures from the NTC or with opposition organizations such as the Muslim Brotherhood and the NFSL.[71]

Despite these challenges, Libyan activists accomplished some milestone achievements in the first year of transition. They succeeded in pressuring the NTC to amend some of the glaring flaws in the Constitutional Declaration of August 2011 and republish it in March 2012. Civil society groups also played a central role throughout the election process, reviewing the draft election law and holding the NTC accountable on issues of representativeness and transparency using radio, social media, newspapers, magazines, television, and protests. By these actions activists working for civil society organizations demonstrated their insistence on a new form of interaction with the state, one that maintains avenues for open, free, and independent activism and holds the government accountable to the people.

Activists also successfully prevented encroachments on freedom of speech. Article 13 of the Constitutional Declaration guarantees "freedom of opinion for individuals and groups, freedom of scientific research, freedom of communication, liberty of press, printing, publication and mass media."[72] After the ousting of Qaddafi, media multiplied in all forms—print, television, radio, and electronic—and a number of groups have formed to lobby for rights and freedoms. One such leading organization is the Libyan Civil Rights Lobby (LCRL) created on Facebook by like-minded activists from various Libyan civil society organizations both inside and outside of Libya. It used Facebook to criticize the lack of transparency of the NTC, to interrogate several of the laws passed in the transitional period, and to expose violations of human rights. Its most noteworthy accomplishment came in response to the NTC-issued Law 37 in May 2012. This "anti-glorification law" in effect criminalized any "acts of speech deemed 'damaging' to the efforts of the February 17 Revolution including the 'glorification' of Qaddafi or his regime."[73] The LCRL and many other Libyan activists such as Lawyers for Justice in Libya, Free Generation Movement, and Libya Outreach Group openly contested the law in a public

February 15, 2011: Over five hundred protesters gather in front of the police headquarters in Benghazi to protest the arrest of activist Fathi Terbil, leaving at least thirty-eight injured.

February 16, 2011: To appease demonstrators, the government releases 110 members of the Libyan Islamic Fighting Group. As protests continue in Benghazi, new protests begin in Quba, Derna, and Zintan.

February 17, 2011: Protests take place in four cities throughout Libya, bringing the day's death count to at least fourteen.

February 20, 2011: After several days of fighting, with total death tolls estimated at three hundred, the rebels take Benghazi.

February 26, 2011: As former Minister of Justice Mustafa Abdul Jalil forms an interim government, the U.S. urges Qaddafi to step down from power. The UN Security Council unanimously votes to impose an arms embargo, to refer the Libyan case to the International Criminal Court, and to freeze the assets of Libyan leaders.

February 27, 2011: The Italian government suspends its Libyan "friendship" treaty, which forbids warfare between the two countries. The newly formed National Transitional Council in Benghazi issues a release saying that it is completely against foreign intervention.

February 28, 2011: The United States freezes $30 billion of governmental assets.

March 5, 2011: The National Transitional Council declares itself Libya's only representative.

March 10, 2011: As France and Portugal officially recognize the National Transitional Council, Libya severs diplomatic ties with France.

March 17, 2011: The UN Security Council approves a no-fly zone and all measures necessary to protect Libyan civilians.

March 19, 2011: For the first time in its history, Denmark authorizes direct military action. In the afternoon, French fighter jets enter Libyan airspace and hit military vehicles. Operation Odyssey Dawn, under the command of AFRICOM, begins with Italian, American, British, French, and Canadian support.

March 28, 2011: Qatar becomes the first Arab country to recognize the National Transitional Council as the official government of Libya.

March 30, 2011: Foreign Minister Moussa Koussa resigns and defects to the United Kingdom.

April 10, 2011: In Tripoli, a NATO attack kills Qaddafi's youngest son and three of his grandchildren.

May 15, 2011: After months of bombardment, pro-Qaddafi forces withdraw from Misrata.

June 1, 2011: NATO extends its mission for ninety days. Top oil official Shukri Ghanem appears in Rome saying that he has defected and is now loyal to the NTC. At least 120 top military and government officials loyal to Gaddafi have defected since the uprising began.

June 27, 2011: The International Criminal Court issues an arrest warrant for Qaddafi, his son Saif al-Islam, and the Libyan head of intelligence.

July 15, 2011: The International Contact Group formally recognizes the NTC as the legitimate governing body of Libya.

August 9, 2011: The Qaddafi government accuses NATO of killing eighty-five civilians, which NATO later denies.

August 15, 2011: Opposition forces take Zawiya, enabling them to surround Qaddafi-controlled Tripoli.

April 19, 2011: Former Libyan prime minister Abdessalam Jalloud defects to the opposition. Opposition forces claim the town of Zliten.

August 20, 2011: The battle for Tripoli begins.

August 21, 2011: Qaddafi addresses Libyans on state TV, urging them to fight opposition forces until the end.

August 22, 2011: Qaddafi's son Saif al-Islam, previously thought to have been captured by opposition forces, appears in Tripoli.

August 24, 2011: Deputy intelligence chief Khalifa Mohammad Ali resigns and defects to the opposition.

August 26, 2011: In its first press conference from Tripoli, the NTC pledges to move its cabinet from Benghazi to Tripoli.

September 11, 2011: Libya begins producing oil again.

September 16, 2011: The UN Security Council unfreezes oil companies' accounts, permits the sales of weapons to Libya, and resumes flights.

September 20, 2011: The United States announces that it will redeploy its ambassador to Libya.

September 21, 2011: Opposition forces capture one of the remaining Qaddafi loyalist towns, Sabha.

October 17, 2011: After a six-week siege, NTC forces capture Bani Walid.

October 18, 2011: Unannounced, U.S. Secretary of State Hillary Clinton arrives in Libya and urges the opposition forces to unite.

October 20, 2011: After taking control of Sirte, transitional government soldiers capture Qaddafi. He dies in custody in transit to Misrata.

October 23, 2011: In Benghazi, the NTC chairman officially declares Libya free and the war over.

October 25, 2011: The NTC buries Qaddafi and his son in an undisclosed location.

October 31, 2011: NATO announces the completion of its military operations in Libya.

November 19, 2011: Qaddafi's fugitive son, Saif al-Islam, is captured in southern Libya.

November 20, 2011: Qaddafi's military intelligence chief, Abdullah Senussi, is captured.

November 23, 2011: In a reminder of tribal dynamics, some leading clans say that they will not recognize the new Libyan government.

campaign, leading the Libyan Supreme Court to declare the law unconstitutional a month later.

Women's rights activists also won a meaningful victory in the transitional period. Under Qaddafi, many laws aimed at improving the position of women in society were promulgated, but these were seen as tainted by association with the Qaddafi system and contradictory to traditional social mores. Although women played a pivotal role in the uprising and during the conflict, they were very poorly represented in the NTC.[74] To mitigate the political marginalization of women, women's rights advocates including the Libyan Women's Platform for Peace and Women4Libya lobbied for the implementation of a women's quota for political parties running in the National Assembly election. The quota requirement that they eventually passed in effect guaranteed almost 20 percent women's representation.[75]

A number of challenges remained, of course. Youth and women continued to be underrepresented in activism, possibly more so in the formal political institutions. Post-revolutionary activism empowered women and youth, allowing them to gain recognition in the public sphere—many of the women elected to the National Assembly in July 2012 were activists who had worked in civil society organizations and who had gained recognition and respect through their activism, and some youth, like Fahmi Abu Rakhis, a young independent candidate from Gharyan, enjoyed a degree of exposure in the media.[76] Yet, neither women nor youth enjoy full representation; well-known male activists in their fifties and sixties dominated the NTC as well as the party lists during the election.[77]

Nevertheless, the transformation in activism from the Qaddafi period to 2012 was remarkable. The days of repressed, fragmented activism at home and isolated groups abroad were replaced by a period of struggles for the emergence and institutionalization of new groups. The nearly unchallenged, repressive playing field of the pre-revolutionary period was transformed into an active contestation over the freedoms of expression, association, and representation. The contests were far from solved, and some challenges went unmet, but the revolution irrevocably changed the face of Libyan activism.

Notes

1. Human Rights Watch, "World Report 2011: Libya," April 4, 2011, available at www.hrw.org/world-report-2011/libya, accessed July 12, 2013.

2. Ali Abdullatif Ahmida, "Libya, Social Origins of Dictatorship, and the Challenge for Democracy," *Journal of the Middle East and Africa* 3(1) (2012): 70–81.

3. Ibid.

4. Jacques Roumani, "From Republic to Jamahiriya," *Middle East Journal* 37 (1983): 151–168, p. 164.

5. Amal Obeidi, *Political Culture in Libya* (Richmond, U.K.: Curzon, 2001), 29.

6. Dirk Vandervalle, *Libya since Independence* (London: I.B. Tauris, 1988), 134.

7. Mohamed Eljahmi, "Libya and the U.S.: Qadhafi Unrepentant," *Middle East Quarterly* 13(1) (Winter 2006): 11–20, 13, available at www.meforum.org/878/libya -and-the-us-qadhafi-unrepentant, accessed July 12, 2013.

8. Obeidi, *Political Culture in Libya,* 48.

9. Ibid., 49.

10. Eljahmi, "Libya and the U.S."

11. James C. Scott, *Weapons of the Weak: Everyday Forms of Peasant Resistance* (New Haven: Yale University Press, 1987).

12. Lisa Wedeen, *Ambiguities of Domination: Politics, Rhetoric, and Symbols in Contemporary Syria* (Chicago: University of Chicago Press, 1999); Mabroka al-Werfalli, *Political Alienation in Libya: Assessing Citizen's Political Attitudes and Behavior* (London: Ithaca Press, 2011).

13. Dr. Ibrahim Ighneiwa (ed.), "The Libyan Students Movement Documents," *Libya: Our Home,* available at www.libya-watanona.com/libya/student1.htm, accessed July 12, 2013.

14. Tasbeh Herwees, "Libyan Remember April 7th as a Day of Rage and Grief," *Neon Tommy,* April 7, 2011, available at www.neontommy.com/news/2011/04/april -7th, accessed July 12, 2013.

15. Ighneiwa (ed.), "7 April 1976," *Libya: Our Home,* available at www.libya -watanona.com/libya/7apr76c.htm, accessed July 12, 2013.

16. David Pugliese, "One Year Later, Libya's Future Still Very Much in the Air," FactDrop, February 18, 2012, available at http://factdrop.blogspot.com/2012/02 /one-year-later-libyas-future-still-very.html, accessed July 12, 2013; Chris Hedges, "Qaddafi Reported to Quash Army Revolt," *New York Times,* October 23, 1993, available at www.nytimes.com/1993/10/23/world/qaddafi-reported-to-quash-army -revolt.html, accessed July 12, 2013.

17. Ighneiwa (ed.), "Libyan Students Movement Documents."

18. Omar Ashour, "Libyan Islamists Unpacked: Rise, Transformation, and Future," Policy Briefing, Brookings Doha Center, May 2012, p. 1.

19. Ibid., p. 2.

20. Michel Cousins, "The Executioner of Benghazi," *Revolutionary Program,* June 4, 2011, available at http://revolutionaryprogram.blogspot.com/2011/06/exe cutioner-of-bengazi.html, accessed July 12, 2013; Redah Ben Yousef, "A Noble Stand against Tyranny in the Absence of Justice," *The Libyan Youth Movement Feb*

17th, October 30, 2011, available at http://feb17.info/editorials/a-noble-stand-against-tyranny-in-the-absence-of-justice/, accessed July 12, 2013.

21. Nick Meo, "'Huda the Executioner'—Libya's Devil in Female Form," *The Telegraph,* March 6, 2011, www.telegraph.co.uk/news/worldnews/africaandindianocean/libya/8363587/Huda-the-executioner-Libyas-devil-in-female-form.html, accessed July 12, 2013.

22. Human Rights Watch, "World Report 2011: Libya."

23. "Timeline: Libya Sanctions," BBC News, October 15, 2004, available at http://news.bbc.co.uk/2/hi/africa/3336423.stm, accessed July 12, 2013.

24. Talis Aghil, "To Be a Libyan!!" *Global Changemakers Blog,* November 6, 2011, available at www.global-changemakers.net/other/to-be-a-libyan, accessed July 12, 2013.

25. Children born in those years did not know these fruits; to this day bananas and apples are favorites in Libya because Libyans were deprived of them during the 1980s, in addition to chocolate and chewing gum.

26. Ian Black, "The Libyan Islamic Fighting Group—from Al-Qaida to the Arab Spring," *The Guardian,* September 5, 2011, www.guardian.co.uk/world/2011/sep/05/libyan-islamic-fighting-group-leaders, accessed July 12, 2013.

27. Eljahmi, "Libya and the U.S.," 15.

28. "List of Countries by Number of Internet Users," Wikipedia, available at http://en.wikipedia.org/wiki/List_of_countries_by_number_of_Internet_users, accessed April 30, 2012.

29. Fozia Mohamed, "Libya 2011: A Seminal Year through Citizen Media," *Global Voices Online,* January 9, 2012, available at http://globalvoicesonline.org/2012/01/09/libya-2011-a-seminal-year-through-citizen-media/, accessed July 12, 2013.

30. Roschanack Shaery-Eisenlohr, "From Subjects to Citizens? Civil Society and the Internet in Syria," *Middle East Critique* 20(2) (2011): 127–138.

31. "Libya: Families of Victims of Abu Salim Prison Massacres Targeted in Attack," Alkarama, April 19, 2010, available at http://en.alkarama.org/index.php?option=com_content&view=article&id=501:libya-families-of-victims-of-the-abu-salim-prison-massacre-targeted-in-attack&catid=27:communiqu&Itemid=138, accessed July 12, 2013.

32. Jim Thorne, "Families of Massacre Victims Hope to Learn Full Story of Abu Slim," *The National,* September 27, 2011, available at www.thenational.ae/news/world/africa/families-of-massacre-victims-hope-to-learn-full-story-of-abu-slim, accessed July 12, 2013.

33. Nora Amalia Femenía and Carlos Ariel Gil, "Argentina's Mothers of Plaza de Mayo: The Mourning Process from Junta to Democracy," *Feminist Studies* 13(1) (1987): 9–18.

34. See, for example, Elisabeth J. Friedman, "Paradoxes of Gendered Political Opportunity in the Venezuelan Transition to Democracy," *Latin American Research Review* 33(3) (1998): 87–135.

35. "Libya," Alkarama.

36. Sydney Tarrow, *Power in Movement: Social Movements, Collective Action, and Politics* (Cambridge, U.K.: Cambridge University Press, 1994).

37. Eitan Alimi, "The Dialectic of Opportunities and Threats and Temporality of Contention: Evidence from the Occupied Territories," *International Political Science Review* 28(1) (2007): 101–123.

38. Reinoud Leenders and Steven Heydemann, "Popular Mobilization in Syria: Opportunity and Threat, and the Social Networks of the Early Risers," *Mediterranean Politics* 17(2) (2012): 139–159.

39. Khadija Teri, "A Sleepy Saturday . . . What Stress Does to Me," *Khadija Teri Blog*, February 26, 2011, available at http://khadijateri.blogspot.com/2011/02/sleepy-saturday-what-stress-does-to-me.html, accessed July 12, 2013.

40. "Full Text of Saif Gaddafi's Speech," February 20, 2011, Available at http://mylogicoftruth.wordpress.com/2011/02/20/full-text-of-saif-gaddafis-speech/, accessed July 12, 2013.

41. Rana Jawad, "'Tripoli Witness' Recounts Life in Hiding," BBC News, August 26, 2011, available at www.bbc.co.uk/news/world-africa-14686402, accessed July 12, 2013; "Green Square Tripoli, Libya February Revolution 2011," video uploaded by "WadiTr," YouTube, February 22, 2011, available at http://youtu.be/oNPVtAm160c, accessed July 12, 2013; "Protest Almegaryaf St/Green Square Tripoli Libya February 20, 2011," video uploaded by "Awsmg1," YouTube, June 26, 2011, available at http://youtu.be/FNoBwHh3cYo, accessed July 12, 2013.

42. Garrett Therolf, "Libya: YouTube Videos Show Protests in Tripoli's Green Square," *Babylon & Beyond* blog, *Los Angeles Times,* February 23, 2011, available at http://latimesblogs.latimes.com/babylonbeyond/2011/02/libya-youtube-videos-show-protests-in-tripolis-green-square.html, accessed July 12, 2013.

43. "Tripoli Eyewitness: Trapped in the Libyan Whirlwind," BBC News, March 2, 2011, available at www.bbc.co.uk/news/world-africa-12621030, accessed July 12, 2013.

44. "Tripoli Witness: Tales of Defiance and a Mystery Man," BBC News, April 21, 2011, available at www.bbc.co.uk/news/world-africa-13154055, accessed July 12, 2013.

45. "Tripoli, Libya after Friday prayers. . . . ," video uploaded by "Egypt1Feb," YouTube, February 28, 2011, available at http://youtu.be/OXK6lRvbz94, accessed July 12, 2013; David Kirkpatrick, "Qaddafi Forces Violently Quell Capital Protest," *New York Times,* February 25, 2011, available at www.nytimes.com/2011/02/26/world/africa/26libya.html, accessed July 12, 2013.

46. "Protests in Tripoli after Friday Prayer," video, *Libya 17th February 2011 Archive Site,* posted February 25, 2011, available at http://archive.libyafeb17.com /2011/02/protests-in-tripoli-after-friday-prayer/, accessed July 12, 2013.

47. Pugliese, "One Year Later."

48. "Abdul Fatah Younis," Wikipedia, available at http://en.wikipedia.org/wiki /Abdul_Fatah_Younis, accessed April 4, 2012.

49. Nicola Nasser, "Opinion: Qatar and U.S.: Collusion or Conflict of Interests?" *Tripoli Post,* January 28, 2013, available at www.tripolipost.com/articledetail .asp?c=5&i=9829, accessed July 12, 2013.

50. *Voices for Libya,* April 12, 2012, available at http://revolutionaryprogram .blogspot.com/2012/01/voices-4-libya-book.html, accessed July 13, 2013.

51. Cyber Security Forum Initiative (CSFI), "Project Cyber Dawn v1.0 Libya," *Unveillance,* April 17, 2011, 1–60, 14, available at www.unveillance.com/wp-content /uploads/2011/05/Project_Cyber_Dawn_Public.pdf, accessed February 1, 2012.

52. *Voices for Libya.*

53. Fozia Mohamed, "Libya: Bloggers Between Dictatorship and War," *Global Voices Online,* August 21, 2011, available at http://globalvoicesonline.org/2011/08 /21/libya-bloggers-between-dictatorship-and-war/, accessed July 13, 2013.

54. "Most Powerful Arabs in the World: In Pictures," *Arabian Business,* June 7, 2012, available at http://power500.arabianbusiness.com/power-500-2012/photos /dummy-industry/2012/jun/7/253032/, accessed July 13, 2013.

55. Paul Collier, Anke Hoeffler, and Måns Söderbom, *On the Duration of Civil War* (Washington, DC: World Bank, Development Economic Research Group, 1999).

56. Caroline Donati, *L'Exception Syrienne: Entre Modernisation et Résistance* (Paris: Editions La Découverte, 2009).

57. Ibrahim Elbadawi and Nicholas Sambanis, "External Interventions and the Duration of Civil Wars," paper presented at the workshop on the Economics of Civil Violence, Princeton University, Princeton, New Jersey, March 2000.

58. Tarrow, *Power in Movement.*

59. Parallels exist here with the geographic patterns of mobilization during the Syrian uprising; see Leenders and Heydemann, "Popular Mobilization in Syria."

60. Elham Saudi, "Letter from Our Director," *Mizan: The Newsletter from Lawyers for Justice in Libya,* no. 1, April 2012, available at www.libyanjustice.org /downloads/Mizaan%20newsletter%2023rd%20april%20-%20FINAL.pdf?utm_ source=smartmail&utm_medium=email&utm_campaign=Mizaan+-+Issue+1+, accessed July 13, 2013.

61. "Tripoli Witness: Afraid to Watch TV," BBC News, March 17, 2011, available at www.bbc.co.uk/news/world-africa-12770318, accessed July 13, 2013.

62. "Tripoli Witness: Tales of Defiance and a Mystery Man."

63. "Tripoli Witness: Covert Protests and Black Humour," BBC News, April 14, 2011, available at www.bbc.co.uk/news/world-africa-13087062, accessed July 13, 2013.

64. Rana Jawad and Penny Dale, "Tripoli Underground: Handbags, Dinghies, and Secret Emails," BBC News, December 3, 2011, available at www.bbc.co.uk/news/magazine-16001247, accessed July 13, 2013.

65. Ibid.

66. Ibid.

67. James Reevell, "Libya: How 'Operation Mermaid Dawn,' the Move to Take Tripoli, Unfolded," *The Telegraph*, August 21, 2011, available at www.telegraph.co.uk/news/worldnews/africaandindianocean/libya/8714522/Libya-how-Operation-Mermaid-Dawn-the-move-to-take-Tripoli-unfolded.html, accessed July 13, 2013.

68. Jamie Dettmer, "Exclusive: Libya's Civil Crackdown Worries Democracy Advocates," *The Daily Beast,* May 28, 2012, available at www.thedailybeast.com/articles/2012/05/28/exclusive-libya-s-civil-crackdown-worries-democracy-advocates.html, accessed July 13, 2013.

69. "Libya New Leaders Legalise Political Parties," *Tripoli Post,* January 5, 2012, available at www.tripolipost.com/articledetail.asp?c=1&i=7616, accessed July 13, 2013.

70. Mohamed Eljarh, "The Libyan Elections Law 2012 and the Muslim Brotherhood," *Middle East Online,* January 2, 2012, available at www.middle-east-online.com/english/?id=5-383, accessed July 13, 2013.

71. The National Forces Alliance, a coalition of fifty-eight political parties identified as "liberal" and affiliated with the NTC's former interim prime minister Mahmoud Jibril, won 39 of the seats in the July 2012 election. The Justice and Construction Party, formed by the Muslim Brotherhood, came second with 17 seats. The National Front, which replaced the NFSL, the longest-running opponent of the Qaddafi regime, based largely in Benghazi, won 3 seats. The al-Watan Party, led by Abdulhakim Belhaj, a former LIFG fighter, and backed by Islamic cleric Ali al-Sallabi, did not win any seats. The Federal Alliance of Benghazi was formed in August 2012, after the election, with the aim of regrouping the federalist elements from the east following the failure of their secessionist efforts. Some of the candidates that ran in the election for the 120 seats reserved for independents were unofficially allied with some of these parties. Therefore, it remained to be seen which group, if any, would dominate the National Assembly.

72. Project on Middle East Democracy, *Draft Constitutional Charter for the Transitional Stage,* uploaded August 2011; p. 5, available at pomed.org/wordpress/wp-content/uploads/2011/08/Libya-Draft-Constitutional-Charter-for-the-Transitional-Stage.pdf, accessed July 13, 2013.

73. Paul Salem and Amanda Kadlec, "Libya's Troubled Transition," *The Carnegie Papers,* Carnegie Endowment for International Peace, June 2012, p. 12, available at carnegieendowment.org/files/Libya_transition.pdf, accessed July 13, 2013.

74. Yusra Tekbali, "Libya's Women Coming Out Now!" *Nahla Ink Online Journal*, September 16, 2011, available at www.nahlaink.com/features.php?article=90yusra%20tikbali%20activists, accessed July 13, 2013.

75. Women4Libya, "Why Women? Why Now? Engaging and Promoting Libyan Women," *Libya Herald*, June 30, 2012, available at www.libyaherald.com/?p=10144, accessed July 13, 2013.

76. "Libyan Women Win 33 Seats in First National Assembly Elections since 1952," Libyan Women Platform for Peace, July 30, 2012, available at http://lwpp.org/libyan-women-win-33-seats-in-first-national-assembly-elections-since-1952/, accessed July 13, 2013; "The Young Face of Libya: Exclusive Interview with Fahmi Abukhris," *Youth Libya*, July 2012, p. 9.

77. Adequate representation of women and youth remains a concern, despite the quota requirement. The requirement for women applied only to party lists, which made up only 80 seats of the 200-seat National Assembly, while the remaining 120 seats were reserved for independents, most of which were won by men in the July 2012 elections. So, too, the brief campaign period disadvantaged new and younger candidates, who found it difficult to introduce themselves to the public fully. A few efforts to establish youth parties emerged, but these were not effectively organized. However, one party—the Centrist Youth Party—did win one seat in the National Assembly.

CHAPTER 4

Explaining Political Activism in Yemen

GAMAL GASIM

Tʜᴇ ʏᴇᴍᴇɴɪ ᴜᴘʀɪsɪɴɢ began in mid-January 2011, when a small group of youth led by a prominent activist, Tawakkol Karman, organized a march in Tahrir Square (Liberation Square) in Sana'a to send a message of support and congratulations to the Tunisian people following the ousting of Zine El Abidine Ben Ali. The regime briefly arrested Karman and then released her due to popular anger driven in part by widespread Yemeni views that detaining women is a socially intolerable and offensive act. The Ali Abdullah Saleh regime also sent regime loyalists and supporters to occupy Tahrir Square as a preemptive measure designed to abort attempts by protesters to replicate the events then occurring in Egypt and Tunisia. Karman's group then moved to Sana'a University and camped out in what was later branded as "Taghyeer Square" (Change Square), demanding political reforms and the resignation of President Saleh. Activists organized similar protest camps in other cities across the country. Most of these activists in the early weeks of the movement were university students—these were the genuine faces of the Yemeni uprising.

These striking events—prompted by the surprise successes of the Tunisian and Egyptian uprisings—were the initial spark of the Yemeni uprising. Yet the roots of the unfolding struggle can be found in events that occurred some years earlier. The rise of the southern al-Hirak (Mobility) movement during 2007 and al-Hirak's nonviolent strategies in challenging Saleh's tight control in the south of the country threatened the Yemeni president for the first time in his tenure since the end of the civil war of 1994. It set the stage for what followed because it empowered youth activists, who are now acting mostly independent of political parties and demonstrating that continuous civil protests can have a significant impact in bringing about political reform.

This chapter will examine the evolution of political activism before and during the Yemeni uprising as well as the ways in which political activism has changed since 1990. The chapter will begin by describing the domestic context in which activism by Yemen's oppositional movements has taken place over the years. It will then address the ideological orientations, political demands, strategies, and relationships among Yemeni political activists as well as the regional and international contexts in which they operate.

The Domestic Political and Social Context

The Republic of Yemen does not enjoy a Weberian monopoly on the legitimate use of coercive power. Yemen is the home of strong and independent tribal communities that have sustained a pivotal role within Yemeni politics for centuries. A key feature of traditional forms of interaction in this tribal structure is that it harbors strong elements of civil society and political engagement.[1] Daily social gatherings to chew qat, for example, provide important informal platforms to discuss and debate various social and political issues.[2] Tribal customs and traditions play an effective role in settling disputes, calling for justice, and mobilizing masses. This tribal structure has made it difficult for state institutions to be effective.

President Saleh capitalized on this weakness. Shortly after seizing power in North Yemen in 1978, Saleh demonstrated a crucial understanding of the sway that tribal leaders held in Yemeni society. He established close ties with Sheikh Abdallah bin Hussein al-Ahmar, the most powerful tribal leader in the country. Sheikh al-Ahmar headed the tribal federation of Hashid (to which Saleh's own tribe, Sanhan, belonged) after the execution of his father and brother at the hands of Imam Ahmed.[3] It has been said that Sheikh al-Ahmar once described this unique relationship by saying that "Saleh is my president, but I am his Sheikh."[4] The support of al-Ahmar was vital to key Saleh military triumphs, such as the civil war of 1994. Saleh understood the importance of this alliance and maintained a close association with Sheikh al-Ahmar until his death, keeping him as speaker of parliament even though al-Ahmar's party had never won a majority of parliamentary seats. Former president Saleh achieved his thirty-year tenure in part because of his political skill in using tribal leaders to his advantage and, in some cases, against each other, an experience he once described as "dancing over snakes' heads."

This maneuvering further impeded the development of state institutions. It thwarted the establishment of strong agencies that could have provided critical public services, such as security, a stable legal system, and public education. It also undermined the political party system. After the 1990 unification of North Yemen and South Yemen, the door opened for a remarkable proliferation of political parties. Indeed, Francesco Cavatorta and Vincent Durac argue that the political union between the politically conservative North and the socialist South resulted in competing ideologies, which, in turn, helped to establish a sensibly competitive party system and allowed for civil society actors to work in a uniquely effective political context in the Arabian Peninsula.[5] Yet although some Arab nationalist and traditional Islamic parties enjoyed increasing support, the dominant and broadly supported political parties remained the General People's Congress (GPC), affiliated with President Saleh; the Yemeni Socialist Party (YSP), which had ruled South Yemen and became an oppositional party after the civil war of 1994; and al-Islah, a coalition of tribal sheikhs and Islamists.

Political parties in Yemen are not well organized or institutionalized, and the relationships among them are shaped by shifting alliances and a lack of political trust. Until the late 1990s, the conservative wing of al-Islah Party was highly suspicious of the YSP because of its history of social engineering attempts in the South, which had weakened the role of the *ulama* (scholars of Islamic jurisprudence) and Islamic laws before the unification. In fact, al-Islah's prominent leader, Abdul Majeed al-Zindani, was concerned that the unification would come at the expense of the hard-won Islamic prominence in the North, so he led a massive campaign under the slogan "Yes to the unification and No to the constitution." Because of this political pressure, the constitution explicitly states that Islamic sharia is the source of all legislation. However, it is not Islamic law but the lack of the rule of law that has shaped Saleh's regime since Yemeni unification.

Activism before the Yemeni Uprising

Political activism before the Yemeni uprising can be broadly categorized into three phases. The first phase started with the formation of the Republic of Yemen in May 1990. The second phase began with the end of the 1994 civil

January 1, 2011: Parliament agrees to make constitutional amendments that would allow President Ali Abdullah Saleh to rule for life.

January 7, 2011: In the southern city of Lawdar, al-Qaeda fighters kill at least ten Yemeni soldiers.

January 12, 2011: Amid fuel shortages and public debate, President Saleh suspends his oil minister and the head of the national oil company.

January 23, 2011: Police arrest female activist Tawakkol Abdel-Salam Karman.

January 27, 2011: At least ten thousand Yemenis gather at Sana'a University and another six thousand outside the capital to demand the ouster of President Saleh.

February 2, 2011: To appease protesters, President Saleh addresses parliament, stating that he will not seek another term in office nor take any measures to change the constitution.

February 3, 2011: At least twenty thousand antigovernment protesters gather for a "day of rage." Proregime and proreform supporters clash, leaving one protester critically wounded.

February 12, 2011: At least three people are injured when four thousand protesters, mostly students, march in central Sana'a to demand the removal of President Saleh.

February 13, 2011: As one thousand protesters continue marching in Sana'a,

President Saleh and the opposition agree to resume talks.

February 15, 2011: In the fifth straight day of protests, police and government supporters clash with proreform protesters, leaving three injured.

February 16, 2011: In a protest in Aden, two protesters are fatally shot by police. In Sana'a, protests continue for their sixth straight day, leaving ten injured.

February 17, 2011: Amid continued clashes between proreform protesters and progovernment supporters, a group of senior clerics calls for the formation of a national unity government.

February 18, 2011: On the "Friday of Rage," five protesters are killed as Yemen goes into its eighth straight day of protests.

February 19, 2011: As many as four hundred protesters in Aden hold a peaceful sit-in. In Sana'a, clashes between protesters and police leave five more injured.

February 21, 2011: Despite nationwide chaos, President Saleh refuses to step down until he is defeated in the elections. In Aden, one student is killed and four are injured as protesters clash with soldiers. Authorities take southern opposition leader Hasan Baoum into custody.

February 22, 2011: Thousands continue protesting throughout Sana'a, Aden, Taiz, and Ash-Shihr. Twelve protesters are wounded, and at least one is killed.

February 23, 2011: Seven legislators from Saleh's party resign, stating that they will form a new bloc. In a strange twist, President Saleh says that he has ordered forces to protect the protesters.

February 25, 2011: As many as 180,000 people take to the streets for another "Day of Rage" in Sana'a. At least forty-three are wounded; death estimates range between four and eleven.

February 26, 2011: As a sign of President Saleh's waning power, leaders of the Hashid and Baqil tribes announce that they will join the opposition forces.

March 1, 2011: Yassin Ahmad Saleh Qadish, a senior separatist movement leader, calls for an independent southern territory. Abdul-Majeed al-Zindani, head of the Council of Islamic Clerics, joins the tens of thousands of protesters in Sana'a.

March 3, 2011: Despite an exit strategy by clerics and leading opposition, President Saleh says that he will not step down.

March 4, 2011: In northern Yemen, soldiers fire on protesters in Harf Sofyan, killing two and injuring thirteen. One hundred thousand protesters gather in Sana'a and Taiz to demand President Saleh's ouster.

March 5, 2011: Just a day after the resignation of tribal presidential ally Ali Ahmad al-Omrani, Deputy Minister Hashid Abdullah al-Ahmar offers his resignation.

March 8, 2011: In Sana'a, two thousand inmates join antigovernment protesters and stage a revolt in a prison.

March 11, 2011: Security forces open fire on the estimated forty thousand protesters on the "Friday of No Return." Protests continue throughout the country.

March 16, 2011: At least 120 people are wounded in the southern port of al-Hudayah as proregime and proreform forces clash.

March 18, 2011: Unidentified gunmen fire on antigovernment protesters in Sana'a, killing at least fifty-two people and injuring hundreds. Authorities declare a state of emergency.

March 21, 2011: At least eleven senior commanders defect and join the protesters calling for President Saleh's ouster.

March 23, 2011: Parliament enacts a thirty-day emergency law, suspending the constitution, allowing media censorship, and banning street protests.

March 25, 2011: Amid clashes between pro- and antigovernment protesters, President Saleh says that he will step down if he can leave the country "in safe hands."

March 29, 2011: President Saleh addresses the nation stating that despite losing six of the country's eighteen provinces, he will not step down.

April 3, 2011: In the southern town of Taiz, security forces and plainclothes policemen clash with antigovernment demonstrators, killing at least twelve. In the southern port of al-Hudayah, police fire on protesters, wounding 250 people.

April 5, 2011: As the United States calls for President Saleh to step down, fighting continues throughout Sana'a.

April 8, 2011: As three people are shot dead in Taiz and thirty are in critical condition, President Saleh addresses his supporters stating that he will not tolerate a coup attempt by Gulf states to oust him from power.

April 13, 2011: Six people are killed in Sana'a as hundreds of thousands continue protesting throughout the country.

April 16, 2011: In opposition to President Saleh's call that it is un-Islamic for women to protest, over five thousand women join the nearly one hundred thousand protesters in Taiz calling for an end to President Saleh's rule.

April 23, 2011: President Saleh announces that in exchange for immunity for him and his family, he will hand over the government to his vice president.

April 27, 2011: In eighteen cities throughout the country, over one hundred thousand people take to the streets to launch a civil disobedience campaign. Twelve protesters are killed and more than 190 are wounded.

May 11, 2011: In the worst violence in months, police open fire on protests in three cities throughout Yemen, killing at least eighteen.

May 20, 2011: In an attempt to stay in power, President Saleh calls for early presidential elections.

May 24, 2011: In Sana'a, forces loyal to tribal leader Sheikh al-Ahmar battle with those loyal to President Saleh. At least thirty-eight die; dozens more are injured.

May 27, 2011: After several days of fighting with a death toll near 110, tribal leader al-Ahmar calls for a ceasefire.

May 29, 2011: In the largely ungoverned province of Abyan, Islamist militants take control of Zinjibar.

May 30, 2011: Soldiers loyal to President Saleh storm Taiz, killing at least twenty people.

May 31, 2011: The ceasefire in Sana'a is broken after government forces attack the home of tribal leader al-Ahmar.

June 1, 2011: As troops loyal to President Saleh and troops loyal to al-Ahmar face off, at least forty-one people are killed.

June 3, 2011: President Saleh survives an assassination attempt as shells strike his palace.

June 4, 2011: Fatal fighting continues through the night, as rumors circulate that a wounded President Saleh has fled the country for Saudi Arabia.

June 6, 2011: Reports confirm that President Saleh is seeking treatment in Saudi Arabia for wounds sustained during the attack on the presidential palace. New fighting breaks out in Taiz, where the death toll this week mounts to fifty.

June 11, 2011: In clashes in the southern Abyan province, at least thirty soldiers and militants are killed.

June 15, 2011: One soldier dies and three are wounded as two hundred militants from Ansar al-Shariah launch an attack on Houta, capital of the southern Lahj province.

June 20, 2011: Tens of thousands of antigovernment protesters take to the streets to demand President Saleh's departure from government.

June 24, 2011: Security forces clash with thousands of activists at the funeral of activist Ahmed Darwish, killing five people.

June 30, 2011: President Saleh calls for dialogue as fighting continues in Zinjibar.

July 1, 2011: Hundreds of thousands of protesters continue to call for President Saleh's resignation in protests throughout the country. Meanwhile, the president's son, Ahmed Saleh, begins arrests of military officers suspected of defecting.

July 7, 2011: As clashes continue in Zinjibar, Taiz, and Loder, a weakened and bandaged President Saleh appears on state TV in his first appearance since his arrival in Saudi Arabia.

July 15, 2011: Opposition groups announce the formation of a seventeen-member body to take control of the government in the event of the collapse of President Saleh's government.

July 19, 2011: More than twenty militants, including senior leader Ayed al-Shabwani, are killed in Jaar.

July 21, 2011: Fighting continues in Taiz, where death toll estimates are as high as ten and thirty-three wounded over the past twenty-four hours of fighting.

July 30, 2011: Government air strikes accidentally kill fourteen tribal allies in southern Yemen.

August 6, 2011: President Saleh leaves the hospital and moves to a private compound in Saudi Arabia.

August 10, 2011: Antigovernment and progovernment supporters enter into a truce in Taiz.

August 11, 2011: Despite the new ceasefire, clashes continue in Taiz, leaving four injured.

August 12, 2011: Hundreds of thousands of antigovernment protesters clash with tens of thousands of President Saleh supporters in Sana'a.

August 16, 2011: As President Saleh gives another address from Saudi Arabia calling for presidential elections, twenty-three Bakil tribal fighters are killed in clashes with government forces in Arhab.

August 17, 2011: The opposition coalition elects 143 members to the newly formed National Council for the Forces of the Peaceful Revolution.

September 9, 2011: Nearly a million antigovernment protesters take to the streets.

September 12, 2011: From Riyadh, President Saleh authorizes the GCC power transfer, which would hand over power to Vice President Abd Rabbuh Mansur Hadi.

September 16, 2011: In Sana'a and Taiz, hundreds of thousands march under the protection of al-Ahmar's First Armored Division.

September 18, 2011: Just after Hadi agrees to sign the GCC deal, government forces fire on protesters in Sana'a, leaving more than twenty-six dead and two hundred wounded.

September 19, 2011: In the bloodiest day of fighting yet, twenty-two are killed and 350 wounded as security forces clash with antigovernment protesters.

September 23, 2011: As President Saleh returns to Yemen, hundreds of thousands of protesters gather in Sana'a for the country's largest-ever antigovernment rally.

October 4, 2011: Security forces shell Taiz, killing seven and injuring twenty-two.

October 7, 2011: Massive protests throughout the country in commemoration of Ibrahim al-Hamdi, the president of North Yemen who was assassinated in 1977, draw as many as three million demonstrators.

October 21, 2011: The United Nations Security Council unanimously passes a resolution condemning the violence and, under the GCC plan, calls on Saleh to transfer power.

October 25, 2011: After several days of fighting, President Saleh's government and al-Ahmar sign a ceasefire deal.

October 26, 2011: Despite the ceasefire, fighting continues in Sana'a and Taiz, leaving twenty-five dead.

October 30, 2011: The General People's Congress nominates Abd Rabbuh Mansur Hadi as a presidential stand-in upon completion of the GCC deal.

November 9, 2011: Houthi rebels defeat the progovernment tribes of Kashir and Ahm and advance toward Sana'a.

November 15, 2011: In response to the Gulf Cooperation Council's request,

President Saleh announces that he will resign in ninety days.

November 20, 2011: Nearly four hundred soldiers defect from the Yemeni Army.

November 23, 2011: Saleh flies to Saudi Arabia to attend the GCC deal signing. United Nations Secretary General Ban Ki-moon says that Saleh will travel to the United States for medical treatment after the signing.

December 7, 2011: Hadi-appointed prime minister Mohammed Basindawa announces that the national unity government shall be comprised of anti-Saleh and pro-Saleh members.

December 11, 2011: Hundreds of thousands of protesters gather in Sana'a to call for the trial of Saleh.

December 16, 2011: Protesters march in eighteen cities across the country rejecting an amnesty given to President Saleh.

December 24, 2011: The United States defends the government's decision to attack a group of more than one hundred thousand demonstrators calling for Saleh's trial. At least nine protesters are left dead.

December 25, 2011: As anti-U.S. sentiment grows after the decision by the United States to support the attacks, tens of thousands of Yemenis march from Taiz to Sana'a demanding justice.

December 31, 2011: Hundreds of thousands of protesters take to the streets demanding Saleh's trial and execution as he decides to remain in Yemen through the elections.

war and the defeat of the YSP, and the third phase stretches from the presidential election campaign of 2006 until the Yemeni uprising in 2011. Political conditions and patterns of activism distinguish these phases from each other. Political activism has evolved from being essentially a party-based affair to encompassing mass movements and grassroots activism. Since 2006, political activism in Yemen has helped remove all forms of political taboo, including criticisms of Yemen's President Saleh, calls for separation from the union, exposés of government corruption, and demands for comprehensive political and economic reforms.

From May 1990 to April 1994

Despite the inherent problems that accompanied a hasty and understudied unification process, the Republic of Yemen was born with a vibrant democratic transition enshrined in a new constitution, which allowed for a multi-party, semi-presidential system as well as freedom of the press and freedom of political association.[6] Political parties facilitated activism during this period. The key political parties included the General People's Congress (GPC), the Yemeni Socialist Party (YSP), and the newly emerged Islamic party, al-Islah (Reform). The GPC and the YSP had been the former ruling parties in North Yemen and South Yemen, respectively, before unification.

Political activism in the early years of unification, before the first democratic parliamentary elections of 1993, focused mainly on party recruitment and mobilization. The GPC maintained its party membership, except for the majority of Muslim Brotherhood members within the party, who left to join al-Islah. The GPC also maintained its strategic alliance with some tribal leaders and supporters of the former president of South Yemen, Ali Nasir Muhammad. The YSP reached out to its former allies in the North, including some tribal leaders in the Bakil federation and central areas. But al-Islah succeeded in gaining the most tribal support by recruiting Sheikh Abdallah bin Hussein al-Ahmar, who became the president of al-Islah until his death.

Immediately after the unification, Yemen's key political parties expanded their social and youth organizations beyond their traditional support base. For example, the YSP expanded its youth outreach to the northern provinces, where its Youth Union (Ashid) became reasonably active in urban centers. Ashid was primarily dedicated to ideological indoctrination and party mobilization. Al-Islah, on the other hand, expanded its charity work and informal Islamic education for women through *nadwat* (Islamic seminars or symposiums). As

Janine Clark explains, "While women generally do not mix party politics into their *nadwa* discussions, during the segment of the *nadwa,* an *Islahi* woman may quietly approach another and suggest that she join her at another *nadwa* or social event on a different day. At this second *nadwa,* she may be introduced to a social group which is more openly supportive of al-*Islah* or Islamist goals."[7] Political activism during this period was shaped in part by organizations and activists asserting both religious (al-Islah) and secular (Ashid) identities.

This period also witnessed a sudden increase in the number of partisan newspapers, which attracted hundreds of journalists affiliated to these parties. The GPC maintained its tight control over state media, including such highly circulated daily official newspapers as *al-Thawra*, while some independent newspapers such as *al-Ayyam* in Aden provided a free platform independent of political parties and government control.

However, these developments took place in the context of a great deal of political uncertainty. The assassination of many politicians and activists such as Majid Murshid and Amin Numan, chiefly from the YSP, helped generate enormous political mistrust between the YSP and the GPC. There were also several failed assassination attempts, including an infamous attempt to kill Yasin Said Nu'man, who was speaker of the parliament at the time. No official investigation report was ever issued on who was behind these assassinations, but it became evident that President Saleh had benefited politically from them.[8] Moreover, Saleh shrewdly exploited the preexisting political divisions within the YSP, which had resulted from the 1986 civil war in the south, to his great political advantage. He also claimed excessive gains from the historical political mistrust between the YSP and Yemen's Islamists. The support of al-Islah and such tribal leaders as al-Ahmar played a crucial role in tipping the balance of power in Saleh's favor during the civil war.

From July 1994 to Early 2006

In the aftermath of the 1994 civil war, strong negative sentiments of injustice and discrimination prevailed not only in the south but also in the north. The situation worsened following the consolidation of political power by Saleh's family and political supporters in the 1997 parliamentary elections, as political activism in Yemen entered its most repressive period since unification. The YSP suffered severely during the civil war. The party's top leaders fled the country, causing a significant vacuum in the party's leadership. The YSP found itself in a soul-searching phase as it looked for new strategies to deal with the aftermath of the civil war. Two opposing views had emerged prior to the 1997 parliamentary elections with regard to whether the YSP should participate in elections or not. Jarallah Omar, a top YSP leader who was assassinated in 2002 by an extremist while attending al-Islah's general conference, believed that "the YSP should participate in the elections and continue its dialogue with the two ruling coalition parties (GPC and *Islah*)."[9] However, the secretary general of the YSP, Abbad Muqbil, succeeded in persuading his party to boycott the parliamentary elections of 1997 in protest against Saleh's policies toward the party after the civil war.[10] This move may have been pivotal in helping the GPC secure the majority of parliamentary seats, ending its government coalition with al-Islah.

Political activism began to lose ground after 1994. The GPC sustained its complete control of government through its majoritarian mechanism in the parliament, but after the 1997 elections, President Saleh began to exercise more authoritarian power in the country. Very few activists, mainly journalists, continued their criticisms of Saleh's post–civil war policies, and some paid a heavy price for expressing disapproval of Saleh's regime. For example, Abd al-Aziz al-Saqqaf, a college professor and activist who founded Yemen's first English-language newspaper, died in a mysterious car accident while walking in Hadda Street in Sana'a in 1999. Other journalists like Abdulkarim al-Khaiwani were sent to prison after criticizing Saleh's war in Sa'dah.[11]

The weakness of the opposition parties, mainly the YSP, coupled with Saleh's growing authoritarian power spurred the proliferation of civil society organizations that addressed various political, social, and economic issues in Yemen. Hundreds of civil society organizations were established, and they sought financial support from local and international donors.[12] Organizations such as the National Organization for Defending Rights and Freedoms (HOOD), the Yemeni Institute for the Development of Democracy, and the Yemeni Association to Raise Awareness of Mines Dangers fought for the protection and promotion of human rights.[13] For example, HOOD used such sophisticated means as media appeals, petitions, and organized protests to draw attention to human rights abuses in the country. Other civil society organizations focused on educating the Yemeni public about the merits of democratic society and political institutions. Organizations working in this area include the Civic Democratic Initiatives Support Foundation and Democratic School. Several organizations focused on advancing women's and children's rights, such as the Childhood Forum Society (Taiz), the Yemeni Society to Protect the Child Legal Rights (Sana'a), and the Women Economic Empowerment Association (Sana'a).

The radicalization of an insurgent religious group, the Houthis, took place parallel to these events. This group was founded in 1992 under the name Believing Youth (*Shabab al-Moumineen*) in Sa'dah, a northern Yemeni province that has been a stronghold for Zaidism, an offshoot of Shiism.[14] Believing Youth began to recruit thousands of supporters at its summer centers.[15] However, after 2004, the group opted for the use of violence, making it a militant opposition group against the Saleh regime. The group later became known as the al-Houthi group (or the Houthis) after its founder Hussein al-Houthi, a former member of parliament and the son of a prominent Zaidi scholar.[16] Al-Houthi accused Saleh of allowing the United States to intervene in Yemen's domestic politics and blamed both the United States and Israel for problems in the Muslim *Ummah*.[17] Al-Houthi borrowed many of the anti-American slogans used by Hezbollah in Lebanon, leading some Yemeni critics to believe that the Houthis have adopted a foreign agenda that could make Yemen the battleground for a proxy war between Iran and Saudi Arabia. Saleh's regime also complained about Iranian support for this group. Despite several rounds of civil war with Saleh, the political demands of the Houthis remain unclear to this day. Nevertheless, this group has succeeded in becoming pivotal to the overall political stability of Yemen.

By the end of this period, political activism took a new turn when the major opposition parties banded together in 2005 to establish a new opposition alliance against Saleh's regime: the Joint Meeting Parties (JMP). Some have argued that Jarallah Omar, who was assassinated in 2002, was the true architect behind the establishment of the JMP. He had worked tirelessly to reach out to al-Islah leadership to form an effective opposition coalition. Both al-Islah and the YSP came to realize that their profound ideological differences—Islamist vs. socialist—had hindered any possibility of political cooperation between them in the past. But the primary beneficiary of this state of affairs was Saleh, whose party had controlled all branches of government since the 1997 parliamentary elections. The JMP was established in part because both al-Islah and the YSP decided to downplay their ideological differences and focus instead on promoting democratic reforms and ending Saleh's authoritarian power. The JMP's main objective was "to replace the current system of 'one person rule,' in which power is concentrated in the president's hands and corruption is encouraged, with a parliamentary system with a separation of power, an independent judiciary, and administrative decentralization."[18] The JMP represented a serious challenge to Saleh in 2006 when it presented an independent and highly respected statesman and former oil minister, Faisal Bin Shamlan, as its presidential candidate. Bin Shamlan lost the elections, but he garnered tremendous support in several Yemeni towns and cities and represented a strong alternative to Saleh.

From September 2006 to January 2011

The period beginning in late 2006 was marked by increased political activism in response to deepening grievances. The reelection of Saleh in September 2006 and his older son's prospects as his heir apparent extinguished any tangible hope for significant political change. The situation in the south became politically toxic as corruption and lawlessness became the rule rather than the exception. After the presidential election and the emergence of al-Hirak, the southern peaceful movement called on Saleh to correct grave mistakes committed after the civil war. Al-Hirak started in 2007 when former high-level military officers who had lost their financial benefits after the civil war and were forced into semi-retirement wrote to the president's office demanding their right to return to work and calling for political reforms in the South. They organized a protest on July 7, 2007, after Saleh rejected their demands. This was not the first time that public protest was used as a tool of activism, but it was the largest organized antigovernment mass protest in the previous decade. It is clear that the al-Hirak movement, despite its secessionist leanings, has breathed a new life into the overall political process in Yemen.

Although Saleh won the presidential election of 2006, the period represented a remarkable turning point for challenges to Saleh's grip on political power.[19] Opposing Saleh overtly and earnestly was no longer as taboo as it had been. The number of newspapers and articles criticizing Saleh increased significantly, and key opposition leaders, such as Hamid al-Ahmar, called for Saleh's resignation on Al Jazeera television.[20]

The movement also attracted large numbers of youth activists in the South and some members of the Yemeni Socialist Party (YSP). The political demands raised by al-Hirak evolved from grievances about the general economic and political conditions in the South after the civil war into strong demands for complete secession from the union established with the North in 1990. The movement continued its adoption of peaceful protests and other nonviolent strategies such as writing opinion articles in opposition newspapers and making appeals for regional and international support.

Because of its controversial political slogans, however, al-Hirak failed to develop political momentum in the North. Many activists in the North agreed with al-Hirak's grievances, but they argued that the separation of the North and the South is not the best solution. Moreover, opposition parties, including the YSP and some of al-Hirak's leadership such as former Yemeni president Ali Nasir Muhammad, believed that federalism could achieve al-Hirak's basic demands through a significant decentralization of power in which the South would gain greater political autonomy. At the same time, one of the biggest challenges that al-Hirak faced was its lack of strong, unified leadership. The past political struggles and domestic military conflicts in the South, before the unification with the North, cast a shadow on any serious attempts to unify al-Hirak's leadership.

Political Activism during the Yemeni Uprising

Yemen is one of the poorest countries in the world, with high levels of illiteracy, weak state institutions, and strong tribal communities, but Yemeni activists have used various strategies to move the country toward substantial democratic transition. During the 2011 uprising, youth activists endured a year-long period of oppression and intimidation by Saleh's political machine, including the use of military and police forces to arrest and kill some of the activists. Like other dictatorial Arab regimes in the Middle East, the Saleh regime also used *baltajia* (or *balatijah* in Yemeni dialect, meaning "thugs") to target and coerce activists.

Unlike previous phases, political activism during this period was not primarily facilitated by political parties. This period is distinguished by the emergence of grassroots activism in relative independence from political parties. However, this should not suggest that Yemen's political parties lack youth representation or support. Many political parties and political movements like the Houthis and al-Hirak are very active in colleges and youth organizations. However, the occupiers of what became known as Change Square in many cities and towns were essentially youth groups independent from any political party. Much as they had in Egypt (see chapter 2), these youth groups have rightly claimed ownership of the Yemeni uprising. The same period also saw the tremendous presence of women activists, who displayed a great deal of political skill in mobilizing and in drawing the world's attention to their cause.

Moreover, political activists during this period sought comprehensive rather than partial solutions to Yemen's political and economic problems. They demanded a new Yemen, where the rule of law and democracy would prevail. An emerging tool for making such demands public was information technology. The internet had become available to the Yemeni public in the late 1990s, spurring the rise of social bloggers, as happened in most Middle Eastern countries in the previous decade. Although it is difficult to evaluate the impact of Yemeni bloggers in a country with high levels of computer illiteracy, the initially limited use of online forums such as Mareb Press for political debate helped pave the way for the use of social media by political activists and freelance writers to spread their message of political and economic reforms during the Yemeni uprising of 2011.

Youth and Student Activists

By the spring of 2011, Yemeni youth—especially Yemeni college students—had become the engine driving the surge of political activism in Yemen. College campuses across the country played a central role in political mobilization and activism.[21] Most of these students were young men and women representing almost all segments of Yemeni society. They came from all social and economic backgrounds—middle- and low-income families, tribal and nontribal communities, Sunni and Zaidi—and had been victims of Saleh's flawed economic policies, political corruption, and deceitful promises. Their messages of urgent political and economic reform resonated with the public.

The killing and wounding of hundreds of youth activists on Karama Friday (Friday of Dignity) on March 18, 2011, during the early months of the Yemeni uprising, was a huge turning point. Youth activists became not only the heroes but, more important, also the martyrs. Heartened by such sacrifices, hundreds of top diplomats, civil servants, and military officers including Ali Mohsen al-Ahmar—previously Saleh's right-hand man—denounced the Karama Friday massacre and proclaimed their support and loyalty to the youth revolution.[22]

Occupation of public squares, especially on university campuses, was one of the most effective strategies adopted by student and youth activists. College campuses became forums for political gatherings and poetry nights in which healthy intellectual debates emerged on various political and social issues pertaining to Yemen's future. Many opposition leaders paid visits to these protest areas to show their allegiance to the Yemeni uprising.

Yemeni activists adopted strategies similar to those used by their counterparts in Tunisia and Egypt—occupying public squares, establishing protest camps, and exploiting social media and modern technology to spread their message and appeal to domestic and international audiences; however, they also employed distinctive modes of collective action that had not been used by other Arab activists in Egypt or Tunisia. For example, the March for Life, which traveled from the city of Taiz on December 20, 2011, and arrived in Sana'a four days later, was intended to preserve the momentum of the Yemeni uprising movement since many youth activists had rejected the Gulf Initiative, a proposal the Gulf States presented for a power transition, aimed at avoiding civil war. The Gulf Initiative sought to facilitate this transition by offering Saleh amnesty in return for his resignation. The marchers demanded that Saleh and others involved in the murders of hundreds of protesters since the outbreak of the Yemeni uprising not be granted any kind of amnesty. This march revealed the sophistication Yemeni activists had developed to increase political pressure for real and meaningful democratic change. The marchers galvanized political support in many small villages and towns along the road from Taiz to Sana'a. For example, families and restaurant owners provided free meals and came out in support of the marchers, while journalists and bloggers continued their daily coverage of the march, emphasizing the importance of keeping the torch of Yemeni uprising alight.

However, like al-Hirak, the student activists lacked a unified, charismatic leadership, possibly because many students were also members of some of the opposition parties. The presence of al-Islah youth members among Yemeni activists, for example, was substantial. The lack of a unified leadership explains why the Joint Meeting Parties (JMP), and not student activists, negotiated and signed the Gulf Initiative with Saleh's regime. Some argued that youth activists should establish their own political organization, but given that these students came from diverse ideological and political backgrounds, the establishment of such a wide-ranging political umbrella was unlikely. This problem also existed in other Arab countries that have undergone similar political changes, such as Egypt and Tunisia, where youth activists were unable to unite under one political organization.

Women Activists

That Tawakkol Karman is widely recognized as the mother of Yemeni uprising speaks volumes about the role women activists played in the year leading up to the uprising. Prior to 2010, it would have been almost impossible to imagine Yemeni women publicly demanding political reform. Yet, as already mentioned, the political engagement of women was taking place mainly through

Nobel Peace Prize winner Tawakkol Karman. Photo by Munir Mawari. Used with permission.

nadwat, civil society activism, and journalism. Karman is a journalist and the founder of a civil society organization, Women Journalists without Chains, that campaigns for freedom of expression and women's rights. Karman's rising public profile and her leadership of the youth movement spurred the involvement of other female activists in the Yemeni uprising, who became key participants in public protests.

One of the remarkable contributions of Yemeni women activists is their ability to adhere to local cultural norms while pursuing political and economic change. In response to a crackdown by Saleh's regime, women activists in Yemen were very creative, sometimes adopting protest strategies used by women in rural and tribal areas, such as burning their headscarves in public, as effective tools to prompt tribesmen to act on their behalf. This fascinated the international media. During one such incident, which took place in October 2011, Mohammed Jamjoom and Hakim Almasmari reported a woman activist warning Yemeni tribesmen that "they will not be respected by Yemeni women if they stay quiet while their women are being attacked by the Saleh regime. Tribes who ignore our calls are cowards and have no dignity."[23]

The remarkable presence of women within the Yemeni uprising is likely to change women's roles in Yemeni society. Activism among Yemeni women was not limited to big cities, where women are more likely to attain higher education and demand more prominent roles in public life. Tens of thousands of Yemeni women have marched for freedom both in major cities and in small towns across the country. Moreover, women have paid with blood and treasure in their substantial backing of the Yemeni uprising. A number of women became martyrs for Yemeni freedom and equality.[24] While it is true that some women played important roles in the past Arab nationalist and liberation movements, such as Algeria in the 1960s and Palestine in the 1970s, only to be consigned to the private sphere again, the current participation of women was significantly different and expected to have long-lasting effects. The massive expansion of education for women in the last three decades, combined with the increased global awareness of women rights, has affected women in urban areas in Yemen and the Arab Middle East.

The picture of women activists wearing headscarves and *niqāb* (veils) is an indication of the role played by women Islamists in the Yemeni uprising. In the very traditional and conservative Yemeni society, religious piety and commitment often helps empower women and protect their political involvement, as it gives them a "legitimate" framework for their public action. As Yadav argues, "A woman's sign of religious commitment (public piety practices, in particular) may be seen within an Islamizing public sphere as strengthening her ability to work as a social activist and agent of change."[25]

Women activists were particularly successful in drawing international attention to their political struggle. For example, international and regional media outlets such as Al Arabiya reported how a portrait of a veiled Yemeni woman embracing her wounded relative won the top prize in the World Press Photo awards in 2011.[26] Moreover, Karman was awarded the Nobel Peace Prize in October 2011. This award boosted the morale of Yemeni youth and also deconstructed several misconceptions about Yemeni politics and society. First, that Karman is a female journalist shows how roles for Yemeni women have progressed over the last several years. Second, as a member of al-Islah,

Yemen's largest Islamist party, Karman proved not only that Islamists be positive forces for democracy and women's rights, but also that their contributions can also be recognized internationally. Indeed, Karman's position within al-Islah provides her with a rare opportunity for the advancement of women's causes. The prize boosted Kamran's status, allowing her to act as an unofficial ambassador for youth activists: She visited several Western countries, including the United States, met with top policymakers, and led campaigns pressuring the U.S. government to help prosecute former president Saleh.

Other Participants in the Yemeni Uprising

Other activists participated in the Yemeni uprising as members of specific organizations and institutions. The most important group was the *ulama*. The increased and organized role of *ulama* in Yemen and other Arab countries is unmistakable. In Yemen, some *ulama* attempted to replicate the Saudi model in which they would significantly impact the overall political process. Most of these *ulama* are associated with the al-Eman University, headed by Sheikh Abdul Majeed al-Zindani, who once represented al-Islah Party in the presidential council after the 1993 parliamentary elections. During the early months of the Yemeni uprising, this group of *ulama* worked as intermediaries between Saleh and the protesters focused on finding a peaceful resolution to the political standoff that paralyzed the country. However, the *ulama* ended their mission when they felt that Saleh was not serious about reaching a peaceful settlement and was, instead, attempting to use them to his own political advantage.

Throughout the Yemeni uprising, the *ulama* enjoyed the privilege of a unique platform to address hundreds of thousands of Yemeni activists during Friday prayers, which played a pivotal role in rekindling revolutionary sentiments among the protesters. Friday prayers in Sana'a were held on Al-Siteen Street, the largest street in the capital city. Other major cities such as Aden and Taiz also organized prorevolution Friday prayers. Importantly, Saleh's supporters also organized their own Friday prayers in Al-Sabeen Square, which were also broadcast live to the Yemeni public via Yemen's official television.

Another example of institutional actors were Yemeni activists who led the so-called revolution of institutions. Many protesters and activists, some of whom were public servants, took matters into their own hands by organizing general civil disobedience strikes and demanding that heads of government agencies known for corruption and close ties with the Saleh family be ousted. This effort expanded to include some military divisions, such as the Yemeni air force. Certainly, the revolution caused fear among top Saleh supporters, who began to feel that they were losing power at all levels of leadership. As a result, Saleh's supporters resumed organization of Friday prayers in Al-Sabeen Square on December 30, 2011, and cautioned the activists involved in the uprising of the potential consequences of continued efforts toward reform of state institutions. By the end of 2012, the revolution of institutions had accomplished very little; corruption was widespread, and Saleh's cronies still controlled many state agencies.

The Regional and International Context

As the confrontation between Saleh and the protesters heightened, the Gulf Cooperation Council (GCC) proposed the Gulf Initiative to facilitate a smooth transition of power that included protecting Saleh and his immediate relatives and advisors from future prosecution.[27] Saleh signed the Gulf Initiative agreement in Riyadh, capitulating to pressure from the United States and Saudi Arabia.[28] The Gulf Initiative stipulated that Saleh would delegate all of his executive power to Vice President Abd Rabbuh Mansur Hadi.[29] Saleh retained his title as president of the republic, without any real authority, and was granted immunity from subsequent prosecution. Youth activists opposed this particular clause on the ground that it represented an utter betrayal of the blood of the youth martyrs. Although a large majority of youth activists, including Karman, welcomed the promotion of Hadi, they intensely urged Hadi to recognize the youth revolution publicly. Moreover, some youth activists did not believe that Saudi Arabia, given its controversial history of meddling in Yemen's domestic politics, would play a positive role in bringing about democratic change in Yemen. So it is fair to argue that the stance of Yemeni activists toward the Gulf Initiative reflected, in part, their reaction to the role played by Saudi Arabia in Yemeni politics. The Houthis also opposed the Gulf Initiative because of ideological differences with Saudi Arabia and a recent history of military confrontations. In contrast, most tribal leaders, whether pro-opposition or progovernment, accepted the Gulf Initiative because of their strategic alliances with the oil-rich kingdom. Since they have been the beneficiaries of a long history of Saudi patronage in Yemen, opposition to Saudi influence would have simply meant losing a great source of financial backing.

Al-Hirak activists also opposed the Gulf Initiative, complaining that it ignored their political demands of withdrawing from the political union established with North Yemen in 1990. While the youth, al-Hirak, and the Houthis did not endorse the Gulf Initiative, the JMP accepted and signed the agreement. A cornerstone of the Gulf Initiative was the formation of a consensus government headed by the opposition parties. The initiative stipulated that this government be shared equally (50% each) by the ruling Saleh party and the opposition parties under the umbrella of the Joint Meeting Parties. The Gulf Initiative was thus another source of division among activists, particularly among southern activists, some of whom support a unified Yemen, while others, mainly those from al-Hirak, insist on secession. Confrontation between the two sides led to a violent clash in early February 2012. Several leaders of al-Hirak who boycotted the presidential election of February 21, 2012, believe that even the election of a southern politician to the presidency would not solve the fundamental problems of the south and the lack of trust toward the Sana'a government.

Divisions and Alliances among Opposition Actors after the Uprising

Opposition actors during the uprising were united regarding the end of Saleh's reign of power, but differences arose between them after the uprising. The Houthis were concerned about the increasing role of Saudi Arabia and the United States via the Gulf Initiative. The Houthis' close ties with Iran are a source of huge concern for Yemen's neighbors.[30] At the time of writing it was still uncertain whether this group would participate in the national dialogue on Yemen's political future, which was intended to include all Yemeni political actors. Another key difference among opposition actors had to do with the relationship between South and North Yemen, namely between the proseparation elements in al-Hirak and the rest of the political activists. It is unclear whether the adoption of a federal system will be an acceptable solution for all parties. Like al-Hirak, the Houthis decided to boycott the presidential election of February 2012. Both groups have similar interests in defeating the agenda of the Gulf Initiative.

Another important difference is between a group of *ulama* and other opposition actors on the nature of the state. Many *ulama* opposed the regime, but they were often in complete disagreement with youth activists and other political factions over calls for the establishment of a civil state (*dawlah madaniyyah*) in Yemen. The *ulama* viewed this proposal as way to undermine Islamic sharia in Yemen's political institutions, even though advocates of *dawlah madaniyyah* based their arguments on Islamic teachings that suggest that the very nature of the Islamic state is *madaniyyah* (civil). They referred to a famous statement issued by the Muslim Brotherhood in Egypt in which they declared no contradiction between Islam and the *dawlah madaniyyah*. In spite of this rationale, the debate remained intellectual in nature. It is uncertain whether the dispute will become a campaign issue in future parliamentary elections.

The only functioning alliance among opposition actors, so far, has been the JMP. During the early weeks of Yemeni uprising, the JMP took a back seat, allowing youth activists to take a leading role in challenging former president Saleh. The JMP avoided showing any form of political custody of youth activists. However, many of the members of the JMP, such as the YSP and al-Islah, were in Change Square in Sana'a working together with various groups of youth activists. The transitional coalition government formed after the presidential election of 2011 showed reasonable coordination within the parties of JMP. The parliamentary and presidential elections, however, posed serious challenges to such coordination.

Prospects for Activism and Pressure for Reform

In Yemen, political activism has undergone momentous changes since the country's unification in 1990. In the early 1990s, political activism had been greatly facilitated by political parties focusing on party recruitment and mobilization. However, the civil war of 1994 represented an enormous setback to the political gains of the transitional democratic era from May 1990 to April 1994. This resulted in a reasonable decline of partisan political activism and the rise of new political movements such as the Houthis and al-Hirak. Both movements succeeded in attracting youth activists and calling for regime change. While al-Hirak persisted as a nonviolent movement, the Houthis transformed into a militarized movement using violence to accomplish its political goals. However, the public appeals of these two movements were limited to specific regions because they lacked a comprehensive national agenda. Several civil society organizations became moderately active after the end of the 1994 civil war. However, with the establishment of the JMP, political activism of opposition parties resurged, especially during the 2006 presidential election.

The Yemeni uprising of 2011 initially saw the JMP and political parties being overshadowed by youth activists who, even when they did belong to parties, did not engage in protest as a top-down action directed by the parties. Those new activists adopted the nonviolent strategies employed by al-Hirak following the eruption of Arab Spring in Tunisia and Egypt, helping empower both youth and women activists in Yemen in unprecedented ways. But opposition political parties became the immediate beneficiaries of the Yemeni

Hijacking of the Uprising
ABDUL-GHANI AL-IRYANI

Abdul Ghani Al-Iryani is a Yemeni analyst, activist, and consultant.

Behind the masses of youth who were the faces of the Yemeni uprising was a less visible tripod of military, religious, and tribal centers that had formed the backbone of Saleh's regime. A military faction, led by General Ali Mohsen; a tribal clan, the al-Ahmars, led by Sheikh Hameed; and an Islamist cleric, Abdul Majeed al-Zindani—all previously supporters of Saleh—later joined the youth in the uprising against Saleh. Yet their participation turned the revolution into a power struggle between Mohsen and Saleh.

A few weeks into the uprising, I was invited to speak at the Academic Forum in Change Square, the massive antigovernment sit-in at Sana'a University. I made the argument that the revolution had already triumphed the day that sit-ins started, first in Taiz, then Sana'a, Aden, and around the country. The corrupt ruling elite had managed to control the country specifically because the people did not have the will or ability to mount sustained collective action. That the people have come out in a sustained collective action to protest that corruption and concentration of power in the hands of the few is in itself a successful revolution.

The task ahead, I preached, is to protect the revolution from potential hijackers. The Saleh regime stood on a tripod of elite power—the military, the tribes, and politicized Islam. "I see, here in the Square," I lamented, "the military, the tribes, and politicized Islam." Upon saying that, conflict ensued. A Sana'a University professor stood up in defense of the tribes, while a brood of Islamist al-Eman University sheikhs and professors expressed disbelief over my use of the phrase "politicized Islam." "All Islam is political, and saying otherwise is heresy," they said—a charge with serious implications. The most astonishing defense came from a Sana'a University professor, who shouted in my face, "When you speak of the military, you cannot equate the butcher Saleh and the patriotic General Mohsen."

Saleh used coercive power to try to end the sit-ins at Sana'a University, and clashes between Mohsen's faction and the regime intensified. This led to severe military confrontations in central Sana'a, the northern al-Hasaba district, and other areas around the country. I witnessed a demonstration of that confrontation in the Kentucky Junction confrontation in September 2011. As I walked toward the sound of high-caliber gunfire, I saw a cartoon-like figure chanting the name of Mohsen's 1st Armored Division and waving the youth toward the source of the sound of gunfire. I got closer, and saw a high-caliber gun firing across the junction. The gun was surrounded by a thousand youth providing a human shield for the gun. At that particular moment, I witnessed the peaceful protesters being used by Mohsen's army to gain grounds in the battlefield.

uprising. The new transitional government was headed by the JMP, with their share of government representation increasing from zero to fifty percent after the signing of the Gulf Initiative.

Meanwhile, the number of youth activists camping "permanently" in Change Squares across the country declined. Youth activists continued their political pressure on the transitional government to broaden the agenda of political and economic reforms through public action. However, the majority of Yemeni youth activists did not have a coherent political agenda to address Yemen's economic and political challenges. Those who remained active after the uprising were either already members of the main opposition parties or were likely to be recruited by these parties, and ultimately they followed the different directions of their parties.

Some civil society organizations continued to have a strong commitment to modernizing Yemen and maintaining sustained political pressure on the government to advance political reforms. These groups had established credibility through adamantly criticizing Saleh's abuses of power before the commencement of the Yemeni uprising. Key activist groups that have established effective organized political activism include Yemen Journalists against Corruption and Tawakkol Karman's Women Journalists without Chains, which focus on exposing government corruption, restrictions on freedom of the press, and human rights abuses. Both organizations include active Yemeni journalists from different political and ideological backgrounds. These activists are poised to ensure political transparency and accountability among various Yemeni political institutions.[31]

Many outside observers of Yemeni politics have good reason to be pessimistic about the overall situation. Yet there are still many signs of hope which are held high by thousands of youth activists. Only time will tell.

Notes

1. On the growing civil society in Yemen, see Sheila Carapico, *Civil Society in Yemen: A Political Economy of Activism in Modern Arabia* (Cambridge, U.K.: Cambridge University Press, 1998); Lisa Wedeen, "The Politics of Deliberation: *Qāt* Chews as Public Spheres in Yemen," *Public Culture* 19(1) (2007): 58–84.

2. A Yemeni plant used widely in Yemen and some eastern African countries but banned in several other countries. For further discussion of the role of qat chews in Yemen, see Wedeen, "Politics of Deliberation."

3. Imam Ahmed succeeded his father Imam Yahya, who was murdered by the leaders of the 1948 revolution, which failed to end the rule of the imamate in North

Yemen. Imam Aḥmed succeeded in aborting the 1948 revolution and continued to rule North Yemen until his death in 1962, a few days before the eruption of the revolution on September 26, 1962. The revolutionary forces of 1962 were backed by President Gamal Abdel Nasser of Egypt, who sent thousands of Egyptian troops to aid the newly established Arab republic in North Yemen. Saudi Arabia, on the other side, supported the Imamate forces fueling the civil war in Yemen, which lasted from 1962 until early 1970s.

4. The relationship between the families of Saleh and al-Ahmar began to deteriorate dramatically shortly after al-Ahmar's death. After failing to persuade al-Ahmar's sons not to side with the youth revolution, former president Saleh opted to use the stick instead of the carrot when his government issued an arrest warrant against Sadiq al-Ahmar and his brothers, accusing them of conducting an armed rebellious movement. Indeed, this move was viewed as part of Saleh's psychological war, since executing such an arrest was deemed next to impossible in Yemen. To delegitimize their political claims, Saleh asserted that al-Ahmar's sons were supporting and financing some of the protests for political and economic gains. Ironically, Saleh went further and warned the youth that opposition parties and al-Ahmar's family were planning to hijack their revolution.

5. Francesco Cavatorta and Vincent Durac, *Civil Society and Democratization in the Arab World: The Dynamics of Activism* (London: Routledge, 2010).

6. The military remained literally divided after unification, and the former ruling parties, the YSP and GPC, sustained their rigid control over state media and government agencies.

7. Janine A. Clark, *Islam, Charity, and Activism: Middle-Class Networks and Social Welfare in Egypt, Jordan, and Yemen* (Bloomington: Indiana University Press, 2004), 140.

8. Some had accused Islamic extremists from the south, who returned from Afghanistan after the unification of Yemen, of conducting these assassinations as political revenge against the YSP, which had a long history of political oppression against the *ulama* and Islamists in the south before 1990. Later these extremists joined Saleh's forces against the YSP in the 1994 civil war.

9. Michaelle Browers, "Origins and Architects of Yemen's Joint Meeting Parties," *International Journal of Middle East Studies* 39(4) (2007): 565–586, 572.

10. Ibid.

11. In 2008, al-Khaiwani was the recipient of the "Special Award for Human Rights Journalism under Threat" awarded by Amnesty International for his political activism advocating human rights.

12. International support for such civil society organizations raised serious questions about their degree of autonomy and effectiveness and whether such organizations would create principal-agent problems in the sense that they would pursue their own interests rather than the interests and goals of international donors. For

more on U.S. monetary support from the National Endowment for Democracy to Yemeni civil society organizations, see "Yemen," National Endowment for Democracy, available at www.ned.org/where-we-work/middle-east-and-northern-africa/yemen, accessed July 15, 2013.

13. HOOD was established by Yemeni lawyers and human rights activists in the late 1990s. In 2008, HOOD was very active in defending the rights of al-Ja'shin villagers who were forced out of their own villages, setting up camps in Sana'a demanding that the government end the brutal and harsh punishment of their sheikh.

14. Other important religious groups that are ideologically at odds with the Houthis are Salafi groups, which in 2012 established the first Yemeni Salafi political party, al-Rashad (Upright). The political development of the Salafi movement has gradually progressed from its early focus on Islamic education and active charity works in the last two decades to active political participation and mobilization during the rise of Yemeni Uprising.

15. Jack Freeman, "The al Houthi Insurgency in the North of Yemen: An Analysis of the Shabab al Moumineen," *Studies in Conflict and Terrorism* 32(11) (2009): 1008–1019.

16. Zaidism is a Shia school of legal thought that is close to that of the Sunnis. Zaidism had been the official school of *fiqh* (jurisprudence) in North Yemen before the 1962 revolution.

17. George Joffé, "The Al-Houthi Rebellion: The History behind Yemen's Long-Simmering Rebellion," *Journal of International Peace Operations* 5(4) (2010): 8, 10.

18. Browers, "Origins and Architects," 578.

19. Prior to his 2006 presidential campaign, Saleh surprised many observers, including members of his own party, by announcing his intention to step down and not seek another presidential bid. However, he later changed his mind and ran for president.

20. Before the 2006 presidential election, calling for Saleh's resignation or regime change was never tolerated by Saleh's security apparatus.

21. Student activism is not limited to Sana'a, Aden, or Taiz. College student activists organized regular protests in several Yemeni cities and small towns, a development that was enabled by the horizontal expansion of Yemeni education since the 1990s.

22. The decision of General Ali Mohsen al-Ahmar to join the revolution against Saleh was a major blow to Saleh's regime. General al-Ahmar helped protect protestors in Sana'a University and in a large section of Sana'a.

23. Mohammed Jamjoom and Hakim Almasmari, "Yemeni Women Burn Veils to Protest Regime," CNN Online, October 26, 2011, available at http://articles.cnn .com/2011-10-26/middleeast/world_meast_yemen-protests_1_saleh-regime-veils -president-ali-abdullah-saleh?_s=PM:MIDDLEEAST, accessed July 13, 2013.

24. Several Yemeni blogs and opposition newspapers have documented, in highly emotional narratives, the sacrifices of these women. They were called martyrs of the revolution.

25. Stacey Philbrick Yadav, "Segmented Publics and Islamist Women in Yemen: Rethinking Space and Activism," *JMEWS: Journal of Middle East Women's Studies* 6(2) (2010): 1–30, 11.

26. "Portrait of Veiled Yemeni Woman Cradling Wounded Relative Wins Top Photo Award," Al Arabiya, February 10, 2012, available at www.alarabiya.net/articles /2012/02/10/193758.html, accessed July 13, 2013.

27. In addition, a democratic Yemen is likely to increase pressure for political reforms in Saudi Arabia. Indeed, the attitude of the Saudi government toward the Arab Spring reflects political caution and suspicion that similar demands for political change might eventually breach Saudi borders. Yemen is the neighbor of several oil-rich Gulf countries, which has added an interesting layer to the challenges that political change and possible civil conflict bring to the region. The unpredictable political climate is likely to increase anxiety among key regional and international actors, most particularly Saudi Arabia, which raises the stakes for Yemen. Saudi Arabia had granted Yemeni immigrants special status in its labor market until 1990 as a way to ease tensions between the two nations. President Saleh reached a border agreement with Saudi Arabia in 2000 that included exchange of some lands to compensate Yemen for the loss of its 1934 territories. Any future government will ultimately have to disclose its position with regard to this controversial agreement.

28. In fact, former president Saleh delayed signing this agreement three times before he was ultimately pressured to do so.

29. Before his election to the presidency, Hadi served as vice president for more than fifteen years. He played a significant role in the 1994 civil war. He lived, however, under Saleh's shadow without any real power or influence in the government. Hadi showed little political ambition, which made him the preferred choice among all domestic and international actors to lead Yemen during the two-year transitional period.

30. See, for example, Thom Shanker and Robert F. Worth, "Yemen Seizes Sailboat Filled with Weapons, and U.S. Points to Iran," *New York Times,* January 28, 2013, available at www.nytimes.com/2013/01/29/world/middleeast/29military.html, accessed February 4, 2013.

31. I have excluded al-Qaeda in the Arabian Peninsula (AQAP), which has increased its violence in Yemen since the outbreak of Yemeni mass protests in early 2011, because AQAP is part of a transnational terrorist organization with political objectives and militant activities that fall beyond the scope of this study.

CHAPTER 5

Activism in Syria

Between Nonviolence and Armed Resistance

WAEL SAWAH *and* SALAM KAWAKIBI

WHEN THE TUNISIAN revolution started, the entire world, including the Syrian population, watched with amazement and admiration. But only when the revolution's spark moved to Egypt did the people elsewhere in the region wonder if the embers could reach their countries. The Syrians were no exception. However, very few believed that the miracle could happen there.

There were several reasons for this. First, fear in Syria was remarkably all-encompassing. As one Syrian scholar put it, only Saddam Hussein's Iraq compared to Syria, describing Syria as "the kingdom of fear, silence, and worshiping Leviathan."[1] Second, as the Assad family was Alawi, with support from other minority groups who sought protection for their communities, any public action against the Assad regime risked igniting sectarian strife. Third, Assad enjoyed a degree of popularity among a portion of the Syrian population: sections of the Alawi, Christian, and other minorities as well as the newly emerged middle class in Sunni cities, who had come to enjoy a new lifestyle and good income working in banks, insurance companies, media, fashion, and other growing sectors helped by Bashar al-Assad's economic "liberalization" policy, which was nevertheless based on cronyism and favoritism. Fourth, the occupied Golan Heights and the sensitive national conflict with Israel historically took center stage in Syria, pushing back other struggles. Finally, despite poverty, Syrians did not suffer from hunger. The Syrian government was eager to continue paying public sector employees regularly, supporting public hospitals, and maintaining the price of bread and other basic commodities as pre-emptive measures to contain dissent.

Therefore, the uprising that broke out in Daraa in March 2011 took almost everyone by surprise, including the regime and the opposition itself. In an interview with *The Wall Street Journal* on January 31, 2011, President Assad said that the protests in Egypt, Tunisia, and Yemen would not find their way to his country, as his anti-American position and confrontation with Israel had strengthened his relationship with the grassroots in Syria. "Syria is stable. Why?" Assad said, "Because you have to be very closely linked to the beliefs of the people. This is the core issue. When there is divergence ... you will have this vacuum that creates disturbances."[2]

The Syrian opposition, too, was busy working out its own problems. The major opposition coalition, the Damascus Declaration (DD), was suffering from several problems. Since 2008, twelve of its leaders had been imprisoned for thirty months. The pan-Arab nationalists and Marxist parties had suspended their membership and activities in the coalition. The Muslim Brothers were also suffering from many difficulties: They did not have many supporters inside Syria, since Law 49 would sentence any member of the group to death. In addition, their image had been blemished by the 2008 announcement of a truce with the Syrian regime in appreciation of Syria's stance toward the Israeli war on Gaza that year. Therefore, when the uprising broke out, the opposition watched from afar for quite a long time. The Damascus Declaration's first response did not come until March 23, eight days after the first demonstration in Damascus and five days after the massacre in Daraa.

This chapter examines activism during the Syrian revolution and the phases through which it evolved while placing it in the context of the dynamics of activism in Syria before the uprising started. Activism in Syria has immensely changed under the Syrian revolution. It has shifted from nonpolitical activism that focused mainly on issues like human rights, the empowerment of women, the environment, and trafficking to political activism by a mixture of actors: peaceful resistance actors and nonviolent actors but also militants. The chapter examines the complexity of activist groups, their strategies, and challenges. It demonstrates how activists shifted from working independently or in small groups to groups that attained a higher level of cooperation and coordination. The chapter concludes with an assessment of the impact of this change on activism in Syria.

The Domestic Context before the Uprising

The political context for the current uprisings traces back to the Baath Party coup d'état in 1963, which represented a historic break with Syria's past. The era before 1963 was neither fully democratic nor fully peaceful. In 1936, when Syria signed an independence treaty with France, it had a vibrant opposition; a parliament was elected; the leader of the National Bloc, an alliance of national bourgeois, Hashem al-Atassi, was chosen as president of the republic; and a nationalist government took office.[3] However, the period following the 1948 Arab-Israeli War saw increasing instability. The first coup d'état took place in 1949, and between then and 1954, Syria witnessed a series of coups followed by an illiberal era during the life of the United Arab Republic that united Syria and Egypt from 1958 till 1961. When the Baathists came to power, however, it fundamentally changed the political playing field. It denied liberalism, abjuring its values as "imperialist," shifting the Syrian pathway into a longstanding dictatorship. For decades to come, Syrian society knew no kind of legal political opposition that operated in public. Those who opposed the regime had to work underground, which deprived them from learning new political skills and interacting with peers from other countries.

If one examines the Syrian political party landscape since this era, one can see that most political parties came from two traditional parties: the Baath Party and the Communist Party. In the early days of Baathist rule in the 1960s, the Syrian opposition was mainly made up of members of the upper class who had lost property and assets as a result of the regime's nationalization policies. As the opposition was not united, the regime managed to contain it. By the late 1960s, a new opposition had emerged, mainly from the middle class. This opposition, which emerged through a series of party splits, shared much the same political ideologies and social background as the regime. From these splits, the Baath and Communist parties produced about a dozen others that shared similar political ideologies but were divided between the ruling National Progressive Front (NPF) and the opposition. Both the ruling party and the opposition parties called for unity among Arab countries, socialism, liberation of the occupied territories, and solidarity with developing nations. Where they competed was the monopoly of power exercised by the Baath Party.

This arrangement broke twice before the 2011 uprising, in the early 1980s and early 2000s. In the 1980s, the Muslim Brotherhood conducted a violent campaign against the rule of the late president, Hafez al-Assad. Unlike the regime and the leftist opposition, the Brotherhood—which was initially founded in the mid-1940s as an Islamic society adopting the principles of Egyptian founder Hassan al-Banna—had a platform based on religion and maintained strong political alliances with conservative Arab regimes. During the 1940s and 1950s, the Muslim Brotherhood played a modest role in Syrian political life, but it managed to send a number of representatives to the Parliament and participated in government coalitions until 1963. After the rise of the Baathist regime, the group was banned. Several clashes occurred between the Baathists and the Muslim Brotherhood between 1963 and 1982, when Hafez al-Assad militarily destroyed the Muslim Brotherhood forces by his assault on Hama. During that time, particularly between 1979 and 1982, the Muslim Brotherhood had a radical Islamic agenda that decisively differed from both the regime and the secular opposition.[4]

The second break with traditional regime-opposition relationships came in 2000. Shortly after Hafez al-Assad passed away in June 2000, ninety-nine intellectuals signed a petition known as "the Statement of 99." This paved the way for other intellectuals and politicians to demand a number of political reforms, including the end of the state of emergency that had been imposed by the Baath regime since 1963. Thus began the Damascus Spring. Subsequently, hundreds of petitions were signed, dozens of forums and salons were initiated, and a totally new phenomenon appeared: sit-ins. After decades of absence of open debate, a new expression was introduced for the first time in Syria: "civil society."

The two breaks differed tremendously. The Muslim Brotherhood, which had started as a popular movement involving a cross section of Syrian society, turned in the late 1970s and early 1980s to armed struggle against the regime, with the Brotherhood becoming a closed group that had, for tactical reasons, both a political and a military wing. The Damascus Spring movement, on the other hand, was short-lived and narrowly based—depending on and enhancing Syrian civil society. However, whereas the violent confrontation between the Muslim Brotherhood and the regime effectively wiped out political opposition in the 1980s, the Damascus Spring opened the door to a new form of nonpolitical activism.

A new generation of activists, influenced by the Damascus Spring, created a framework centering on individual liberties and economic rights. Whereas the older generation fought for democracy and political freedoms, the new generation fought for the right of every individual to act according to his or her own free will. To outside observers, the campaigns and topics that preoccupied new civil society activists appeared to be disconnected from democracy and political freedoms, focused as they were on the arts, culture, women's empowerment, human rights, the environment, disability, internal migration, and human trafficking. However, many of those fields, such as the arts, culture, and human rights, have always played a prominent role in Syrian political life.

It should finally be noted that activism was no longer limited to the urban middle class. Non-movements are another kind of change that had been occurring on the ground well before the uprising, although slowly and almost unnoticeably. Millions of the new urban dispossessed (displaced persons and immigrants from rural areas) had left their homes and moved to live in squatter settlements in Damascus and other major cities in Syria. They embarked on steady and strenuous campaigns relating to the acquisition of land and shelters, which were followed by demands for such basic services as electricity, running water, sewage system, and telephone services. Hundreds of thousands of men, women, and children continued to leave their villages and come to the major cities looking for jobs and a better life, usually seeking to escape droughts and harsh farm life. These immigrants came from different ethnicities, sects, and geographic provinces, creating a kind of an imperium in imperio in their squatter settlements.[5] They built houses, connected illegally to water and electricity, and established parallel economies in their own way to earn "their right to the city."[6] They also implemented nearly autonomous laws and regulations in their areas, resolving their conflicts without seeking the government's assistance, and bought and sold their illegal houses with documents that were not worth the paper they were written on.[7] The first decade of the current millennium demonstrated a bigger gap between the reality of these people and their dreams. They had very little and could provide very little to their children and families, even as they watched the gap between the haves and have-nots increase. One cannot but notice that the revolution started in one of the poorest provinces in Syria and that most people who took to the streets and participated in the protests did not have much to lose.

Despite this activism, the first decade of the 2000s saw little in the way of openings. Bashar al-Assad's regime focused on regional issues—the invasion of Iraq, the assassination of former Lebanese prime minister Rafik Hariri, and the 2006 war between Hezbollah and Israel that isolated the Syrian regime— but paid little attention to the social fabric. While his father had kept a kind of equality among people, not allowing the corrupt to show their wealth, Bashar opened the space for his entourage to multiply their wealth through corruption, monopoly, and favoritism. He focused more on the Syrian capital and the other major cities such as Aleppo, Homs, and Latakia while ignoring outlying areas. To multiply wealth, the regime shifted toward the open market economy, dropping subsidies and raising prices. The economy was stronger in a neoliberal sense, but society suffered setbacks. The gap between rich and poor widened. Actual unemployment figures hovered officially around 20 percent, while unofficial figures painted an even darker picture. Problems were particularly acute for the remote regions, such as the northeast and the south, which felt deserted by the government.

The Syrian Uprising: A Miracle Happens

When the spark of revolution speedily moved to Egypt, Libya, and Yemen, Syrians started to ask, Why not? In January and February 2011, a group of young men and women started to meet in cafes, homes, and public places to ask, Can we do the same in Syria? If the Tunisians could revolt in Tunisia, they argued, there was no reason why Syrians could not do the same, as in many respects Tunisia was—like Syria—a police state. But the first calls for a sit-in in front of the Parliament on February 5 failed. Brave young men and women then started to organize sit-ins at the Egyptian and the Libyan embassies to express solidarity with the revolutions in both countries. The regime's attempts to stifle these demonstrations may inadvertently have helped foster them. At least one activist argues that what made her resolutely persist in the uprising was the slap that she got from one of the security policemen while she was demonstrating at the Libyan embassy against the Qaddafi regime.[8]

However, the revolution did not start in Damascus. It started elsewhere. On March 6, the Syrian security arrested and tortured schoolchildren for spraying graffiti on walls in the southern city of Daraa calling for the end of the regime. When the security forces refused to release them, a great many people took to the streets. The regime responded by shooting demonstrators, killing a number of them. The spark spread to other cities and towns, and the entire world watched in surprise.

The demonstrations opened the battle between regime and opposition. They started out peacefully, including people from across the social and cultural spectrum.[9] The slogans were general, calling for freedom and political reform. Both government and demonstrators recognized that the battle was not only on the ground but also in the media. The government expelled all foreign media from the country, and state media portrayed the demonstrators as sectarian thugs who wanted to create chaos and establish an Islamic state.[10]

Protesters reached out to the media, creating a new phenomenon called *tanseeqiat*—groups of young activists who participate in demonstrations, document them via mobile phones, and are aware of the power of media to help organize or coordinate opposition activities.[11] As the uprising moved from Daraa to many other Syrian cities and villages, the *tanseeqiat* mushroomed and gained popularity among the protesters. These small groups of activists, spread across the country, needed to coordinate their efforts, to exchange information, and to improve their strategies in reaching the international media. This prompted the *tanseeqiat* to join and expand their efforts, forming a larger, loosely structured group that called itself the Local Coordination Committees (LCC). The LCC became a major player on the ground, organizing demonstrations, coordinating the efforts of the activists, exchanging information through a newsroom set up on Skype, and then reaching out to the media with news, videos, and eyewitness reports to narrate the unfolding events. But the LCC did not remain the only umbrella that united all of the *tanseeqiat*. It was only a few weeks after its birth that other umbrellas started to exist and to claim that they were the true representatives of the *tanseeqiat*. This happened because of serious differences in ideological background among the different opposition groups, such as between LCC and the Syrian Revolution General Commission, as well as personal conflicts. In addition to the *tanseeqiat,* a host of small political civil society organizations started to emerge. Some of them were genuinely grassroots in nature; others were mere vocal experiences that lasted for months or weeks or even days before fading away.

The Syrian revolution led to the development of larger, more organized coordination efforts between activists. This has come partly from grassroots pressure, which was exerted directly and indirectly on activists. Tens of thousands of ordinary people took to the streets, facing the military machine of one of the fiercest and most ferocious regimes in the region. Their courage and persistence put pressure on politicians and activists to unite their efforts in larger coalitions. It was also a result of the international and regional forces that have repeatedly encouraged, and sometimes pressured, the Syrian activists to unify their efforts. Another factor is the role of the media. President Hafez al-Assad had for decades arrested thousands of citizens, and when he destroyed the city of Hama in 1982, killing between twenty and forty thousand citizens, the massacre went largely unnoticed. Today, however, due to the development in communication technologies and the efforts of activists at home and abroad, Syria has been at the heart of the international news. The Syrian activists knew that to take advantage of international pressure, they had to coordinate.

The Commitment to Nonviolent Resistance
KHAWLA DUNIA

Khawla Dunia is a Syrian writer and human rights activist. She was a member of the first Syrian human rights organization, the Committees to Defend Democratic Freedoms and Human Rights in Syria, between 2000 and 2002. She has been a columnist for the London-based al-Quds al-Arabi newspaper and other websites and was a member of the editorial board of Muqarabat Review, issued by the Damascus Center for Theoretical Studies and Civil Rights from 2007 to 2011. She is coauthor of "The People Want," sponsored and published by the Heinrich Böll Foundation. Since the revolution, she has dedicated her life to supporting the uprising through peaceful resistance.

From among the remains comes the demonstration, just as the Free Syrian Army fighters are busy preparing for another demonstration somewhere in the Damascus suburbs. There are no arms in people's hands; the military jets are hovering above in the sky, threatening to shell any minute, if they have not already started bombing.

This is one of the remaining faces of peaceful resistance in Syria, persistent in spite of the devastating war that swarms the country, launched by a regime that kills its own people. The Syrians had resisted taking up arms for a long time—over a year. They spared no effort to create new means to send their message to the world and to declare their rejection of a regime that has responded to them only through repression, detention, bullets, and killing.

For more than a year, Syrians insisted on remaining peaceful: They took to the streets facing live bullets, buried their beloved in other demonstrations that would be faced with more bullets. They resisted all the regime's efforts to push them to fight back. This was the outcome of the endeavor of the young people who believed in their revolution: They adopted it and were arrested, tortured, and killed for it. Later, many of them found themselves in exile for their support of the revolution and for their peaceful contribution to it, and because they could not find a venue for themselves in the face of the increasing wave of violence and the shift the revolution made to become an armed revolution.

The Syrian uprising was a great motivation for women to take part. Women, in fact, have played an exceptional role, as peacefulness is a domain that they can enter, participate in, and have an impact within. Contrary to that, the armed rebellion would make them pay the price of violence and revenge in a pure masculine battle.

Calls for demonstrations, graffiti on walls, pamphlets, emitting balloons and lighting fires on Mount Qasioun that read "FREEDOM," and, best of all, the spontaneous demonstrations that dominated the streets, to express rejection of repression and support to the revolution—all of these characterized the Syrian revolution and the creativity of the Syrians. Even when the revolution became armed, these peaceful activities did not stop. In fact, in some areas, these activities became even stronger, simply because they were more needed than before. Even when armed struggle escalated, peaceful activities started taking place in new domains that had not existed before.

With the escalation of bombing, shelling, and military confrontations, many Syrians left their homes seeking refuge in safer areas and neighborhoods. In some cases, complete cities were emptied of their citizens, such as Homs and its countryside. This reality created new responses. Activists now had a new mission: relief. Many activists actually became involved in ensuring and providing relief to the displaced families, which was not an easy task to do. Rather, it was a dangerous one, as the regime especially targeted relief workers. Relief did not mean simply food and shelter; it also meant communication and moral and psychological support. The displaced have become attached to the activists who became not only the reason behind survival but also the source of communication with the external brutal world, where they may be again a target for arrest, killing, or further displacement.

The huge waves of displacement created new forms of peaceful activities, such as providing food and medication, teaching and entertaining children, and other activities.

In addition, there were areas that were fully under the control of the armed rebellion. These created the need to establish ways to run the cities and villages. Local committees emerged to fill in the role of the absent government and to run the daily affairs of the citizens. In these areas, people resumed peaceful demonstrations in order to send a message to the new people in charge (the armed opposition). The message was that despite the fact that people had to take up arms to defend themselves, this does not mean that arms have the upper hand; the people do.

The Syrians have acquired their peaceful weapon, and they will never give it up. This is precisely what makes us hopeful and optimistic about the future and about our ability to rebuild our country despite all of the destruction.

Opposition Forces

Nevertheless, many inside the country and in exile criticized the opposition, arguing that it did not form a unified force. They exhorted it to gel into a more unified coalition, with a uniform vision on how to overthrow the regime and how Syria would be run in the post-Assad era. Months after the uprising started in Syria, the complex charts of the Syrian opposition remained a puzzle for observers, reporters, and analysts. It was divided into categories like old opposition vs. new opposition, internal vs. external, and reconciliatory vs. rejectionist.

The Old Opposition

The old opposition included mainly the traditional opposition parties, who, after awakening from their initial surprise, tried to keep pace with the protesters on the ground. The old opposition refers here to the traditional leftist-nationalist parties that formed an umbrella for "national-democratic" change in the 1980s, which include Marxist parties, pan-Arab ideologists, and semi-democratic groups. It also includes the Islamic parties and the liberal forces that had rallied under the auspices of the Damascus Declaration. This opposition is itself divided into several groups, reflecting historical differences in strategy, ideology, and personality.

The most outspoken and quickest old opposition group to join the uprising was the Damascus Declaration. The DD is a secular opposition coalition, named after the statement drafted in 2005, that calls for a gradual and peaceful transition to multiparty democracy and the equality of all citizens in a secular and sovereign Syria. The experienced opposition leader Riad al-Turk, who spent eighteen years in solitary confinement; former liberal Damascene MP Riad Seif; and the former Muslim Brotherhood leader Ali Sadreddine al-Bayanouni played an essential role in forming the coalition.[12] In 2007, the liberal trend in the DD, then led by Riad Seif and Riad al-Turk, won the internal elections in the movement, which led to a complete shift in the political discourse of the coalition toward an open liberal discourse as opposed to the old national-socialist discourse. This prompted nationalist-socialist groups, led by the Arab Socialist Union Party, to leave the coalition, but it also strengthened the relationship between the political movement in Syria and the West.

The old opposition also includes groups from the Islamic movement, although, as discussed above, these groups were in a weak position when the 2011 uprising began. The largest Islamic group, the Muslim Brotherhood, was mainly in exile because of Law 49. In addition, their image had been tainted after they quit the Damascus Declaration and formed an alliance with former vice president Abdul Halim Khaddam.[13] The second-largest Islamic group in Syria as the uprisings began was Hizb ut-Tahrir al-Islami (Islamic Party of Liberation), which was founded in 1953. This is a pan-Islamic political organization commonly associated with the goal of all Muslim countries unifying as an Islamic state or caliphate ruled by Islamic law and with a caliph head of state elected by Muslims.[14] The Islamic Party of Liberation has never been widely popular in Syria due to its elitist nature and to continuous government clampdowns. The third major Islamic group was the Movement for

Justice and Development, which was founded in London in 2006. It describes itself as "committed to peaceful, democratic change in Syria and the creation of a modern state which respects human rights and promotes economic and social development."[15] The Movement for Justice and Development itself was suffering from internal troubles following a split between its two major leaders, Anas al-Abdeh and Osama al-Munajed, and the embarrassment that followed when the leaked U.S. State Department cables on WikiLeaks revealed that the group was secretly funded by the State Department.[16] As a result, the Islamist groups got stronger and more radical during the course of the revolution. The endless conflict, which has led to an everlasting suffering and loss of lives, freedom, and property, has helped them gain more momentum, especially with the regime's persistence in fanning sectarian strife.

Finally, the old opposition contained a number of Kurdish parties. Most of these come from the nationalist party known as the Kurdistan Democratic Party of Syria. Established in 1957, this party was closely connected to the Democratic Kurdistani Party (Iraq). When Jalal Talabani and Mustapha Barazani split in Iraq, a similar split took place in Syria and a new party emerged, the Kurdish Democratic Progressive Party. The two parties reproduced a dozen of smaller parties that were very active in the northeastern province of Hassakeh. After Bashar al-Assad came to power in 2000, the Kurdish parties pressed hard to abolish an old decision made by the Syrian government in the 1960s that deprived thousands of Kurds of Syrian citizenship. In 2004 protests broke out across the areas heavily inhabited by Kurds; in an eight-day period, forty people (thirty-three Kurds and seven Arabs) were killed, four hundred were injured, and over two thousand Kurds were arrested. Calm was restored only after tanks were sent into all major Kurdish towns.[17] Despite their longstanding grievances, the Kurdish parties did not participate actively in the first year and a half of the Syrian uprising, perhaps, as some argued, because Bashar al-Assad had granted citizenship to two thousand Kurds in the wake of the uprising seven years earlier.[18]

In addition to the formal political groupings, the first decade of the twenty-first century saw many intellectuals, former political prisoners, writers, filmmakers, scholars, and lawyers voicing their opposition to the government of Bashar al-Assad and calling for serious reforms. As presented above, the role of intellectuals in the political process had begun in June 2000, when the Statement of 99 was published.[19] These individuals helped inflame the Syrian scene and inspired a new generation of political dissidents who followed a different political path.

Finally, in this context, it is essential to mention that the opposition in exile also played a growing role in Syrian politics during the revolution. Before the revolution, the opposition in exile was small and had little influence on Syrian politics. The Syrian Salvation Front, which included the Muslim Brotherhood and former vice president Abdul Halim Khaddam, had almost no influence inside the country but managed to play a role in the Western media. The Damascus Declaration in Exile played a slightly bigger role and communicated the DD's political views abroad. The U.S.-based Reform Party did not have any popularity because of its relations with Israel. Once the revolution started, however, the political balance shifted in favor of the external opposition. This became especially clear after the formation of the Syrian National Council and the huge support it received from the international community and the regional forces, as will be shown below.

The New Opposition

The new opposition refers to groups of activists who joined their efforts in new opposition movements and organizations that started to work on the ground, both on the political and the civil levels, in order to fill the vacuum that the older, weakened opposition had left behind. The phrase "new opposition" indicates both new on-the-ground activist groups as well as new political frames. In mid-2011, the structure of the new opposition was not, however, any less complicated than that of the old opposition. It experienced similar divisions—which created similar confusion for observers and stakeholders—as the old opposition groups.

The most active part of the new opposition was the *tanseeqiat*, which were formed spontaneously in towns and cities across Syria after the uprising began. These committees took responsibility for meeting, planning, and organizing events on the ground within their own communities. They were made up of activists who came from different political and ideological backgrounds: secular and religious, liberal and conservative. They came together either because they were friends or because they worked in the same area. The *tanseeqiat* varied greatly in size and structure. In some areas, the *tanseeqiat* included men and women; in other areas, they mostly contained moderate religious young men. There were also professional *tanseeqiat*, a good example of which is the doctors' *tanseeqiat*.[20] Over time, the *tanseeqiat* sought greater coordination among themselves in order to synchronize their activities, movements on the ground, and political positions. Together the committees formed the Local

Coordination Committees of Syria, an umbrella organization with members from most cities and many smaller towns across Syria. The existence of the LCC was announced in May 2011 and played an important role in coordinating between protesters, documenting protests, contacting the media, and spreading news of the uprising locally and abroad. As with the membership of individual *tanseeqiat*, the LCC was made up of activists from different political backgrounds, including liberals, seculars, Islamists, socialists, and others. The main LCC center in Damascus contained young men and women and people from different sects and religions.

Islamist activists, who rushed to catch up with the developing events, also formed their own body: the Syrian Revolution Coordinators Union, which was announced early in June 2011. But the latter was soon absorbed by a bigger organization, the Syrian Revolution General Commission, which represents the official political Islamist group: the Muslim Brotherhood. The Muslim Brotherhood benefited from several factors to occupy a leading position in the old opposition as well as the new opposition. First, it benefited from the Muslim Brotherhood experience in Egypt. It thus joined the revolution early but did not take on Islamic slogans, instead adopting the same slogans as the protesters; second, it benefited from regional support, particularly Turkish and Qatari support; and third, despite all the setbacks that it had suffered, it was the most organized political group in exile and had excellent relations with regional Islamic groups such as the Tunisian an-Nahda Party, the Palestinian Hamas, and the Lebanese Sunni Islamist groups. The Syrian Revolution General Commission was formed in mid-August 2011 and claimed that forty-four groups had joined it as part of "merging all visions of all revolutionaries from all coalitions and coordinators mutually focusing primarily on toppling the oppressive and abusive regime."[21] It has been described as having an "aggressive platform," seeking removal of President Bashar al-Assad and "actively supporting armed rebels through provincial military councils."[22]

Differences among the Syrian Islamic groups also led to the creation of additional Islamist bodies such as Supreme Council for the Syrian Revolution (SCSR), which is made up of *tanseeqiat* that represent other Islamic views. Islamic leaders who are not affiliated directly or indirectly with the Muslim Brotherhood, such as Imad al-Din Rasheed, inspire this group. The SCSR set the outlines for a political solution while also recognizing the importance of armed struggle.

The new opposition also includes Kurdish youth who did not abide by the Kurdish political parties' policies to refrain from joining the uprising. In July

2011, they formed their own *tanseeqiat,* which was seen by both the regime and the traditional Kurdish parties as defiance. The Kurdish Youth Coordinating Committee celebrated its first anniversary on July 7, 2012. The committee emphasized its dedication to peaceful tactics, claiming that it would prioritize nonmilitarized solidarity with all aspects of the Syrian revolution.[23]

Other political groupings emerged as well, often from civil society activists and politicians reacting to the new conditions. Perhaps the most notable is a political group, known as the Building the Syrian State movement, that claims to be working for "Syria as a civil democratic state impartial towards all ideologies and doctrines; a state of citizenship and equality among all citizens regardless of their race, gender, religion, sect or culture; a state based on a social contract reflecting the free will of all citizens; and a state of laws that avoid the reproduction of a totalitarian regime like the one governing Syria now."[24] This group emerged in June 2011, when activist Louay Hussein, who had just completed five days of imprisonment, called for a conference for the Syrian opposition. Held in the Semiramis Hotel in Damascus with two hundred opposition members, the meeting marked the first time the opposition had met openly in Syria.[25] Opposition members came out from hiding and openly called for reform, the removal of the totalitarian regime in Syria, and a peaceful transition to democracy. In a final communiqué, participants declared their support for a "popular uprising seeking a peaceful transition to a democratic, civil and pluralistic state" and called for an immediate end to the security crackdown and for the army's withdrawal from towns and villages.[26] Another notable movement is the Ma'an (Together) movement, formed by Alawi activists, mainly located in Latakia, that started in June 2011. This group, too, aims to "support the peaceful struggles of the Syrian people for democracy, freedom, and building a civil, democratic state; and to expose violence in all its forms and wherever it comes from."[27]

Just as before the uprising, there was no clear demarcation between the spheres of civil society and political activism. An example is a group formed in Damascus in 2011 called the Mouatana (Citizenship) movement. Mouatana started as a civil group to hold public discussions about the uprising and to promote the concept of citizenship. However, it was not long before the group decided to turn into an active political group insisting on promoting peaceful resistance values and calling on the activists on the ground to produce a united leadership to work "whether independently or in alliance with other traditional political groups" to overthrow the "repressive, totalitarian" regime.[28] Other small groups included Nabad (Pulse), a civil group based in Homs and

"Syria: God is protecting it": This slogan was used by the Assad regime and was appropriated by the Syrian opposition during the Syrian uprising. Photo by Lina Khatib.

Damascus and made up of activists from different sects, including Alawis and Christians; the Social Secular Democratic movement, which focuses on the importance of secularism in the Syrian uprising; and the Coalition of Leftist Forces, a small group of leftist activists who had left communist parties because the parties did not support the revolution and in this way declared their participation in the uprising.

Activist Demands

The relative inactivity—and ineffectiveness—of the traditional opposition gave new opposition activists a strong justification for developing their own political position. Although, as presented above, the new opposition was structurally fragmented, it recognized the need to take a stance that would both support the revolutionary activities and sustain their political demands. Thus, in April 2011, the LCC released a statement that moved the Syrian revolutionary movement to enter a new phase.[29] The statement called for stopping the killing, releasing all political prisoners, forming an independent investigation commission, disbanding the disreputable security forces, creating a special commission for reconciliation among all elements of the Syrian nation, and amending the constitution to guarantee free elections. Overall, however, it boiled down to four primary demands:

1. Overthrowing the regime and moving into a civil, democratic state. To this end activists adopted "Ashaab yureed isqat al-nizam" ("the people want to overthrow the regime"), the spontaneous slogan raised by the people on the street.
2. The unity of the Syrian people. The slogan "The Syrian people are one" was one of the major slogans used by demonstrators. This was reflected in the demands of the new opposition activists for the people not to be divided into their sectarian affiliations by the regime's efforts.
3. Equity, dignity, and equality. All activists called for justice and equal opportunity among all Syrians, regardless of their political, family, or sectarian affiliation. They denounced the dominating method of *wasta* (favoritism) which qualifies some young people for positions and excludes others based on their loyalty and the circle of influence they have. The retrieval of property that had been confiscated by the government without proper compensation and then given to "loyal" people was a major demand. Another demand was to stop humiliating the Syrian people. One remarkable slogan, in fact, went "The Syrian people cannot be humiliated."
4. An end to arbitrary detention, the release of all prisoners, and justice for the officials who killed and tortured people.

By so doing, the new opposition escalated the confrontation with the regime. Before the revolution, the Syrian opposition's demands had been limited to freedom of expression, freedom of political action, and political reforms that would abolish the state of emergency and change Article 8 of the Constitution that presented the ruling National Progressive Front as "the only framework for legal political party participation for citizens."[30] Now they were openly calling for regime change. The statement dumbfounded the government and the traditional opposition: The former rushed to silence the newly born creature through a cruel campaign of arrests and torture; the latter started to work vigorously to develop a political platform that would contain the dramatic developments.

Activist Strategies: Nonviolent Resistance

The opposition generally converged on its demands, but opposition forces differed significantly over the strategies used to achieve those demands. A key division centered on the militarization of the uprising. The uprising started off as a peaceful movement, and some opposition groups were firmly committed to nonviolence as a strategy, including advocating dialogue with the regime. Other opposition groups, however, concluded that the regime's ongoing brutal crackdown on protesters left the opposition no choice but to engage in armed struggle against the regime.

Nonviolent protest was a key feature of the Syrian uprising, persisting despite the continuous regime brutality. Civil resistance activists used a variety of nonviolent tactics: street protests; humor and sarcasm; relief aid to victims and displaced families; petitions; persuasion campaigns; group statements; noncooperation, including strikes, sit-ins, and civil disobedience; and unarmed blockades. Humor featured prominently both in online posts and in street demonstrations as a method of countering the regime, its security forces, and *shabeeha*—regime thugs disguised as regular civilians.[31] In Kafr Nebel, a small town in the province of Idlib, several sarcastic banners were raised. One banner portrayed President Vladimir Putin of Russia giving electric shocks to President Assad as he lay on a bed in a hospital; another portrayed the Syrian people as Sisyphus carrying the rock of the Syrian revolution; a third read, "We demand increasing the number of tanks in Kafr Nebel to reduce the pressure on Homs."

Nonviolent protest was a strategy centered on bringing together different sectors of Syrian society under the banner of national unity. Through their online outputs (videos, photographs, and written communiqués) and offline demonstration banners, as well as through the names they gave to "protest Fridays" that followed the Tunisian and Egyptian model of using Friday prayers as a starting point for street demonstrations, activists called for unity and cooperation among all components of Syrian society. With mounting anger at government oppression tools like the mostly Alawi *shabeeha*, activists, such as the LCC, were concerned about rising sectarian tension, particularly as some popular calls began to be made to engage in violence against the *shabeeha*. Thus, one emphasis of the call for unity was on sectarian harmony. In a gesture toward the Christian community, one Friday was named "The Good Friday." In another directed at the Alawi community, a Friday was named "Saleh al-Ali Friday," referencing a renowned Alawi fighter against the French Mandate.

In some areas, it was not only a matter of peaceful uprising but also a matter of nonviolence as a principle. For example, in Darayya, a small town to the south of Damascus, citizens organized peaceful demonstrations in which they declared their commitment to nonviolence. The regime's response was to imprison and kill the activists involved, such as the young activists Yahiya Shurbaji and Ghayath Matar, respectively. In Damascus, Razan Zeitouneh—a thirty-five-year-old lawyer, human rights activist, blogger, and leading member of the new opposition—was forced into hiding, as her family members were detained and her fellow activists jailed, killed, or forced to flee the country for their prodemocracy activities. Still she adhered to nonviolence.

Activists also engaged in capacity-building efforts. This was done internally and externally, covering all needed domains, including networking, using internet technology and new media, filming, documenting, preparing media reports, organizing demonstrations, creating mechanisms for dealing with tear gas and electrical batons, delivering first aid, and distributing pamphlets. It also included relief, offering food, shelter, and medication, including surgeries. My Home is Yours and Homs in Our Hearts are good examples of collective efforts of relief. The first built a network of groups working on the ground to provide relief to displaced families, especially those who had to leave their homes in Homs. The second was the product of some twenty young men and women who collected two truckloads of food and clothing and took them to the city of Homs, which was being shelled in March 2012, to help the hundreds of thousands of displaced people in the city.

Other civil resistance strategies included the dissemination of position statements by activist groups and signed petitions. One of the most famous petitions was known as the "milk petition," signed by a good number of well-known artists and writers, asking for humanitarian access to deliver food, water, and milk to suffering children in the city of Daraa. Another strategy was civil disobedience in the form of sit-ins and strikes, such as the strike held in Damascus in June 2012 in reaction to the al-Houla massacre, where, according to the UN, over one hundred people, including forty-nine children and thirty-four women, were killed on May 25, 2012, allegedly by the Syrian military and *shabeeha*. Citizens also formed neighborhood committees that used unarmed blockades to prevent the penetration of the military into their areas, such as the case of the human shields formed by the residents of the coastal city of Baniyas in the first weeks of the revolution. The response of the regime to those strategies was either to try to prevent sit-ins from taking place, as in the city of Homs in April 2011, or to continue to attack unarmed protesters.[32]

In addition to the on-the-ground strategies discussed above, on more than one occasion the new opposition actors found themselves obliged to take further steps in assuming the role of a political actor. In an attempt to contain the increasingly urgent calls to arm the revolution or to seek foreign intervention, the LCC adopted a political position cautioning against the threat of sectarianism that could be catalyzed by such a development. The new political actors, including some *tanseeqiat* and Building the Syrian State movement, also had to jump in and take a position on the issue of dialogue with the regime. In 2011, the regime had started to meet individuals from the opposition to find out what the possibilities for talks were. The opposition was divided on the issue and started to exchange accusations without defending their views. In the end, the new opposition presented a unified position. They argued that there was no alternative to a political process, provided that four conditions were met: "end the killing and violence, release prisoners, allow peaceful demonstration, and allow the media to cover the uprising in Syria." These four conditions would become the common ground for all stances of the different opposition groups whenever they spoke about dialogue with the government.

The Militarization of the Revolution

The regime did not respond positively to the activists' demands or to the opposition's attempts to maintain a nonviolent revolution. Indeed, perhaps seeing itself under an existential threat, the regime pushed the revolution toward sectarian strife and a militarized uprising. The regime increasingly divided the people according to their religions and regions. It promoted an indirectly sectarian discourse, accusing the protesters of being radical Islamists and intimidating the Alawis and Christians by speaking of a Sunni hegemony. In many areas it encouraged the arming of the progovernment Alawi population, and in the Kurdish areas, it supported a progovernment faction, which many believe might have been responsible for the killing of Kurdish antigovernment rebels.[33] The regime had been working on this goal from day one. When the people of Daraa took to the streets asking merely for justice, the regime asked the influential progovernment cleric Saeed al-Bouti to appear on television and tell the people that the regime had responded to the people's demands and consequently ordered the launch of a religious television channel. Then it started to portray the protests as a Salafi intifada aiming to establish a Salafi emirate.

The regime also chose a military solution. After it held a first meeting for dialogue in July 2011, none of the meeting recommendations were actually implemented. Instead, it rushed in August to march into the city of Hama, which had been a stronghold of the revolutionaries. Later, the military and the security forces shelled and destroyed one third of the city of Homs and continued to attack other protest areas like Idlib. Tens of thousands of families had to leave their homes and seek refuge in Damascus or other cities and villages. Many others had to flee to Turkey, Lebanon, or Jordan. The mass killings intensified; the more the international pressure on Assad increased, the more brutal the regime's reaction became.

The regime's excessive use of force pushed many to support a more militarized uprising and pulled the rug out from under the nonviolence advocates. After August 2011, one would hear more and more people say that they had had enough, that the regime would not listen to the "voice of reason," as one banner put it in Binnesh, a village in the province of Idlib. Syrians increasingly called for retaliating against the regime's attacks, and an increasing number of defectors from the Syrian army—soldiers who refused to kill their people—were executed or defected to create the Movement of Free Officers, which later became known as the Free Syrian Army (FSA). Although the LCC and others would repeatedly appeal to defectors to "leave their weapons and join the protesters in the street," others—such as the General Commission for the Syrian Revolution—hailed the FSA and use of force.[34]

Militarization grew. People began to speak more about the Free Syrian Army than they did of the demonstrators. They raised banners that read "The Free Syrian Army protects me" in place of ones bearing the words "peaceful, peaceful." And, instead of "Neither Christians nor Muslims, we want national unity," talk on Facebook slowly changed into *we* and *they*. This violence and disunity increased, and when the Syrian army shelled the suburb of Baba Amr in Homs in 2012, stories about rape, looting, and killing spread across the country like wildfire. In fear and despair, many others took up arms as well, saying that they would not allow the army to rape their women and destroy their property.

In general, while the demonstrations continued to exist and people continued to take to the streets in most areas (as many as 850 demonstrations on certain Fridays), the nature of activism shifted from peaceful resistance to armed resistance due to the escalating violence by the regime. The number of demonstrators, which had reached tens of thousands in the city of Hama in

July 2011, shrank to just a few hundred. The FSA controlled complete areas, neighborhoods, towns, and sometimes cities.

Both the new and the old opposition were divided over how to respond, and particularly over the issue of foreign intervention. While the majority approved the diplomatic pressure exerted by the Western countries on President Bashar al-Assad, some went a step further and called for military interventions, under different labels, including safe corridors, or safe havens for defectors. Others, however, strived to adhere to their opposition to any military intervention. As Yaseen Haj Saleh, a writer and activist close to new activist circles in Damascus, put it in 2011, militarizing the revolution would cause it to lose its moral superiority with no guarantee that it would mean the regime's defeat in the end. Because of these sharp divisions, the new opposition actors bickered over who was the "genuine" representative of the Syrian people, a competition that played out both internally and internationally, leading some observers in Western countries to criticize the lack of unity among the Syrian opposition and cite it as a factor hindering further international support for the opposition.

New Activist Coalitions and New Actors

The uprising's substantial transformation into armed struggle catalyzed changes in the composition of the opposition. By October 2011, larger coalitions called the Syrian National Council (SNC) and the National Coordination Committee (NCC) were formed—albeit with markedly different levels of credibility and impact—but engaged in a seemingly endless conflict on who represents the Syrian opposition and consequently the Syrian people. At the same time, new actors emerged, namely civil society movements and small business owners in the Damascus Bazaar.

After the uprising broke out in March 2011, activists, politicians, and ordinary Syrians had called for a political umbrella to cover and represent the revolution. Very little was achieved in this regard, as the historically divided opposition was not ready to put aside its differences and reach an agreement among its parties. But the efforts to reach this goal did not stop. The SNC, which came about as a result of sustained efforts to unify the Syrian opposition, includes the Muslim Brotherhood, the Damascus Declaration, the Istanbul Working Group, the LCC, the Supreme Council for the Syrian Revolution, and a number of liberal scholars and activists, including the first SNC President, Burhan Ghalioun.[35] The Istanbul Working Group is a team of experts, technocrats, and political figures who worked collaboratively to formulate a new mechanism by which they could establish a council that includes competent national figures while considering the diversity that reflects Syrian society.[36] In many ways, the SNC represented the hardline opposition whose ultimate goal was to overthrow the regime and build a democratic state. It refused talks with the regime and (as it stated) would only negotiate the regime's departure. Although the Muslim Brotherhood and the Damascus Declaration had experienced leaders, the majority of the members of the SNC lacked such experience as well as the eloquence, charm, and charisma needed to lead the street.

The NCC, on the other hand, was created on June 21, 2011. The main components of the NCC are the National Democratic Rally, which was formed in 1980 and included most traditional nationalist and socialist parties, as well as the Arab Socialist Union Party, headed by Hasan Abdul Azim, and the Communist Action Party, both of which quit the Damascus Declaration after losing the internal elections there. Smaller leftist groups joined the coalition, including the Independent Leftist movement, in addition to (oddly enough) a progovernment Kurdish Party, the Parti Yekiti Demokrati (Kurdish Democratic Union Party). This trend thus stands in stark contrast to the DD, both in economic positions (the socialist orientation of the NCC versus the liberal orientation of the DD) and in its stance toward the West. The NCC claimed to represent the internal opposition with a more reconciliatory approach toward the regime in Syria. It was involved in the protests that took place in the beginning of the revolution, especially in Daraa and Rif Dimashq as well as in the city of Douma. However, this role diminished as the revolution developed. The undetermined position of the coalition on the issue of overthrowing the regime and its eagerness to find conciliatory political solutions contributed to this.

The SNC and the NCC differed from each other in most of their strategies and details, but above all in three areas: dialogue with the regime, the Free Syrian Army, and foreign intervention. In July 2012, the two groups held a meeting in Cairo to try to reach common ground, but they failed except for a vague agreement to support the Free Syrian Army and to exclude Assad and other senior regime figures from a place in the transition. They also failed to reach an agreement on forming a unified body to represent the opposition. In late August, the NCC issued an initiative for a "temporary truce by all parties involved in armed actions," the release of "all detainees, prisoners, captives, and kidnapped" by "both sides" (meaning the regime and the FSA), permission to relief organizations to deliver aid, and the "start of a political process based on negotiations between all opposition forces and a regime delegation with full negotiation powers."[37] The SNC soon responded to the initiative, noting that it is "a violation of the national consensus agreed upon in the opposition meeting in Cairo on 2–3 July. It is a retreat from the most important article that calls for the removal of the regime and its head and the refusal to deal with him and for supporting the Free Syrian Army and the people's resistance. The initiative gives the regime more time to stay in power while the entire people of Syria absolutely rejected this by continuing to protest for seventeen consecutive months."[38]

The increasing use of violence made the nonviolent actors in Syria more aware of and vocal about its disastrous consequences. In the beginning of 2012, particularly after the first anniversary of the uprising on March 15, new civil society entities appeared in response to the mounting violence. This was inspired by the release of some peaceful activists from prison who immediately resumed their peaceful resistance and wanted to send a message about the importance of the nonviolence movement. Among these groups, the most important one was the Syrian League for Citizenship, which was founded to promote the values of citizenship, equity, and equal opportunities. The Syrian League for Citizenship, which included lawyers, professors, writers, human rights activists, and women's rights defenders, worked on four programs: a knowledge program (lectures, books, and so on); a capacity building program; a media program; and a relief program. Another nonviolent civil initiative was Stop the Killing, a campaign that called on all parties to stop engaging in violence. It called on the regime to stop killing the people and at the same time called on the opposition to stop its armed operations "because we want to build a homeland for all Syrians," as the campaign founder Rima Dali put it in July 2012.[39] It was a brave, solitary act when Dali stood in the middle of a busy Damascus street holding a banner that called on the government to stop killing its citizens. For this, she was arrested and put into detention. To honor her, supporters recreated her protest two days later. Dali was released, but the campaign continued, and many participants were arrested for it. Another group was the Civil Enlightenment Movement, a nonpolitical movement that aimed to "direct the compass to the political and social culture" and get "totally involved in the Syrian revolution and to defend the values of justice, freedom, and equality as individuals."[40]

In addition to those new civil society actors, the second phase of the Syrian revolution witnessed another new player: the Bazaar. It had been repeatedly said that unless the Damascus Bazaar moves, there is little chance for the Syrian revolution to succeed. Activist and scholar Hassan Abbas eloquently described how the regime's economic policy has produced groups of affluent people who are organically tied to it and act as its protectors, since it is the source of their own wealth and the guarantor of their continuing survival and accretion of further wealth. They all rely on set rules of business, which oblige them to include the regime entourage in their investments, and relinquish a share of their profits to them in return for the administrative and legal services that they provide.[41] Syria's big business elite is also closely intertwined with the ruling Baath Party through financial and family ties.[42] Disloyalty to the government can mean not only loss of lucrative government contracts but also political isolation and even jail. Consequently, a Syrian former World Bank economist interpreted the support of big business leaders for the regime as pragmatism: "They expect the unrest to end sooner or later. The regime is well entrenched. The Army is certainly loyal to the government."[43]

This remained the case for the big businesses, but the traditional merchants of both Damascus and Aleppo began to lose their patience. They sent a number of signals to the regime to express their dissatisfaction. Among these signals were the labor strikes that stunned the regime in June 2012. The May 25 massacre in al-Houla, however, was the landmark event that changed the Bazaar's attitude. On May 28, an unexpected strike took place to protest the massacre. The strike paralyzed most commercial and semicommercial districts in Damascus, including key markets and commercial areas such as al-Hamidiya, al-Hariqa, al-Maidan, and al-Salhiya.[44] Earlier, the regime had tried to find a way to contain the Bazaar. Successive news reports were leaked in May about a meeting between President Assad and a carefully selected group of the most prominent businessmen in Syria. This was an extremely tense and stormy meeting that represented a humiliation for the Syrian businessmen, who were subjected to explicit violent threats that required no interpretation, namely that either these businessmen and merchants clearly and explicitly support the regime and comprehensively refuse to support the revolution or face the consequences.[45] Slowly, perhaps, but steadily, the traditional merchants and manufacturers made their way to backing the revolution and offering financial and moral support to the opposition.

On November 11, 2012, the Syrian opposition managed, after months of debate, to form a coalition that comprised the broadest representation of the opposition. The National Coalition for Syrian Revolutionary and Opposition Forces, which was unveiled in Doha, elected Sheikh Ahmad Moaz al-Khatib president of the coalition and prominent dissident Riad Seif and female opposition figure Suhair al-Atassi vice presidents. Khatib had served in the past as the imam of the central Umayyad mosque in the Syrian capital before he was banned from leading prayers. He was arrested in 2011 and in 2012 for supporting the uprising before he left the country.

With more than a hundred countries recognizing the new Syrian opposition coalition as the legitimate representative of the Syrian people, the door was open to a new era of activism. The international community was expecting the new entity to play the leading role in the revolution and also in the creation of a new Syria. This expectation changed the picture of activism in Syria as it began to move from fragmentation into institutionalization, as has the change in the balance of forces on the ground. The new political actor that came into being in the first phase of the revolution has faded away, and the techniques that the young peaceful resistance activists invented every day became old and beautiful memories, but the weight of the competition between the regime and the opposition became more apparent to both sides as well as to the regional and international powers.

Conclusion: Activism Changes and Challenges

The initial dreams that a peaceful revolution could lead swiftly to the downfall of the Syrian regime—much as it had in Egypt and Tunisia—were not realized. Activism did not remain entirely peaceful. The massacres committed by proregime militias inflamed many activists and made them reconsider their position. Some peaceful activists joined the Free Syrian Army. Others who did not approve of violent action withdrew from the streets and took refuge on Facebook. Indeed, the very discourse of peace became an object of sarcasm. But the hope for a peaceful revolution for a unified Syrian nation was not entirely defeated: the LCC launched a festival in June 2012 entitled, "Our Streets are Colorful: The Syrian Day for Diversity" in areas free of regime control to celebrate Syrian diversity. Yet hopes for unity, peace, and a new regime were dealt serious blows, and even the LCC eventually changed its stance about militarization.

It is important to understand how the challenges activists faced contributed to the militarization of the conflict. The first challenge was that they lacked a key strategic element in their struggle: *planning*. Oppression is usually not overcome solely through spontaneous and improvised acts of resistance, even if the acts themselves are well executed. Planning is needed in order to direct

January 26, 2011: Hasan Ali Akley from al-Hasakah self-immolates.

February 2, 2011: At Bab Tuma in Damascus, a group of twenty civilians violently clashes with fifteen people holding a vigil for Egyptian demonstrators.

February 5, 2011: In al-Hasakah, hundreds of protesters participate in mass demonstrations calling for political reform and an end to emergency law, which has been in place since 1962. Though many protests are planned, none come to full fruition, indicating the far-reaching and strict security measures, presumed presidential popularity, and a fear of the aftermath of sectarian violence.

February 17, 2011: In the al-Hamidiya market in Damascus, fifteen hundred demonstrators are quickly dispersed by police officers.

March 6, 2011: In Daraa, several young boys are arrested for writing antiregime graffiti.

March 7, 2011: Thirteen political prisoners go on a hunger strike, demanding an end to political arrests and injustices throughout Syria.

March 10, 2011: Dozens of jailed Kurds from the Yakiti Party and the Democratic Union Party begin a hunger strike in solidarity with other prisoners.

March 12, 2011: In al-Qamishli and al-Hasakah, thousands of Kurds protest on the day of Kurdish martyrs.

March 15, 2011: In the first time since the 1980s uprisings, demonstrations take place in Damascus, al-Hasakha, Daraa, Deir ez-Zour, and Hama. As clashes break out, some three thousand protesters are arrested.

March 16, 2011: Authorities clash with some two hundred demonstrators outside of the Syrian Ministry of the Interior. Among the arrested are activists Suhair al-Atassi and Kamal Cheikho.

March 18, 2011: In the largest day of unrest in recent Syrian history, thousands of protesters clash with government officials in demonstrations in Damascus, Daraa, Homs, Baniyas, al-Qamishli, and Deir ez-Zour. Unconfirmed reports indicate that four protesters are dead and hundreds more injured.

March 21, 2011: Protests spread from Daraa to Jasim, Baniyas, Homs, and Hama, where police fire live ammunition into protesting crowds.

March 24, 2011: Twenty thousand protesters march at funerals in Daraa. Death estimates range from thirty-two to more than a hundred.

March 25, 2011: Demonstrations continue throughout the country in what protesters call the "Friday of Glory." Reports from Sanamayn say that security forces have killed twenty-five people, In addition three deaths are reported in Tafas, seventeen in Daraa, forty near the Omari Mosque, four in Latakia, and three in Damascus.

March 26, 2011: As a sign of good will, two hundred political prisoners are released. In Latakia and Tafas, Baath Party buildings are set on fire. In Homs, the governor is dismissed from his post.

March 27, 2011: As Buthaina Shaaban, the president's media adviser, states that emergency law will be lifted, twelve people are killed in clashes in Latakia.

March 29, 2011: Hundreds of thousands demonstrate in support of President Assad in Damascus, Aleppo, al-Hasakah, Homs, Tartous, and Hama. Muhammad Naji al-Otari resigns from his post as prime minister.

March 30, 2011: In an address on national TV, President Assad blames foreign conspirators for the uprisings and states that the emergency law will not be lifted. In response to the president's speech, protesters take to the streets in Latakia, where police fire on them. Twenty-five are killed, bringing the countrywide death total to over two hundred.

March 31, 2011: President Assad announces that he will increase the wages of state employees, effective April 1.

April 1, 2011: In response to the recent killings, thousands of protesters take to the streets on the "Friday of Martyrs."

April 2, 2011: In President Assad's village of Buq'ata, two thousand people gather to protest in support of the president. Security forces arrest more than twenty people in Daraa and Homs.

April 3, 2011: President Assad appoints Adel Safar to be the new Syrian prime minister.

April 6, 2011: In an effort to appease Sunnis and Kurds, President Assad allows teachers to wear the niqab again, promises that thousands of Kurds will soon be granted Syrian citizenship, and closes the country's only casino.

April 8, 2011: Protests erupt throughout the country on the "Friday of Resistance," leaving twenty-seven antigovernment protesters killed in Daraa, three in Damascus, and two in Homs.

April 18, 2011: More than ten thousand antigovernment protesters march in Homs amid a massive funeral for six protesters from Homs. Security forces clash with protesters, killing at least thirteen people as the protest is dispersed.

April 21, 2011: President Assad signs a decree that will lift the state of emergency, end the Supreme State Security Court (SSC), and recognize the right to peaceful protests.

April 22, 2011: In the bloodiest day in the uprising thus far, at least seventy-two are killed by security forces during protests in Daraa and Damascus.

April 25, 2011: The Syrian army occupies Daraa, killing at least twenty-five people as it moves in. The United States moves to freeze Syrian assets in the United States, as France and the United Kingdom push for international sanctions.

April 29, 2011: Security forces kill at least seventy-three civilians at protests throughout the country.

May 5, 2011: As the Syrian army moves out of Daraa, forces move to occupy Homs.

May 6, 2011: Following Friday prayers, demonstrations break out throughout the country. Security forces clash with antigovernment protesters in Homs and Hama, leaving at least three antigovernment protesters and eleven army officials dead. After the demonstrations, major opposition activists go into hiding.

May 12, 2011: The death toll climbs to over eight hundred since the uprising began two months earlier. The sieges on Homs, Tafas, Baniyas, Dael, Jasim, and al-Harah continue as troops move toward Hama.

May 19, 2011: The United States places sanctions on senior Syrian officials, including President Assad.

May 28, 2011: The army moves into the towns of al-Rastan and Talbiseh. Thirteen-year-old martyr Hamza Ali al-Khateeb from Daraa is returned to his family after having been abused and mutilated. Internet media sources circulate the boy's story, and he becomes a national and international hero for the antigovernment protests.

June 3, 2011: Security forces clash with fifty thousand protesters in Hama, killing at least sixty-four people. The government shuts down most of Syria's internet.

June 14, 2011: For the first time, the Arab League condemns the atrocities in Syria. Residents in Daraa continue to face famine, and Syrian troops expand the siege to Maraat al-Numaan, Ariha, and Abu Kamal.

June 17, 2011: In mass demonstrations throughout the country, protesters clash with security forces on the "Friday of Saleh al-Ali," leaving nineteen dead.

June 18, 2011: The Syrian army storms Bdama, a town near the Turkish border. Nearly ten thousand refugees have fled to Turkey since the uprisings began.

June 19, 2011: Opposition forces establish the Syrian National Council to lead the Syrian revolution.

June 20, 2011: President Assad addresses the public, saying that while he will engage in talks with the opposition, he refuses to reform Syria under such a dire situation.

June 24, 2011: Mass demonstrations occur throughout Syria, with protesters taking to the streets in central Damascus.

June 30, 2011: Demonstrators take to the streets in Aleppo, calling for mass protests on July 1.

July 1, 2011: Security forces kill at least twenty-eight people as more than half a million people take to the streets in Hama.

July 8, 2011: In Hama, in the presence of French and U.S. ambassadors, five hundred thousand protesters call for an end to the regime. Demonstrations take place around the country, leaving thirteen dead and forty wounded.

July 11, 2011: President Assad supporters attack the French and U.S. embassies in Damascus.

July 22, 2011: Mass protests draw 450,000 supporters in Deir ez-Zour and 650,000 in Hama. Protesters clash with the Syrian army in Aleppo, leaving eight dead.

July 31, 2011: One hundred and thirty six are killed throughout the country as the Syrian army cracks down on demonstrations before Ramadan.

August 3, 2011: In the wake of the forty-five deaths on this day and over the course of the uprising, the UN Security Council for the first time condemns the violence in Syria.

August 4, 2011: President Assad issues a decree authorizing the formation of multiple political parties as well as moderate electoral reform.

August 7, 2011: After seventy people are killed countrywide, the Arab League for the first time condemns the actions of the government.

August 8, 2011: As Saudi Arabia says that it will withdraw its ambassador, the attack on Deir ez-Zour begins. President Assad fires his minister of defense and replaces him with General Dawoud Rajiha. The day's death toll estimates are between twenty-four and eighty-seven.

August 10, 2011: Led by former minister of information Mohammed Salman, forty-one former and current officials announce an initiative for transition in *The New York Times*.

August 18, 2011: For the first time, the governments of Canada, France, Germany, the United Kingdom, and the United States call for Assad's resignation.

August 22, 2011: The UN issues a report saying that the protesters' death toll has reached 2,200 and votes to launch an investigation into crimes against humanity.

August 23, 2011: In Turkey, the Syrian National Council is inaugurated.

August 25, 2011: Political cartoonist Ali Farzat is kidnapped.

August 28, 2011: The Movement of Free Officers claims large numbers of defectors from the Syrian security forces.

September 1, 2011: The attorney general of Hama resigns in reaction to the seventy-two political prisoners supposedly executed by the regime on July 31, 2011.

September 11, 2011: As fighting continues in Deir ez-Zour and Daraa, Sawasiah, a Syrian human rights organization, claims that at least 113 civilians have been killed.

September 12, 2011: Three prominent Alawi clerics denounce the violence committed by the regime.

September 14, 2011: In an unprecedented diplomatic showing, representatives from the United Kingdom, France, Germany, Canada, Japan, the Netherlands, the United States, and the EU take part in a vigil for Ghayyath Matar, believed to have been tortured to death by security forces.

September 21, 2011: Prime Minister Recep Tayyip Erdoğan announces that Turkey has cut off all relations with Syria.

September 29, 2011: The Free Syrian Army claims more defectors as fears mount that a civil war could break out.

October 2, 2011: Burhan Ghalioun, chairman of the Syrian National Council, announces that a general assembly of 190 members will convene in November to discuss reforms.

October 4, 2011: At the United Nations Security Council, China and Russia veto sanctions against Syria.

October 7, 2011: At protests to support the SNC, security forces kill at least twenty-one people. Syrian security forces assassinate activist Mashaal Tammo.

October 21, 2011: As protesters take to the streets to celebrate the death of Muammar Qaddafi, security forces continue to clash with antigovernment forces throughout the country.

October 23, 2011: Iranian President Mahmoud Ahmadinejad, Syria's key ally, condemns the killings of more than three thousand people since the uprisings began.

October 26, 2011: Nabil el-Araby, secretary-general of the Arab League, arrives in Damascus for talks.

November 3, 2011: Only one day after the government approves an Arab League plan to halt the violence, security forces in Homs kill at least nineteen people.

November 7, 2011: After more than 110 people have been killed in Homs in the past week, opposition forces appeal for international intervention in Homs.

November 27, 2011: The Arab League agrees on economic sanctions against Syria.

December 1, 2011: The death toll in Syria reaches over four thousand and the UN characterizes the uprising as a civil war.

December 2, 2011: Tens of thousands march to demand that Turkey create a buffer zone to protect civilians. More defections continue as soldiers join the Free Syrian Army.

December 3, 2011: The Syrian government condemns a UN vote on human rights violations, claiming that the vote is unfair.

December 4, 2011: At least a dozen secret police defect from President Assad's loyal intelligence service.

December 7, 2011: In an interview with Barbara Walters, President Assad claims that the government is doing nothing wrong.

December 12, 2011: The UN says that more than five thousand people have been killed since the uprisings began.

December 21, 2011: Syrian security forces are accused of massacring more than one hundred people in the village of Kfar Owaid. Under new Syrian law, the government is able to execute anyone smuggling weapons for the sake of committing a terrorist act.

December 23, 2011: Two car bombs detonate in Damascus, killing forty-four and leaving 163 wounded.

December 24, 2011: Sudanese General Mohammed Ahmed Mustafa al-Dabi arrives in Syria as the leader of the Arab League observers.

December 28, 2011: Despite the Arab League observers, at least thirteen people are killed in demonstrations in Hama, Homs, Aleppo, and Idlib.

December 29, 2011: Protesters march throughout the country demanding the ouster of Arab League monitoring team leader al-Dabi.

December 30, 2011: Over six million people across the country participate in demonstrations against President Assad.

December 31, 2011: Security forces attack activists throughout the country. The SNC signs an agreement with the National Coordination Committee to work together on political reforms.

these spontaneous acts and benefit from the positive charge in the population so as to achieve targeted and focused goals. Syrian activists did not have the time or the luxury to plan their revolution. And one of the major setbacks of the Syrian revolution is that activists assumed in the beginning that the regime would fall in a short time, as had happened in Egypt and Tunisia. Therefore, they did not think of planning their activities, and later, they found themselves rushed and had little time to do that.

The second challenge that imperiled the Syrian revolution is the division among its major actors. The Syrian revolutionary actors were divided among old vs. new, internal vs. external, radical vs. reconciliatory, and violent vs. non-violent. The major split between the Syrian National Council and the National Coordination Committee threatened the entire transition into democracy. The two largest opposition groups showed great mistrust toward one other. Members of the SNC accused the NCC of being too close to the regime, while the NCC accused the SNC of being a front for the Muslim Brotherhood and Western powers.[46]

The third challenge was that both the SNC and the NCC failed to reach out to the Syrian street and to the activists and protesters on the ground. In fact, the Syrian protesters on the ground, both the peaceful resistance actors and the fighters, seemed to be left alone to decide what to do in a rather amorphous way. The SNC, possessing the means and funds to support the protesters, was often more interested in playing politics with the regional and international players than engaging with the Syrian street.

The fourth challenge was that the Syrian opposition focused more on the post-Assad era than on how to get there. The SNC showed little interest or enthusiasm in working with the different components of the Syrian population, especially the Alawi and Christian communities, the officers of the Syrian army, and the business community to assure them all about their positions in the new Syria.

Finally, the fifth challenge was the attitude of the international community toward the Syrian revolution. In the first year and a half, the international community did not take a steady unified approach toward the Syrian crisis.

Just like the Syrian opposition, which often took a spur-of-the-moment approach to its decisions, the international community allowed itself to proceed in the Syria case without having a coherent vision about Syria or any Plan B. On the one hand, it seems to have underestimated the regime's powers and its capacity to destroy the country and the population. Therefore, it rushed to have strong positions against President Assad and asked him to step aside. It certainly escalated sanctions on the regime. On the other hand, however, this policy had its share of ups and downs. This fluctuating policy influenced the performance of individual protesters and opposition groups alike. The calls for arming the opposition in particular were hugely controversial. While a big part of the opposition, including the SNC, the Free Syrian Army, and regional powers such as Qatar and Saudi Arabia, were in favor of such a step, other opposition players, such as the NCC were opposed to it.[47] This exacerbated deep societal divisions and increased the possibility of jihadists taking a more prominent role in the resistance. Although the number of al-Qaeda fighters in Syria remained relatively small a year after the uprising began, other foreign fighters, many of whom are not directly affiliated with al-Qaeda, were either in or headed to Syria.[48]

With the 2011 uprising, the challenges to the regime in the political field in Syria were and continue to be mainly the work of a younger generation that had long considered itself to be apolitical. But the foundations of this movement go back to the work of the older generation since the 1970s through 2001's Damascus Spring, which failed due to state repression, and to the Damascus Declaration in 2005, which suffered the same fate. The great challenge for activism in Syria seems to be coexistence between the political leadership of the old opposition and the active enthusiasm of the new opposition. Beyond that there are proposals to overcome divisions within the new opposition itself, whether religious, ethnic, or political. Yet despite those divisions, the dynamics of activism during the revolution have planted the seed for a new form of political activism in Syria.

Notes

1. Abdulrazak Eid, interview with sooryoon.net, July 20, 2010.

2. Interview with Syrian president Bashar al-Assad, *Wall Street Journal,* January 31, 2011.

3. Effective independence from France did not happen until 1946, when French troops finally left Syria.

4. On the Muslim Brotherhood, see Johannas Reisner, *Ideologie und Politik der Muslim Brüder Syriens* (Berlin: K. Schwarz, 1980); Robin Wright, *Dreams and Shadows: The Future of the Middle East* (London: Penguin, 2008).

5. On non-movements, see Asef Bayat, *Life as Politics: How Ordinary People Change the Middle East* (Stanford, CA: Stanford University Press, 2010).

6. Ibid., p. 15. See also Henri Lefebvre, *Le droit à la ville* (Paris: Éd. Anthropos, 1968).

7. On this issue, see Wael Sawah, "Al-ashwaiyat al-arabiya wa al-zahf al-hadi lil aadiyeen," *Al-Hayat*, January 11, 2011.

8. Marwa Ghamian, a female activist from Damascus who has revealed her experience in the Syrian uprising on her page on Facebook.

9. Hassan Abbas, "The Dynamics of the Uprising in Syria," Arab Reform Brief 51 (October 2011), available at www.arab-reform.net/sites/default/files/ARB_51_Syria_Oct_2011_H-Abbas_En.pdf, accessed July 16, 2013.

10. All of LCC's statements can be found at the LCC website: www.lccsyria.org/category/statements, accessed July 16, 2013. The website also contains a wealth of information on the LCC's origins.

11. The word *tanseeqiah* comes from the noun *tanseeq*, which means "coordination."

12. For more on the Damascus Declaration, see "The Damascus Declaration," Carnegie Middle East Center March 1, 2012, available at http://carnegie-mec.org/publications/?fa=48514, accessed July 16, 2013.

13. Khaddam was vice president under Hafez al-Assad. He defected in 2005 and, together with the Muslim Brotherhood, formed the "Syrian Salvation Front" and managed to recruit a good number of Syrian activists in exile. His website once was a major source of information and opinion pieces for the opposition in Syria. But due to his role in the Syrian regime as a major assistant to Assad over more than three decades, he was not popular inside Syria.

14. See the Constitution of the Islamic Party of Liberation.

15. On the Movement for Justice and Development, see "What We Stand For," an introductory article on MJD website, available at www.forsyria.org/What_westandfor.asp, accessed July 1, 2012.

16. "U.S. Secretly Backed Syrian Opposition Groups, Cables Released by WikiLeaks Show," *Washington Post*, April 17, 2011.

17. Gary C. Gambill, "The Kurdish Reawakening in Syria," *Middle East Intelligence Bulletin* 6(4) (2004), available at www.meforum.org/meib/articles/0404_s1.htm, acccessed July 16, 2013.

18. Zeina Karam, "Syria War Empowers Long-Oppressed Kurdish Minority," *Denver Post*, August 21, 2012, available at www.denverpost.com/nationworld/ci_21358095/syria-war-empowers-long-oppressed-kurdish-minority, accessed July 16, 2013.

19. A very long list of these individual dissidents who became active in the uprising includes Antoun Makdissi, Aref Dalilah, Tayeb Tizini, Yaseen Haj Saleh, Omar
Amiralai, Osama Mohamad, Colette Bahna, Samar Yazbek, and many others.

20. For a deeper understanding of *tanseeqiat,* see Abbas, "Dynamics of the Uprising in Syria."

21. AFP, "Syrian Coalition against Assad Formed: Statement," AAJ News, August
19, 2011, available at www.aaj.tv/2011/08/syrian-coalition-against-assad-formed
-statement/, accessed July 16, 2013.

22. Elizabeth O'Bagy, "Disorganized Like a Fox," *Foreign Policy,* June 29, 2012,
available at www.foreignpolicy.com/articles/2012/06/29/disorganized_like_a_fox,
accessed July 16, 2013.

23. "Kurdish Youth Coordinating Committee Celebrates Its First Anniversary,"
Alliance for Kurdish Rights, July 9, 2012, available at http://kurdishrights.org/2012
/07/09/kurdish-youth-coordinating-committee-celebrates-its-first-anniversary/, accessed July 16, 2013.

24. See the official website of the group at http://binaa-syria.com/B/en, accessed
July 16, 2013.

25. Joshua Landis, "Syrian Opposition Conference: Semiramis Hotel: 200
members—First Impressions," Syria Comment, June 27, 2011, available at www
.joshualandis.com/blog/?p=10504&cp=all, accessed July 16, 2013.

26. The final communiqué in Arabic can be found at www.levantnews.com/index
.php?option=com_content&view=article&id=8088:-q-q&catid=78:civil-society
-releases&Itemid=79, accessed July 16, 2013.

27. The group's statement in Arabic can be found at www.syrianparties.info
/?page_id=1124, accessed July 16, 2013.

28. Mouatana's statement in Arabic on the first anniversary of the Syrian revolution can be found at http://almwatana.net/wathaak/w7.aspx, accessed July 10, 2012.

29. "Statement of the Syrian Local Coordinating Committees," Local Coordination Committees website, April 22, 2011, available at www.lccsyria.org/1103, accessed July 16, 2013.

30. Bureau of Democracy, Human Rights, and Labor, "Human Rights Report
2010: Syria," U.S. Department of State, April 8, 2011, 29, available at www.state
.gov/documents/organization/160478.pdf, accessed July 16, 2013.

31. *Shabeeha* are paramilitary groups who come from poor neighborhoods with
a significant rural-urban migrant sector. The regime bribed them with public sector
jobs and allowed them to rent rooms in illegal housing areas. Although a good proportion of these *shabeeha* came from the Alawite community (the president's community), many others were Muslim Sunnis and Christians.

32. On April 18, 2011, the people of Homs gathered at Clock Square in the
afternoon and staged the first sit-in in Syria since the start of the revolution. Hundreds
of thousands of residents gathered from all over Homs and its suburbs to demand

the regime's ouster and emphasize the unity of the Syrian people. The sit-in continued until the dawn of April 19, coming to an abrupt stop when Assad forces stormed the square to disperse the crowd. Forces opened fire on unarmed, peaceful civilians, killing and injuring many in the process.

33. For example, there is a controversy regarding the killing of the Kurdish anti-government leader Mashaal Tammo, who was assassinated on October 7, 2011. Some believe that the Syrian security forces eliminated Tammo using a faction within the Kurdish Democratic Union Party as a tool. Basel Dayoub, *Man qatala Mishaal Tammo* [Who killed Mishaal Tammo?], 2011, available at http://ishtar-enana. blogspot.com/2011/11/blog-post_04.html, accessed July 16, 2013.

34. Khaled Yacoub Oweis, "Syrian Activist Lawyer Says Non-Violence Key to Success," Reuters, October 10, 2011, available at http://uk.reuters.com/article/2011 /10/10/uk-syria-lawyer-idUKTRE7991V920111010, accessed July 16, 2013.

35. The Supreme Council for the Syrian Revolution sent representatives to the SNC but was not formally a member.

36. Ibid.

37. See the full text on the group's official website at "An Initiative to Stop the Violence and Achieve a Smooth and Safe Transition to Democracy," available at syrianncb.org/2012/08/14/an-initiative-to-stop-the-violence-and-achieve-a-smooth -and-safe-transition-to-democracy/, accessed July 16, 2013.

38. "SNC: The National Coordination Committee Initiative Violates National Consensus, Equates Victim with Murderer," Syrian National Council, August 15, 2012, available at www.syriancouncil.org/en/press-releases/item/779-snc-the-national -coordination-committee-initiative-violates-national-consensus-equates-victim-with -murderer.html, accessed July 16, 2013.

39. Rima Dali, communication with the author, July 16, 2012.

40. The official page of the Civil Enlightenment Movement on Facebook is www .facebook.com/tanwer.madni/info, accessed September 7, 2013.

41. Abbas, "Dynamics of the Uprising in Syria."

42. Bassam Haddad, *Business Networks in Syria: The Political Economy of Authoritarian Resilience* (Stanford, CA: Stanford University Press, 2012).

43. Nabil Sukkar, a former World Bank economist who now heads an economic consulting firm in Damascus, quoted in Reese Erlich, "Christian Science Monitor: Why Businessmen Support Assad in Syria," *Christian Science Monitor*, October 28, 2011, available at http://reeseerlich.com/2012/02/18/christian-science-monitor-why -businessmen-support-assad-in-syria/, accessed July 16, 2013.

44. Basel Audat, "Syria: Business Abandons the Regime," *Al-Ahram Weekly*, June 7–13, 2012.

45. Hussein al Shobakji, "Syria: Assad's Businessmen Have Defected," Alarabiya. net, May 14, 2012.

46. See, for example, Rania Abuzeid, "Just When They Needed It Least: The Syrian Opposition Fractures Again," *Time Magazine,* February 27, 2012; and an interview with Haytham Mannaa at http://syrianncb.org/2012/08/20/, accessed July 16, 2013.

47. The LCC reactivated its membership in the SNC after freezing it due to disagreements, including on the wisdom of armed struggle, and changed its stance to accepting at least the establishment of safe zones.

48. Neil MacFarquhar and Hwaida Saad, "As Syrian War Drags On, Jihadists Take Bigger Role," *New York Times,* July 29, 2012.

CHAPTER 6

Activism in Bahrain

Between Sectarian and Issue Politics

LAURENCE LOUËR

B AHRAIN HAS A rich history of political activism dating back to the beginning of the oil industry in the early 1930s, an activism that is characterized by the recurring resort to street politics. The collective memory of Bahraini activists of all ideological persuasions is thus filled with stories from the great uprisings that have punctuated the country's political life, referred to as *intifadhat* (*intifadha,* in the singular). The longest of these uprisings lasted more than four years, stretching from 1994 to 1999; it helped set the context for the month-long uprising that occurred in 2011. The uprisings that emerged during the first year of the Arab Spring did not come as a surprise; mass demonstrations and riots are tools to which Bahraini activists have resorted throughout history. Yet they were nevertheless a shock to the Bahraini political system, fundamentally altering the relationship between the opposition and the regime.

That is, while the Bahraini 2011 uprising from February 14 to March 18 was triggered by the regional context, it was also deeply rooted in domestic politics. Bahrain had seen escalating tensions between the regime and its opposition since 2002, when King Hamad bin Isa Al Khalifa unilaterally promulgated a new constitution that curtailed the powers of the parliament. Emulating the modus operandi of their Egyptian counterparts, the Bahraini demonstrators camped on the Pearl Roundabout, a strategic location in the capital Manama. The regime's response to the protest alternated between brutal coercion and dialogue. The situation appeared to be heading in the direction of major concessions to the opposition when some 2,500 troops from the Peninsula Shield, the Gulf Cooperation Council's (GCC) joint military force, arrived in Bahrain. This signaled the end of dialogue and the beginning of all-out repression. On March 18, the monument of a pearl at the center of the roundabout was razed. It had become the symbol of the revolt.

The 2011 uprising represented a turning point for Bahraini political activists. It put an end to a period of "liberalized autocracy" in which previously clandestine political movements were allowed to organize legally and compete during elections.[1] The uprising profoundly reshaped the landscape of activism. The regime closed the field of opportunity by clamping down on and imprisoning its most radical opponents, accentuating existing fault lines within the opposition, while the uprising also fostered the emergence of new types of movements. The Shia Islamic movements that have been the main actors of opposition since the 1980s had to deal with the increasing popularity of nonsectarian movements. These movements were more radical in their demands, expecting nothing less than full regime change, while the major Shia Islamic movement–al-Wefaq–had accepted the premise of playing by the rules of the cooptation game. Informal youth movements, with their close ties to the blogosphere and human rights organizations, became a key player. The emergence of new Sunni Islamic movements that used harsh anti-Shia rhetoric further complicated the situation. So did the fragmentation of the regime itself, whose internal balances have been profoundly upset in favor of the hardline factions.

All together, these phenomena broadly reflected the deep fragmentation of the Bahraini political landscape, which made it increasingly difficult to speak about "the regime" and "the opposition" as if they were homogeneous entities and, in particular, as if they were uniquely based on sectarian identities, as conventional readings of Bahraini politics often suggest. For this reason the post-uprising period became highly unpredictable.

Shia Institutions as a Place of Activism

For Bahraini activists, a major challenge has always been to overcome the sectarian divide between Sunnis and Shias. This cleavage has structured the society since the founding of the modern state of Bahrain at the end of the eighteenth century. At that time, the Al Khalifa ruling dynasty, which adheres to the Sunni creed, conquered an overwhelmingly Shia population in Bahrain with the help of a handful of Sunni tribes, appropriating many of the country's riches. This continued to 2011, when an estimated 35 percent of Sunnis in Bahrain dominated the roughly 65 percent of the population that was Shia.[2]

After independence from the British in 1971, the division between the Sunnis and the Shias became increasingly political. Before then, the divide had affected political mobilization only occasionally; for example, during the 1954–56 uprising when protesters created the Supreme Executive Council, a body endowed with the task of presenting their demands to the rulers in which Sunnis and Shias were represented at parity.[3] It is only after independence that sectarian identities became politicized in the form of political movements and that Shia religious institutions became the locus of political activism.

In the early independence period, Bahraini rulers gave in to demands–made since the late 1930s–for an elected assembly with legislative powers. A constituent assembly was elected in 1972, followed by a parliament in 1973. This first parliamentary experiment saw the polarization of the opposition between the progressive bloc and the religious bloc.[4] Inspired by Marxism and Arab nationalism, the former constituted the most important political group in the parliament. The second-largest group, the religious bloc, was made up of Shia Islamic activists from a clandestine cell of the party al-Da'wa al-Islamiyya (the Call to Islam). Based in Iraq, the party aimed at combating the influence of secular ideologies and had as an ideological horizon the establishment of an Islamic state based on the Shia version of Islam. The party was particularly influential in the religious seminaries of the city of Najaf, then the main center of Shia religious learning worldwide, where it recruited and socialized many non-Iraqi students, including a handful of Bahrainis. In Bahrain, al-Da'wa was since its inception intimately tied to segments of the younger rural Shia clerical class, including Sheikh Isa Qasem, one of the founders of al-Da'wa in Bahrain and a member of the 1973 parliament, who emerged as the main high-ranking Shia cleric with a political profile in the 2000s. Al-Da'wa also attracted many young middle-class laypersons from the Shia villages.[5]

The appearance of al-Da'wa in Bahrain was only one manifestation of the impact of the politicization of the Shia centers of religious learning in Iraq, to which the Arab Shia communities were intimately tied through thick transnational clerical networks. Another Shia Islamic movement, which made itself known as the Islamic Front for the Liberation of Bahrain (IFLB) in 1976, emerged from these networks as well, and it came to adopt a more confrontational attitude toward the Bahraini regime. Embedded in the transnational networks woven around Ayatollah Mohammed al-Shirazi from the shrine city of Karbala in Iraq, it was a proponent of the exportation of the Islamic Revolution to Bahrain and was responsible for a failed coup in 1981 that had been supported by segments of the Iranian regime. Unlike al-Da'wa, its first recruits came from the urban areas, mainly the pious merchant nobility as well as young middle-class men. A number of them were from the minority of Iranian Shias who had settled in Bahrain's urban areas around the turn of the twentieth century.[6]

The Shia political field evolved after the early 1980s. Al-Da'wa was disbanded in 1984 and has since ceased to have a formal existence. As for the IFLB, a handful of its members founded a new body named the Islamic Action Society in 2001, which has played a peripheral role since then. A new Shia Islamic movement was created in 2001 in the context of political liberalization, gathering ex-members from al-Da'wa and the IFLB as well as a new generation of Shia Islamic activists: the Islamic Society for National Concord (hereafter al-Wefaq, which means "the Accord").[7] Headed through the present day by Sheikh Ali Salman, it has quickly become the dominant force of the opposition, with nearly half of the forty parliamentary seats in both 2006 and 2008.

There has been much speculation about Bahraini Shia Islamic movements' transnational relations. As compared with the history of al-Da'wa and the IFLB, which reflect the strength and positions of transnational Shia networks, the career of al-Wefaq shows a drift towards domestication and autonomy. Sheikh Ali Salman himself was never a member of al-Da'wa, although he was socialized politically by leading al-Da'wa activists. Like other leading members of al-Wefaq, he built his political standing on his leadership role during the 1990s uprising. That uprising was mainly triggered by socioeconomic hardship and, contrary to the 1981 coup attempt, received no backing from Tehran, which at the time was at the apex of the reconciliation process with the Gulf monarchies.[8]

Because they were all deeply embedded in the Shia population, al-Da'wa, the IFLB, and al-Wefaq did not attract Sunni activists. All could be described as Shia identity movements, promoting a revival of Shia religious identity and expressing deep resentment toward what they saw as the Sunni domination of Bahrain's political institutions and economic resources. Al-Da'wa and the IFLB were chief actors in the diffusion of a Shia nativist narrative, which, drawing on elements of Bahrain's history, presented the Shias as the "original inhabitants" of Bahrain and portrayed the Sunnis as alien invaders.[9] Al-Da'wa and the IFLB hence signaled the polarization along sectarian lines, which divided opposition groups and also separated the ruling dynasty from the opposition.

Issue-Based Activist Coalitions

Although the competition between the progressive and the religious activists has often been bitter, activists within those groups have engaged in a number of coalitions over the years, working together on specific issues and joining forces against the regime. Such issue-based coalitions between Shia Islamic and secular activists–who by 2011 were colloquially referred to as "liberals"– are a recurring feature of the Bahraini political field, signaling the ability of activists from competing ideologies to overcome their differences in order to promote a common political platform focusing on the demand for democratic reforms. Sometimes, joint action took place within the parliament. In 1974, leftists and Shia religious activists formed a coalition to oppose a bill on state security submitted by the Amir Isa bin Salman Al Khalifa that curtailed civil liberties. As a consequence, the Amir decided to disband the parliament in 1975.

Other times, joint action took the form of electoral boycott. On February 14, 2001, the Amir issued a referendum proposing to the Bahraini people the transformation of Bahrain into a constitutional monarchy. The proposed National Action Charter was adopted by just over 98 percent of voters, with a turnout of roughly 95 percent. The country consequently witnessed a period of calm and political revival. Political parties were still banned, but political "societies" were authorized, as were trade unions and various types of civil society associations. An independent newspaper, *al-Wasat* (the Middle), was created by Mansur al-Jamri, a former member of an offshoot of al-Da'wa based in London known as the Islamic Bahrain Freedom Movement. All of this enabled the leftist and Shia Islamic movements from the 1970s to reorganize on a legal basis.

However, the opposition's hopes were short-lived. In February 2002, the king unilaterally promulgated a new constitution, breaking the commitments made in the National Action Charter one year before. Compared to the 1973 constitution, which was voted on by an elected constituent assembly, the 2002 constitution severely curtailed the powers of the parliament, making all its decisions subject to veto by a consultative council appointed by the king in a discretionary manner.

The opposition immediately rejected the new text. In protest, and in a move typical of Bahraini politics, two liberal movements (the National and Democratic Gathering, which would become al-Wa'd in 2006, and the National Action Society) and two Shia Islamic movements (al-Wefaq and the heir of the

IFLB, the Islamic Action Society) jointly boycotted the October 2002 parliamentary elections in an effort to repeal the new constitution.

Importantly, the boycotting groups did not intend to undermine the regime in general. They emphasized that their decision did not mean a rejection of the regime but rather was simply a tactic to bring about the implementation of the reforms announced in the National Action Charter. They also explicitly rejected any resort to violence. In other words, they wanted to be seen as a legal opposition, hence accepting the constraints of the liberalized autocracy to the extent that popular suffrage was respected.

In 2006 the leading opposition force, al-Wefaq, decided to cease boycotting the parliamentary elections and sealed an electoral alliance with the liberal National and Democratic Action Society, known as al-Wa'd (the Promise), the heir of the leftist Popular Front for the Liberation of Bahrain, which was active in the 1960s and 1970s. The aim of the alliance–though not achieved–was to gain the majority of seats in the parliament and, more broadly, to promote democracy.

Issue-driven coalitions also spurred the formation of new political societies. In the 2000s, the Haqq Movement for Liberties and Democracy (hereafter al-Haqq, which means "the Right") emerged when the opposition underwent a profound reshaping after the decision by al-Wefaq and al-Wa'd to end their boycott of the parliamentary elections. A number of prominent activists who disapproved of this shift split off from al-Wefaq and, under the leadership of Hasan Mushaima, founded al-Haqq, which promoted the boycott of the ballot because it believed that participation would only legitimize the regime. Contrary to al-Wefaq and despite the fact that it included many Shias and old Shia Islamic activists, its name bore no allusion to any kind of Islamic identity. The movement instead focused on the establishment of a genuine democracy and, during the 2011 uprising, came out in favor of a republic. Accordingly, it strove with some success to recruit beyond the milieu of Shia Islamic activists, having several Sunnis in its ranks.

Sunni Islamic Activism

In the absence of systematic academic enquiry, we lack many details about Sunni political Islam in Bahrain. It appears that Bahraini students coming back from Cairo University established a cell of the Muslim Brotherhood in the 1940s, in the form of a charitable association named al-Islah (the Reform), which is active to this day.[10] A member of the Al Khalifa dynasty and uncle of the king, Isa bin Mohammed Al Khalifa, reportedly became the president of the association, which is why it was generally considered to have intimate links with the dynasty. Many also suspect that the movement was directly financed by the Royal Court Ministry.[11] The other face of Sunni Islamic activism by 2011 was the Salafi movement, which emerged in the 1980s.[12] They, too, were said to be under the influence of a particular faction of the ruling dynasty, which emerged as a forceful center of power in 2009. This faction was headed by the Royal Court Minister, Khaled bin Ahmed Al Khalifa, and his brother Khalifa bin Ahmed Al Khalifa, the defense minister who has served as commander in chief of the army since 2008.

Both the Muslim Brotherhood and the Salafis have long conducted charitable and educational activities. They first created political societies in 2002 when the parliament was reinstated: respectively, al-Minbar (the Tribune) and al-Asala al-Islamiyya (the Islamic Authenticity). Their presence in the parliament fluctuated from one election to another. Al-Minbar's share of seats has ranged from eight seats out of forty in 2002, when opposition movements boycotted the elections, to only two seats in 2010. It rose to seven seats thanks to the by-election of 2011, which was organized to replace the deputies from al-Wefaq who had stepped down during the uprising to protest repression; the opposition boycotted the by-election. Al-Asala followed roughly the same route, with six seats in 2002, three in 2010, and seven in the 2011 by-election.

That opposition forces generally considered Sunni Islamic groups to be pro-regime forces stemmed from the regime's strategy. The regime attempted to turn the Sunni population into a captive constituency by presenting itself as the best bulwark against a Shia appropriation of the country, which would reduce Sunnis to a marginalized minority. A particularly telling example was the "Bandargate" scandal that erupted in 2006. Saleh al-Bandar, a British national of Sudanese origin who had worked at the Royal Court Affairs Ministry, gave the pro-opposition Bahrain Society for Human Rights a 200-page report describing how, under the supervision of the Royal Court Affairs minister, a secret network was acting in order to reinforce the Sunni population's identification with the regime while keeping the Shias out of the key power sectors.

However, a closer examination reveals that it is difficult to place al-Minbar and al-Asala in one of the two definite categories of "proregime" or "opposition." On the one hand, it does seem that the polarization of the Bahraini political field around sectarian identities pushed them toward the ruling dynasty. On the other hand, their attachment to religious identity made them wary of many government policies. Hence, like the Shia Islamic opposition,

Al-Wa'd campaigners during the 2010 election. A poster of al-Wa'd candidate Munira Fakhro can be seen in the background. Photo by Jasem Redha.

they were vocal against tourism and "business-friendly" policies, which imply a relaxed approach to the sale of alcohol and prostitution. Moreover, in the course of the 2006 legislature, the Muslim Brotherhood and the Salafis made it clear that they were in favor of increasing the parliament's powers and even seemed to be willing to support a set of such proposals submitted by al-Wefaq in 2009.[13] During the 2011 uprising, the presence of at least one Salafi among the protesters gathered on the Pearl Roundabout showed that some Sunni activists are tempted to advance an agenda that does not fully support that of the regime.[14] In other words, there was probably no consensus on a strategy of unquestioned support of the regime.

Al-Wefaq and the New Political Opportunity Structure

Al-Wefaq's conciliatory position towards the regime, bolstered early in its lifetime by its stance towards the National Action Charter in 2001, made it susceptible to cooptation. But a closer look reveals a more complex picture: al-Wefaq's cooptation was also the result of the new political opportunity structure that came out of the political and economic reforms undertaken by the regime in the 2000s, which created internal division within the ruling family.

The enthronement of King Hamad in 1999 and the following political reforms entailed an upsurge of factionalism within the ruling dynasty. In the previous reign, the regime's strongman was the brother of the Amir and prime minister, Khalifa bin Salman Al Khalifa, whom the opposition regards as the main architect of the repression of the 1990s uprising. Succession kept the latter in place, which, at the time of this writing, made him the Arab world's longest-serving prime minister; he has held the position since 1971. Understandably, King Hamad struggled to gain much leeway in front of his powerful uncle.

Relatively compliant toward the political liberalization launched by his nephew, the prime minister was more alarmed at the economic reforms conducted under the supervision of the crown prince Salman bin Hamad Al Khalifa. The king's son Salman had garnered increasing power throughout the 2000s. The crown prince's economic reforms hurt the economic interests of the prime minister, a major stakeholder in Bahrain's economy, taking bribes on most of the big projects and investing heavily in the country's real estate market. The reforms mainly aimed at enhancing the share of the private sector in the economy to diminish the country's dependence on oil but also to provide new job opportunities for the citizens in the context of persistent high unemployment rates among the youth.

Of course, like other rentier states in the Gulf, Bahrain had widely distributed oil revenues to citizens as a way of placating dissent, having established a relationship of dependency with citizens through various forms of social subsidies. A key policy in this context concerned employment. From the 1970s onward, the regime practiced a policy of almost guaranteed public employment for male citizens, especially those who hold degrees. The employment policy is based on the segmentation of the labor market: nationals are mainly employed in the public and semi-private sectors (companies in which the state holds the majority of the capital), while the jobs in the private sector are overwhelmingly occupied by expatriates. This did not prevent the persistence of a particularly lively political activism, but it did lead citizens to have high expectations toward the state's capacity to provide social well-being and, in particular, to provide job opportunities. However, from the 1990s onward, the state became unable to absorb the national population into the public and semi-private sectors due to a number of factors: low oil prices, high population increase, and the saturation of the bureaucracy.

Thus, the labor market reform launched in 2006 aimed to foster the integration of nationals in the private sector by raising the cost of hiring expatriates and improving the nationals' professional training. This reform faced hostility from the business community, which preferred to continue to rely on cheap and compliant expatriate labor rather than employing higher-paid and less submissive nationals.[15] Labor market reform also aggravated divisions within the regime. As a businessman, the prime minister, regarding the increased cost of expatriate labor as harmful, became the main ally of the opponents to reform. Thanks to him, the business community, in which he has extensive patronage networks, succeeded in their efforts to reduce fees on expatriate employees. More broadly, the old guard and the business community were joined in their belief that unemployment is widely overestimated by the opposition, which has used it as a tool to pressure the king.

The labor market reform thus fostered the formation of an unprecedented configuration of political forces in Bahrain. Faced with the opposition of the business community and the prime minister, the king and the crown prince dearly needed al-Wefaq's support, not only to promote labor market reform but, more broadly, to fight the encroachment of the old guard. The struggle over labor market reform within the ruling dynasty modified the political opportunity structure for the opposition, showing that the regime was not monolithic and that siding with the reformist faction of the dynasty against the old guard could be a way to encourage more reforms, whether economic or political. Hence, the inclusion of al-Wefaq in the 2006 parliament following its support of the labor market reform and again in 2010 was a form of cooptation typical of liberalized autocracies. It also signaled the reshaping of the dominant coalition in the context of a major split inside the ruling dynasty.

The 2011 uprising should be understood in this context. As with the other Arab uprisings, the majority of the first demonstrators were not members of the existing opposition groups, be they al-Wefaq or other political societies. The only major figure present the first day was Abdulwahab Hussain–a hero of the 1990s uprising and leader of al-Wafa' (the Loyalty), an offspring of al-Haqq created in 2009 that emphasizes Shia Islamic identity. However, the violent repression of the demonstration pushed the formal opposition to join the demonstrators as a sign of solidarity. This move was natural for al-Haqq, which always had a predilection for street politics, but it was harder

Activism, al-Wefaq Way
JASIM REDHA

Jasim Redha is a member of al-Wefaq.

My experience as an activist has been shaped by the changing political tides in Bahrain and the region more broadly. I was born in 1962—an era of independence in the Gulf—and as I became politically aware in the early 1970s, I was influenced by friends and acquaintances involved in politics and especially student activities. It seemed the Arab world was buzzing with calls for freedom, and Bahrain itself was taking its first steps toward independence and the election of its first parliament.

My turn toward Islamic activism came in the late 1970s, after Khomeini led the successful revolution in Iran, and the Islamic tide started to expand across the region. I joined Islamic groups at the university and was detained for the first time at the age of seventeen. Though interrogated and tortured, I was released a week later. The next time, when I was arrested for participating in the 1981 corrective movement, [the failed coup of 1981 by the Islamic Front for the Liberation of Bahrain.—Ed.] I was not so lucky. I was charged with espionage and served fifteen years.

When I was released in 1996, the world around me had changed once again. The country was bubbling with a struggle for democracy and calls for constitutional changes. Although violence was a prominent feature of the demonstrations at the time, my detention had brought me to appreciate peaceful approaches to demanding political and civil rights. I was still pursuing a democratic civil state and seeking full political rights for the people of Bahrain, but I was also determined to do so peacefully.

It seemed the chance for real change had come in 1999, when His Majesty King Hamad came to the throne after the death of his father. Seeing the chance for real democratization, I helped found Bahrain's largest Islamic society, al-Wefaq National Islamic Society, and I became the first head of the society's public relations office. I joined the municipal councils and became a member of al-Wefaq's high committee for election, proudly contributing to the election committee's best achievement, winning all 36 seats for al-Wefaq candidates both in parliament and municipality in 2006. I worked with many parliamentarian committees, reviewing and amending laws and legislations, and witnessed the evolution of political societies as one of the main pillars for democracy alongside relatively free elections and media.

Some Bahrainis felt that participation would stifle the movement for change—and they went so far as to boycott the first parliamentary elections in 2002. I believed, though, that participation was the best chance for democratization. The decade of 2000–2011 was the golden age for the development of democracy in Bahrain.

This changed dramatically after the demonstrations of February 14, 2011. Inspired by the Arab Spring, they led to an escalation of violence and counter-violence and the constriction of political participation and democratic development. Today, many political societies are working hard to reestablish a role in any foreseen national dialogue. But we are left to react to the situation and see few openings. I am in no better a situation than other activists. My own political involvement today is minimal. I am awaiting a breakthrough and a chance to help reestablish the country's political life.

---

for al-Wefaq, whose strategy of rapprochement with the dynasty's reformist faction was at stake. It also considered the regime's security policy to render pointless any attempt at a revolutionary overthrow per the Tunisian or Egyptian model. Since the 1980s, the regime has endeavored to create a hyper-loyal security apparatus by excluding the Shias from the security forces almost entirely and instead recruiting Sunni nationals and foreign mercenaries.

After it joined the uprising, al-Wefaq signaled its desire to retain the status of "moderate" opposition. Forced to withdraw from parliament to protest the brutal repression and to boycott the September 2011 by-elections for the same reason, it nevertheless strove to maintain its moderate status and to restrain the protesters' demands. Al-Wefaq tried to bring protesters together around the demand for a genuine constitutional monarchy, which would, among other things, imply that the prime minister be appointed from the ranks of the parliamentary majority. In contrast to calls for the fall of the regime, al-Wefaq promoted the slogan "The people want reform of the system." This demand was perfectly in line with its strategy of joining forces with the dynasty's reformists against the old guard. Al-Wefaq's position stood in stark contrast to the calls of many protesters. The state-sponsored violence radicalized many protesters, and they started demanding not just the implementation of the National Action Charter but the fall of the regime. The Coalition for a Bahraini Republic formed around these demands, with Hasan Mushaima, the leader of al-Haqq, announcing in March 2011 its creation by the boycotting societies, namely al-Haqq, al-Wafa', and the Islamic Bahrain Freedom Movement.

On March 14, 2011, when the troops of the Peninsula Shield arrived in Bahrain to help the local security forces put an end to the uprising, all signs suggested that the regime's young guard and al-Wefaq were willing to continue with the coalition created in 2006 as a way out of the crisis. What was less evident was the game played behind the scenes by the old guard. They were the obvious beneficiaries of the foreign intervention: The dialogue between al-Wefaq and the crown prince was broken, the leaders of the prorepublic societies were jailed and henceforth condemned to life sentences, while thousands of the protesters and medics who treated the injured among them were arrested and condemned during hasty trials.

Al-Wefaq was the only political society to be spared from repression: It was not banned and none of its leaders have been arrested. Rather, al-Wefaq continued to pursue the cooperation strategy, as it worked with regime reformists, agreed to participate in a dialogue with the crown prince, and, in October 2011, released the "Manama Document," which reiterated a reformist approach to the process, in conjunction with al-Wa'd and three other minor liberal groups. This was, however, a mixed blessing for the movement: It confirmed that the regime considers al-Wefaq its main interlocutor within the opposition and made it the object of suspicion from the societies that have paid a high price for their participation in the uprising.

The Limits of Informal Activism

The above discussion shows that the formal opposition in Bahrain until 2011 was broadly divided into three segments: first, al-Wefaq, which became coopted by the regime; second, other political societies like al-Haqq, which engaged in street politics periodically and boycotted elections in protest of the regime; and third, Sunni Islamic groups, which the regime allowed to operate on the basis of sectarian loyalty and hence were not viewed as a threat to the ruling family. However, other forms of opposition to the regime existed before the uprising, mainly within civil society and through youth activists.

Before the uprising, the Bahrain Center for Human Rights (BCHR) was the main civil society pressure group opposing the regime on a nonpartisan and nonsectarian basis. The group was created in 2002 in the context of the political liberalization process. Gathering former secular and religious activists, it quickly gained recognition as the main trustworthy human rights organization in Bahrain by international human rights NGOs (most notably Human Rights Watch and the International Federation for Human Rights) in which BCHR's president, Nabil Rajab, held positions. From its inception, the regime saw BCHR as a component of the opposition and treated it accordingly, harassing its leading members, who suffered numerous arrests. In 2004, the regime revoked BCHR's authorization to exist as a legally recognized association, but the group managed to continue to operate.

The 2011 uprising put BCHR under the spotlight. It became a major source of information on the events, and some of its members became for this reason internationally known figures, notably Abdulhadi al-Khawaja, who was arrested in the aftermath of the uprising and condemned to life imprisonment together with al-Haqq and al-Wafa' activists. While the organization had no official political position, it was leaning toward al-Haqq and the other prorepublic societies that prioritized boycotts.

Youth activism was the driving force of the 2011 uprising. It was primarily embodied by the February 14 Coalition. Typical of a new type of informal issue-based movements that have emerged in the context of the Arab Spring, this movement consisted of a loose network of activists and insisted on its goal to set aside sectarian identities and create a "democratic current." Its members were mainly people not previously engaged in the established opposition movements who indeed resent them for having been unable to achieve anything tangible. However, many of the movement's members were previously active online, in internet forums that have flourished since the late 1990s. These were the main places to express controversial political views, including direct attacks on the king, which the law banned in officially licensed media.[16]

The forums also played an important role in organizing demonstrations, be they spontaneous–for example, to protest the arrest of this or that person–or formally organized by political societies.[17] The most influential forum was the bahrainonline.org forum, which has been active since 1998 and whose founder, Ali Abdul Imam, has been arrested several times for "spreading false information." In 2011, a few days before the uprising, he went into hiding after his umpteenth arrest. Relying extensively on internet social platforms and social networks to spread information and organize its activities, the February 14 Coalition was voluntarily decentralized and, in order to protect itself from repression, claimed no identified leaders.

The name of the coalition itself reveals its approach to politics, since it derives from a founding event, that of the first demonstration of the 2011 uprising. One should add that February 14 was chosen as the day for the first demonstration organized within the framework of the Arab Spring because it came exactly ten years after the vote of the National Action Charter. In the eyes of the 2011 demonstrators, the Charter is Bahrain's only legitimate political contract, along with the 1973 constitution, since only those two texts have ever been submitted to a popular vote. At the inception of the uprising, it does seem that the activists of what subsequently crystallized as the February 14 Coalition were merely taking on the objective of the pro-boycott societies to

Activism Challenges in Bahrain
MARYAM AL-KHAWAJA

Maryam Al-Khawaja is the deputy director of the Gulf Center for Human Rights and acting president of the Bahrain Center for Human Rights.

To be a human rights defender or a member of the opposition in Bahrain means that there is a very good chance that you are in prison. Several members of my family have been imprisoned for exercising their right to freedom of expression in peaceful opposition to the authoritarian regime—my sister has faced thirteen politically motivated cases against her in court and my father is serving a life sentence.

But political opposition in Bahrain is nothing new. Every decade since the 1920s has seen a protest movement. The response of the authorities has varied to some degree, but the methods of quelling the political dissent have repeated themselves in alarming detail.

At present Bahrain remains a strong ally of the West, and much of the struggle we face as human rights defenders is to convince the international community to act in consideration of the people of Bahrain and not merely in accordance to Western geopolitical interests. Much of my contribution to the struggle for human

Maryam al-Khawaja. Photo by Lina Khatib. Used with permission.

rights is centered on international advocacy and meeting with people who can influence the current situation, as I would face certain arrest and imprisonment upon my return to Bahrain. A large part of my advocacy is aimed at rebutting the notion that a sectarian divide is the defining characteristic or motivation of the opposition movement, as it is often portrayed in Western media outlets.

The attacks that activists face within Bahrain come in many different forms. Activists can expect judicial harassment from a system that is not independent or fair. Torture is commonly practiced and never seriously investigated; several people have died while in police custody. Dozens more have died on the streets as a result of the brutal police tactics unleashed upon peaceful, prodemocracy demonstrations—in 2011, at least nine of the people who died in this manner were minors under the age of eighteen. Injured activists who seek medical attention in hospitals are typically arrested from their hospital beds, brutalized, forced to sign confessions, and imprisoned.

The regime has demonstrated a unique ability to appease the international community with promises of reform, while continuing—and at times intensifying—its attacks on the political opposition. Although we have seen some signs that the international community's patience is running thin with the regime, it is yet to be seen if any concrete steps will be taken to stop the widespread practice of human rights violations.

---

have the 2002 constitution repealed and the Charter implemented, that is, to transform the system into a constitutional monarchy. As happened with al-Haqq, however, the movement radicalized over the course of the events; in February 2012 it released a document, the "Pearl Charter," in which it unambiguously demanded that the Al Khalifa dynasty be ousted from power and that the people be democratically consulted on the political regime they want. Having a predilection for street politics, the February 14 Coalition also became increasingly violent in the aftermath of the uprising, engaging regularly in confrontation with the police during illegal demonstrations.[18]

Some have considered the February 14 Coalition as the main political actor of the post-uprising period.[19] It would exceed al-Wefaq in influence and popularity because al-Wefaq's moderation in face of the repression alienated it from popular support. The relations between the Coalition and al-Wefaq have been tense, with the Coalition accusing al-Wefaq of being too moderate and lionizing the imprisoned leaders of the republican societies al-Haqq and al-Wafa'.[20] But the February 14 Coalition suffered from the recurrent problem of informal opposition: Its resentment toward traditional political formalization and negotiation made it liable to splits and incoherence. Hence, the coalition did not always speak with one voice, and several subgroups exhibiting local identities sometimes acted autonomously. These characteristics also made it difficult for the movement to shift to political negotiation, given that it would need a leadership capable of deciding controversial issues and assuring the group's compliance with any agreement.

Activism after the 2011 Uprising

The uprising resulted in restricting the political opportunity structure for the opposition. Contrary to Tunisia and Egypt, where popular protests led to expanding opportunities for activists and fostered democratic reforms, in Bahrain the institutions of the liberalized autocracy were emptied of their substance, and participation was restricted. The parliament ceased to be a place of dialogue for the opposition and the government and thus no longer offered a legal outlet to protest. With the leaders of all the other established political societies in prison and with the February 14 Coalition committed to "the revolutionary path until victory," al-Wefaq by 2012 remained the only major opposition movement that would engage with the regime.[21] However, its fate was highly dependent on that of the reformists inside the dynasty who, in the immediate aftermath of the uprising, were outflanked by the hardliners.

The 2011 uprising also reshaped the landscape of Sunni activism. New Sunni Islamic movements emerged after the mobilization of hitherto rather marginal political actors gathered around a handful of Sunni clerics trained in al-Azhar religious seminaries in Egypt and members of a religious society created at the end of the 1970s and named the Islamic Society. In the 1990s, the chairman of the society, Sheikh Abdullatif al-Mahmoud, participated in a petition demanding the reinstatement of the parliament, which cost him his job as professor of Islamic studies at the University of Bahrain. In early February of 2011, when calls for the rally of February 14 spread throughout the internet, al-Mahmoud began seeking to unite a group of Sunni public figures, including members of the Muslim Brotherhood and Salafis, to decide what kind of action should be undertaken.[22] On February 21, 2011, he initiated a rally at the al-Fateh Sunni mosque in Manama, where he condemned the Pearl Roundabout protesters. For this reason, the rally was seen by many as a progovernment gathering.

At first glance, the National Unity Gathering (NUG) seemed perfect for the role of mobilizing the Sunni population in support of the regime, but in the event, it was not. Indeed, Sheikh 'Abd al-Latif al-Mahmoud was not in favor of the status quo ante and defined his movement as a "national opposition" in contrast with the sectarian rationale he detected in the Pearl Roundabout protesters.[23] Hence, while he espoused part of the regime's language against the Shia Islamic activists, stigmatizing them for their anti-Sunni tendencies and subservience to Iran, he also favored increased legislative powers for the parliament, a position in line with his previous engagements. Moreover, he sought a voice for Sunnis in negotiations to solve the crisis, hence refusing to be spectator in a dialogue between the regime and the opposition. This largely reflected a growing trend within the Sunni population, that the regime's policy of coopting al-Wefaq had led the government to endorse policies favoring the Shias to the detriment of the Sunnis. The labor market reform was clearly seen in this light, as was the crown prince's program of scholarship to study abroad; both were seen as having been hijacked by the Shias.

Toward the end of 2011, various subgroups within the NUG began to have significant disagreements, which had the effect of weakening the credibility of the movement as an umbrella for the various Sunni movements. Unable to secure positions in the movement's Central Committee, the Muslim Brotherhood and Salafis split off and began to criticize al-Mahmoud openly for attempting to marginalize them. For his part, al-Mahmoud underlined that they were afraid that the NUG would tilt too harshly against the government and in particular against the prime minister. In a controversial interview to *The Washington Times*, Abdul Latif al-Mahmoud expressed the view that the prime minister should consider stepping down.

The dispute between al-Mahmoud and his Muslim Brotherhood and Salafi associates led to the breakup of NUG, giving birth to Sahwat al-Fatih (al-Fatih Awakening). A Sunni youth movement, Sahwat al-Fatih was initiated by a group of young members of the Muslim Brotherhood who built on the growing discontent in the Sunni population at the way the government was dealing with the opposition.[24] Using rhetoric strikingly similar to that of the February 14 Coalition, al-Fatih Awakening affirmed its rejection of established political entities, showing that wariness toward the old political frameworks cuts across sectarian lines. It organized a rally every Friday evening in which the speeches were uncompromising.

Al-Wefaq was a major target for the movement. This was largely because one of al-Fatih Awakening's main objectives was to prevent any government concession to the Shia opposition, urging the government instead to reward its true supporters among the Sunni population. This showed that some Sunni

February 4, 2011: In solidarity with Egypt, several hundred people gather outside the Egyptian embassy in Manama. Ibrahim Sharif, secretary general of the National Democratic Action Society, calls for local reform.

February 14, 2011: Despite cash payouts from the ruling family to assuage citizens, "day of rage" protesters gather to call for constitutional, political, and socioeconomic reforms. Protesters clash with police forces, leaving several dead and injured in Nuwaidrat, Sitra, and Manama. That evening, police fatally shoot twenty-one-year-old Ali Mushaima.

February 15, 2011: Police open fire on the more than ten thousand people attending Ali Mushaima's funeral, killing Fadhel Al-Matrook and injuring twenty-five others. Protesters march from the funeral to the Pearl Roundabout in Manama, reaching ten thousand by sundown. King Hamad goes on national TV and expresses sorrow for the two deaths. Former defense force officer Mohammed al-Buflasa addresses protesters at the Pearl Roundabout, calling for national unity between Sunnis and Shias. He is detained by government forces after his speech but is not reported to be in their custody until March 4.

February 17, 2011: An early raid on the 1,500 camped-out protesters in Pearl Roundabout by five hundred policemen leaves three dead, two hundred injured, and thirty-one missing. By late after-noon, nearly four thousand protesters gather outside Salmaniya Hospital.

February 18, 2011: Clashes between security forces and protesters carry on into the night, leaving 230 injured and at least five people dead. The United States, whose fifth naval fleet is stationed in Bahrain, expresses "strong displeasure" at the regime's handling of the situation.

February 19, 2011: As police withdraw from the Pearl Roundabout, protesters return to set up camp.

February 21, 2011: Progovernment supporters gather outside al-Fateh Mosque to show their support for the royal family. Crown Prince Salman bin Hamad Al Khalifa calls off the Formula One opening race.

February 22, 2011: Tens of thousands join an antigovernment rally in Manama, demanding the release of prisoners, the resignation of the government, and radical political reforms. Opposition leader in exile Hassan Mushaima, on trial in absentia for his connection to an alleged coup plot, begins talks of returning to Bahrain.

February 23, 2011: King Hamad orders the release of 308 political prisoners.

February 25, 2011: Tens of thousands gather in Manama on the day of mourning for the seven people killed since the clashes began on February 14.

February 26, 2011: Opposition leader Hassan Mushaima returns to Bahrain. King Hamad attempts to appease protesters by dismissing several ministers and canceling 25 percent of housing loans.

February 27, 2011: In solidarity with the protesters, eighteen opposition members of the al-Wefaq Shia bloc submit their resignation.

February 28, 2011: Antigovernment protesters, many of whom are from the February 14 Youth Movement, block the entrance of the National Assembly building.

March 1, 2011: Tens of thousands gather at the National Unity Rally, a protest organized by seven of the main opposition groups.

March 2, 2011: Antigovernment protesters continue to occupy the Pearl Roundabout, while progovernment protesters gather at al-Fateh mosque.

March 3, 2011: Police intervene in a sectarian clash between Sunnis and Shias in Hamad Town.

March 4, 2011: Six opposition groups officially place their demands to the government, calling for the abolition of the 2002 constitution and the election of a constitutional assembly.

March 8, 2011: Three Shia groups form the Coalition for a Bahraini Republic aimed at toppling the monarchy and establishing a republic.

March 9, 2011: Thousands of Shias march to the immigration office demanding that the Sunni majority government stop granting citizenship to Sunnis from other countries.

March 10, 2011: Clashes break out between naturalized Sunni parents and native Bahraini Shia parents at a school in Saar. In Isa Town, protesters call for the resignation of the minister of education.

March 13, 2011: Riot police clash with antigovernment protesters at Pearl Roundabout, leaving 200 injured.

March 14, 2011: At the request of the Bahraini government, the Gulf Co-operation Council sends in a six-nation regional force to secure key facilities. The same day that GCC troops entered the country is one of the last days of open protest at the Pearl Roundabout.

March 15, 2011: King Hamad declares a three-month state of emergency as clashes continue throughout the country.

March 16, 2011: A twelve-hour curfew is enacted after security forces clash with protesters leaving six dead and hundreds wounded. Several major opposition leaders and physicians are detained.

March 18, 2011: The hub of Pearl Roundabout is destroyed. It will later be renamed Farouq Junction, a controversial reference to Umar ibn al-Khattab, the second caliph who is perceived as having been uncompromising to the Shias.

March 20, 2011: Opposition groups call for the removal of troops from the streets before they will engage in negotiations with the government.

March 25, 2011: Internet-organized protests erupt in nine sites throughout Bahrain.

March 29, 2011: Eleven of the eighteen remaining MPs of al-Wefaq resign.

March 30, 2011: Police arrest blogger Mahmood al-Yousif at his home.

April 3, 2011: The government shuts down independent newspaper *al-Wasat*.

April 9, 2011: Prominent human rights activist Abdulhadi al-Khawaja is arrested. He is later given a life sentence.

April 11, 2011: Prominent human rights activist Nabeel Rajab is accused of faking pictures of beatings.

April 13, 2011: The University of Bahrain suspends operations in Sakhir and Issa Town amid mass student protests.

April 15, 2011: Shia businessman Karim Fakhrawi becomes the fourth man to die in government custody. The Ministry of Justice holds off on banning al-Wefaq and the Islamic Action Society.

April 21, 2011: Medical staff nationwide report systematic abuses and threats by Bahraini military forces.

April 28, 2011: In the first time since 1996, four Bahrainis are given the death sentence for their role in killing two police officers on March 16. The remaining three protesters are sentenced to life in prison.

May 11, 2011: Bahrain's oil company fires three hundred workers for their involvement in antigovernment protests.

May 21, 2011: Unknown assailants attack activist Nabeel Rajab's house.

May 22, 2011: The National Safety Court of Appeal overturns two death penalty decisions for the protesters charged for killing two police officers.

May 23, 2011: Activist Nabeel Rajab claims that government forces have taken his uncle and are torturing him due to his relation to Rajab.

May 31, 2011: The military prosecutor summons major opposition leaders and interrogates them for their role in the uprisings.

June 6, 2011: In a sign of continued pursuit of the opposition, the government puts forty-seven medical personnel on trial for treating antigovernment protesters.

June 11, 2011: At least four thousand attend the "Homeland for All" rally in Saar.

June 12, 2011: Ayat al-Gormezi is sentenced to a year in prison for reading a poem at a prodemocracy rally.

June 22, 2011: Twenty-one civilian activists are given lengthy sentences by Bahrain's special military court.

July 13, 2011: Ayat al-Gormezi returns home a national hero.

August 28, 2011: King Hamad pardons some protesters, including al-Gormezi, for their "abuse" of Bahraini officials.

August 30, 2011: More than one hundred jailed activists begin a hunger strike.

August 31, 2011: In Sitra, a fourteen-year-old-boy is killed in clashes between antigovernment protesters and security forces.

September 1, 2011: Thousands demonstrate in Sitra at the funeral of the fourteen-year-old boy killed in the attack of the previous day.

September 23, 2011: Protests throughout the country turn violent as dozens are injured.

September 25, 2011: In an election with low voter turnout, two more women join the lower house of the Bahraini parliament.

September 29, 2011: Twenty medical professionals are jailed for their role in the Bahraini uprisings.

October 6, 2011: Seventeen-year-old Ahmed Jaber is killed during clashes between antigovernment supporters and security forces in Abu Saiba.

October 7, 2011: Security forces open fire on the ten thousand protesters attending Jaber's funeral, wounding eleven.

October 11, 2011: The Bahrain High Criminal Court fines the editors of four independent newspapers 1000 dinars (about US$2,500) for publishing "fake" stories.

October 13, 2011: An opposition coalition headed by al-Wefaq publishes the Manama Document calling for dialogue and political reform.

November 23, 2011: The Bahrain Independent Commission of Inquiry releases a report confirming that the government used torture and excessive forms of violence in the uprising earlier in the year.

December 15, 2011: Zainab al-Khawaja, daughter of prominent dissident Abdulhadi al-Khawaja, is arrested in a peaceful protest in Manama.

December 23, 2011: Security forces attack al-Wefaq headquarters in Manama.

December 31, 2011: During New Year's Eve protests in Sitra, fifteen-year-old Sayed Hashim Saeed is killed at close range by the police.

activists were becoming increasingly aware that in this time of crisis they held bargaining power with the regime that they could use to position themselves as third players somewhere between the regime and the various components of the opposition. Beyond that, the details of their program are rather elusive.

International Influence

Finally, it is important to consider how international forces influenced Bahraini activism and its outcomes. More particularly, a clear understanding of the changing nature of Bahraini activism requires recognizing how Bahrainis maneuvered within the context of strong competing international forces.

There is evidence that Saudi Arabia supported both the old and new Sunni Islamic movements. The increased Saudi leverage in Bahraini domestic politics was another direct result of the uprising, constraining both the regime–in particular the reformist faction—and the opposition's room for maneuver. The old tutelary power in Bahrain, Saudi Arabia was alarmed at the developments fostered by the Arab uprisings and steadfastly decided to do everything in its power to make sure that the revolutionary fever would not reach its territory. It is in this perspective that it instigated the Peninsula Shield intervention in Bahrain and chose to support the regime's hardliners against the reformists.

The Saudi influence was partially counterbalanced by that of the United States. As the other major foreign player in Bahrain, having maintained a military presence in the country since 1950 and the headquarters of its Fifth Fleet there since 1995, the United States took a less hardline position during the uprising. This explains why it became the object of fierce criticism in the ranks of the regime's hardliners supported by Saudi Arabia, especially the inner circles of the royal court minister and his brother, the defense minister and army's commander in chief. The commander in chief himself openly accused the United States of being part of a foreign plot to destabilize Bahrain. These accusations, though far-fetched, revealed a widely shared perception among the Sunni population that the United States had failed to support the Bahraini ruling dynasty at a time when its very survival was at stake in front of a Shia crowd motivated by anti-Sunni hatred and acting on Iran's behalf.

In reality, the American position was to support a negotiated solution between the regime and the opposition. Washington did not support the opposition as such but rather the forces of dialogue and reform, namely al-Wefaq and the dynasty's reformist faction. When the hardliners and the Saudis decided to put an end to the negotiations with the reformists, the United States was caught in between its conviction that a measure of reform was to be implemented for the sake of stability and its equal conviction that its alliance with Saudi Arabia was vital. The U.S. administration ultimately chose its camp in the regime's ongoing factional struggle, notably striving to empower the crown prince by having President Barack Obama receive him several times in Washington.[25]

But what of Iran? Iran had ceased sponsoring revolutionary activities in Bahrain and the Gulf monarchies overall years earlier, seeking instead to maintain a modus vivendi with them. Contrary to the thesis that holds sway in GCC ruling circles, the 2011 uprising was not triggered by Iran, and while Tehran retained networks of influence in Bahrain, they were outmatched by the Saudi and American ones. Al-Wefaq was in no way another Hezbollah in the Iranian orbit; when the Iranian Ministry of Foreign Affairs released a communiqué disapproving of the Peninsula Shield intervention, Sheikh Ali Salman was quick to demand publicly that Iran not meddle in Bahrain's internal affairs,

knowing that any Iranian support of the protesters would go against the interest of the entire opposition by adding weight to the regime's propaganda that
the uprising had been initiated by Iran.

In short, while it is important to recognize the role that Iran, Saudi Arabia,
and the United States play in Bahrain, it is equally important not to see regime-
opposition relations as being determined from abroad. Just as in Syria, it was
the combination of domestic and international forces that drove events (see
chapter 5). Within the constraints of the international forces, Bahraini domestic political forces maintained their own agency.

Bahraini Activism: Changes after the 2011 Uprising

The 2011 uprising reshaped Bahraini activism. It altered the political playing
field, weakening institutions that had previously served as venues of opposition-
regime engagement, exacerbated the internal divisions among the Al Khalifa,
and led to the repression of formal political opposition groups. Altering the
political playing field in this way has strengthened the more acephalous groups
that embrace the agenda of radical change while weakening more traditional
opposition parties. This leads to distinct challenges for activists engaged in the
struggle for political reform.

The main challenge for activists after the Arab uprisings was not the survival of the newly mobilized, more radical groups but rather their ability
to engage with the regime. This would require first and foremost to have a real
interlocutor within the regime capable of delivering reform. The Al Khalifa's
internal divides, which were exacerbated during the uprising, has remained
problematic in this regard. International players can influence these—indeed,
Saudi pressure played a decisive role in upsetting the balance between the reformists and the hardliners in 2011, and Western support has in turn been
important in allowing the reformists to retain some leeway—but ultimately the
emergence of interlocutors within the regime capable of credibly committing
to reform would depend on the intricacies of domestic politics.

Indeed, the emergence of new Sunni Islamic movements demonstrated the
deep discontent among much of the Sunni population at the regime's cooptation policy with al-Wefaq throughout the 2000s, which was perceived as favoring the Shias. These new movements were not entirely autonomous from the
regime, but the Sunni activists did coalesce into a third actor in the political
landscape. The presence of these groups made a return to the status quo
ante virtually impossible. Because the Sunni opposition believed that its

empowerment depended on the weakening of al-Wefaq, it was willing to fight any return of al-Wefaq in institutional politics.

Finally, the uprising also altered activism among the predominantly Shia opposition in important ways. The opposition's internal divides were deepened, but far from being stifled, opposition activism managed to survive repression and remained vivid. This was particularly true of the groups that embraced a radical agenda of regime change. With the leaders of the formal republican societies serving life sentences, the informal opposition took the lead in organizing the demand for regime change. This apparently leaderless opposition somehow became a functional substitute for the formal radical opposition, to the point that some speculated that al-Haqq's Hasan Mushaima was the leader of the February 14 Coalition.

Thus, the 2011 uprising has significantly reshaped not only the playing field and nature of activism in Bahrain but also the potential for negotiations and reform in the country. The uprising was not unprecedented; indeed, unlike many other countries in the region, Bahrain had a long history punctuated by *intifadhat*. However, it was unparalleled. Never before had an uprising so fundamentally altered the Bahraini political landscape. The effects will be felt for decades to come.

Notes

1. Following the concept put forward in Daniel Brumberg, "The Trap of Liberalized Autocracy," *Journal of Democracy* 13(4) (2002): 56–68.

2. In 2009, the Pew Research Center did a survey of the world Muslim population and estimated the Shia population in Bahrain to be between 65% and 75%. Pew Research Center, "Mapping the Global Muslim Population: A Report on the Size and Distribution on the World's Muslim Population," October 2009, available at http://pewresearch.org/pubs/1370/mapping-size-distribution-worlds-muslim-population, accessed September 9, 2011. Since then, due to the naturalization of numerous foreign Sunnis as part of an attempt at rebalancing Bahrain's sectarian demography, there is a tendency in Bahrain to estimate that the Sunnis represent 40% and the Shias 60%. In the absence of a census that takes into account sectarian belongings and the politicization of the demographics, there is no way to ascertain those figures precisely.

3. Fuad I. Khuri, *Tribe and State in Bahrain: The Transformation of Social and Political Authority in an Arab State* (Chicago: University of Chicago Press, 1980).

4. Emile A. Nakhleh, *Bahrain: Political Development in a Modernizing Society* (Lexington, MA: Lexington Books, 1980); Mohammed Ghanim Rumaihi, *Bah-*

rain: Social and Political Change since the First World War (London: Bowker, 1976).

5. Laurence Louër, *Transnational Shia Politics: Religious and Political Networks in the Gulf* (New York: Columbia University Press, 2008), 104–111.

6. Ibid., 126–129.

7. Several members of the IFLB joined al-Wefaq, the most noteworthy being Murtadha Badr, who became mayor of Manama in 2002. However, the IFLB wanted to exist independently and created the Islamic Action Society in this perspective.

8. Louër, *Transnational Shia Politics,* 238–239.

9. Ibid., 23–30.

10. This was explained in an article of the Bahraini daily *al-Watan* (the Nation) published in 2005 as part of a series of articles on the history of political Islam in Bahrain. See Mohammed al-Banki, "The Story of Political Islam in Bahrain 10" (in Arabic), *al-Watan* (Bahrain), December 30, 2005.

11. Not to be confused with the Royal Court Affairs Ministry, a distinct entity. See International Crisis Group, "Popular Protest in North Africa and the Middle East (III): The Bahrain Revolt," *Middle East/North Africa Report* 105 (2011): 12.

12. Ibid., 13.

13. Mansoor al-Jamri, "Are Constitutional Amendments Possible in Bahrain?" *Arab Reform Bulletin,* Carnegie Endowment for International Peace, 2009, available at www.carnegieendowment.org/2009/04/02/are-constitutional-amendments -possible-in-bahrain/1yxk, accessed July 17, 2013.

14. Justin Gengler, "Bahrain's Sunni Awakening," *Middle East Research and Information Project,* 2012, available at www.merip.org/mero/mero011712, accessed July 17, 2013.

15. Laurence Louër, "The Political Impact of Labor Migration in Bahrain," *City and Society* 20(1) (2008): 32–53; Laurence Louër, "The Politics of Employment Policy Reform in the Gulf States," *Les Etudes du CERI,* no. 185, April 2012, available at www.sciencespo.fr/ceri/en/content/politics-employment-policy-reform-gulf-state, accessed August 5, 2013.

16. Luke Schleusener, "From Blog to Street: The Bahraini Public Sphere in Transition," *Arab Media and Society* 1(1) (2007): 5, available at www.arabmediasociety .com/?article=15, accessed July 17, 2013.

17. Ibid.

18. Jane Kinninmont, *Bahrain: Beyond the Impasse,* Chatham House, June 2012, p. 7, available at www.chathamhouse.org/publications/papers/view/183983, accessed July 17, 2013.

19. Toby C. Jones and Ala'a Shehabi, "Bahrain's Revolutionaries," *Foreign Policy,* January 2, 2011, available at http://mideast.foreignpolicy.com/posts/2012/01/02 /bahrains_revolutionaries, accessed July 17, 2013.

20. Kinninmont, *Bahrain*, 7.

21. As stated in the conclusion of the Lulu Charter.

22. Hasan Tariq Alhasan, "On-Air, Online, and on the Street: Understanding Bahrain's 2011 Counter-Revolution," unpublished paper, presented at the Gulf Research Center annual meeting, Cambridge, U.K., July 11–14, 2012, p. 15.

23. Ibid., p. 20. The author calls the NUG a "soft opposition."

24. Ibid., p. 18.

25. Josh Rogin, "Obama Administration Seeks to Bolster Bahraini Crown Prince with Arms Sales," *The Cable* blog, *Foreign Policy,* May 11, 2012, available at http://thecable.foreignpolicy.com/posts/2012/05/11/obama_administration_seeks_to_bolster_bahraini_crown_prince_with_arms_sales, accessed July 17, 2013.

CHAPTER 7

Morocco's Makhzen and the Haphazard Activists

AHMED BENCHEMSI

O N FEBRUARY 20, 2011, one month after Zine El Abidine Ben Ali fled Tunisia and eleven days after Hosni Mubarak stepped down from Egypt's presidency, crowds of protesters flooded the streets of Morocco to demand democratic change. The Minister of Interior said thirty-seven thousand were involved, whereas the organizers claimed a turnout of three hundred thousand. Yet both parties agreed on the number of towns—fifty-three, mostly urban—where protests were held. Never since the kingdom's independence had so many demonstrations been held simultaneously. That the government readily admitted the number says a lot about its state of dismay at that moment.

Two weeks later, King Mohammed VI responded to the pressure by announcing dramatic reform to the Constitution in order to implement "authentic democracy and wise governance [based on] the principle of accountability for those in charge."[1] The quick succession of events took everyone by surprise. What happened in such a short time that enabled a protest movement led by young activists bursting seemingly out of nowhere to generate a mobilization so immense that the mighty monarchy had to comply? Was it a "spontaneous generation" triggered by the ripple effect of the Arab Spring, or had the dynamics of Morocco's "new" activism been building quietly for years? If so, how did that happen? What was the role of traditional political actors, and

February 15, 2011: The government announces a 15-billion-dirham (US$1.8 billion) increase in the government subsidy fund to offset regional unrest and to ease price hikes for staples.

February 20, 2011: According to the Ministry of the Interior, thirty-seven thousand protesters in fifty-seven towns across Morocco call for a new Constitution and diminished powers for King Mohammed VI. Protesters estimate that over three hundred thousand people attended the countrywide protests.

February 21, 2011: King Mohammed VI announces the creation of the Social and Economic Council.

March 9, 2011: For the first time in fifteen years, King Mohammed VI announces a far-reaching revision to Morocco's constitution.

March 13, 2011: Security forces bar about two hundred activists from the February 20 movement from staging a protest in Casablanca.

March 20, 2011: Tens of thousands of Moroccans stage protests throughout the country demanding better civil rights and an end to corruption.

April 14, 2011: King Mohammed VI pardons or lessens the sentence of 190 prisoners.

April 24, 2011: Despite attempts by King Mohammed VI to assuage Moroccans, tens of thousands peacefully protest demanding more regime changes.

April 28, 2011: At least sixteen die and twenty are injured in a bombing in a tourist café in Marrakech. Al-Qaeda in the Islamic Maghreb denies involvement in the bombing.

May 1, 2011: Thousands of people protest throughout Morocco denouncing the latest attack and demanding a transition toward democracy.

May 8, 2011: Protests continue throughout the country condemning the attack and demanding reforms.

May 15, 2011: Several people are injured as Moroccan security forces disperse prodemocracy protesters in Rabat.

May 22, 2011: Police violently stop protesters from challenging a ban on demonstrations throughout the country.

May 29, 2011: Twenty-nine people are wounded in proreform demonstrations in Casablanca.

June 5, 2011: Thousands of protesters gather in Rabat for a peaceful prodemocracy rally in which they express their anger at the death of February 20 movement's member Kamal Amari, who was beaten to death in the May 29 protest.

June 17, 2011: King Mohammed VI proclaims constitutional reforms, calls for a "yes" vote in a referendum to be held on July 1.

June 18, 2011: The February 20 Movement rejects the constitutional reforms and calls for nationwide protests. Clashes break out between progovernment and prodemocracy protesters.

July 1, 2011: The Ministry of Interior claims that 73 percent of registered voters turned out to vote and that 98.4 percent voted in favor of the new constitutional reforms that will allegedly lessen the king's power and increase governmental power. Fraud reports emerge in several locations (open ballot boxes, unregistered voters, and so on). The February 20 movement denounces the 98 percent figure as "grotesque, à la Ben Ali."

July 3, 10, and 17, 2011: Despite recent reforms, thousands of prodemocracy activists take to the streets throughout Morocco to demand more reforms. However, compared to the protests on February 20, March 20, and April 24, the attendance is noticeably lower.

July 30, 2011: King Mohammed VI addresses his population for the first time since the July 1 referendum calling for parliamentary elections.

September 18, 2011: Three thousand people in Casablanca and two thousand protesters in Tangiers take to the streets in an attempt to revitalize prodemocracy protests.

November 25, 2011: Forty-five percent of Moroccans turn out to vote in the first parliamentary election since new constitutional reforms were enacted. The Islamist Justice and Development Party (PJD) wins 107 seats in the 395-seat assembly.

November 29, 2011: Abdelilah Benkirane of the Justice and Development Party is named prime minister of Morocco.

how did it combine with that of the new activists? These are the main questions that will be addressed in this chapter.

From the Palace to the Outskirts

On January 2011, right before the protests began, four major political actors populated the political landscape in Morocco: the monarchy, political parties, civil society organizations, and Islamist groups[2]—with the first actor having a clear edge over the other three. That supremacy was the result of a half-century-old political struggle between the monarchy and the rest of Morocco's political forces: a historic mix of repression, cooptation, and corruption that finally led to an über-dominant royal palace hardly challenged by weak, divided, or corrupt opponents. Before analyzing 2011's new dynamics of activism, let's review the country's main political players and examine their respective strengths and weaknesses.

The central player is, of course, the king. Mohammed VI, twenty-third ruler of the more than 350-year-old Alaouite Dynasty, enjoys absolute power by dint of the Constitution. He appoints the prime minister and cabinet members at will,[3] has the power to dissolve parliament for any reason, and controls the judiciary personnel who render justice in his name. Even though the king keeps a tight leash on the three branches of government (executive, legislative, and judiciary), he still has the power to bypass them by taking personal executive steps, issuing laws, and pardoning convicts. He is also the military commander-in-chief and the religious commander-of-the-faithful.

Royal authority is relayed by a power structure known to Moroccans as the Makhzen,[4] an unofficial network of patronage- and allegiance-based relationships built around the king. It includes the royal court (Mohammed's family, friends, former schoolmates, advisers, and secretariat), the Ministry of the Interior, and high-ranking civil servants appointed by the king or sponsored by his cronies. It also includes the armed branches, from the nation's "Royal Armed Forces" to intelligence agencies, police forces, and the "Gendarmerie royale." Such a concentration of power, resources and positions—complete with control over the lion's share of the public budget—explains why the Makhzen is so indisputably in command of Morocco's public affairs, leaving all but crumbs to the other political forces.

Thirty-four political parties operate legally in Morocco. While a handful have historic roots stemming from the fight for independence, the majority were created under former King Hassan II to act as political minions of the Makhzen. Yet whether they are outright puppets or not, thirty parties abide by the Makhzen's rules and do not challenge—or even dare question—the king's absolute supremacy. Those are called "legitimist" parties, and they were totally irrelevant to the 2011 protests.

Out of those thirty, one legitimist party has a specific position: the Islamist formation known as Justice and Development Party (PJD). Even though its leaders wisely steer clear of the Makhzen, their political virginity (they had never been in government before 2011) and religious leanings give them a reputation of probity, which appeals to the voters. Consequently, the PJD has a solid constituency, one that has been continuously growing since the party's creation in 1997. In 2011, the PJD was the second-most-represented party in the parliament, a striking progression from fourteen years earlier, when it had occupied the tenth position.

The remaining four parties constitute what is known as the radical left. They do oppose the Makhzen,[5] and three of them demand an alternative system à la European monarchies, where an elected government would be fully in charge, leaving only symbolic powers to the monarch. In 2007, these three parties joined forces and created a common group called "Democratic Alliance of the Left," or DAL. (The most prominent DAL member, in terms of historical roots and territorial extension, is the Unified Socialist Party, or PSU.)[6] That same year, the DAL parties offered joint lists of candidates for parliamentary elections, yet ended up winning just 1 percent of the parliament's seats in all, thus becoming the least-represented political group in the kingdom.

The DAL parties' lack of political attractiveness is paradoxically explained by their hyper-politicization. Their central motto is that constitutional reform (one that would reallocate power resources to elected officials and confine the monarchy to a symbolic role) is the precondition for any other significant reform. They are right in principle, but their abstract focus on the Constitution makes them look out of touch with reality in the eyes of many voters, for whom the struggles of everyday life—low purchasing power, unemployment, housing difficulties, the corruption of state officials—are more concrete.

The fourth and last party opposing the Makhzen, an-Nahj ad-Dimocrati,[7] is the country's most radical (albeit legally recognized) formation. Its hardline Marxist-Leninist members want the end of the monarchy but consider themselves unable to speak out about their republican views under the current political constellation. Until "working masses rise up," so they say, their strategy is to boycott everything related to the Makhzen—including elections.

On the social side, Morocco's civil society has long impressed foreign observers. It is a very large network made up of thousands of NGOs scattered around the territory, many of which achieve outstanding grassroots work: microcredit systems, community organization, social development—but when it comes to politics, the circle narrows down to a handful of human right groups, the most influential of which is the Moroccan Association for Human Rights.

Up until 2011, the AMDH[8] did not engage in political activism per se—since its creation in 1979, its leaders have claimed that defending human rights was their one and only concern, regardless of political ideologies.[9] However, the AMDH has consistently been visible on the ground, organizing countless sit-ins to denounce specific cases of human rights violations (torture in police stations, unfair trials against activists and journalists, and so on) and to demand the liberation of political prisoners. These activities usually drew a few tens of participants, occasionally a hundred or two. Yet each of them was reported by the independent media—especially when the sit-ins were brutally dispersed by police forces, which happened quite often. Over time, this helped build the image of the AMDH as a courageous and relentless NGO. Indeed, its ten thousand listed members and more than ninety regional branches make the AMDH one of the largest grassroots organizations in the country.[10]

Starting in 2006, the AMDH enlarged its scope of interest to economic matters by initiating the "National Coordinating Committee against the High Cost of Living." A coalition of leftist parties (including an-Nahj and DAL members), antiglobalization groups, and labor unions, the committee pushed a left-leaning economic agenda—opposition to the privatization of public services, support for price regulation, and so on—and organized a series of sit-ins to protest the price increases of staple goods and services such as transportation and electricity. The popular success of these protests triggered the creation of as many as seventy local coordinating committees (*tanseeqiat mahallia*). Within two years, the "*tanseeqiat,*" as they became known, seemed to function independently from the national structure, which eventually became irrelevant. Yet the decentralized movement retained a high mobilizing capacity, and some sit-ins attracted up to five thousand protesters. This movement also led to the emergence of an organization called ATTAC Maroc,[11] which gained large popularity upon its radical denunciation of French companies holding urban concessions of water and electricity distribution in Casablanca, Tétouan, and Tangiers.

It is worth mentioning that the success of ATTAC and the *tanseeqiat* was largely based on their reputation as apolitical movements. This indicates two important things: up until 2011, Moroccan citizens were eager to protest against their economic conditions as long as it didn't mean directly challenging the monarchy.[12] Also, even though many of them were members of anti-Makhzen political organizations, the *tanseeqiat* activists demonstrated discipline in putting their political grievances to one side in order to guarantee high turnouts to their protests. In doing so, the leftist leaders managed to involve scores of new followers in recurrent protest activities. This would later prove instrumental in mobilizing the 2011 crowds.

The last—but certainly not least—group of political significance is al-Adl wal-Ihsan.[13] A semi-clandestine Islamist organization[14] focused on social work and religious education, it is concentrated in the outskirts of major cities, and its members do not recognize the king's legitimacy as a religious leader. One of al-Adl's mottos, "*la malika fi-l islam*" (no king in Islam), suggests that the organization rejects the monarchy altogether—yet its leaders are unclear about what should replace it.[15] Even though a "political circle" (a replica of the legal parties' political bureaus) was created in 1998 to bring out its brightest leaders, the unelected and yet uncontested leader of al-Adl was eighty-two-year-old "general guide" Abdessalam Yassine, a Sufi mystic turned political dissident who had spent nearly twenty years in prison or under house arrest during the reign of Hassan II. In 2006, Yassine's mystic "vision" of an impending mass uprising set the agenda for his supporters and for other actors in the kingdom—not least the security services and the press. Ultimately, nothing happened, and the ageing leader lost credibility. That probably explains why he has been increasingly less visible in the media since then, yielding to younger cadres of al-Adl.[16] The organization is believed to have around one hundred thousand listed members,[17] which makes it, while not formally legal, the biggest political group in Morocco.

Back in January 2011, none of the above-mentioned groups was strong enough or willing enough to confront the Makhzen head-on. DAL parties were going through an internal crisis, many of their members despairingly questioning their own "political utility" in the light of their weak electoral scores. For their part, the AMDH and ATTAC were visible and energetic but confined their grassroots action to social and economic combat—which was tolerated by the Makhzen as long as the crowds the sit-ins attracted were not too large. As for al-Adl, its leaders were quietly focusing on social work and educational activities (they also tried to join the *tanseeqiat* but were not welcomed by their leftist leaders)—as if the goal was to re-consolidate the group's cohesion after Yassine's failed prophecies.

Two months later, a coalition of the very same groups would corner the Makhzen so implacably that King Mohammed would hastily take to the airwaves, promising "comprehensive constitutional change." What enabled such a dramatic turn of events is of course the Arab Spring's contagion but also—and more importantly—the sudden burst of a new player in the game: the February 20 movement, also called Feb20, a group led by as-yet-unknown activists. In fact, the emergence of Feb20 as a political counterforce had been playing out for years. Yet very few identified them as a meaningful trend until they found themselves spearheading the 2011 protests.

Meanwhile, on the Web . . .

The young secular activists who would later give birth to Feb20 never planned to create a political movement. They formed in 2009 as an elusive network of internet users (many operating under aliases) defending individual freedoms after the MALI incident (described below) became a cause célèbre in the kingdom. The underground community's most active early members were twentysomething middle-class students or recent graduates from politically engaged families and living in big cities such as Casablanca and Rabat.[18] They barely knew each other in real life, but they progressively firmed up their virtual group (even though it had no name, structure, or admission criteria) by engaging in common online advocacy campaigns to defend victims of police abuses and to protest against the nepotistic behavior of the El Fassi "government family." Still, they remained little more than a network of Facebook friends, with little impact outside of the online world.

Some young activists (the ones who would later play a leading role in transforming the virtual network into a street movement) did have links with the AMDH and radical left parties: they were members of these organizations' youth sections or had family ties with their leaders. This political affiliation and education would later facilitate addressing Feb20's logistical needs, most notably in terms of a headquarters and venues for meetings. But the synergy never went further, and Feb20 never was an extension of established political parties or civil society organizations. On the contrary: its leaders always insisted on their independence vis-à-vis established political groups. Notably because of their experiences in the latter's youth sections or their family histories, the young web activists knew firsthand the flaws of traditional political groups: bureaucratic rigidity, lack of inventiveness, and, to various extents, the blasé attitudes of its leaders. That, along with the popular rejection of the "abstract," "out-of-touch" radical left (and also, maybe, a hint of generation-gap defiance) is the main reason why Feb20 leaders missed no opportunity to reaffirm their independence from the older activists and politicians.

Feb20 is in fact a spontaneous movement, generated by a succession of unexpected events and unplanned chain reactions. As a network of virtual activists mainly based on Facebook, it was in place and operational in the beginning of 2011. Yet it needed a catalyst event to burst into "real life" and to morph into a street movement. That catalyst event was the Arab Spring. But before we get there, let's examine how and by whom the virtual network was formed and how it evolved before becoming Feb20.

The Origins of Feb20

It all started in September 2009 when a group page named "Alternative Movement for Individual Freedoms," or MALI,[19] was launched on Facebook. In order to "open a debate on freedom of conscience," its two female administrators—a journalist and a psychology intern—called a daylight picnic during the month of Ramadan, when Muslims can eat only before dawn and after dusk.[20] On D-Day, only six persons, all of them in their twenties, showed up at the scheduled time with sandwiches in their backpacks. They found themselves surrounded by fifty policemen determined to stop the MALI action for the sake of "preserving public order." The six activists were brutally interrogated in police stations, and the failed picnic was front-page news for days, resulting in a national scandal.

The conservative uproar against MALI's initiative was so vociferous that the rare supportive voices went almost unheard. Human rights organizations (notably the AMDH), a handful of weekly magazines, and some noted leftist activists personally backed the young secularists. On the web, two thousand youngsters joined MALI's Facebook group within two days, continuing the debate. According to many leaders of what later became Feb20, the MALI affair was "a catalyst event"—the "pretext young Moroccans needed to engage in political activism."[21]

Starting in early 2010, successive small events contributed to firming up this elusive virtual community. Mounting talk about the nepotistic El Fassi family[22] spurred the creation of a Facebook group titled "All against Bequeathing Public Positions." A protest march was discussed but never held. Another Facebook group titled "All for Justice: The Minister's Son Should Stand Trial" was created after Communications Minister Khalid Naciri appeared on a YouTube video, ordering a policeman to discharge his handcuffed son who had assaulted a man in public. More than eight hundred supporters joined the Facebook group. This time, a real sit-in ensued, allowing forty virtual activists to meet for the first time. It was later argued that the opposition to the rich and powerful El Fassi and Naciri families might denote a class struggle dimension in the early dynamics leading to the formation of Feb20 as a political group—a notion even more plausible given the leftist background of many of the founders of the movement. Yet all of the activists interviewed by the author refuted that notion, insisting that their only driver was the urge to fight injustice.[23]

What became known as the "Aberkan affair" marked a milestone for the virtual network, since it triggered its first structured action—including coordination with senior organizations—that had a significant impact offline. On September 15, 2010, Fodil Aberkan, a thirty-seven-year-old mason, was tortured to death in a police station during what started out as a routine interrogation for marijuana possession. Confronted by press coverage, police officials denied mistreatment. A Facebook group named "All for Disclosing the

Truth on the Aberkan Affair" was promptly created, and it attracted thousands of members. The online discussion quickly turned into a planned action with a distribution of tasks: while some activists designed leaflets explaining what had happened and announcing a forthcoming sit-in, others raised money from the AMDH and DAL parties to have the leaflets printed. Then a third group distributed the leaflets in the victim's neighborhood and campaigned for the sit-in, which ended up attracting four hundred participants. Serious press coverage ensued, and the policemen were finally charged with mistreatment.

The Aberkan action was a tangible success, to the credit of the virtual activists—plus, it was widely advertised through mainstream media—which boosted the rising virtual movement. Discussion groups mushroomed on social media platforms, and thousands of internet users joined in. Starting out with individual freedoms and the defense of human rights, the debate broadened to liberal ideas and later to proposals about democracy in general. In January 2011, tens of thousands of Moroccan internet users were passionately discussing various topics on abundant politically engaged Facebook groups. The Aberkan affair had given the virtual activists a sense that they could have a significant impact if they were to export their activism to real life. In other words, the mobilization tool was ready, it just needed a catalyst event. That event would be the Tunisian revolution.

Of hundreds of Facebook groups, one in particular would make history: "Moroccans Converse with the King," as it was called, invited the public to address King Mohammed VI with questions, concerns, and comments. On January 14, just days after the group was created, President Ben Ali fled Tunisia. The news electrified Facebook users, who filled the group's page with daring statements and demands addressed to the king. As days passed and revolutionary fervor spread like wildfire in the Arab world—thanks, notably, to the round-the-clock coverage on Al Jazeera—the demands grew bolder. The group's members were now asking the king to change the Constitution, fire the cabinet, dissolve the parliament, put "those who steal public money" on trial, and so on.

On January 25, as Egyptians started gathering in Tahrir Square, thus adding fuel to the fire of revolutionary fervor, the Facebook page administrators[24] took new steps to benefit from the growing momentum: they changed the page name to "Freedom and Democracy Now" and sorted the commentators' demands by recurrence, keeping only the seven most popular ones (respectively: changing the Constitution, dismissing the cabinet, dissolving the parlia-

The Revolution's Internet Branch
HISHAM ALMIRAAT

Hisham Almiraat, thirty-seven, is a Moroccan "medical doctor, blogger, and citizen media enthusiast"—as he defines himself on Facebook—living in El Jadida, Morocco. While he was a graduating physician in Nantes, France, he cofounded mamfakinch.com, a "citizen-driven website dedicated at aggregating, curating, and disseminating unfiltered, uncensored prodemocracy movement related news." Launched merely days before the Arab Spring protests hit Morocco on February 20, 2011, Mamfakinch quickly became the protest movement's mouthpiece. On July 2, 2012, Mamfakinch won the Google/Global Voices Breaking Borders award, honoring organizations that have made "significant impact in their communities to defend and promote freedom of speech rights on the Internet."

Online coordination between Moroccan prodemocracy activists started a couple of years before the Arab Spring. We were a network of engineers, doctors, junior executives, and students, many of us part-time bloggers and most of us living abroad but all very concerned by our home country. We used to get together every once in a while in cafés or restaurants in Paris or elsewhere in Europe and discuss the situation in Morocco. Then we'd continue the discussion online via a thirtyish-person mailing list.

By mid-February 2011, we had all heard about a call for national protests on February 20. Yet save for the nasty smear campaign conducted by the regime's media apparatus, we had very little information about what was going on. For us living abroad, the frustration was immense. So the idea started as a mailing list discussion: we would start fresh and launch a website that would provide credible information by giving a voice to the activists on the ground, without the filter of mainstream media. The name Mamfakinch, or "We won't give up," came up in brainstorming—it would later become a street mantra!

Our Tunisian colleagues from Nawaat, a website that played a crucial role in exposing Ben Ali's regime, suggested we adopt Posterous as a blogging platform. Because it allows cross-posting on multiple other platforms (Facebook, Twitter, etc.) via simple emails, it would facilitate information circulation and collection, even from activists with limited internet skills. We started with correspondents covering thirty-five cities in Morocco. The list included bloggers, journalists, and leftist party and human rights activists. The AMDH (Moroccan Association for Human Rights) helped us a lot in setting up the network.

The site was launched three days before February 20, and content started to flow very quickly. Within its first three months of existence, Mamfakinch received half a million unique visitors—to our astonishment! The ad hoc nature of our organization and day-to-day planning led us to commit a couple of mistakes, like publishing inaccurate information. We weren't journalists, but we progressively learned how to proofread and cross-check. Also, for editing as much as security purposes, we decided that logins, codes, and passwords would be handled by just eight of us, all living outside Morocco.

After a few months of hectic activity, we started to feel some kind of "revolutionary fatigue" emerging from the ground. We had to find out new ways of covering the protests without getting trapped in daily routine. Inspired by Ushahidi, a website launched by Kenyan prodemocracy activists, we began making techie mappings of the protests, implementing demonstration videos on Google Maps.... That was cool, and it revived the visitors' interest. In June, as fewer and fewer people were attending the protests, we engaged in strategy making. We started with "Noss Noss," a campaign claiming fifty-fifty airtime sharing between the "yes" and "no" arguments in the constitutional referendum campaign. Then in September, we launched "Open Makhzen," an initiative to encourage whistle-blowing and document leaking (WikiLeaks-style) in order to expose the government's corrupt practices. By January 2012, Mamfakinch had received visits from 1.2 million unique IP addresses. We're thinking of refurbishing the site's layout and are still looking for new, creative ideas.

Hisham Almiraat. Used with permission.

ment, installing an independent judiciary, setting corruption trials, making Tamazight (Berber) an official language alongside Arabic, and freeing all political prisoners). Then one of the group's administrators posted a video of himself online wearing a beret and a Palestinian scarf and reading the seven demands, his clenched fist raised.[25] The video would turn viral, the young man would be dubbed the "Ché Guevara of Salé," and the seven demands would soon become the protesters' official platform. In order to "take the action to real life," the group members decided to publish a call for nationwide protests on February 20.[26] As it turned out, the short Facebook post would trigger the biggest national protests since the country's independence.

Bubbling up to D-Day . . .

In the days to follow, multiple internet users, inspired by the "Freedom and Democracy Now" activism, created Facebook groups urging the citizens of many Moroccan towns and villages to take to the streets on February 20. No real coordination happened among the local groups, except for sharing the "Freedom and Democracy Now" platform and agreeing on a common time—10 a.m.—for the protests to start on D-Day. On February 8, a second video was released: with classical piano in the background, thirteen young web activists appeared in turn, each proclaiming one line starting with "I am Moroccan, and I will go out on February 20 because. . . ." (followed by reasons stemming from the "seven demands" platform). That video far overshadowed "Che Guevara of Salé": within a few days, it got half a million hits on YouTube. Public media smear campaigns to discredit the movement's thirteen new "faces" only resulted in generating more publicity for the upcoming Feb20 protest. Whether to support or discredit it, the press was talking about nothing else.

. . . in Rabat

Meanwhile, Tunisia's and Egypt's revolutions were boosting the morale of civil society and leftist groups. The Moroccan Committee to Support the Masses, a group initiated by the AMDH and including DAL parties, an-Nahj, and ATTAC, organized a sit-in on February 12 to salute the ousting of President Mubarak of Egypt. Sitting on the parliament's sidewalk in Rabat, about two hundred senior activists chanted slogans in support of fellow Arabs . . . and quickly diverted their focus to the protests planned in Morocco for February 20. Before the sit-in was called off, all of the organizations present decided to issue a joint communiqué supporting the nascent "February 20 youth movement"—this was the first time the expression was used—to host its spokespersons in the AMDH's headquarters for a press conference and to unite to print promotion leaflets for the upcoming protest. With these acts, the logistical synergy between web activists and traditional anti-Makhzen political groups started.

The above discussion describes the dynamics that played out in Rabat, the kingdom's capital city. But the platform claims impersonated by the local "Ché Guevara" and, more decisively, the video clip featuring the thirteen actors, did inspire people throughout Morocco, prompting tens of thousands to "go out" on February 20. For that reason, the Rabat group would always be credited with a certain "moral leadership" over the local Feb20 groups throughout the nation. Yet this prevalence would never translate into concrete, hierarchical terms. Depending on the city, developments would bubble up in different ways, involving different kinds of activists or political and civil society groups, and featuring varying forms and levels of interaction.[27] In fact, the form of each local branch of Feb20 would result from two main factors: on the one hand, the spirit, background, and personal abilities of local web activists, and on the other hand, the status of local "senior" activism, itself a product of the way that local branches of traditional groups had cooperated (or not) in the past. In other words, the formation of every Feb20 local group is a case study of how a new dynamic transforms (and is transformed by) older strategies.

...in Casablanca

The Casablanca Feb20 dynamics started on February 6, 2011, with a casual meeting in a bar between two twentysomething web activists and four senior leftist party members. The agenda was to discuss the "Freedom and Democracy Now" Facebook page activities, including the call for a protest on February 20. A decision was taken to extend the discussion to a larger audience by organizing a public meeting. On February 12, around fifty people, representing two generations of activists from various leftist groups, convened in the Casablanca headquarters of the PSU for a conference titled "The Meeting of Hope: The Youth and the Protest Movements." After two senior politicians explained the basics of popular protests—"in quite a pontificating way," one of them later admitted[28]—younger activists were invited to take the stage. Within minutes, they swept the audience away with their passionate arguments in favor of the February 20 protest and platform. When the meeting ended, impressed PSU leaders placed their offices at the disposal of the young activists, vowing to "help but not interfere" with their future action—just as the youth, eager to demonstrate their independence vis-à-vis the elders, had requested. That was the starting point of the Feb20 Casablanca branch.

Six days later, a "Founding General Assembly" held in PSU's Casablanca offices attracted more than 150 young activists. About half of them were members of the youth sections of leftist parties and civil society organizations, while the other half were made up of independent bloggers and Facebook activists. Some of the latter took the initiative to invite al-Adl wal-Ihsan youth leaders to join in—a bold and audacious step, as strategic coordination between radical-left parties and Islamists had never happened before in Casablanca. What enabled this was the willingness of the independent bloggers to cross boundaries in order to ensure a high turnout for the upcoming protest. The Islamist cadres accepted the invitation, and a behind-the-scenes discussion ensued between them and the General Assembly organizers. At the latter's request, the Islamists agreed to instruct their followers to avoid gender segregation and religious slogans during the protest. Every group—this would soon become a national rule—would have to put its specific agenda aside and align behind a unique banner: that of the Feb20 movement.

. . . in Marrakech

In Marrakech, no political group sponsored the Feb20 movement. Internet contacts led to a meeting in a café on February 14 for the purpose of discussing the platform shared on Facebook. Out of the twenty-two persons who attended, three-fourths were either independent activists or members of the Amazigh movement,[29] and the last fourth was made up of leftist university students. Inspired by the Rabat video, they decided to make a video of their own, raising local concerns specific to the Marrakech area, such as the forced rehousing of four thousand families due to a real estate project, sexual tourism, underfunded local hospitals, and so forth. The video was posted on YouTube and quickly generated a buzz in the city. This resulted in a swift response by local police, who violently cracked down against the video actors, some of whom were beaten during detention. That, more than the video, became the talk of the town and prompted Marrakchis to take to the streets on February 20.

Why did Marrakech's police take action, while those of Rabat and Casablanca remained quiet? The reason may be that, unlike their counterparts from these two cities, Marrakchi activists were not backed in any way by traditional political groups. This would later change, as PSU and another DAL party would make their offices available for Feb20 meetings. But the interaction between the young and elder activists always remained limited in Marrakech, for no other apparent reason than a certain wariness between the city's two generations of activists.[30] Plus, Islamists would later join the local dynamics without any coordination with leftist groups—which would eventually generate vehement conflicts within the Feb20 local branch.

... and in Tangiers

Things played out very differently in Tangiers—sometimes in the exact opposite way—than elsewhere in Morocco. There were indeed local young activists, who created at least one "Feb20 Tangiers" group on Facebook. Yet their influence would never compare to that of the city's senior political activists, generally in their forties, who have a history of efficient cross-partisan collaboration. Left parties, Islamist organizations, and labor unions had started to coordinate in order to mount protests against the U.S. invasion of Iraq in 2003 and then against the Israeli attacks on Lebanon in 2006 and Gaza in 2009. Such coordination is unique to Tangiers. Common anti-U.S. and anti-Israel marches did also happen in Casablanca, but the only coordination between Islamists and leftists consisted of agreement on a schedule and itinerary. During the marches, the physical separation between the atavistic foes was visible, with each group raising its own placards and chanting its own slogans; for example, both groups would defend Palestine, but the Islamists would chant pro-Hamas slogans while the leftists would claim their support to Fatah. In Tangiers, coordination went beyond schedule and itinerary and included banners, slogans, and promotion leaflets—in other words, both the logistics and the message were coordinated. As a result, Tangiers's protests in 2003, 2006, and 2009, though less massive than Casablanca's (simply because the former city is not as populated as the latter), looked more compact and homogenous.

Tangiers was also the only big city in Morocco where Islamists were invited to participate in the *tanseeqiat* against rising prices. Everywhere else, such movements were the domain of leftist groups, labor unions, and antiglobalization organizations like ATTAC. The "Tangiers exception" deserves a study of its own, but it is safe to say that the main reason for cooperation was the common ground found in the city's labor unions. Partly because of their leaders' personalities, Tangiers's labor organizations have long been governed through careful consensus—the main principle being "whatever their ideology, workers have the same rights and deserve the same improvements to their status." This encouraged cross-partisan contacts, which later proved instrumental in defending other causes than those of the workers. Another—quite peculiar—facilitating factor for Tangiers's cross-partisan coordination is the Laasri brothers: while Khalid is a top local leader of al-Adl, his sibling Jamal is a top local leader of PSU, and both are respected and trusted to act in the best interests of their respective organizations. Thus, many cross-partisan conflicts in Tangiers were settled with the resolution "let the brothers sort it out."

By mid-February, talk of a tentative protest had spread in Tangiers, as it had everywhere else in the country. Yet the cross-partisan collaboration did not take Facebook seriously. Moreover, it was busy supporting ATTAC, whose activists were at that time mobilizing big crowds for daily demonstrations against the city's water and electricity company, which had been accused of unjustified price raises. On February 17, after an ATTAC sit-in was called off, a group of hooligans set a bank agency on fire. Worried that an unsupervised Feb20 demonstration would turn into chaos, local leaders of ten different leftist and Islamist groups decided to hold an urgent meeting on February 18. Within two days, a start-to-end itinerary was agreed upon; banners and placards were crafted; common slogans were fixed; megaphones, stewards, and other logistical needs were addressed, and a joint communiqué was written, signed, and published. In terms of organization, no other local Feb20 group would ever rival Tangier's. In no other place did Feb20 appoint spokespersons in charge not only of giving interviews to the media but also of coordinating with the police to prevent the protests from getting out of control.

As we have seen, every branch of Feb20 grew organically, drawing on the specifics of the local situation. Yet there is a general lesson to be learned: the deeper the coordination between the two generations of activists and among the various political groups in the city, the stronger and better organized the Feb20 group—and the more immune it is against police action. This was a concrete illustration of the conventional wisdom that "unity is strength."

Yet unity, present to varying degrees inside Feb20's local branches, was still totally nonexistent on a national level. A few days before February 20, the only common feature of all local groups was the seven-demand platform that had been distributed on Facebook. On February 18, al-Adl wal Ihsan published a communiqué stating that its youth section members would join the protest throughout the country. That gave the nascent Feb20 movement an ultimate boost before D-Day.

Connecting Networks and Surfing the Momentum

The turnout on February 20 came as a surprise to everyone, including the protest organizers themselves. Whatever the city, Feb20 leaders shared the same feeling: "We thought only a few hundreds of people would join us: comrades from the AMDH and leftist organizations—the 'usual suspects' when it comes to street protests—plus, maybe, a bunch of al-Adl youth and our most dedicated Facebook friends. . . . But we were astonished to see that protesters turned out by the tens of thousands. We had never seen the great majority of those people before."[31] The most widely given explanation of this success is a combination of the state of white heat induced across the nation by Tunisia's and Egypt's revolutions (most specifically, by their 24-7 Al Jazeera coverage) and the persistent media buzz that preceded Feb20, including smear campaigns by pro-Makhzen media, which only publicized the protest further.

The February 20 protests hit fifty-three Moroccan towns simultaneously. The protesters did not openly call for the fall of the king but still they chanted political slogans including "Down with corruption and absolutism," "The people demand a new Constitution," and other demands derived from the "Freedom and Democracy Now" Facebook platform. As the police backed off everywhere for fear of sparking a Tunisia- and Egypt-like snowball effect, the protesters' triumph spurred a wave of exaltation throughout the kingdom. Thousands of fired-up comments on the monarchy's corruption suddenly popped up on the internet. Overnight, café customers started discussing King Mohammed VI's prerogatives out loud. A Moroccan immigrant in the United States created a sensation by filming himself addressing the monarch with a crude and populist tone—within a few days, his video had received more than half a million hits on YouTube. Astonishingly, the wall of fear that had paralyzed large segments of the population for decades had fallen in a single day.

On February 23, the "National Council for Support of the Feb20 Movement," or the "Support Council," was created in Rabat by forty political and civil society groups including the AMDH, the DAL parties, an-Nahj, and AT-TAC—as a continuation of the Moroccan Committee to Support the Masses, the coalition that had decided to provide the youth movement with logistical support eleven days earlier, upon its sit-in on the sidewalk outside the Parliament. With a few exceptions, this coalition was formed by the same groups that had created the *tanseeqiat* movement five years earlier. In other words, a network of cross-partisan collaboration was already up and running; it just seized the opportunity offered by the Feb20/Arab Spring context to rename itself and push a new agenda—the "Freedom and Democracy" platform—that happens to match its members' convictions. Yet this time, a new member was solicited: al-Adl wal-Ihsan.

Incorporating the Islamist organization within a left-dominated coalition didn't occur without intense debate. Al-Adl was finally allowed in, provided it committed to the same rules that the Feb20 Casablanca group had spontaneously set days before: No distinctive features, slogans, or banners would be tolerated for any group; everyone would line up behind the Feb20 banner and accept the youth's slogans and overall guidance; and all groups would mingle in the crowd. This last instruction was directed especially at al-Adl's Islamists, who usually created separate spaces to allow "their" women to demonstrate while avoiding male contact—discarding that practice was a way to reaffirm the secular character of the Feb20 demonstrations. The Support Council's deputy secretary general stated: "Aside from instructing our respective members to join the protests and helping with providing logistical means, we, senior political and civil society groups, were taking great pains in not looking directive or intrusive. Otherwise, the kids would have been wary of us. We had to win their trust before anything else."[32]

During the euphoric weeks that followed February 20, the youth movement's meetings—mainly in the premises provided by members of the Support Council; except al-Adl, whose leaders seemed unwilling to push their association with the secular protest movement too far—became the place-to-be in every city of the kingdom. Word was quickly out for the next national day of protest, set to happen on March 20. Neither the government's hastily granted economic perks (the minimum salary and civil servant wages were raised by 15 to 35 percent, and the budget of the equalization fund—which holds down the prices of consumer staples—was almost tripled) nor the public media's change of tone toward the protest leaders (some were even invited on live TV shows) was able to temper the excitement of the youth.

Nothing seemed able to stop the growing momentum when, on March 9, Mohammed VI took to the airwaves unexpectedly. In a very dramatic speech, the king promised a spectacular constitutional reform featuring the "rule of law," an "independent judiciary," and an "elected government that reflects the will of the people, through the ballot box." The media and the public were flabbergasted. Forcing the head of state to make such bold concessions in such a short time—this was unprecedented in Morocco's modern history. Undoubtedly, many observers said, the Feb20 movement had scored a major victory against the monarchy. In fact, the game was just starting.

Strategy Beats Improvisation: The Royal Trap...

As it quickly turned out, the king's promises were more a clever preemptive move than any genuine intention to implement change. To be convinced of that, one only needs to examine the constitutional reform committee that Mohammed VI appointed the day after his speech. Composed of eighteen loyal civil servants and presided over by a scholar with a history of condoning autocracy,[33] it was unlikely to produce meaningful change. Still, the monarchy had successfully reversed the momentum by seizing back the initiative—a perfect Clausewitz-type "offensive action."[34] By launching a new reform agenda, however spuriously, the king was taking the helm, forcing Feb20 leaders to position themselves according to *his* agenda—not the other way around.

In a seemingly democratic move, Mohammed VI ordered the reform committee to "undertake vast consultations with all political groups and the nation's lifeblood." The royal strategy, as it quickly appeared, was a classic Makhzen move, the template of which was crafted and applied many times under Mohammed's father, Hassan II. It consisted of generating countless versions of the needed reform in order to cloud the issue under the cover of a democratic debate. Then, under the royal palace's guidance, the reform committee would produce a draft of its choice, claiming that it is a "synthesis of the propositions received." Of course, no mechanism would ever be set to guarantee that the final draft reflects the propositions in a fair and proportionate way. Any group who would complain that its own propositions were not taken into consideration would be answered that they indeed had been, but given the number of other propositions, compromises and arbitrations were necessary—is this not the spirit of a democratic process? In other words, any group who would engage in the royal committee's "consultations" would in fact participate in an outflanking maneuver from which it could not emerge as a winner—unless it sided with the Makhzen. Boycotting the royal committee would not be an option, either: the Makhzen and its media would easily dismiss those who would make that choice as "talkers, not doers" and, worse yet, as people who do not believe in the virtues of debate—and thus in democracy.

Indeed, the trap was well set for Feb20. After "consulting" every political party, association, trade union, or notable group in the country (including a great majority of Makhzen supporters), the press reported, the royal committee contacted "100 young Moroccans, 45 of whom are members of different Feb20 local coordinating committees" to engage in constitutional talks. The strategy here was the same: the more participants, the blurrier the discussion and the unlikelier the outcome. Feb20 local groups declined the invitation one after the other, arguing that the commission was "appointed and not elected" and demanding a "democratically elected constitutional assembly." That was the right thing to say to escape the royal trap, but it came too late. Had the demand for an elected assembly been raised prior to the king's speech, it would have been more credible. But as a political riposte, it sounded "unconstructive," as pro-Makhzen media outlets immediately pointed out, questioning the youth's "true commitment to democracy."

...and Feb20's Organizational Collapse

Maybe the Feb20's noble democratic excuse for not producing a constitutional draft of its own was hiding something more pragmatic: the protest movement's intrinsic difficulty of producing a common position on anything. This brings us to Feb20's coordination techniques, and how they quickly became the movement's major weakness. Except in Tangiers, all Feb20 local groups relied on weekly, open, and pretty chaotic "general assemblies," during which everyone spoke in turn without a time limit. After hours of talk—sometimes it would take all night—decisions would be made according to the "general trend"—a method the activists favored over voting because, they said, "alienating minorities with majority votes could result in a split of the movement."[35] Consequently, decisions would almost never go beyond "let's demonstrate."

Narrowing the decision circle by establishing a formal organization and leadership was the obvious solution. But the activists took pride in Feb20 being an unstructured, leaderless movement because "structures are a target for the government, and leaders eventually get arrested, or corrupted" and also because "electing leaders means allowing an ideological current to prevail over the other ones, which means the beginning of the end of the movement."[36] In other terms, the unstructured, leaderless aspect of Feb20 was seen as the guarantee of its inclusivity because it allowed large numbers of people with different opinions and ideologies to coexist in the same environment without having to compete for control. To the great majority of Feb20's leaders (a status earned through charisma and deep commitment to the movement, in the absence of actual votes), having no formal organizational structure or official leaders was in fact the movement's principal strength. However, not electing representatives condemned Feb20 to strategic paralysis, since no one could make decisions in the movement's name and no clear group decision could be made by the unwieldy general assemblies. Indeed, this system was unable to produce any agenda—let alone constitutional reform propositions—beyond slogans such as "Down with absolutism!"

Yet until late April, sloganeering seemed enough. Even in the absence of reliable statistics, it is widely believed that the second and third days of national protest attracted a turnout that was at least twice as large as that of February 20. It is certain that more towns were involved—63 on March 20 and 110 on April 24.[37] The first explanation for such mass enthusiasm was the continuing ripple effect of the Arab Spring. With breaking news on Al Jazeera several times a day, January–May was the most eventful period of 2011 in the Arab world. That certainly helped to keep the momentum going in Morocco. Another explanation is that, devious as it was, the royal promise of constitutional reform appeared to be a bold concession and thus a recognition of the people's power. That boosted the protesters' morale and encouraged them to turn out in important numbers.

Reversing the Tide

However, the climate eventually changed. By mid-May, the Arab Spring fervor was tempered by civil war in Libya and ruthless crackdowns in Syria, Yemen, and Bahrain—repression had even resumed in Egypt despite Mubarak's ouster. All of that certainly contributed to decreasing the general revolutionary fever. Besides, Moroccans were getting used to protests—and perhaps bored by their apparent pointlessness—after all, the Constitution was being reformed, wasn't it? By mid-May, protesters started turning out in reduced numbers. That is when the government began to take tougher action against them. On May 15, a tentative sit-in by Feb20 outside a detention center near Rabat was brutally dispersed by police forces. May 22, one week later, was the date of the first nationwide crackdown on protesters. Truncheon beatings and police round-ups happened all over the country. Dozens of activists were wounded, and one of them died.

The government's change of strategy is explained by Feb20's loss of momentum starting in mid-May but also by the decrease in international attention on the Arab Spring (and thus on Morocco). With the Libyan and Syrian uprisings becoming bogged down, the Western media were less interested in covering the Arab world than they had been three months earlier. Still, to the government's dissatisfaction, one can surmise, European media outlets picked up wire news stories about "police repression against peaceful protesters in

Morocco." In early June, two weeks after the first police beatings, the authorities consequently readjusted their strategy: Violence against the protesters would continue, but it would be outsourced to unofficial police auxiliaries. To that effect, the Ministry of the Interior began mobilizing proregime thugs, Morocco's version of the famed Egyptian *baltagiya*.[38] Unlike the Feb20 activists who had vowed to remain nonviolent, their opponents were armed with stones and clubs, openly looking for fights while the police looked elsewhere. Each time a Feb20 local group announced a protest venue, "resident associations" suddenly mushroomed there, pledging to "defend" their neighborhood against "extremists" and "troublemakers." These were in fact pro-Makhzen goons, largely manipulated by local authorities, as some YouTube videos clearly demonstrated.

The draft Constitution was released at the peak of this tension. As expected, it featured cosmetic changes. Behind an elaborate rhetorical smokescreen, the monarchy was still tightly controlling the three branches of government and had firmed up its grip on security forces and the religious sphere.[39] In a televised speech on June 17, the king disclosed the constitutional draft and urged Moroccans to approve it through a referendum scheduled for July 1—no more than two weeks later. The rushed course of events was obviously intended to take full advantage of the new pro-Makhzen momentum, leaving insufficient time for the opposition to organize.

Local Feb20 groups and the Support Council immediately called for a boycott, complete with nationwide protests against the "imposed Constitution." This triggered violent clashes with hordes of semi-naked thugs[40] who roamed the streets, bawling that Mohammed VI was their "only king." Meanwhile, the government mobilized state-controlled mosques and public TV to preach the Constitution's virtues. On Election Day, fraud reports flooded the internet. A video posted on YouTube showed officials rummaging through an open ballot box. Another one featured a polling station staffer revealing that his manager had ordered him to manipulate voter listings. Scores of voters testified that their identities had not been checked—which enabled widespread ballot stuffing. Finally, the Ministry of the Interior claimed Ben Ali–esque scores: a turnout of 73 percent and an approval rate of 98.5 percent for the new Constitution.

Despite the blatant fraud, the general perception was that the Makhzen had severely defeated Feb20. Not only was the plebiscite seen as a stinging disavowal of the protest movement, but it also appeared as a renewed, massive tribute to the monarchy—or at least for those who did not trust the results, a spectacular demonstration of how much the Makhzen remained in

"The Arab Spring Prompted Us to Rebuild Our Organization"
KHALID LAASRI

Khalid Laasri, forty-two, is a leading member of the Tangiers section of al-Adl wal-Ihsan (Awl), Morocco's most prominent Islamist organization. He has been an Awl activist since he was nineteen. He speaks about his organization's strategy and how it transformed to adapt to the "tidal wave" of the 2011 protests.

What are al-Adl wal-Ihsan's strategic goals, and how are they served?

Our two main strategic goals are included in our group's name. "Al-Ihsan," which is usually translated as "charity," means literally "doing good" (in an Islamic way). This is our religious objective. We serve it through organizing activities such as companionship programs (forming groups of worshipers to pray and invoke God jointly), educational programs (delivering classes on proper religious attitudes), etc. "Al-Adl," or justice, is our second strategic goal, the political one. The way we serve it is based on this assumption: reforming the Makhzen (Morocco's monarchic system) from the inside is a vain pursuit. Therefore, we boycott all political institutions, including elections. Instead, we aim at building a grassroots movement big and strong enough to stand up against the government's tyranny through various forms of peaceful protests. Many of our activists are regularly arrested and harassed, but the organization itself has always survived, simply because it is too big and too deeply entrenched in the society for the government to uproot it and take it down.

Have these goals and strategies evolved in 2011, particularly with the advent of the February 20 movement?

The writings of the organization's guide Abdessalam Yassine repeatedly refer to the concept of *qawma,* or mass uprising—a tidal wave that must be prepared and accompanied up until the stage of civil disobedience. The Arab Spring empirically confirmed the theoretical narrative of Awl, which provided its members with renewed confidence. By joining the Feb20 protests, three key aptitudes that Awl teaches to its members were put to the test: (1) the aptitude to adapt to rapidly changing situations; (2) the aptitude to mobilize the people, help them overcome their fear, and make them take to the streets in protests; (3) the aptitude to bridge the gap between Awl's activists and leftist groups' members, in order to organize protests. These three challenges were met to varying degrees, depending on the city. In some cities, the leftist activists were mature enough to transcend their ideological differences with Awl and build unity—in others, they weren't. Also, some young independent Feb20 activists proved more able than others to build bridges with activists from established political groups. Finally, a key factor for success was the ability to prevent police infiltration in Feb20's ranks. In some cities, it was severe enough to cripple the protest movement.

Why did Awl withdraw from Feb20 in December 2011?

That decision was taken for three reasons. (1) Some of Feb20's groups insisted to establish a "ceiling of demands"—meaning: they were claiming specific forms of political organization, while we wanted a democratically elected constitutional assembly, thus allowing the people to choose the political system they want. (2) Some of Feb20's groups insisted on giving the movement an identity that conflicted with the country's identity in provocative ways. For example, they steadily refused to chant any slogan with a religious connotation, which we deemed an unacceptable blow to the country's Muslim character. (3) Awl saw Feb20 as an important stage of activism for the Moroccan people, but not as the decisive one. Awl considered that Feb20 had played its role but that it was over. Continuing the same tactics even though the Makhzen had adapted to them would have been political naiveté.

Did the Feb20 episode drive strategic changes in Awl?

Yes indeed. The main lesson learned from our Feb20 activism period was that we needed to interact differently and more efficiently with the masses, interiorize the people's needs and concerns in a better way. This prompted us to transform our organizational structure from a recruitment-oriented organization to what we call a social movement. The transformation is now fully enacted, but the organization didn't decide yet to communicate on the new structure.

Khalid Laasri. Used with permission.

control. Either interpretation might explain why Western governments rushed to congratulate the king, saluting the constitutional referendum as "an important step toward democratic reform" (U.S. Secretary of State Hillary Clinton), "an exemplary process" (French President Nicolas Sarkozy), or a "demonstration of political maturity" (Spanish Foreign Minister Trinidad Jiménez). As for global media, they broadly applauded the kingdom's "peaceful" reforms. Whatever the objections of Moroccan oppositionists, their situation was not as bad as the Libyans' or Syrians', was it?

Drowning in the Swamp: The Seniors' Discords ...

Despite the summer season, which coincided in 2011 with Ramadan—traditionally a month of religious contemplation and sociopolitical apathy—Feb20 groups kept calling protests every Sunday to denounce the "Makhzen's masquerade." But the turnouts dwindled visibly throughout the country. At least at face value, the movement's most important demands had been met: the Constitution had been reformed, the parliament would soon be dissolved and the government dismissed, upon forthcoming legislative elections. "Why protest now?" many citizens thought.

In addition, an internal conflict paralyzed Feb20's Support Council: whereas the PSU and fellow DAL parties were calling for a "parliamentary monarchy" (in the European style), an-Nahj and al-Adl refused any "ceiling of demands"—an ambiguous way of saying that they did not renounce the prospect of taking the monarchy down (though with two very different replacement plans: a proletarian republic for an-Nahj and an Islamic State for al-Adl).

This raises an important issue: Why did the question of "what system next?" come into play in Morocco so much earlier than in other Arab countries during the Arab Spring? Arguably, there wasn't that much more agreement among Tunisia's or Egypt's political groups about what system would be best to replace Ben Ali's or Mubarak's. Yet it didn't prevent the activists from putting this question aside and remaining united until their regimes fell. The difference is that while the Tunisians and Egyptians effectively united under a clear objective—namely: the head of state must go—Moroccan activists could not raise such a sharp demand.

There are three main reasons for this. First, the Moroccan monarchy has a deep legitimacy, rooted in twelve centuries of history. Second, the current king, as undemocratic as he might be, has not stifled his people or behaved tyrannically enough to give way to a general revolutionary sentiment among his subjects.[41] Finally, Moroccans widely credit the monarchy for holding the ethnically and culturally diverse population together. Were this symbol of unity to disappear, they rightly or wrongly believe, the nation would fall apart and dissolve into bloody sectarian conflicts. Whatever their convictions and ideology, Morocco's activists are well aware that calling for the monarchy's demise would alienate the great majority of their followers (that is why al-Adl's and an-Nahj's antimonarchic views are never expressed openly in public but rather are implied by the semantic detour of refusing a "ceiling of demands"). Since removing the king is not a viable option, the question of "what next?" is really "what now?"

As long as activism consisted of chanting anti-Makhzen slogans alongside fired-up kids, unity could be preserved among otherwise ideologically opposed groups. After the constitutional sequence, denouncing absolutism was no longer sufficient. The Makhzen had engaged in a strategy, which required in return a counter-strategy. After this moment, unity could no longer be found among the members of the Support Council: some called for radical reform, others wished for a revolution. There is no way to reach a compromise between these two options: either the monarchy is maintained (in whatever form), or it is not. The reformists have repeatedly invoked the monarchy's popular legitimacy to call their revolutionary comrades to realism, but to no avail. Abandoning the ultimate objective they have been pursuing for decades was too great a sacrifice for al-Adl and an-Nahj. And since the two groups are keys to the cross-partisan coalition (the former because it provides large troops during the protests, the latter because it is closely linked with the AMDH, the coalition's dynamo), the "ceiling of demands" soon became a serious obstacle. Because of it, the Support Council was incapable of providing the Feb20 movement with a unified and consistent political strategy to counter the Makhzen's.

. . . and the Youth's Haphazardness

However, even assuming that the Support Council could produce a unified strategy, its endorsement by Feb20 would be far from certain. The first reason is that, as we saw, there is no centralized structure and decision-making process in the Feb20 movement. Each Feb20 local group would have to discuss the strategy in a general assembly, and nothing would guarantee that the same course of action would be adopted everywhere. Moreover, the very notion of Feb20 following a policy determined by elder activists is scarcely conceivable by most of the young activists, who are rebelliously determined to preserve their "independence."[42] The youth's wariness vis-à-vis established political parties or civil society organizations is rarely expressed in a blunt manner, if only because they are using their offices and logistical support. Yet this wariness is implicitly and constantly present.

The official explanation is that Feb20 must preserve its "political virginity" to remain attractive to the larger masses—which implies that a closer association with traditional groups would be a corrupting factor. Yet, we are not talking here about the—indeed corrupt—"legitimist" political parties but rather about the AMDH, an-Nahj, PSU, and the DAL parties, all groups that the Makhzen never succeeded in coopting. Why the enduring mistrust, then? There may be a vindication of a subtler, psychological nature. One should consider that the youth led huge prodemocracy crowds to take to the streets, a success that senior activists (with whom they often have family ties) have consistently failed to achieve over several decades. The youth may ultimately believe that they know better.

Yet examining the youth movement's evolution does not confirm this assumption. Ultimately, the haphazard nature of the Feb20 movement caused its collapse. The lack of organizational structure and legitimate leadership in the local groups led them to be hijacked by their most radical members. The latter took advantage from the "general trend," the General Assemblies' functioning method, to impose their views by commotion or by force. In the absence of a voting system, the "general trend" method gradually led to a general radicalization of the movement, which in turn resulted in a diminution of public support.

As time passed, the general assemblies became venues for venting frustrations—which grew even as the Makhzen was successfully reversing the momentum. In the absence of legitimate leaders who would play a moderating role, the loudest and most vociferous activists tended to monopolize the debate. Anyone who proposed taking a step back to look at the big picture or considered even a slight tactical compromise with the Makhzen would be immediately accused of treason. As a way to showcase their uncompromising spirit, the most radical activists obstinately continued to propose weekly protests (even though their recurrence was visibly alienating the people) in working-class neighborhoods (even though the latter harbored Makhzen-manipulated "resident associations," which guaranteed violent clashes with the protesters). But since the most vociferous activists were now dominating general assembly discussions, the "general trend" was always in their favor, and their propositions were systematically adopted.

In Rabat, the creative Facebook activists who directed the movement in its early weeks (remember the video with the thirteen actors that launched the Feb20 original fervor) were gradually pushed aside in favor of radical activists. While a lot of time was once devoted to conceiving original slogans and arty banners, when the autumn of 2011 came, the protesters went mostly empty-handed, chanting outdated mantras—which rang hollow now that a new Constitution had been adopted and the political atmosphere had been altered by imminent legislative elections. The same thing happened in Casablanca, but with a twist: after the Support Council's dead-end dispute over the "ceiling of demands" contaminated the Feb20 activists, they resolved it by simply . . . abandoning political claims. After a heated general assembly, the "general trend" concluded that the only way to avoid a split was to set politics aside and focus on slogans denouncing poverty, unemployment, poor social services, and so on. This move definitely altered the image of the Feb20 Casablanca group: what used to be a movement claiming change and raising hope became perceived as a group of bitter and frustrated malcontents.[43] The protests' attendance diminished as a consequence.

In Marrakech, no compromise could be reached to ease the conflict between the two dominant local forces: university students from al-Adl and the "Basists" (*qa'idiyin*)—an extreme-left group with some members defining themselves as "Stalinists." The two groups have a history of violent clashes on university campuses, involving knives and even artisanal swords.[44] After they infused general assemblies with militant rhetoric, thus creating a vacuum in the Feb20 group, the Adlists and the Basists faced off and ended up "fighting with chairs," as a frustrated local activist put it. Pretty small crowds have attended Marrakech's protests ever since.

At the other end of the spectrum, Tangiers's demonstrations have long remained the most crowded ones in Morocco—and the local Feb20 group remained the country's most efficient. Even though they eventually created a "youth branch," mainly for communication purposes, the disciplined coalition of senior activists (from established groups and parties such as DAL, an-Nahj, al-Adl, the AMDH, ATTAC, and so on) remained firmly in command. However, the problem with being disciplined is that is also requires abiding by the decisions of one's mother organization—which are set in the organization's central headquarters in Rabat. Thus, as efficient as it was, Tangiers's cross-partisan coalition got eventually bogged in the same sand as the Support Council: that of the insoluble "ceiling of demands" dispute.

The Free-Rider Islamists

This was the context for the parliamentary elections, held on November 25. Feb20 and the Support Council called once again for a boycott, but in the end, the participation rate was higher than they had expected.[45] More noticeably, the electoral winner was the Justice and Development Party. Throughout ɔ11, the Islamist party played what many called a "double game" vis-à-vis the Makhzen and Feb20. At first, the PJD's secretariat general announced that the party would not back the protest movement, but it also stated that if some party members were to take to the streets, their "personal decision" would be "respected." Indeed, some of the PJD's most charismatic leaders were photographed on the front lines of the first demonstrations. Though refusing to officially support the protesters for the purpose of "preserving the kingdom's stability" (which implied that the protesters put the latter in jeopardy, an argument the royal palace cherished), the PJD continually highlighted its "points of agreement" with Feb20 and kept calling them to "constructive dialogue." At the same time, it was studiously participating in the "consultations" of the royal committee for constitutional reform. In other words, during the first phase of the 2011 events (those that ended with the constitutional referendum), the Islamist party kept a foot in both camps, as if it was playing for time, waiting to pick a winner.

By the time King Mohammed VI disclosed the constitutional draft, Feb20 had lost momentum and the monarchy had clearly regained the edge. The PJD unequivocally chose its side by calling for a "yes" vote. Feb20 immediately opened fire on Abdelilah Benkirane, the Islamist party's secretary general, calling him "another servant of the Makhzen." Benkirane struck back, dismissing the protest movement as an "isolated minority"—and, at the same time, using Feb20's rhetoric on change and democracy to campaign for the new Constitution's approval and later for his own party during the legislative elections campaign.[46] This ultimately led the PJD to a big victory at the polls, with an unprecedented 27 percent of the Parliament's seats (the incumbent Istiqlal Party won only 16%).

In fact, democratic claims were not new to the PJD or to the country. The advocacy for democratic reform has always been the soundtrack of Moroccan politics. Yet for most political actors, it mainly consisted of taking rhetorical postures while preserving the status quo, that is, the Makhzen's interests. The 2011 sequence of events and the emergence of Feb20 gave the same rhetoric new credibility—or, more accurately, it made the public realize two things: that calling for democracy can make sense, depending on who's making the call; and that it can work, judging by the way the monarchy complied and changed the Constitution.

Ultimately, Feb20 did not change political activism in Morocco. Rather, it improved the public's perception of political activism—provided it is performed by a group deemed credible and not corrupt. That was the case for Feb20 and also for the PJD, a party with an image of "political virginity" since it had never before been associated with the government. Finally, while the PSU and fellow DAL parties were stuck in their support of Feb20 (which led them to boycott both the constitutional referendum and the legislative elections), the PJD had it both ways: it benefited from the new context of hope created by Feb20's activism, and it capitalized on its support of the monarchy, branded as a "wise move that preserved the country's stability" (an appealing argument to voters). Therefore, with PJD's Benkirane appointed prime minister and the formation of a PJD-dominated cabinet, the Islamist party ended up as 2011's ultimate winner—alongside the Makhzen, of course.

The Quest for Survival

With a reformed Constitution and a fresh government, the general impression on December 2011 was that the people of Morocco had been granted a new political deal. That Feb20 and its last diehards were still unhappy and willing to protest seemed incomprehensible—and quite annoying—to the majority of the public. That explains the very low turnout of some sit-ins in December 2011, when only a few dozen protesters showed up, compared with the earlier turnouts of thousands. The protest movement's crisis deepened on December 18: in a surprising twist, al-Adl proclaimed through a communiqué that it was "ending its participation" in Feb20—an announcement immediately put into effect in all local Feb20 groups. Said Fathallah Arsalane, spokesman of the Islamist organization: "Going on protesting in the streets every Sunday with repetitive slogans is pointless and leads nowhere. The movement is a victim of its internal blockages and therefore, we don't see any more margin of progress within it."[47] Arsalane also referred to the "ceiling of demands" dispute by affirming: "The Feb20 movement has become the hostage of some groups who want to limit the threshold of its claims." In other words, the Islamist organization was willing to coalesce with its secular leftist foes as long as their coalition rocked the Makhzen's boat. But now that this approach was not working any more, it saw no point in continuing the alliance.

The Islamists' secession, however, may turn out to be a good thing for Feb20. Re-focusing on its original secular dimension may enable the protest movement to cater to middle-class constituencies (the latter had been neglected when Feb20 had started focusing on working-class neighborhoods, which are either pro-Makhzen or full of Islamists). Secularism and individual freedoms are highly polarizing concepts in Morocco since the independent press started to raise them in the mid-2000s.[48] In other words, both their adversaries and supporters are fervently passionate about these concepts. Yet while the Islamists do have political structures of their own, the secularists are not politically represented. Filling that gap could be a good political redeployment for Feb20: It would enhance the movement's commitment to democracy in a way that is consistent with its MALI origins and also affirm its newfound ideological independence vis-à-vis the Islamists. In a public speech delivered on January 6, 2012, the Support Council's vice president (also a top member of the AMDH and an-Nahj) urged Feb20 activists to add "gender equality" to their fundamental demands. An indirect blow to Islamists, this claim fits with the "secularist redeployment" direction explained above.

Still, what Feb20 needs first and foremost is organization. At least among the original nucleus of web activists, there seems to be a growing awareness that structure, hierarchy, and leadership are indispensable to the movement's revival, if there is to be any revival.[49] How exactly these things will be implemented remains unclear. There was some talk about transforming the movement into a regular political party, but it seems a daunting challenge given the current status of Feb20 local groups and the lack of interconnection between them. Another solution would be to join an existing political party. The PSU, which sided with the activist movement since its onset, seems the most appropriate choice. During its December 2011 convention, the leftist party adopted an openly secular platform and offered one-fifth of its congress seats to Feb20 activists. Many of them, notably in Casablanca, seized the opportunity and joined the leftist party. Yet this falls short of soaking up the movement's lifeblood. More efforts are needed to integrate maximum numbers of Feb20.

At the time of writing (March 2013), press reports suggest that the Benkirane cabinet is losing popular support after a series of increases in staple good prices (although no opinion poll was conducted to back this assumption). More decisively, no structural economic reform was conducted by the PJD. The sources of the 2011 revolt are still in place. Corruption, a major factor for discontent, is at peak level. Morocco's position on Transparency International's Corruption Perceptions Index has been worsening for years, going from 52nd in 2002 to 80th in 2011 and all the way to 88th at the end of 2012, one year into the Benkirane term. Unemployment is also higher than ever, especially among university graduates (the official rate is 25% in 2012).[50] On January 18, 2012, five militants of the "jobless graduates" hardline group set themselves on fire in Rabat to protest unemployment. Given the depth of these problems and the profound structural reforms that they require, the odds are long that Benkirane and his government will assuage popular anger quickly enough.

With months passing and the economy degrading, in the absence of democratic freedoms developed enough to act like a safety valve, serious street protesting is likely to resume sooner or later. The question is which group will channel the next round of popular anger; and if so, whether or not it will seize the momentum while exerting efficient—and this time, focused—pressure on the Makhzen. The PJD cannot play that mobilizing role anymore, now that it has been closely associated to the Makhzen and even held responsible for the degradation of purchasing power. The remaining activist movements that can do the channeling are al-Adl wal Ihsan or, maybe, a reformed Feb20-like coalition—provided that Morocco's democratic and secular activists learn lessons from the 2011 fiasco and manage to build a real grassroots movement with an identified and appealing agenda. Will this ever happen? The answer depends on the ability of Morocco's liberals to overcome their divisions, to build effective unity, and to rally behind legitimate national leaders—ones who are able to balance charisma and strong convictions with political wit and strategic finesse. That such leaders exist, however, is yet to be proven.

Notes

1. King Mohammed VI's speech, March 9, 2011.

2. In Morocco, the common understanding of "civil society" (notably established by the independent press in the mid-1990s) encompasses NGOs, advocacy groups, professional and labor unions, charities, think tanks, sports clubs, and other urban or rural groups that are active on the social, economic, or cultural fronts. Their common denominator is their refusal to engage in political activity. In some cases—mostly among human rights groups and labor unions—their activity has obvious political connotations. But officially, all of these groups pledge to stay away from partisan activity and to desist from taking political sides. That is why Islamist groups that have openly political positions and agendas are considered a category of their own, distinct from civil society.

3. This has changed slightly since July 2011's constitutional reform. Now the king is obliged to pick the prime minister from the political party that wins the parliamentary election. Yet the king can still pick any member he wants from that party. Also, the notion of "winning" the elections is vague, tricky, and insufficient to guarantee a true democratic outcome. The key factor remains Morocco's biased electoral system—which did not change despite the new Constitution. For more details, see Ahmed Benchemsi, "Morocco: Outfoxing the Opposition," *Journal of Democracy* 23(1) (2012): 57–69.

4. *Makhzen* is the Arabic word for "warehouse." It was originally used to name the treasure chest where Sultans stored the taxes collected from the people. The meaning has evolved throughout history. It first broadened to mean, symbolically, the contents of the chest—that is, the Sultan's assets. Later, it expanded to include the personnel paid with these assets and later still the whole government, administration, and army. Since the Alaouite dynasty was installed in the seventeenth century, the term *Makhzen* is used in reference to anyone who contributes in relaying the king's power to the population. In its current political usage, however, the word refers to the clique surrounding the king, which often operates as a club of shadow decisionmakers.

5. In fact, they are the only parties that use the term *Makhzen* in their lexicon.

6. French acronym for "Parti Socialiste Unifié." The two other members of the DAL coalition are the Democratic and Socialist Vanguard Party (PADS) and the Ittihadi (Unionist) National Congress (CNI).

7. Arabic for "the Democratic Path"—the party is commonly known as Annahj or an-Nahj (the Path).

8. French acronym for Association Marocaine des Droits de l'Homme.

9. The AMDH is formally an independent NGO. However, many of its leaders are also members of the republican an-Nahj Party. Even though double-hatted leaders take particular pains to insulate their human rights advocacy from their party activism, the Makhzen-leaning media often accuse the AMDH of "extremism," highlighting its an-Nahj penchants.

10. For more on this, see the AMDH's website at www.amdh.org.ma/ar/about -amdh/presentation, accessed July 24, 2013.

11. Local branch of ATTAC, French acronym for "Association pour la Taxation des Transactions financières et pour l'Aide aux Citoyens" (Association for taxing financial transactions and helping citizens). ATTAC was created in France in 1998 to "oppose neo-liberal globalization and develop social, ecological, and democratic alternatives."

12. Many protesters against high prices were also carrying pictures of King Mohammed VI as a signal of loyalty directed at the police forces who might be tempted to repress them.

13. Arabic for "Justice and Charity"—the group is commonly known as al-Adl (Justice).

14. The authorities never formally authorized it but generally tolerate its activities.

15. Some evoke the "philosophical prospect" of "reinstalling the Islamic caliphate," others mention a hypothetical "Islamic republic" . . . but no one gets into the particulars of such options, and the organization's literature is no clearer on the matter.

16. Yassine would die on December 13, 2012, at the age of eighty-four, to be immediately replaced by his lieutenant Mohammed Abbadi. At the time of writing, it is

too early to say whether the leadership succession would induce significant changes in al-Adl's structure and political strategy.

17. "Al-Adl vs. the Monarchy: A Secret War," *TelQuel* magazine, July 15, 2006.

18. Rabat's public school of journalism is arguably the country's most fertile breeding ground for web activists.

19. French acronym for "Mouvement alternatif pour les libertés individuelles."

20. By a provision of Morocco's penal code, breaking the Ramadan fast in public is prohibited, and those who commit this offense are subject to six months in jail.

21. The author conducted twenty-five interviews with Feb20 activists in Casablanca, Rabat, Marrakech, and Tangiers in April, May, and December 2011. A majority evoked the MALI affair as their "awakening to activism."

22. Four members of this family were then serving as cabinet members (including Prime Minister Abbas El Fassi), and at least four other family members occupied top government positions. When the prime minister's son Majid El Fassi was made a high-ranking executive in public television right after his college graduation—his position reportedly came with a car and chauffeur—an outcry ensued, both on- and offline.

23. Another fact may debunk—at least partially—the notion of a Feb20 driven by class warfare: The presence of multimillionaire industrialists Karim Tazi and Miloud Chaabi at the forefront of the Feb20 manifestations would never be seen as a problem by Feb20's leaders—on the contrary, the latter would gladly accept Tazi's financial help to acquire megaphones, print flyers, and address other logistical needs; as for Chaabi, he would distribute thousands of water bottles—which he manufactures—during the protests.

24. At that time, they were three: a student from Meknes and two unemployed young men, one from Fes and the other one from Salé.

25. Oussama El-Khlifi, a twenty-three-year-old unemployed computer science graduate from Salé (the twin town of Rabat, on the other side of the Bou Regreg River), is the son of a police officer and a former member of the socialist party's youth section.

26. Oussama El-Khlifi, interview with the author, April 2011. The first date they picked was February 27. After realizing that this was also the anniversary date of the Polisario Front (an armed group at war against Morocco because of its independence claim for Western Sahara), they moved it to February 20 in order to avoid confusion.

27. Even though some local Feb20 groups emerged in rural areas, the movement was mainly an urban phenomenon—simply because the typical actors of Feb20 local groups (internet-savvy youth, radical left party members, and civil society organization activists) are mainly found in cities. Since independence, Morocco's countryside has generally been the bastion of the Makhzen (through either one of its satellite parties) or, in rare cases, of nationalist-conservative formations like the Istiqlal

Party or Hizb ash-Shoura. Leftist parties and left-leaning civil society organizations were never able to take significant root in rural areas—except for some rare mining localities where labor unions managed to establish themselves among the rural working-class populace.

28. PSU's Mostafa Meftah, interview with the author, Casablanca, April 2011.

29. A dense and loosely structured network of NGOs throughout Morocco, the movement claims recognition and implementation of Amazigh (Berber) language and culture in the Constitution as much as in the public administration and public education curricula.

30. Feb20 local activists, interviews with the author, Marrakech, December 2011.

31. Feb20 leaders, interviews with the author, Casablanca, Rabat, Marrakech, and Tangiers, April, May, and December 2011.

32. AMDH's Abdelhamid Amine, interview with the author, Rabat, April 2011.

33. Constitutional law professor Abdeltif Menouni once explained the notion of "royal prerogative" as "the monarch's discretionary privilege to act for the good of the country in the absence of constitutional provisions or by his personal interpretation of any." Abdeltif Menouni, *Revue juridique, politique et économique du Maroc,* Mohammed V University, Rabat, January 1984, p. 42.

34. Carl von Clausewitz, *Principles of War* (Princeton: Princeton University Press, 1976).

35. Interviews in Casablanca and Rabat, April–May 2011.

36. Ibid.

37. The lists of cities were provided by al-Adl wal-Ihsan, and the government never contested any of it—that would not have made sense, since every local march was documented by at least one YouTube video, largely shared through social networks.

38. Visual proof of the connection between the authorities and proregime demonstrators largely circulated online. In a couple of videos posted on YouTube, some of them openly admitted being paid to chant "Long live the king."

39. Benchemsi, "Morocco: Outfoxing the Opposition."

40. Oddly enough, going shirtless was a common mark of recognition of the proregime goons. Many explain that strange habit by the consumption of *qarqoubi,* a cheap and popular psychotropic drug known for raising the body's temperature.

41. Opinion polls on the monarchy are de facto forbidden in Morocco, as can be seen by the August 2009 seizure of one hundred thousand copies of the weekly magazines *TelQuel* and *Nichane* by police forces for running and publishing a national survey titled "The People Judge the King." That was the first and last article of the kind in the country. Paradoxically, the survey banned "on principle" (as a way to signify that conducting polls about the "sacred" monarch was out of range) showed

that the king enjoys overwhelming popular support: 91% consider the track record of Mohammed VI either "positive" or "very positive" after ten years on the throne. Also, 49% consider Morocco a "democratic monarchy," while 33% consider it an "autocratic monarchy"—but the majority of the latter, according to *TelQuel,* mean that "as a compliment." The *TelQuel/Nichane* poll was also featured in the French daily *Le Monde,* which partnered with the two Moroccan magazines for the project. The print issue of *Le Monde* (August 4, 2009, pp. 1, 6) was censored in Morocco. However, the article was—and still is—available online: Florence Beaugé, "Maroc: le sondage interdit," *Le Monde,* August 3, 2009, available at www.lemonde.fr/af- rique/article/2009/08/03/maroc-le-sondage-interdit_1225217_3212.html, accessed July 24, 2013.

42. Interviews in Casablanca and Rabat, April and May 2011.

43. Interviews in Casablanca, December 2011.

44. Al-Adl wal-Ihsan is a nonviolent organization—except on campuses, where its members form militias to maintain "Islamic order." As for the Basists, one of their ideological features—assertive atheism aside—is to consider violence a "class behav- ior" (*suluk tabaqi*). Therefore, they condone it and, sometimes, practice it.

45. The official participation rate for the November 25 election is 45%, but the figure's legitimacy is disputed. The participation rate in Morocco is derived from the number of registered voters (13 million in 2011) rather than the number of citizens above voting age (21 million). Had it been derived from the latter number, critics say, the participation rate would have been 24%—below the official 2007 partici- pation rate of 37%. This argument intends to demonstrate that Feb20's call for a boycott was successful, since the participation rate had receded. Yet, it is fallacious because the 2007 rate too was derived from the registered voting population. There- fore, it makes sense to compare 45% to 37%, but it is irrelevant to compare 24% to 37%. In other words, Feb20's call for a boycott was numerically unsuccessful.

46. Speech by Benkirane, 2011, available at www.youtube.com/watch?v= -IyUdQ3_aCE, accessed September 4, 2013.

47. Interview published in *Maroc Hebdo* magazine, December 23, 2011.

48. Particularly the weekly magazines *TelQuel* (in French) and *Nichane* (in Arabic).

49. Interviews with the author of Feb20 activists in Rabat and Casablanca, De- cember 2011.

50. Haut Commissariat au Plan du Royaume du Maroc, "Taux de chômage na- tional selon le diplôme," available at www.hcp.ma/Taux-de-chomage-national-selon -le-diplome_a267.html, accessed July 25, 2013.

CHAPTER 8

Jordan

Evolving Activism in a Divided Society

MOHAMMED YAGHI *and* JANINE A. CLARK

SINCE EARLY JANUARY 2011, Jordan has witnessed ongoing protests demanding social justice and democratic reform.[1] Starting as a demonstration against the rise of commodity prices and unemployment in the southern town of Thieban, the protests spread to all Jordanian cities and soon evolved into demands for political reform. Tensions reached their peak on March 24, 2011,[2] when fourteen youth groups associated with the opposition tried to emulate the sit-in in Egypt's Tahrir Square by holding a permanent sit-in in Amman, only to be attacked by the Jordanian riot police (*darak*).[3] Jordan's opposition did not demand a change of regime, as in the cases of Tunisia and Egypt, but it did call for constitutional reforms aimed at limiting the king's executive authorities, namely his prerogatives to appoint and dismiss the government, dissolve the parliament, and appoint deputies to the Upper House of Parliament, as set forth in articles 34, 35, and 36 of the Jordanian constitution. However, it is not the opposition's demands per se that have attracted the attention of political analysts and the concern of the regime but the widespread nature of the protests, both demographically and geographically, and in particular their presence in Transjordanian areas—areas that for a long time have been considered the regime's social base.[4]

In order to minimize the political concessions it is being pressured to make, the regime has attempted to exacerbate divisions within the opposition. The

opposition is divided along lines of both identity and ideology, with Transjordanian activists primarily demanding reforms related to issues of social justice
and Palestinian Jordanian activists seeking greater political inclusion. The
chance that the king would relinquish part of his executive authority to elected
deputies remains high. However, the realization of any political reforms will
depend to a large extent on the opposition's ability to unify and advance a
common reform agenda, one that bridges longstanding divides between Transjordanians and Jordanians of Palestinian origin.

   This chapter traces the rise of new opposition groups in Jordan as a result
of the "Jordan Spring" and examines their different and often conflicting political demands, their impact on the structure of mobilization of the opposition, and their significance for long-term political reform.[5] The chapter is divided into six parts. The first section provides a concise historical background
to the sources of division within the opposition and the institutional factors
that affected the mobilization of opposition forces beginning in the late 1980s.
The second section examines the changes in the structure of mobilization of
the opposition, based on the forms of organization, places of engagement, and
the demographic profile of activists. The third section identifies the most important new actors in the opposition and their significance. This section draws
specific attention to the rise and demands of four new opposition actors from
the regime's traditional support base: Transjordanian youth, tribal leaders,
retired military generals, and reformist elites. Section four addresses the relationship between activists in the opposition, underscoring the sources of disagreement over reform priorities and the impact of events in Syria on the unity
of the opposition. It also tracks and assesses initiatives by different actors to
unify the opposition's agenda and activities. The fifth section highlights the
changes in the regime's strategy in response to the domestic crisis and regional
developments. The chapter concludes by identifying opportunities for positive
reforms.

Identity and Institutional Context

Structural factors have shaped Jordan's opposition, specifically the nature of
its mobilization, its demographic and geographic reach, and its demands.
These are largely but not solely a result of regime strategies that both build on
and entrench the identity divisions within Jordanian society. Three structural
factors—the design of political institutions in favor of Transjordanians, the
division of labor according to identity, and the increasing role of the Palestinian

January 7, 2011: Almost five hundred people gather in Theiban, Madaba, southern Jordan to protest unemployment and poverty.

January 21, 2011: More than five thousand people gather in Amman to protest declining economic conditions and demand that Prime Minister Samir Rifai step down from power.

January 28, 2011: On the third consecutive Friday of protests, 3,500 opposition protesters gather in Amman to denounce Prime Minister Samir Rifai and demand economic and political reform.

January 31, 2011: To appease the protesters, King Abdullah II sacks his government and asks former army general Marouf al-Bakhit to form a new cabinet.

February 3, 2011: For the first time in nearly a decade, King Abdullah II meets with members of the Muslim Brotherhood.

February 9, 2011: Amid demands for economic improvements, King Abdullah II swears in a new twenty-seven-member cabinet, though the foreign, interior, and economic ministers are a holdover from the old guard. The Muslim Brotherhood declines an offer to participate in the new government.

February 15, 2011: To appease protesters, Interior Minister Saed Hayel Srour says that demonstrations will no longer need government permission.

February 18, 2011: In Amman, eight people are injured as three hundred protesters clash with government supporters.

February 25, 2011: Six thousand people march in Amman calling for lower prices, new elections, and changes to the constitution that would give King Abdullah II absolute power.

March 4, 2011: Thousands of people march in Amman demanding the ouster of newly appointed prime minister Marouf al-Bakhit, who is suspected of election fraud.

March 11, 2011: Clashes between proreform protesters and government loyalists occur in front of the Ministry of the Interior, leaving scores of people injured.

March 24, 2011: In the main square in Amman, hundreds of Jordanians set up a protest camp to demand political and social reforms.

March 25, 2011: Clashes between government supporters and protests leave one person dead and at least 120 injured in one of the most violent demonstrations since the start of the unrest in January.

March 26, 2011: Seven thousand progovernment supporters take to the streets to show their loyalty to the crown.

April 7, 2011: Forty-five-year-old Mohammed Abdul-Karim immolates himself outside of the Prime Minister's office.

April 15, 2011: Dozens are wounded as 350 Salafi hardliners clash with progovernment protesters in Zarqa.

June 27, 2011: Prime Minister Marouf al-Bakhit survives an impeachment vote amid angry cries from protesters who want him fired for his role in approving the country's first casino.

June 2, 2011: King Abdullah II signs a decree admitting nine new members to the newly reshuffled cabinet.

July 8, 2011: Police clash with hundreds of proreform protesters, leaving at least seventeen people injured.

July 22, 2011: Three hundred youth join together to protest the oppressive measures used on protesters by the government.

July 29, 2011: Three thousand protesters, the majority of whom are members of the Muslim Brotherhood, demonstrate in Amman.

October 1, 2011: Outspoken opposition leader and former MP Laith Shbeilat is stoned while making a speech criticizing the slowness of the reforms.

October 7, 2011: Former prime minister Ahmad Obeidat leads a march of over two thousand people outside the Grand Husseini Mosque in Amman.

October 15, 2011: Progovernment and proreform protesters clash during demonstrations in Salhub, leaving thirty-five people injured.

October 17, 2011: King Abdullah II sacks Prime Minister Marouf al-Bakhit and replaces him with international judge Awn Shawkat al-Khasawneh.

October 24, 2011: King Abdullah II swears in a new thirty-member cabinet.

November 14, 2011: King Abdullah II becomes the first Arab head of state to call for Syria's President Assad to step down.

December 23, 2011: In Almafraq, loyalists to King Abdullah II from the Bani Hassan tribe clash with hundreds of protesters and attack the offices of the Muslim Brotherhood.

Liberation Organization (PLO) after the 1967 Arab-Israeli War—have impeded the development of a Jordanian national identity that unifies Jordanians of Transjordanian and Palestinian descent. The development of these two separate and distinct identities was then exacerbated by both domestic and regional events. The following section examines these structural factors and how the existence of two national identities, one Transjordanian and one Palestinian, is reflected in the demographic base of Jordan's different political parties and opposition groups, the conflicting political demands of the different opposition parties and groups, the issues over which they mobilize, and even in the different geographic areas in which opposition protests take place.

Transjordan was created by British imperial fiat in 1921 as a means to satisfy the last part of its promise to its Arab allies against the Ottomans during

World War I.[6] Prince Abdullah, son of Sharif Hussein, with support from the British, struggled to achieve the loyalty of various tribes that lived in the newly created state.[7] By "enlisting tribal members in a national army, offering them land grants and expanding employment for them in the emerging civil service," Prince Abdullah was eventually successful in creating "deep bonds between Transjordanians and the regime."[8] From the beginning, therefore, the regime's social base was rooted in Transjordanian tribes who rely on the state for employment and subsidies.

The evolution of a distinct Transjordanian identity, however, was aborted by the 1948 Arab-Israeli War, when hundreds of thousands of Palestinians fled to or were expelled to Jordan.[9] The West Bank itself was annexed to Jordan in 1949, and the unification of the two banks of the Jordan River was officially declared in April 1950.[10] Prince Abdullah became the king of the united two banks. Jordan Law No. 56 of 1949 considered the populations of both the West Bank and the East Bank to be Jordanian. As a result, Jordan's population increased overnight from 375,000 to 1,270,000. The seats of Jordan's Chamber of Deputies were divided equally between the West Bank and the East Bank.[11]

Both the official policies of the Jordanian regime and the rise of the PLO prevented the evolution of one identity for all Jordanians. The Jordanian regime continued to favor the employment of Transjordanians in the army and the state public sector after 1949. At the same time, its investments in East Jordan encouraged hundreds of thousands of Palestinian Jordanians to leave the West Bank and to settle in the East Bank in order to work in the growing private sector. Later, this division of labor was exacerbated by the regime's policy during the 1970s of purging Palestinian Jordanians from state institutions, largely as a response to the regime's tensions with the PLO.[12] Transjordanians thus came to dominate the public sector and Palestinian Jordanians the private sector.[13] At the same time, the rise of the PLO in late 1964 and its conflict with the regime over representation of the Palestinians also prevented the development of one national identity for all Jordanians. The PLO's rejection of Jordan's annexation of the West Bank; the PLO's struggle to create an independent Palestinian state; the Israeli capture of the West Bank in 1967; the 1970–1971 conflict between the PLO militants and the Jordanian army; and finally the 1974 Arab Summit decision in Rabat that made the PLO the sole legitimate representative of the Palestinians all exacerbated the divisions between Jordanians over issues of national identity.[14] Transjordanians came to believe that the state was theirs and developed a narrative of national identity revolving around the role of the Hashemite family in building Jordan and their traditional tribal origins, while Palestinian Jordanians maintained a Palestinian national identity, one revolving around the conflict with Israel.[15]

Transjordanians' fears that Jordan may turn into an alternative homeland for the Palestinians helped to foster a distinct Transjordanian national identity. These fears have been fueled by successive political events beginning, most importantly, with the Israeli Likud Party's position, created on the heels of the Israeli occupation of the West Bank in 1967 and remaining in place today, that Jordan is the Palestinian homeland.[16] Transjordanians became more concerned with the arrival of three hundred thousand Palestinians expelled from Kuwait during the 1991 Gulf War, the failure of the 1993 Oslo Accords, and the Palestinian Second Intifada in late 2000.[17] These events all reinforced the Transjordanians' apprehension that Palestinians fleeing or being expelled to Jordan as a result of the ongoing political unrest in the West Bank, Syria, and even Lebanon would turn Jordan into a homeland for the Palestinians, as a result of which they would lose the Jordanian identity of their land. Thus, Palestinian Jordanian fears that their claim for regaining the West Bank and, more broadly, historical Palestine is becoming more endangered with each successive defeat have accompanied growing Transjordanian fears of losing their own homeland as a result of the increasing numbers of Palestinians settling and buying land in Jordan and, most importantly, seeking Jordanian nationality.

Jordan's political liberalization and economic restructuring of the 1990s also deepened the discourse regarding national identity and the all-important question of who is a Jordanian. The economic crises of the late 1980s forced Jordan to implement a structural adjustment plan that "included monetary stabilization to fight inflation and privatization to encourage economic growth."[18] A political opening followed in 1989, spurred by riots in the southern cities of Maan, Tafilah, and Kerak in response to rising fuel prices.[19] However, the new electoral law implemented as part of the political reform was designed to favor the regime's Transjordanian support base and to provide it with a mechanism to compete over access to state resources.[20] As a result, electoral districts with Palestinian Jordanian majorities, such as Amman, Zarqa, and Irbid were and continue to be underrepresented.[21] This, coupled with the fact that most of the state income tax is derived from the private sector, has deepened Palestinian Jordanians' sense of political exclusion.[22] At the same time, Transjordanians, especially in southern Jordan, are frustrated by the policies of marginalization and privatization, as Jordan's natural resources, such as phosphate, potassium, oil shale, and uranium, are overwhelmingly found in Transjordanian areas. Uneven regional development as well as the weakening of the public sector as a result of the privatization of state companies are both perceived as undermining their domination over state resources.[23] Indeed, as state corruption has accompanied privatization, Transjordanians largely feel that they are losing their own state to a small circle of elite Palestinian Jordanians close to King Abdullah II.[24] In this light it is no surprise that the phrase "the center of Jordan [Amman and Zarqa, where most Palestinian Jordanians reside] is eating from the peripheries" is common among Transjordanian opposition elites.[25]

This structural context, namely the design of political institutions in favor of Transjordanians, the division of labor according to identity, and the increasing role of the PLO, has impeded the development of a unified political opposition that cuts across the identity lines dividing Jordanians and also shaped the kind of oppositional mobilization that has arisen and its demographic and geographic reach; in Tunisia and Egypt, contrariwise the activists were able to overcome their identity divisions temporarily by focusing on ousting the respective regime, considering it the source of all grievances for the moment.[26] Indeed, when the regime initiated the political opening of 1989, old opposition parties such as the Jordan's Democratic People's Party and the Democratic Popular Unity Party were dominated by Palestinian Jordanians who were officially affiliated with the Democratic Front for the Liberation of Palestine and the Popular Front for the Liberation of Palestine.[27] In contrast, both the Arab Socialist Baath Party and the Jordanian Communist Party were dominated by Transjordanians.[28]

The Muslim Brotherhood (MB) was in no way immune from identity-based politics. Registered as a charitable society in 1946, the relationship between the regime and the MB prior to 1989 was based more on cooperation than on competition or opposition. In 1957, the MB supported the regime in its struggle against pan-Arabist and leftist parties.[29] During the 1970–71 conflict between the regime and Palestinian militants, the MB remained neutral; for this stance it was rewarded with the appointment of Ishaq El-Farhan, a prominent MB leader, as minister of education.[30] During the April 1989 uprising, King Hussein similarly thanked the MB leaders for not joining the protests. It was only in 1994, when the regime signed the Wadi Araba Treaty with Israel, that the MB and its newly created party, the Islamic Action Front (IAF), began to take a more oppositional stance toward the regime and to cooperate with other opposition parties.

However, as a result of the MB's focus on the conflict with Israel and its strong bonds with the Palestinian Hamas movement, both it and the IAF were perceived by many Transjordanians as the political representative of Palestinian Jordanians, a perception that was actually reflected in the MB and IAF memberships. This continues to the present day. Although the MB, beginning with the Jordan Spring, now focuses less on the conflict with Israel and support for Hamas[31] and is increasingly engaged with the protests in the southern Jordanian cities and the calls for reform,[32] it is still perceived by the majority of Transjordanians as a Palestinian party.

As a result of these identity-driven politics, the 1989 protests against the removal of fuel subsidies and the 1996 protests against the reduction of food subsidies were concentrated in the regime's social base in the southern cities of Maan, Kerak, Madaba, and Tafilah and were spontaneous in nature in the sense that they were based on the uncoordinated initiatives of local activists.[33] The 1990–91 protests against the American intervention in Iraq, the 1997 protests against the involvement of some Jordanians in cultural and economic activities with Israelis, the 2000–02 demonstrations in support of the Palestinian Second Intifada, and the 2003 protests against U.S. intervention in Iraq, however, were all organized by the party-based political opposition and were concentrated primarily in Amman, Zarqa, and Irbid, where a majority of the inhabitants are Palestinian Jordanians.[34]

Finally, the identity division has limited both the opposition's agenda for political reform and the extent of popular mobilization. The opposition never contested the legitimacy and authority of the king during the era of liberalization in 1989 and beyond. Similarly, the extensive interventions of the General Intelligence Agency (*mukhabarat*) in almost every aspect of Jordanians' lives also had not been a subject of protest.[35] With regard to domestic political rights, the political opposition's activities have historically been limited to demanding changes to the electoral law. After the introduction of the new election law in 1993 (giving one person one vote as opposed to voting for the number of seats the district held), the opposition parties boycotted the parliamentary election of 1997.[36] Opposition political parties, however, did not resist the restrictions on freedom of expression that began in the 1990s. According to Ellen Lust, "Between 1993 and 1997, the government made sixty-six prosecutions for violations of the Press and Publication Law" and in 1998, the government increased the monetary fines for violations to the Press and Publication Law.[37] These changes all occurred largely without any opposition parties defying the regime.

Ideological divisions also hinder the opposition's quest for political reform. Research has shown that cooperation between Jordan's political parties breaks down largely on issues that are ideological in nature. Islamists in particular are unable to compromise on issues relating to Islam, such as the Personal Status Law, which is the part of the law that deals with matters pertaining to the life of a person such as marriage, divorce, inheritance, if a child can depart a country with his mother (or father) without the consent of the father (or mother), and so forth. As Janine Clark explains, while the Higher Committee for the Coordination of National Opposition Parties (HCCNOP), founded in the mid-1990s in response to normalization efforts by Jordan with Israel, was able to agree on a joint rejection of Jordan's normalization of relations with Israel as well as on the quota allocating seats for women in parliament, it failed to reach a common stance on Article 340, also known as the "honor-crimes law," and the Personal Status Law granting women greater divorce rights.[38]

In short, the dynamics of mobilization of the old opposition before the advent of the Arab Spring were strongly affected by structural conditions. As a result, the political opposition of the past was sporadic and limited in both its demographic and geographic profile and in its agenda for political reform.

Changes in the Structure of Mobilization: The Jordan Spring

As stated above, the Jordan Spring began in a small southern town in January 2011. Seven young men independently gathered in front of the main mosque of Thieban to protest unemployment and the rise of gas prices (in excess of 30% in 2010).[39] The seven became seventy when bystanders, who shared their frustrations with the regime's economic policies, joined them; by the time the Friday prayer had finished, the group had become five hundred.[40] During the following week, pan-Arabist and leftist activists as well as retired military officers had contributed to the spread of protests to Kerak and Amman; by the second week, the IAF had joined the protests. By the third week, there had been protests in Jordanian cities from Irbid to Maan.[41] Unlike the protests of the past, the activists linked their economic demands with political demands, asking for the dismissal of the Samir Refai government.[42] As the protests evolved, their dynamics and demands changed significantly from those of the past. Protests that had been sporadic began to occur with regularity. Activists were no longer limited to party members, as had been the case in the past but were comprised mostly of independents and those with Transjordanian roots. Most importantly, activists' fears of the *mukhabarat* increasingly vanished, and their demands for political reform now aimed for the elimination of the king's executive and legislative authorities.

The transition from sporadic protests to a more continuous pattern of activism can be grasped from the number of demonstrations, marches, seminars, conferences, and speeches that have taken place across the country. According to Lieutenant General Hussein Al-Majali, the director general of the General Security Department, there were more than four thousand protest activities in 2011 alone.[43] Al-Majali also claims that the government spent 28 million Jordanian dinars to ensure the safety of the protesters in 2011.[44] The locations of the protests were diverse: While the protest activities in Amman were concentrated in downtown and eastern Amman, the activities in southern Jordan primarily took place in front of governorate buildings.[45] The activists were also diverse. In addition to the old opposition's activists, they were made up of youth, tribal, and retired military members. Some youth activists carried the names of their origins, such as the Kerak Youth Movement and the Hay al-Tafaileh Youth Movement. Other activists have named themselves in reference to a major event, such as the Youth Movement of March 24 (in reference to their call for the sit-in at Gamal Abdel Nasser Circle on March 24, 2011) and the Movement of April 15 (in reference to the uprising of April 1989). Some named themselves after the nature of their demands, such as the 1952 Constitution Movement and the National Commission for Constitutional Monarchy. Still others named themselves according to their profession, such as the Higher National Committee for Retired Military.[46] As Curtis Ryan notes, many Jordanians participate in more than one group.[47] Most of the groups have a Facebook page where its members discuss political reform, report on events across Jordan, and inform their supporters of dates, slogans, and places of protests.[48]

The demographic profile of activists also has changed. Prior to the Jordan Spring, the majority of activists had been young people, while the opposition leaders had been the old guards of political parties. Today, all political parties refer to the protesters as the youth movement (al-hirak al-shababi). The protests also have spread beyond the engineers, doctors, lawyers, and journalists who used to be at the forefront of the opposition in the past and now include schoolteachers and laborers.

Schoolteachers and workers have been particularly active since April 2010. Teachers organized twelve strikes, marches, and sit-ins in the name of the right to establish a trade union.[49] Similarly, in 2010, labor activists at the Ministry of Agriculture organized seventeen protest activities demanding the same working rights as their colleagues performing similar or equivalent jobs.[50] The struggles of both teachers and laborers encouraged other groups to defend their social and economic rights. In the first nine months of 2011, public and private sector employees organized 607 strikes, 61.5 percent of which were carried out by the employees of the public sector, the very base of regime support. This is four times the number of strikes in 2010.[51]

The role of women in the protests has been limited; however, this trend is also beginning to change. Women have participated in protest activities, particularly in Amman and Irbid. The sit-in of March 24, 2011, at Gamal Abdel Nasser Circle in Amman, for example, included women activists from different governorates throughout the country.[52] The formation of the Jordanian Women for Reform Forum, a coalition of women affiliated to the IAF, also draws women to participate in the protests—most of whom are not affiliated with the MB.[53]

It also can be argued that the wall of fear has fallen. The king is no longer immune from criticism. In almost all rallies, protesters chant "Hey Abdullah, the son of Hussein: Where is the people's money?"[54] In this phrase, the words "His Majesty and our beloved king" are replaced by the disrespectful "Hey Abdullah." Indeed, the most daring and popular dance today in Jordan's southern cities is the Corruption Dance (*Dabket al-fasad*), in which the dancers chant "Ali Baba and the forty thieves." The song depicts the king as Ali Baba, the sponsor of corruption, who is assisted by forty thieves, some of whom are explicitly named as royal family members.[55]

The activists have also become bold in both their discourse and activities. It is common to find statements on activists' Facebook pages accusing the regime of not wanting reform and pushing the activists to demand regime change.[56] In fact, following the detention of fourteen activists in Tafilah, the opposition organized a demonstration in that city on March 10, 2012, during which the mother of Majdi Qabaleen, one the detainees, addressed the demonstrators and called for regime change amid cries of support from the gathering.[57] Similarly, in response to regime supporters' attack on the IAF march and the burning of its offices in Mafraq on December 23, 2011, the IAF organized a "Fed Up Friday" march in downtown Amman a few days later.[58] A large group of the IAF's youth activists marched in the front of the rally wearing green headbands similar to those of the Islamic Resistance Movement (Hamas).[59]

Perhaps the most important change in the protests is the nature of the activists' political demands, which focus on two main subjects: constitutional reforms, which would establish Jordanian citizens as the only source of political authority, and economic reforms, which would restore the state's role in the economy and put an end to corruption. Ali Habashneh, head of the Higher National Committee for Retired Military, explains the demands of the activists: We want the king to own but not to govern *"yamluk wa la yatahakam,"* in other words to wield far less power. By using the word *own* he is specifically referring to the throne but not including any of its executive authorities.[60] Similarly, Zaki Bani Rsheid, a member of the IAF's political bureau, has stated that his party will not end its protest activities before the establishment of an elected parliamentarian government and the amendment of the constitutional articles that grant the king authority to appoint the government, dissolve the parliament, and appoint the Upper House.[61] To paraphrase a young activist in Amman, the activists are demanding that responsibility and accountability work hand in hand. The king, he argues, is responsible, but he is not accountable—the constitution makes him immune. As the activist explained, "We want the government to be elected and to have full executive authorities."[62]

However, despite their common agenda, the new opposition and the old opposition prioritize these demands differently. Activists of the new opposition begin their discourse with an overview of how privatization policies and corruption have impoverished Transjordanians and focus mainly on the southern regions of Jordan, while the activists of the old opposition commonly begin with the need for political reforms and conclude with the latter's implication for economic reforms. This division over priorities has weakened the protest movement. In fact, since the sit-in of March 24, 2011, the new opposition and the old opposition, especially the IAF, have organized only a limited number of protest activities together. The nature, demands, and political significance of the new opposition actors play an important role in contributing to this ongoing lack of cooperation between the new and old opposition groups.

New Opposition Actors

The embedded nature of the new opposition actors in and across multiple social network groups and their different motivations make it hard to define them in exact terms. However, as stated above, the new opposition can be said to be a loose alliance that includes Transjordanian youth groups, tribal leaders, retired military generals, and influential elites. As the following section demonstrates, however, the sources of power of these new actors, their specific demands and, ultimately, their political significance differ greatly.

The Transjordanian youth groups that are influential in the new opposition are concentrated predominantly in southern Jordan and in Hay al-Tafaileh in Amman.[63] Several factors contributed to the rise of these youth groups. First among them, according to Khaled Shaqran, the head of the Al-Rai Center for Studies, is the poverty and unemployment of southern Jordan. More specifically, Transjordanian youth rose up in protest against what they perceive as the sons and daughters of the elites taking the places of their fathers. As Shaqran explains, the Transjordanian youth may consider it normal that the king's son inherits the throne of his father, but it is not acceptable that the sons of the elites inherit the positions of their fathers.[64]

Second, the high discrepancy between salaries of public servants with equivalent jobs and status also has created a sense of anger, especially among younger employees. The salary of a driver for the Ministry of Energy and Mineral Resources is approximately 400 Jordanian dinars (US$570), double that of a driver for the Jordanian Atomic Energy Commission, even though both perform the same job and receive their salaries from the Ministry of Finance.[65] A related source of frustration is the prevailing nepotism within the civil service—not all tribes are treated equally. In his attempt to maintain the loyalty of Transjordanian elites, King Abdullah II has created sixty-two independent commissions employing twenty-two thousand people, all of whom are on the public payroll and most of whom are the sons and daughters of former or current ministers and deputies, ambassadors, and tribal leaders.[66]

Finally, and most importantly, there is a general feeling among Transjordanian youth that the regime treats them as subjects. The privileges Transjordanians receive, whether the construction of a new road or an entry scholarship for university, are bestowed by the regime as royal grants. This policy (and attitude) might have worked in the past to uphold the allegiance of Transjordanians; today, however, the majority of young Transjordanians are well educated and seek to be treated as citizens. Unlike their grandfathers and fathers, who used to perceive these privileges as a grant from the royal family for which they should be grateful, the younger generation thinks of them as a right. Indeed, in every demonstration, Transjordanian youth activists can be heard reminding the king that they are asking for rights and not grants (*huqooq la makarem*).[67] This also is a common theme in the posts and comments that appear on the Facebook pages of youth groups.[68] The Transjordanian youth's source of power derives from their status as the sons and daughters of influential tribes; as a result, the regime is hesitant to use coercive power against them, as that might exacerbate the cracks in its own social base. The Transjordanian youth groups, furthermore, do not have one central leadership that can be coopted by the regime.

Tribal leaders, or the "36 Current" as the public has come to call them, comprise a second force within the new opposition.[69] The significance of the 36 Current lies in its achievement of shifting the discourse over the source of Jordanian identity away from the Hashemite family and to the Transjordanian tribes. Rather than attributing the establishment of Jordan to the royal family, the 36 Current attributes Jordan's creation to the tribes that had provided the royal family asylum and protection. This shift in the discourse was clearly articulated in the 36 Current's statement of February 5, 2011. After reminding King Abdullah II that in 1919, the Jordanian tribes provided his grandfather, Prince Abdullah, protection, legitimacy, and identity, the statement demanded that the king take on corruption, including that of his own family, and cease the naturalization of Palestinians by not giving them Jordanian citizenship.[70] One year later, the effect of the 36 Current's statement still reverberates in Jordan, as it effectively removed one of the layers of the regime's sources of legitimacy and has allowed Transjordanians to celebrate their own identity in isolation from the royal family and sometimes even at its expense. When Prince Hassan intervened to defend his family as the builder of Jordan and to remind the opposition that the royal family would not tolerate those who attack it, he was hugely criticized through the traditional and social media; once again, he was reminded that his family arrived in Jordan from Saudi Arabia as impoverished guests.[71]

Working under the name of the Higher National Committee for Retired Military (HNCRM), retired military generals are the third main actor in the new opposition. As with the tribes, the army is considered one of the regime's pillars of support. The Retired Military Committee (RMC) has an extremely large membership base—140,000 retired soldiers and generals elect the RMC leadership.[72] On May 1, 2010, sixty retired generals issued a statement in the name of the HNRMC linking privatization and corruption to a plot conducted by high-ranking officials to turn Jordan into a homeland for the Palestinians.[73] In the statement, Queen Rania and her brother, Majdi Al-Yaseen, and Basim Awadallah, former head of the Royal Diwan (all of whom are of Palestinian origin), were singled out as the source of corruption and the reason for the naturalization of tens of thousands of Palestinians.[74] The statement furthermore demanded the king put an end to state corruption, the policy of naturalization (tajnis), and his family's interference in state policies.[75]

Reformist elites are the fourth and final group of the new opposition. The reformist elites are composed of former officials and deputies, such as Ahmad

Obeidat, Marwan Muasher, Kamel Abu Jaber, and Faris Sharaf, some of whom, such as Obeidat, are directly engaged in opposition activities while others, such as Muasher and Abu Jaber, are pressing the king to take genuine steps toward reform that meet the activists' demands.[76] The mere existence of this group strongly hints at an important crack inside the regime's ruling elites. Insider elites, furthermore, have leaked information regarding corruption. Obeidat, for example, has questioned the wisdom of having a third of the budget reserved for the military at a time when Jordan's foreign debt has reached 14 billion Jordanian dinars (US$20 billion).[77] Similarly, after being forced to resign, Sharaf, the former president of the Central Bank of Jordan, told newspaper correspondents that 80 percent of the government's subsidies go to the affluent and not to those who need them.[78] This information and similar statements have boosted the protest activities, with more and more participants joining and demanding reform.

There can be no doubt that the new opposition must receive credit for changing the dynamics and the structures of political activism in Jordan. However, as a result of the new opposition's refusal to advance a fair electoral law and its insistence on first defining who is a Jordanian and who is not, the new opposition has been accused of being exclusionary by the old (overwhelmingly Palestinian) opposition. The question of identity that underlies the divisions between activists is directly related to state priorities and to the distribution of state resources.

Identity and Ideological Cleavages

Both the new and the old opposition use the identity divide between Transjordanians and Palestinian Jordanians to advance their reform priorities. The new opposition views democratic political reform as a means to end policies of privatization and to restore the state's role in the economy.[79] However, while social justice lies at the heart of the new opposition's demands, it rejects any change to the electoral law that would reflect the true population distribution in Jordan's governorates. The old opposition views political reform as a means to end political discrimination against a large segment of the population, the Palestinians. However, while the old opposition claims to seek political equality, its political discourse exacerbates the new opposition actors' fears that Jordan will become a Palestinian state. The division between the two is aggravated further by disagreements concerning the uprising in Syria—Islamists in the traditional opposition support the Syrian opposition while the leftists and pan-Arabists in the old opposition defend the Syrian regime, together with the new opposition. These multilevel divisions have weakened the opposition's endeavors for democratic reforms.

The privatization program and corruption both have undermined the social contract between the activists in the new opposition and the Hashemite family. As a result, Transjordanians are seeking a new social contract based on their right to govern themselves. The question of identity thus is closely linked to the issues of resource distribution. Central to the issue of resource distribution is the question of who is a Jordanian and who is not. When, during the sit-in of March 24, 2011, Islamists demanded an electoral law based on a fair distribution of people in the governorates, Transjordanian activists in the new opposition left the sit-in.[80] For Transjordanian activists, a fair electoral law is contingent on first defining the electoral constituency which for them has changed since Jordan's decision to disengage from the West Bank on July 31, 1988.[81] The implications of the disengagement, as Salem Bani Sakhr explains, are that Palestinians who received Jordanian nationality or residency after July 31, 1988, are not Jordanians; they should be denied the right to vote, to run in elections, and to obtain employment in the public sector.[82] This narrow definition of Jordanian identity contradicts the notion of citizenship generally believed to be at the heart of any democratic system and raises questions about the new opposition's commitment to democratic ideals.[83]

The old opposition's main priority, especially that of the Islamists, is to change the electoral law in order to give Palestinians better representation in state institutions. Islamists are demanding an increase in the number of deputies for all underrepresented areas.[84] They argue that the low level of participation in the protest activities in Amman, Zarqa, and Irbid is a result of the Palestinians' bitterness at being underrepresented in state institutions and their feeling that it would be futile to try to change that underrepresentation. Indeed, according to one Palestinian Jordanian columnist, the percentage of Palestinian Jordanians in the parliament, which in 2007 was 20 percent, dropped to a feeble 12 percent by 2010. Furthermore, there are no Palestinians in the Ministry of the Interior and the Ministry of Foreign Affairs. Even in the less prestigious ministries, such as the Ministry of Education and the Ministry of Health, all of the high-ranking positions are filled by Transjordanians.[85] It is little wonder that Palestinian Jordanians regard the protests as an internal Transjordanian affair.[86] In short, Palestinian Jordanians believe that the state is not theirs.

The discourse of the old opposition over identity reinforces the new opposition's fears that Jordan may turn into an alternative homeland for the

Palestinians. Islamists consider Jordan's decision to disengage from the West Bank to be constitutionally illegal, as it is contingent on the end of the Israeli occupation of the West Bank before elected deputies in both banks can meet and ratify the disengagement.[87] The old opposition considers the debate over identity as a convenient way for the regime to keep Jordanians divided.[88] According to this view, whether they live in the West Bank or East Bank, Palestinians are Jordanians and have full social and political rights, and the kingdom should assume responsibility in liberating part of its land. Furthermore, Jordanian national identity is still evolving, its final shape contingent on the end of the Palestinian-Israeli conflict.

This division over identity is exacerbated by the disagreement between Islamists and other actors within the opposition concerning the uprising in Syria. With the eruption of the Syrian uprising in March 2011, Islamists have supported a change of regime in Syria in accordance with the Syrian Muslim Brotherhood. Islamists justify this position by arguing that it is in accordance with the will of the Syrian people and that the leftists and pan-Arabists in support of the Syrian regime receive financial support from Damascus.[89] By contrast, other opposition actors perceive the uprising in Syria as a conspiracy to topple a "resistance regime" due to its support of Hezbollah, Hamas, and the Iraqi resistance.[90] They view Jordanian Islamists as opportunistic, seeking to expand their political advantage after the election results in Tunisia, Egypt, and Morocco—even if that happens through direct American military intervention in Syria or, as many interviewees put it, "even if they expand their gains using an American tank" (the controversy over foreign military intervention also has divided the grassroots activists in Syria and Bahrain).[91] The disagreement over the Syrian uprising has frozen the work of the HCCNOP. Since May 2011, the old opposition parties have rarely attempted to coordinate their protest activities. Furthermore, although they have not withdrawn from the HCCNOP, leftist and pan-Arabist parties formed a competing coalition on January 20, 2012.[92]

There have been several initiatives aimed at unifying the opposition, including those of Laith Shbeilat (former Member of Parliament and a longtime rival of the regime), Ahmad Obeidat (former prime minister and former head of the *mukhabarat*), and Salem Fleihat and Rheil Gharaibeh (prominent members of the IAF). Summarizing his initiative in a letter directed to Ahmad Obeidat and published by Al Jazeera's website, Shbeilat called for the entire opposition to unite on an agenda based on reforming the monarchy.[93] According to Shbeilat, Jordan can only move toward genuine political reform after the king has abandoned all his executive authorities. Shbeilat stated that Jordan's prime ministers have no authority in practice, as policies are implemented by the 2,500 employees of the Royal Diwan.[94] As Shbeilat's initiative puts the opposition forces in direct conflict with the king, it has received little to no support from Jordan's opposition parties.

Ahmad Obeidat introduced an initiative in "The Document for Comprehensive Reform." The introduction of the document links the continuation of the regime's constitutional legitimacy to the implementation of twelve major reforms.[95] The document is crystal clear on what unites the opposition (for instance, fighting corruption and limiting the *mukhabarat*'s role in the public sphere) but vague in its treatment of the political issues over which there is little agreement (the electoral law). Article 3, for example, calls for a democratic, fair, and decent election law that "maintains national unity" without defining what national unity means. Obeidat succeeded in bringing the old opposition under his leadership; on May 19, 2011, he declared the formation of the National Front for Reform. He failed, however, to bring the new opposition into the fold, as the document ignored the 1988 disengagement decision.[96]

Finally, Islamists Salem Fleihat and Rheil Gharaibeh attempted to unify the activities of the youth groups. On July 13, 2011, twenty-four youth groups met in Amman and declared the birth of the Popular Gathering for Reform (PGR). Avoiding any discussion of the electoral law, the PGR declared its main goal to be the transformation of Jordan into a constitutional monarchy. A month later, however, the PGR froze its activities and its executive committee resigned. It was accused by some of the youth groups as leaning too strongly toward the Islamists.[97] Although the PGR has renewed its activities, the main actors of the new opposition have remained outside the coalition.

As a result of these divisions, the discourse for political reform has alienated the majority of Jordanians and has largely become an intellectual debate among the opposition elites. The fragmentation of the opposition has also allowed the regime to turn its back on the main demands of the opposition— those that are related to the concentration of power in the hands of the royal family. (Much the same thing occurred in Morocco.)

Assessing the Regime Strategy

The regime remains intent on minimizing the number and nature of political reforms it may have to undertake, with the ultimate goal of preserving the king's executive authorities. It has, however, been forced to tolerate greater

The March 24 Sit-In as Recounted by Jordanian Activists

On March 17, 2011, several youth groups representing independents, leftists, pan-Arabists, and Islamists met in the Social Forum office at al-Weibdeh, Amman. They agreed to hold a permanent sit-in at al-Dakhiliya Circle beginning on March 24. In the following excerpts from interviews with Mohammad Yaghi, activists describe the events.

"We agreed to hold a permanent sit-in at al-Dakhiliya Circle on March 24th until the regime agrees to fight corruption, presents a fair and decent electoral law, and a progressive taxation law." On March 24, "the youth groups from southern Jordan arrived first at al-Dakhiliya Circle, followed by the leftist groups, and lastly the Muslim Brotherhood members arrived."
Mohammad Sneid, activist, interview at Thieban, Madaba, February 3, 2012

"We were almost 3,000 and wanted to imitate the sit-in in Tahrir Square.... The sit-in was a tableau.... Many activists came with their families, young men and women chanted for Jordan, and kids painted their faces with the colors of the national flag." The sit-in "was a great experience" for them as it showed the unity of Jordanians from "all ideologies and origins."
Transjordanian activist, interview in Irbid, February 7, 2012

The regime's counteraction came as a surprise. Ghaith Alqdah, head of Youth Organization in Muslim Brotherhood Movement, explained: "We did not expect the reaction of the regime to be brutal. The leaders of Muslim Brotherhood had met the king just before the sit-in of March 24 and assured him that it would be peaceful and would request reforming the regime, and not ousting it."
Interview in Amman, February 23, 2012

Yet on the dawn of the 25th, as an activist from Fuheis, Amman, recounts, the *darak* (police) "attacked us—at first by tear gas—and the regime supporters mounted the bridge above the circle and hit us with stones, and then the *darak* beat us with batons. While one of the *darak* was hitting me, he recognized from my accent that I am Transjordanian. He stopped and asked me why I was sitting with those Palestinians who wanted to commit a coup and ordered me to go home immediately. Later on, I met one of the regime supporters; he was from Kerak. He told me that the regime supporters were brought from different places to King Abdullah Gardens in Amman. They had been offered meals, each one of them had received 50 Jordanian dinars, and they were told that the Palestinians were organizing a coup against the King."
Transjordanian activist, interview in Fuheis, Amman, January 26, 2012

The sit-in divided the activists. Mohammad Sneid explained, "Not all the youth groups were at al-Dakhiliya Circle when the *darak* attacked the sit-inners. We chose to leave when the MB activists brought with them loudspeakers and dominated the sit-in. The MB activists asked for the dismissal of the head of the General Intelligence Agency (*mukhabarat*) and for an election law based on the demographic distribution of the population in governorates. These demands were not part of our agreement of March 17. We told the MB members our position but they did not listen to us."

Khalid Kaladeh, head of Social Left, confirms Sneid's account: "I warned the youth groups not to hold the sit-in because the MB would use it for its own benefit," adding that the regime also "is scared of permanent sit-ins as they would attract the attention of the media worldwide, something the regime is trying to avoid."
Interview in Amman, January 19, 2012

The next day, as the activist from Fuheis explained, "the national media used the demands of the MB for an electoral law that would give the Jordanians of Palestinian origin more seats in the Parliament as a pretext to depict the sit-inners as Palestinians while most of them were in fact of Transjordanian origin."

A female activist of Palestinian origin adds, "The daily live program of Mohammad al-Wakeel on Rotana FM Radio bluntly accused the Palestinians of working against national unity," adding that "al-Wakeel asked the Palestinians to 'cross the bridge' [return to the West Bank—Ed.] if they cannot live according to Jordan's rules."
Interview in Amman, March 27, 2012

The sit-in was an important junction for opposition activities. As Zaki Bani Rsheid, a member of the Muslim Brotherhood's Shura Council, put it: "The security apparatuses used the 'weapon' of national unity to fragment the people . . . [which] affected negatively the Palestinians' participation in the opposition activities." After the March 24 Sit-In, the opposition preferred that "the activists of the governorates in southern of Jordan to take the lead, as this would end the regime's rumors that the opposition is mainly composed of Palestinians."
Interview in Amman, January 29, 2012

Far from the longstanding, effective demonstration activists had hoped for—following in the steps of the Tunisians and the Egyptians—the March 24 Sit-In left the Jordanian opposition deflated. Tensions between Jordanians of Palestinian and Transjordanian origin had been used, once again, to divide the opposition. Reforms, at least for the time being, were put on hold.

---

freedom of expression. In this regard, the regime now allows public meetings and marches without prior authorization, and it has expanded the margin of journalistic freedoms.[98] The regime also has responded positively to the demands for improved economic conditions for different social groups. It relented to the establishment of a trade union for school teachers and raised their salaries, appointed twenty-one thousand new employees in the public sector, and increased the salaries of retired military.[99] Politically, the regime dismissed two governments in response to the opposition activist demands, and it abolished or amended forty-three articles of the 1952 constitution.[100] The amendments include the establishment of an independent body to run the parliamentary and municipal elections and a constitutional court, and the abolition of all laws that violate the constitution.[101] The anticorruption commission also brought several officials to court, including Mohammed Dahabi, the former head of *mukhabarat*.[102] Finally, the king has urged the government and the parliament to prepare and ratify the parties and elections laws in order to hold municipal and parliamentary elections prior to the end of 2012.[103]

The king, however, has not relinquished any of his executive authorities. He may approve the establishment of an elected parliamentarian government as there is no article in the constitution impeding this from happening, but this would not reflect a change in his authority. He may still dismiss the government at his will.[104] The regime's strategy seems to be a carbon copy of its strategy in the early 1990s, when it expanded freedom of expression, ran relatively fair legislative elections, and invited the Islamists to join the government. Similarly, Awn Shawkat al-Khasawneh, who served as prime minister from October 2011 through May 2012, engaged in intensive dialogue with Islamists in order to convince them to join his government, expressed a willingness to reinstate the 1989 electoral law, and renounced the expulsion of Hamas leaders from Jordan in 1999 as illegal and a constitutional mistake.[105]

The regime's strategy may work in the short term. It has resulted in a decrease in protest activities in Amman, Zarqa, and Irbid while simultaneously exacerbating tensions between the Islamists and the other opposition actors and within the Islamists themselves, as certain factions are now pressuring the IAF leadership to respond positively to the regime's approach.[106] However, the constitutional reforms that the regime has undertaken fall far short of the demands of those of the new and old opposition. The public, furthermore, remains skeptical of the regime's stated intention to combat corruption. The barometer for the public will be whether or not the convictions against high-ranking officials result in prison sentences. Activists point to the resignation of the deputy president of the anticorruption commission in protest against the selective work of the commission.[107] Moreover, the activists believe that the royal family is directly involved in corruption. They point to state lands that are registered in the king's name, the role of Walid al-Kurdi, the husband of Princess Basma, in the corruption case of the Jordan Phosphate Mines Company and the role of Majdi Al-Yaseen, the brother of Queen Rania, in the corruption case of the Umniah telecommunication company.[108]

More importantly, the regime's efforts have failed to satisfy the Islamists. The Islamists do not seem to be in any rush to make a deal with the regime as regional events are in their favor and reinforce their bargaining power. Lastly, regime attempts to satisfy public sector employees by raising their salaries will ultimately result in an increase in taxes on the private sector in order to keep the state's budget under control. Should this happen, according to at least one journalist, Palestinian Jordanians, who dominate the private sector, would join the protests.[109]

In sum, drawing on the experience of the protests in Jordan and in the Arab Spring countries, the regime's failure to respond positively to the activists' earlier claims escalated the protests in terms of their intensity and extent and emboldened the activists to raise the ceiling of their demands.

Conclusions

Jordanian opposition forces still suffer from their historical structural constraints, but the regime today is no longer capable of controlling the reach and content of the reform agenda. The opposition (old and new) is united in terms of demanding limitations on the king's executive authorities, ending state corruption, granting the parliament true supervisory authority, and creating a political system based on checks and balances. Second, fear of the *mukhabarat* among the opposition and the public has substantially abated, as a result of which they are increasingly turning to the streets as a way to achieve their demands. Finally, an increasing number of societal and professional groups are organizing around specific social and economic issues and demanding action from the state. As the state is financially bankrupt, the regime has an interest in bringing the political opposition into decision-making circles in order to share the burden of responsibility with the king.

The extent of democratic reform, however, depends on the ability of the opposition to unify. The rift between opposition groups limits their ability to maximize regime concessions. Towards this end, a collapse of the Syrian regime would most likely encourage Islamists to increase their activities in an effort to wring more concessions out of the regime. The regime continues to play on the divisions within the opposition in order to minimize its political concessions. The regime's core intention is to reintroduce the 1991 reform package.[110] Although the opposition would welcome these reforms, it would not consider them sufficient as the king would maintain his authority and would be able to reverse the reforms at any time.

The future of democracy in Jordan depends to a large extent on breaking the regime-Islamist dyad in order to allow for a better distribution of political power. In other words, the emergence of effective democratic political parties is a necessary condition for the advancement of political reform in Jordan. The old leftist and pan-Arabist parties are simply too weak and do not have a strong enough social base to counterbalance the Islamists and the regime. In response to the rise of new opposition groups, seventeen new parties applied for registration at the Ministry of the Interior. Six were rejected because they could not fulfill the ministry's requirements. Nine are in the process of revision by the ministry; two have been accepted.[111] These parties fall into two categories. The first are those supported by the regime to weaken the opposition while the second are those that reflect the interests of specific social groups. With the exception of the Jordan National Congress Party (established January 2012), which is affiliated with the retired military and the Jordanian Social National Party, none of the new parties are related to the new opposition actors; all are competing for Transjordanian support.[112]

The prospects of any youth groups evolving into a political party appear very slim. Youth activists acknowledge that their influence stems from the fact that they are "a protest movement without a specific leadership." As one activist states, "If you want to kill a movement, give it a leadership."[113] Youth activists admit that while there are issues over which they can unite, it is very difficult for them to agree on a common political, social, and economic platform. This is due, they argue, to tribal and regional divisions as well as their historical experience with political parties.[114] In short, the youth activists see political parties as a source of division.

Finally, in order for the political activism in Jordan to yield any democratic reform, activists need to concentrate on the constitutional reforms that would vest the legislative and executive authority in the elected deputies. These demands are included in the slogans activists raise during their protest events, but they are by no means their top priority. In addition, the majority of protest activities take place on a weekly basis (each Friday) as opposed to a daily basis.[115] Unless activists can transform their protest activities into a large-scale movement—increasing in both frequency and size—the regime will be able to maintain its conviction that the protests can be contained without providing substantial concessions to the opposition.

Notes

1. The only important events prior to these protests were the teachers' strike in April 2010, the retired military committee protest in May 2010, and several strikes organized by the daily workers of the Ministry of Agriculture (see the sections on the changes of the structure of mobilization and the new opposition actors).

2. While some scholars would not consider March 24, 2011, as significant as other protests, we consider it an important turning point not only because the regime was successful in preventing a permanent sit-in (as in the case of Egypt) but also because the opposition was increasingly unable to work together following the event.

3. One activist was killed and several tens were wounded during the sit-in. For more information on the sit-in at Gamal Abdel Nasser Circle (also known as Duwar al-Dakhiliya Circle), see "Jordan's March 24 Youth Sit-In Violently Dispersed (Videos)," Jadaliyya, March 26, 2011, available at www.jadaliyya.com/pages/index /1012/jordans-march-24-youth-sit-in-violently-dispersed-, accessed August 1, 2013.

4. Curtis R. Ryan, "Political Opposition and Reform Coalitions in Jordan," *British Journal of Middle Eastern Studies* 38(3) (2011): 367–390.

5. The research for this chapter is based mainly on interviews with Jordan's party-based opposition, newly-emerging oppositional figures, and government representatives, conducted primarily in January through April 2012.

6. Stefanie Nanes, "Choice, Loyalty, and the Melting Pot: Citizenship and National Identity in Jordan," *Nationalism and Ethnic Politics* 14(1) (2008): 85–116.

7. Joseph A. Massad, *Colonial Effects: The Making of National Identity in Jordan* (New York: Columbia University Press, 2001).

8. Nanes, "Choice, Loyalty."

9. Ibid.

10. Massad, *Colonial Effects*.

11. Ibid.

12. Ibid.; see also Adnan Abu Odeh, *Jordanians, Palestinians, and the Hashemite Kingdom in the Middle East Peace Process* (Washington, DC: United States Institute of Peace Press, 1999); Adnan Abu Odeh, chief of Jordan Royal Diwan (1991–1992), interview with Yaghi, Amman, March 17, 2012.

13. Nanes, "Choice, Loyalty"; Ryan, "Political Opposition"; Massad, *Colonial Effects*.

14. Salah Khalaf, *A Palestinian without an Identity*, 2nd ed. (Amman: Dar Al Jalil for Printing, Studying, and Palestinian Research, 1996). According to Adnan Abu Odeh, the policy of purging the Palestinian Jordanians from state institutions became official after the Arab Summit of Rabat in 1974 when the Arab leaders recognized the PLO as the sole legitimate representative of the Palestinians. Abu Odeh interview.

15. Massad, *Colonial Effects*; see also Hussein Sirriyeh, "Jordan and the Legacies of the Civil War of 1970–71," *Civil Wars* 3(3) (2000): 74–86; Khalaf, *Palestinian without an Identity*. For more on the Palestinian and Jordanian identities, see Laurie Brand, "Palestinians and Jordanians," *Journal of Palestine Studies* 24(4) (1995): 46–61.

16. Marc Lynch, "Jordan's Identity and Interests," in *Identity and Foreign Policy in the Middle East*, ed. Shibley Telhami and Michael Barnett (Ithaca: Cornell University Press, 2002), 26–58.

17. Musa S. Braizat, *The Jordanian Palestinian Relationship: The Bankruptcy of the Confederal Idea* (London: British Academic Press, 1998).

18. Nanes, "Choice, Loyalty."

19. See Sufyan Alissa, "Rethinking Economic Reform in Jordan: Confronting Socioeconomic Realities," Carnegie Paper no. 4, Carnegie Middle East Center, July 2007.

20. See Ellen Lust, "Democratization by Elections? Competitive Clientelism in the Middle East," *Journal of Democracy* 20(3) (July 2009): 122–153.

21. See Ellen Lust, "Elections under Authoritarianism: Preliminary Lessons from Jordan," *Democratization* 13(3) (2006): 456–471.

22. Palestinian Jordanian journalist, interview with Yaghi, Amman, January 26, 2012.

23. Many Transjordanians became unemployed as a result of the privatization of state-owned companies. Exact numbers are not documented, however. Transjordanian activists cite the number of workers in the Cement Company prior to privatization as four thousand and at fewer than fourteen hundred at present.

24. King Abdullah II became King of Jordan following the death of his father in February 1999. His wife, Rania al-Yassin, is of Palestinian origin, from the city of Tulkarm.

25. Ali Habashneh, head of the retired military committee, interview with Yaghi, Marj Al-Hamam, Amman, January 25, 2012.

26. See Ellen Lust, "The Decline of Jordanian Political Parties: Myth or Reality?" *Journal of Middle East Studies* 33(4) (2001): 545–569.

27. Ryan, "Political Opposition." It should be noted that in the 1989 parliamentary elections, all parties candidates ran as independents, as political parties were still illegal.

28. For example, the Socialist Arab Baath Party is mainly concentrated in Kerak.

29. Massad, *Colonial Effects.*

30. Azzam Tamimi, *Hamas: The History from Within* (Grand Rapids, MI: Olive Branch Press, 2007).

31. Rheil Gharaibeh, a leader of the IAF and a columnist at the *Alarab Alyawm* newspaper admitted that MB had focused on the Palestinian question and ignored Jordanian internal affairs until the beginning of the Arab Spring. Gharaibeh, interview with Yaghi, Amman, March 10, 2012. Other Islamists have confirmed this.

32. For example, the IAF organized several activities in solidarity with Tafilah activists after their detention—the activities included marches in Tafilah and Amman in the presence of IAF leaders, visits to the activists' families, and official statements to condemn their detentions.

33. On the 1989 riots, see Alissa, "Rethinking Economic Reform." The reduction of food subsidies in 1996 led to what have been dubbed the "bread riots," which began in Kerak. See Lamis Andoni and Jillian Schwedler, "Bread Riots in Jordan," *Middle East Report* 201 (October–December 1996): 40–42.

34. See Lust, "Decline of Jordanian Political Parties"; Jillian Schwedler, "Cop Rock: Protest, Identity, and Dancing Riot Police in Jordan," *Social Movement Studies* 4(2) (2005): 155–175; Jillian Schwedler, "More Than a Mob: The Dynamics of Political Demonstrations in Jordan," *Middle East Report* 226 (Spring 2003): 18–23.

35. Jordanians' fear of the *mukhabarat* cannot be underestimated, as working, studying, and traveling were subject to and continue to be subject to clearance from the *mukhabarat.* It is a common saying in Jordan that the *mukhabarat* rules the country.

36. Ellen Lust and Sami Hourani, "Jordan Votes: Election or Selection?" *Journal of Democracy* 22(2) (2011): 119–129; Lust, "Elections under Authoritarianism."

37. Lust, "Decline of Jordanian Political Parties."

38. Janine A. Clark, "The Conditions of Islamist Moderation: Unpacking Cross-Ideological Cooperation in Jordan," *Journal of Middle East Studies* 38(4) (2006): 539–560.

39. "A Sit-In in Thieban," Amman Net website, January 7, 2011, available at http://ar.ammannet.net/?p=87975, accessed December 28, 2011.

40. Mohammad Sneid, interview with Yaghi, Thieban, Madaba, February 3, 2012.

41. The first time Islamists participated in "Jordan Spring" protest activities was on January 21, 2011, when they organized a march following the Friday prayers at Al Hussainy Mosque in downtown Amman.

42. Sneid interview. Samir Rifai was prime minister from December 14, 2010, to February 1, 2011.

43. "Almajali: The Protests Cost the General Security Department 28 Million Jordanian Dinar," *Kul Al Urdun*, March 14, 2012, available at www.allofjo.org/index.php?page=article&id=25438, accessed August 10, 2013.

44. Al-Majali did not give detailed information regarding the kinds of protests. Additionally he announced that there were 1,318 protest activities since the beginning of 2012.

45. Downtown Amman is the center of commerce for poorer Ammanis, who most commonly live in eastern Amman, the traditional and the older part of the capital.

46. Hadi al-Shobaki, director of the Al-Rai Center for Studies, interview with Yaghi, January 22, 2012. It should be noted that the number of groups is significant. The Popular Bloc for Reform, for example, a coalition affiliated with Islamists, includes twenty-six different groups.

47. Ryan, "Political Opposition."

48. One activist alone has 3,342 friends who daily exchange information on reform activities.

49. In response to the teachers' protests, the Ministry of Education in July 2010 dismissed two of the leaders, Mustafa Rawashdeh and Adma Izrekat. As a result, the teachers organized a march from Amman to Kerak demanding that the government reinstate the two. In August 2010, the teachers also held a sit-in in front of the Prime Minister's office with the same demand. Mustafa Rawashdeh, interview with Yaghi, Kerak, February 2, 2012.

50. "Worker Protests in Jordan during 2010," *Phoenix Center for Economic and Informatics Studies,* February 2010.

51. "Worker Protests during the First Half of 2011: An Analytical Study," *Phoenix Center for Economic and Informatics Studies,* September 2011.

52. Student female activist, interview with Yaghi, Irbid, February 7, 2012.

53. Ibid. Jordanian Women for Reform was established in January 2012; see "The Conference of Jordanian Women for Reform Launches its Activities," *Assabeel* newspaper, January 7, 2012.

54. In Arabic, "ya Abdullah ya ibin hussayn, massary al-sha'ab rahat wein."

55. "The Corruption Dance at the Entrance of Jweideh's Prison," available at www.youtube.com/watch?v=1m1uPK7B68c&feature=related, accessed March 15, 2012.

56. As one activist stated, the movement demands are changing in an upward direction. He further added that the regime's "delay in meeting our demands may end up with calls for regime change." Another activist said, "In most of our marches we chant the people want *iss iss. . . .* Do you want to make reform or shall we say it?" "*Iss Iss*" refers to the first letters of the Arabic word *Issqat* (toppling). The people want *Issqat Alnizam* (toppling the regime), which is the phrase that was used in the Tunisian and Egyptian's demonstrations that called for the two regimes' departure.

57. "Mother of Detained Majdi Qabaleen: It Is Time for the Regime to Go," available at www.youtube.com/watch?v=rPKp_bgrSjk, accessed March 12, 2012.

58. Issam Mbaydeen, "Thousands in Amman Participate in the March of Fed Up Friday," *Assabeel* newspaper, December 30, 2011.

59. The rally occurred after two statements were issued by the IAF. One, under the name of the MB youth movement in Mafraq, threatened to "cut the hands of those who would dare to attack the IAF offices in the future." For the MB youth statement, see *Zad al-Urdun,* December 8, 2011, available at http://jordanzad.com/index.php?page=article&id=67073, accessed January 22, 2012. The second was issued by the IAF leadership and stated that the regime's actions sent a message to the people that they should defend themselves using similar gang means. See "The Islamic Movement Statement on Mafraq Attack," *Assabeel* newspaper, December 26, 2011. On the Fed Up Friday, see the YouTube clip on the *Ammon News* website, available at www.ammonnews.net/webtv/default.aspx?id=2cc9a727-5e8f-4314 -89d1-9df33ca6b839, accessed January 28, 2012.

60. Habashneh interview.

61. Zaki Bani Rsheid, interview with Yaghi, Amman, January 29, 2012.

62. An activist, interview with Yaghi, Hay al-Tafaileh, Amman, January 28, 2012.

63. Hay al-Tafaileh is located in East Amman. Thousands of families from Tafilah governorate immigrated to Amman in the last three decades in search for work. The area has one of the highest concentrations of inhabitants from one governorate.

64. Shaqran provides the example of the Rifai family, in which three generations in the same family have held the position of prime minister. Khalid Shaqran, interview with Yaghi, Amman, January 22, 2012. This has been confirmed during interviews with approximately thirty activists.

65. The example was provided by Jafar Okaily, journalist, *Al Rai* newspaper, interview with Yaghi, April 7, 2012.

66. Ahmed Awad, director of economic and informatics studies (Phenix), interview with Yaghi, March 12, 2012.

67. For example, on January 20, 2012, the opposition organized demonstrations in all Jordanian cities under the name *Huqooq la Makarem*. See for example "The Governorates Organize Marches on Rights and Not Grants' Friday," *Amman net,* available at http://ar.ammannet.net/?p=141809, accessed March 5, 2012.

68. See for example the writings on the Facebook wall of Tafila Freedom, available at www.facebook.com/groups/tafilafreedom/, accessed August 11, 2013.

69. Many tribes also have created their own movements, such as the Bani Hassan, Bani Humeida, Bani Sakhr, al-Da'ja, al-Hajaya, and al-Aysra. Shobaki interview.

70. "The Complete Statement of Jordanian National Figures," *Arab Times,* March 22, 2011, available at www.arabtimes.com/portal/news_display.cfm?Action= &Preview=No&nid=7759&a=1, accessed December 25, 2011.

71. For Prince Hassan's defense of the role of the Hashemite family in building Jordan, see his interview on the "60 Minutes Program" with the Jordan state television

on February 17, 2012. A transcription appeared in *Alghad* newspaper, February 18, 2012. For the reactions of columnists, bloggers, and tribes, see Nahed Hatar, *Alarab Alyawm* newspaper, February 20, 2012; blogger Inas Musalam, http://enassmusallam.blogspot.com/2012/02/blog-post_19.html, accessed February 20, 2012; for the tribes' statements, see *ammanpost*, http://ammanpost.net/article.aspx?articleno=21398, accessed February 20, 2012.

72. "The National Committee for Retired Military: General Information," *Maraya News* website, available at www.marayanews.com/?p=157718, accessed January 20, 2012.

73. "The Statement of the Higher National Committee for Retired Military," *Ammon News,* May 1, 2010, available at www.ammonnews.net/article.aspx?articleNO=59696, accessed December 25, 2011. The HNCRM is a body that emerged out of the RMC. It should be noted that the head of the HNCRM, Ali Habashneh, was the elected president of the RMC.

74. Ibid.

75. Ibid.

76. Marwan Muasher, "A Decade of Struggling Reform Efforts in Jordan: The Resilience of the Rentier System," *Carnegie Papers,* May 2011. Marwan Muasher and Kamel Abu Jaber are former foreign ministers; Fares Sharaf was the head of Jordan Central Bank.

77. Ahmad Obeidat, interview with *Alghad* newspaper, February 1, 2012, available at www.alghad.com/index.php/article/527608.html, accessed February 7, 2012.

78. For the details on Sharaf's dismissal ten months after his appointment, see *Alarab Alyaom* newspaper, September 21, 2011, available at http://alarabalyawm.net/pages.php?news_id=327353, accessed December 25, 2011.

79. Youth activists, interviews with Yaghi, in Amman, Tafilah, and Kerak; Khalid Kaladeh, the head of Social Left, interview with Yaghi, Amman, January 19, 2012; Khalid Ramadan, leaders of the National Progressive Current, interview with Yaghi, Amman, January 31, 2012.

80. Sneid interview.

81. "A Statement by the Nationalist Progressive Current," *Kul al-Urdun* website, February 28, 2011, available at http://allofjo.net/index.php?option=com_content&view=article&id=9235:2011-02-28-15-05-18&catid=49:2010-09-24-07-31-59&Itemid=1, accessed December 28, 2011.

82. Salem Bani Sakhar, retired general, interview with Yaghi, January 25, 2012. There is no agreement concerning the details of social and political rights for the Palestinians who became Jordanians or who secured residency in Jordan after July 31, 1988. In Kaladeh's view, for example, they have the right to run for municipal elections but not the parliament. Kaladeh interview.

83. For further discussion on this topic, see Hisham Bustani, "Jordan's New Opposition and the Traps of Identity and Ambiguity," *Jadaliyya*, April 20, 2011, avail-

able at www.jadaliyya.com/pages/index/1303/jordans-new-opposition-and-the-traps -of-identity-a, accessed August 1, 2013.

84. According to Zaki Bani Rsheid, Islamists are not demanding an electoral law that represents the population's actual distribution in the governorates. Bani Rsheid interview.

85. Palestinian Jordanian journalist interview.

86. Mohammad Abu Ruman, interview with Yaghi, Amman, February 5, 2012.

87. Saleh Armouti, former head of the lawyers' association and an Islamist leader, interview with Yaghi, Amman, January 20, 2012. See also the interview with Hamza Mansour, *Addustour* newspaper, April 18, 2012.

88. Armouti interview; Bani Rsheid interview; Ramadan interview. Abla Abu Ilbeh, a parliamentarian deputy and secretary general of the People Democratic Party, interview with Yaghi, Amman, January 20, 2012.

89. Bani Rsheid interview; Hamza Mansour, secretary general of the IAF, interview with Yaghi, Amman, February 2, 2012; Armouti interview.

90. Abu Ilbeh interview; Ramadan interview; Habashneh interview; Muwafq Mahadin, head of Jordanian Writers, interview with Yaghi, January 24, 2012.

91. Abu Ilbeh interview; Ramadan interview; Rasmi Aljabiri, head of Palestinian Right of Return Committees, interview with Yaghi, Zarqa, February 3, 2012.

92. For more information on this coalition, see "The National and Leftists Parties Declare a New Coalition," *Alghad* newspaper, January 28, 2012, available at http://alghad.com/index.php/article/526747.html, accessed January 29, 2012.

93. Laith Shbeilat, "Letters that Need Points" (Horoof bihaja ila nuqat), Al Jazeera website, September 7, 2011, available at www.aljazeera.net/NR/EXERES /56891D34-9FFE-4E0A-B2D-9B064AD67800.htm, accessed December 25, 2011.

94. Ibid. According to the National Progressive Current, when King Hussein died the Royal Diwan had only about fifty employees; *Khabarjo* website, "The Jordanian Progress Current: Our Vision for Uniting the Movements of Change," July 23, 2011, available at http://khabarjo.net/mohfadat/12104.html, accessed December 27, 2011.

95. "The Document for Comprehensive Reform," *Addustour* newspaper, May 23, 2011.

96. Interviews with Transjordanian activists in Kerak, Tafilah, and Amman.

97. "Jordanian Progress Current."

98. "The Text of the Modified Public Meeting," *Ammon News,* May 5, 2011, available at www.ammonnews.net/article.aspx?articleNO=86734, accessed March 1, 2012.

99. For the government's decision to increase teachers' salaries, see *Al-Rai* newspaper, "Salah Abadi: Increasing the Teachers' Salaries 30–45% on Three Stages," February 4, 2012. For the appointment of twenty-one thousand new employees in public sector, see the Head of Civil Servant Bureau statement before the parliament

on January 17, 2012, available at www.parliamentjo.net/?p=5555, accessed January 25, 2012. For the increase in retired military salaries, see *Alghad* newspaper, December 25, 2011.

100. The Ma'rouf Al Bakhait government was dismissed on October 17, 2011; the Samir Rifai government was dismissed on February 2, 2012.

101. Shakran interview. For more information about the amendments, see *Addustour* newspaper, October 1, 2011.

102. See, for example, *Alsabeel* newspaper, January 5, 2012.

103. On February 18, 2012, the king met with MPs and asked them to ratify the new laws as the parliamentarian elections are to take place before the end of 2012; see "The King Discusses with Deputies the Political Reform Laws," *Alghad* newspaper, February 19, 2012.

104. On several occasions, the king has announced his desire to see elected parliamentarian governments. See for example "The King's Speech," *Al-Rai* newspaper, June 13, 2011.

105. Mansour interview. For the Al Khasawneh statement, see *Alsabeel* newspaper, October 31, 2011.

106. According to Gaith Alqdah, head of the IAF youth section, the IAF's decision to boycott the next parliamentary elections unless the opposition' demands are met is not reflective of all IAF leaders. A segment of the leadership advocates the acceptance of the current reforms and argues that further reforms can be achieved from within the parliament. Gaith Alqdah, interview with Yaghi, Amman, February 23, 2012.

107. For the reasons for the resignation of Abdulrazeq Bani Hani, deputy president of the anticorruption commission, see *Alghad* newspaper, January 24, 2012.

108. All these claims regarding corruption are mentioned in Jordanian newspapers and discussed by the parliament. For example, in response to claims that the king registered state lands in his name, the Royal Diwan explained that the king did so in order to facilitate investment in these lands. See *Alghad* newspaper, December 8, 2011.

109. Palestinian Jordanian journalist interview.

110. Abu Ruman interview.

111. For details on the new parties, see Amman net website, available at http://ar.ammannet.net/?p=135796, accessed January 25, 2012.

112. The activists of this party are strongly involved in the protests for reform. The leaders of the party are mostly university professors and journalists. One of the main goals of the party is to constitutionalize the 1988 disengagement decision.

113. Sneid interview.

114. Activists in Kerak, Maan, and Tafilah, interview with Yaghi.

115. There are some exceptions. For example, when the *mukhabarat* arrested twenty-two activists from Tafilah in March 2012, the activists stepped up their pro-

tests and held a permanent sit-in in a tent in front of the governorate building. Two weeks later the tent was removed by the *darak,* as it had become a place that received activists from all over Jordan who were coming to demonstrate solidarity with the detainees. On the detention of the activists in Tafilah, see Mohamed Najar, "The Arrest of the Fifth Activists in Tafilah," Al Jazeera TV, March 12, 2012, cited at www.aljazeera.net/news/pages/7e32e628-2d2d-4244-9a2a-8bb5d6e885c2, accessed August 30, 2013; on the removal of the sit-inners' tent, see Feisal Al-Qatamin and Hashal Al-Adailah, "The Security Removes the Sit-In Tent from the Entrance of Tafilah Governorate," *Alghad* newspaper, March 18, 2012.

CHAPTER 9

Political Activism in Kuwait

Reform in Fits and Starts

MARY ANN TÉTREAULT

THE ARAB GULF nations are often viewed as rentier states whose governments trade money and benefits for a politically passive population.[1] In reality and despite differences from place to place, Gulf populations are not passive.[2] Indeed, Kuwait has not witnessed an uprising like those in nearby Bahrain and Yemen, but the Arab Spring did encourage already restive groups in Kuwait to push harder for recognition and policy changes.

Kuwait is a political outlier in the Gulf, and it has often been a bellwether: It was the first Gulf nation to establish a "welfare state," the first to set up a foreign aid program, and the first to venture as an equal into the world of multinational, vertically integrated oil companies.[3] Among the first to pressure their government to recognize the legitimate demands of citizens outside the ruling family, Kuwaitis are noted in the region—not always favorably—for their political activism. Beginning with merchants decades ago, and today including high school and university students and even stateless residents, social groups in Kuwait have taken to the streets to demand civil and human rights from a government that they seek to make accountable for its actions. But activism in Kuwait is not limited to social groups; it very often incorporates cooperation between those working within state institutions—mainly in parliament—on the one hand and formal civil society organizations and informal groups and coalitions on the other.

Kuwaiti activism has constrained autocratic rule even though it has not yet cracked the shield protecting Kuwait's authoritarian executive. Under the radar of most observers, the many and varied cycles of activism in Kuwait constitute transition *in* authoritarianism, politics through which both sides seek and sometimes effect structural changes that alter the landscape in significant ways.[4] This is far from the picture of passive rentierism that still dominates visions of Arab oil-exporting countries.[5] It also contradicts theories of authoritarian persistence by broadening the focus to include opportunity structures and the protest politics that exploit them.[6] Institutional and psychological openings offer alert actors opportunities to alter the balance between themselves and those who have power over them. Some are created by events like the discovery of oil or an invasion by a neighboring state. Others come from ideas able to mobilize crowds, like protests against the crackdown on tribal primaries and demonstrations for women's rights or changes in electoral laws. Still others cascade from actions by the regime. In Kuwait, authoritarianism is challenged by changes in the structural relationship between citizens and rulers that result from activist victories. Although the regime does attempt to under-

A demonstration in Kuwait in June 2011 demanding "an elected government." Photo by Abdullah Fadel Boftain.

mine those results, its ability to do so is constrained by institutions and shifts in social expectations produced by prior successful political activism.

The external environment also affects the emergence and trajectory of activist movements. As we have seen in Bahrain, Syria, and elsewhere, external actors often interfere in confrontations between activists and rulers by providing resources or opening new spaces for activists or assisting rulers to quash such movements.[7] The Arab Spring contributed to Kuwaiti activism by suggesting new repertoires, such as mobilizing after Friday prayers, and by evoking reactions from the regime, which made several attempts first to pacify and then to repress protesters. Both patterns have been evident in Kuwaiti politics since the 1930s, when the first major citizen movement to check the authority of the regime resulted in Kuwait's first constitution. The composition of Kuwaiti activist movements changes constantly, with merchants, leftists, Islamists, women, students, tribalists, parliamentarians, and stateless persons taking center stage at different times, but the regime's responses tend to follow a routine beginning with an attempt to pacify opponents and, if that fails, to crack down on them.

Kuwaitis in the Streets

Citizen activism in Kuwait predates the discovery of oil in 1938, but the socioeconomic and political context surrounding this discovery provided a catalyst for street mobilization and parliamentary action as methods of activism. Consequently, early activism in Kuwait took place both within and outside formal institutions, setting a pattern that activists in Kuwait continued to follow over the years.

Ottoman and British sponsorship of Kuwaiti rulers in the late nineteenth and twentieth centuries shifted power from the merchant oligarchy to the emir by contributing to his fiscal independence from these wealthy taxpayers. In the nineteenth century, the Al-Sabah family acquired date gardens in Iraq whose produce generated an independent income for the clan, while Ottoman subventions and then British payments to the emir added substantially to the ruling family's financial resources. They allowed Shaikh Mubarak, who ruled from 1896 to 1915 and was the only emir to reach his position as the result of a coup, to increase the power of the ruling family as compared to the merchant class.[8]

Resistance to authoritarian rule began during the reign of Mubarak, but the storied beginning of broad-based Kuwaiti activism is the 1938–39 parliament movement, triggered by the discovery of oil in Kuwait, when it was still a dependency of Britain. Kuwaiti merchants feared that oil income would be completely sequestered by the ruler, Shaikh Ahmad al-Jaber. The British political resident shared their concern, supporting a movement by Kuwaiti merchants to establish a representative body to advise—and to direct—the ruler. The merchants chose a set of 150 electors who then voted for the members of Kuwait's first parliament. This all-Sunni institution shook the foundations of Al-Sabah authority by creating government agencies, reforming the tax system, and writing a constitution. It also alienated Kuwaiti Shia, whose sympathies lay with the ruler who protected them. The ruler dismissed the parliament after it demanded that he turn over payments from the oil company, but popular expectations made it impossible for him simply to shut it down.[9] Instead he called for a new parliament to be chosen by an enlarged electorate but, to his chagrin, the second parliament looked very much like the first one.

In the meantime, the British, having second thoughts about the wisdom of encouraging an independent parliament in Kuwait, withdrew their quiet support from the movement. The emir seized this opportunity to force a showdown with the activists. Police were sent to retrieve the parliament's documents and records, including the regime-changing constitution, but they came to blows with its defenders. One person was killed, several were injured, and the rest went into hiding. The lucky ones escaped into exile, but the remainder were arrested and jailed. The emir is said to have danced in Safat Square that evening, delighted with the outcome of the confrontation and convinced that Kuwaitis' parliamentary ambitions had been vanquished for good.[10]

This confrontation has been repeated, with certain variations, for generations. An opportunity to shift the political balance between citizens and the regime is first taken by an aggrieved group, such as the urban merchants whose desire to share national wealth and to improve government services shaped Kuwait's first constitution. The regime shifts its position, as the emir first concedes to the demands but then decides that this path would take too much power away from him. In 1939, his resort to force was limited but effective in ending that experiment in participatory governance. Yet each encounter also validates activism and changes popular expectations. Indeed, the Kuwaitis' brief experience with a parliament convinced them that they were a democratic nation.[11] Constitutionalism became the frame of future confrontations between state and society.

Kuwait's next emir was the Al-Sabah most open to participatory politics. Shaikh Abdullah al-Salim had to fight the authoritarians and rent-seekers in his family as well as navigate the populist wave caused by the victory of

Gamal Abdel Nasser in Egypt, especially its effect on labor and student dissidents.[12] Rather than applying repression against restive workers and students, Abdullah al-Salim instituted a system of popular representation, presiding over the drafting and ratification of a new constitution that remains the most liberal such document in the Gulf region. In addition to a parliament with actual, if limited, legislative powers (Majlis Al-Umma), Kuwait's 1962 constitution established limits on executive authority to curtail citizen expression by guaranteeing civil liberties such as a free press and the right to assemble. Despite its limitations, the 1962 constitution has remained a bulwark against the perpetuation of extralegal behavior by the regime.[13]

The *Diwaniyya* as a Place of Activism

The second venue of activism in Kuwait is the *diwaniyya,* an important traditional institution in Kuwait. *Diwaniyyas* are regular informal meetings held in the homes of persons connected to one another by family or business ties. *Diwaniyya* is the term for the rooms or buildings used for these meetings, spaces ancillary to or closed off from the living quarters of the host's house. They quickly became favored venues for electoral politics after the adoption of the constitution and served as forums for discussing politics and planning strategies whether there were elections or not. *Diwaniyyas* occupy a space that is private and proprietary, that is, controlled by the householder. Because of their inherent privacy, they are especially useful for activists during periods of state repression.

The constitution and the civil liberties it guarantees, along with the parliament, have been constant targets of Abdullah al-Salim's successors, who have tried to weaken both through legal and extralegal means. In their confrontations with the regime, citizen activists in tandem with parliamentarians pushed back against these attempts. When opportunities arose, they worked to strengthen and extend institutional checks on the regime that they hoped would be enduring.

The regime fought these checks, seeking to weaken and delegitimize the parliament and undermine Kuwaitis' commitment to participatory politics. The constitution was suspended twice, from 1976 to 1981 and from 1986 to 1992. Each time, the suspensions came when key cabinet ministers were threatened with interpellation, a procedure requiring them to respond to questions about their activities and, depending on their answers, to face a vote of confidence. The constitutionally required new elections were not held within sixty days after these suspensions, both of which were reactions to the parliament's unwillingness to turn a blind eye to financial and other malfeasance by the regime. Each came to an end in part as a result of political pressure by Kuwaiti activists demanding that "their" constitution be restored.

During both parliamentary interregna, the emir, Jaber al-Ahmad, made de jure and de facto attempts to defang the parliament. When his 1980 bid to amend the constitution was opposed, he mobilized new constituencies to weaken the power of the merchants and Arab nationalists who at that time formed the core of the opposition. In doing so, he initiated structural changes as well. Prior to the reinstatement of parliament in 1981, he forged an alliance with Kuwaiti Islamists and also enlarged the electorate by conferring first-category citizenship on Bedouin populations from Najd in central Arabia, allowing them to vote and run for office.[14] These changes not only reduced the influence of merchants and urban intellectuals in the parliament but also elevated tribal over urban values in the population as a whole.[15] The emir also redrew voting districts, redistributing neighborhoods across urban constituencies and carving out tribally dominated districts, both of which increased the power of the tribes.[16] He raised the number of districts from ten to twenty-five, facilitating electoral interference through such means as vote-buying and supporting frivolous candidacies that could draw votes away from candidates the regime did not like.[17] These changes in campaigns and elections altered the scope of what had been the main forum for citizen activism since the adoption of the constitution.

Not surprisingly, the 1981 parliamentary election returned a conservative body in which Islamists and tribal representatives were highly influential. Yet the emir's new allies in the parliament soon proved to be as demanding as their urban, liberal peers. Islamist and tribal representatives in the 1985 parliament joined other opposition forces to demand answers from cabinet ministers about government policies. Disagreements over education, problems with the Central Bank, and concerns arising from the Iran-Iraq War (1980–88), among other issues, triggered a second illegal suspension in 1986, five years after the previous one had ended. This time, however, the parliament did not disband. The opposition made up a majority of the elected members (cabinet members serve in an ex officio capacity), and it continued to meet at *diwaniyyas* held at the home of the speaker of the Kuwait National Assembly, Ahmad al-Sadoun.

This action set a precedent for the use of *diwaniyyas* as venues for mass activism. In the fall of 1989, during the "prodemocracy movement," a series of "Monday *diwaniyyas,*" presumed to be safe from government intrusion because of their location in a protected space, were held in the homes of members of the rump parliament.[18] The weekly gatherings attracted more and more people even though citizens risked arrest by attending these events. The first Monday *diwaniyya* was held at the speaker's home and was undisturbed. Yet, attendees at the second one, also held in Kuwait City, found riot police and dogs blocking access to the house. Many prominent activists sent telegrams to the emir protesting the police action, and a delegation from the rump parliament met with the foreign minister, who promised that it would not happen again. The two subsequent meetings, both located in the city as the others had been, attracted no visible police presence.

On January 8, 1990, after a break for the New Year's holiday, the Monday *diwaniyya* was scheduled to be held in a tribal area. A key element in the regime's divide-and-rule strategy had been to impose a wedge between urban (*hadhar*) and tribal (*badu*) Kuwaitis, but the composition of the rump parliament, which included *badu* members, showed that the metaphorical wall dividing these two groups was in danger of eroding.[19] Consequently, arriving guests found their host sealed in his *diwaniyya* by troops surrounding his house. No one was allowed to pass without showing an identification card, and as more and more people arrived, the police began to beat them. Several persons were injured, including an elderly former member of parliament and a former ambassador. Some guests were arrested and held overnight. The *diwaniyya* host was arrested and taken to jail in Kuwait City. This proved to be a tactical error, however, because the jail was in a convenient, public location in the city, and activists demonstrated outside until he was released.[20]

When guests arrived for the January 15 gathering, they found that the entire house had been wrapped in barbed wire. But the final Monday *diwaniyya*, on January 22, was met with a show of force reminiscent of the regime's attacks on the parliamentary movement in 1939. The venue once again was in an outlying area, where the regime appeared to be especially concerned to quash citizen mobilization and perhaps to disrupt nascent coalitions between urban and rural Kuwaitis.[21] The tribes were already challenging the regime's plans for their contributions to electoral politics and its efforts to bring about the rhetorical and physical separation of urban and rural populations.

Arriving guests (and reporters) found more than barbed wire. National Guard units, riot police, and tanks shot chemical foam at them. The security forces also used tear gas and stun grenades. When the people sought sanctuary in the mosque, foam and tear gas followed. Kuwaitis and foreign reporters also were arrested and detained.

Afterward, the organizers, most of them members of the rump parliament, changed their tactics. Rather than holding one mass meeting at one designated *diwaniyya*, they took advantage of the relative peace of the private spaces offered by Kuwait's many *diwaniyyas* and the dispersion of and variation in the population of activists (which included, in addition to merchants, numerous professionals, religious leaders, and women) to meet in small groups in homes throughout the country.

Despite the attacks on the Monday *diwaniyyas*, Kuwaitis still perceived the home and the *diwaniyyas* they sheltered to be a protected space.[22] During Ramadan, which began in late March, members of the ruling family went to the *diwaniyyas* of family members and prominent merchants to persuade attendees to support the emir. Members of the opposition also spoke at *diwaniyyas*, arguing for the restoration of constitutional life. The Ramadan interlude was so calm that most activists in and out of parliament expected the emir to call for new elections after the Eid, the holiday that marks the end of Ramadan. But Jaber al-Ahmad had another card to play. He did call for new elections, but to an extraconstitutional "national assembly" (*al-Majlis al-watani*) that would have only advisory power.

Opposition members I spoke to at the time feared that if such a body were elected with their consent, it would become the de facto "parliament" and consign the constitutionally mandated Majlis Al-Umma and civil liberties to oblivion. As a result, few former members ran, leaving the field to middle-class and tribal candidates. Voter turnout was low, but the new body convened as scheduled without challenging the regime. When Saddam Hussein invaded Kuwait on August 2, 1990, constitutionally governed participatory politics in Kuwait seemed to be a thing of the past.[23]

Instead, the opposition in parliament and among Kuwait's professional and merchant classes used the occupation as another opportunity to press for democracy. These mostly urban Kuwaitis confronted their rulers at two mass meetings held in Saudi Arabia where the rulers had sought refuge from the occupation. At the October meeting in Jeddah, the opposition pledged to support the continuation of Al-Sabah rule, and the ruling family pledged to restore the constitution after liberation. The crown prince promised to set up a committee that would include representatives from the opposition "in the critical decision making process undertaken by the government in exile."[24] But the committee was never set up. Instead, after liberation the regime declared martial law. In a stark departure from the arrests and brief imprisonments that formed the usual way that citizen dissidents were dealt with, death squads committed human rights violations against residents whom they accused of collaborating with the invading Iraqis, including some Kuwaitis who had remained in Kuwait during the occupation.[25] When elections resumed in October 1992, they took place only because of persistent pressures from domestic groups and from the few foreign governments in the large coalition that had liberated Kuwait which demanded that the regime make good on the Jeddah promise.[26]

Activism after Liberation: Institutionalizing Organized Activism

After the liberation of Kuwait, activism expanded in formal organizations like voluntary associations and other civil society structures, where it had been suppressed during the suspension of civil liberties protecting the rights to free speech and assembly. Civil society organizations utilized a broad array of methods, including organizing, lobbying, and engaging in public demonstrations, thereby reclaiming citizen entitlement to engage in political life in unambiguously public spaces.

The normal level of popular activism in Kuwait resumed, but with a difference. The experience of the regime's reactions to peaceful mass gatherings to protest the continued suspension of the parliament coupled with the harsh crackdown following liberation pushed the 1992 parliament, with its large portion of Islamist and secular opposition figures, to demand institutional changes they hoped would add to the durability of activist practices. The parliament established a new standing committee on human rights. Citizen activists, many of them professionals, organized several domestic human rights groups to deal with Kuwaiti prisoners of war in Iraq and provide assistance to traumatized families, including children whose needs were unaddressed by the regime. As a result of their experiences during the prodemocracy movement and under Iraqi occupation, these activists were determined to investigate allegations of human rights violations and take measures to stop them. The first such group, the Kuwaiti Association to Defend War Victims, was denied a government license but continued to operate anyway.[27] It cut a path that a few other organizations have followed since. After the groups working on prisoner of war issues organized a mass demonstration outside the parliament building, the government countered by pushing a law through parliament to ban all unlicensed groups. Several decided to carry on anyway.[28]

Kuwaiti human rights activists had external support for their work, not from governments but from transnational human rights organizations. One was the Cairo-based Arab Organization for Human Rights, with which the Kuwait Society for Human Rights, organized in 1993 (and also denied a license to operate), is affiliated. The internationally affiliated Kuwaiti groups, along with NGOs like Amnesty International, were able to carry out investigations and publicize their results more broadly than the domestic groups could have done on their own. International and domestic attention put pressure on the government to respond and also protected the unlicensed groups that were in technical violation of the new law on associations.

Among the issues these groups took up was the treatment of *bidun*, stateless persons living in Kuwait without nationality. Although *bidun* were not citizens, until 1986 they had been treated like Kuwaitis under the law and were even counted as Kuwaitis in government statistics.[29] After liberation and the selection of "out groups," chiefly Palestinians, as scapegoats, *bidun* also were singled out for ill treatment by a government obsessed by fifth columns.[30] Those allowed to return to Kuwait suffered high rates of unemployment unless they had been members of the state security forces. The children of *bidun* men married to Kuwaiti women were, like their fathers, treated as noncitizens and denied pre-1986 benefits such as free schooling and health care. Kuwaiti and *bidun* human rights activists continue today to press for better treatment of *bidun* and, as I note below, have made some progress as a result of regime fears evoked by the Arab Spring.

Human rights activists championed foreign workers abused by their employers, leading to the establishment of a special police station dedicated to complaints of abuse by household workers. Cases of rights abuses, such as the firing of a non-Muslim sales clerk because the store owner was worried that his customers would be put off if they were served by a non-Muslim, triggered spontaneous demonstrations. Women demonstrated for political rights, particularly during voter registration periods and on election days. The civil and human rights campaigns that enjoyed several spectacular successes in the first decade of the new century built on these sturdy foundations.[31]

Activists also protested government corruption, a persistent issue that had contributed to demands to interpellate government ministers prior to the closure of the parliament in 1986. Corruption reached the attention of outside actors when a case was brought in a British court against Kuwaitis and others who had embezzled funds from the Kuwait Oil Tanker Company during the occupation. The oil minister at the time, a member of the ruling family, was not a defendant, but the judge's decision and accompanying opinion made his role in the affair very plain. When these documents were released, masses of

Kuwaitis took to the streets to protest the corruption displayed by high officials at a time of grave national peril.[32] Many continued the fight by mobilizing against the privatization of the domestic oil industry, a move favored by the ruling family, including the errant former oil minister who also had been accused of insider trading when he organized the purchase of a U.S. oil services company some years earlier.

Kuwaiti Activism and Citizens' Rights: The Rise of Multi-Platform Activism

Burgeoning civil society organizations in Kuwait allowed activism to become more sophisticated and diversified in its methods and strategies. Activist groups used a variety of media as well as public protest to mobilize and publicize their demands, while each "wave" of activism provided valuable lessons in methods and approaches for later campaigns.

Activist efforts to extend civil and political rights to women, the last excluded citizen group in Kuwait, demonstrated growing sophistication in tactics used both in the public sphere and behind the scenes. Modernization did not erode men's or women's primary loyalties to families and tribes, patriarchal structures that continued to be pivotal sources of social status and privilege.[33] Indeed, some women expressed a pervasive fear of change in Kuwaiti society, seeing even the enfranchisement of women as too far-reaching.[34] In this sense, Kuwait did not differ significantly from other Middle Eastern societies in which demands for women's rights are perceived as signs of moral decay.[35] Even arguments for women's political rights as human rights were interpreted as threatening and at first resulted in more opposition than support on the part of Kuwaiti women; conservative women organized against suffragist campaigns and collected hundreds of signatures on petitions.[36] This changed after 1999, although unevenly.[37]

In 1999, alarmed at the widespread popular demonstrations and parliamentary action that the revelations of embezzlement by high-level officials had triggered, Jaber al-Ahmad dissolved the parliament and called for a new election within sixty days. This was the first legal parliamentary dissolution in Kuwaiti history. It offered a much-desired opportunity to the emir, who issued sixty-three decrees during the parliament's absence, including several privatization measures. One decree granted women full political rights—that is, not only to vote but also to run for office. Although the parliament had never shown itself to be enthusiastic about women's political rights in the past, many

Kuwaitis hoped that the emir's proposal would be accepted.[38] Yet if the parliament were to accept it and then reject the other laws on the grounds that they were not matters of necessity, parliamentary rejections of emiri decrees would be more difficult to justify in the future. Not surprisingly, the new parliament voted all of the nonbudgetary emiri decrees down. A subsequent attempt to pass the women's rights law as a parliamentary initiative also was defeated, but by a narrower margin.

If at that juncture the antifeminists in the parliament breathed a sigh of relief, it was premature. The emir's apparent support for women's political rights opened the door for Islamist women to join their liberal peers in organizing and lobbying for some version of them. Two weeks after the emiri decree, the liberal Women's Cultural and Social Society (WCSS) created a committee on the political rights of women. Moderate Sunni groups, Shiite groups, and others quickly aligned themselves with the WCSS, and newly formed pro-suffrage groups also joined the movement. In addition to lobbying, they worked hard to keep the women's rights issue on the national political agenda. Their tactics included intensive utilization of media; holding conferences and debates; sponsoring rallies, sit-ins, and marches; putting women's names on candidates' lists; organizing petitions; and filing lawsuits in the courts.[39]

Urban high school and university students, many of whom had begun mobilizing to oppose a law passed in 1996 requiring gender segregation at Kuwaiti universities, joined the experienced feminist activists.[40] Graduates who had returned to Kuwait from overseas studies helped to coordinate pro-suffrage activities. Liberal graduates had honed their political skills in campaigns for leadership positions in the Kuwaiti Overseas Student Union, where they succeeded in winning office against Islamist opponents who had led the organization for years.[41]

Kuwaitis have always been in the vanguard of users of electronic media. In addition to meetings and rallies, women's rights activists employed text messaging to get demonstrators, including high school students, into the streets at a virtual moment's notice. Near the close of the campaign, Kuwaitis of all ages and genders took to the streets to demand women's rights. Beset by feminists' threats to continue their highly effective and media-friendly protests, many couched in the evocative language of human rights, the acting prime minister, Shaikh Sabah al-Ahmad, brought a bill for women's rights to the floor of the parliament as an act of urgency. This allowed it to be passed in a single session on May 16, 2005, thanks to some arm-twisting and alleged bribes to tribal representatives.[42]

The following year, another movement achieved rapid success by applying lessons from the women's rights movement to its campaign to reduce the number of election districts from twenty-five to five. The movement began when about a dozen of the study-abroad returnees who had joined activists in the women's rights movement organized the first "We Want Five" demonstration. They sent text messages to friends to gather outside the Seif Palace on May 5, when a cabinet meeting was scheduled. These messages were forwarded to friends of friends, and about two hundred young Kuwaitis wearing orange T-shirts and waving orange flags showed up. Press coverage and word of mouth ensured that news of the demonstration would spread, but neither guaranteed the intense popular interest it generated. At a second rally, held outside the parliament the following week, more than five hundred gathered to hear speeches by the young activists. Information conveyed in speeches was augmented by blogs reporting news from *diwaniyyas* and "private meetings," some based abroad to prevent the regime from closing them down.[43]

The demonstrations snowballed, attracting members of parliament as well as citizens to the area in front of the National Assembly. The government first sought to pacify the activists, offering a ten-district proposal, which failed because twenty-nine orange-supporting MPs left the building, denying the government a quorum. When demonstrators converged on the National Assembly the next day, repression was applied. The parliament building was surrounded by police and special forces dressed in riot gear and armed with batons. Despite the show of force, about four thousand Kuwaitis returned to demonstrate at the parliament that evening, the anniversary of the adoption of the women's rights law. The next day, the emir dissolved the parliament and called for new elections.

The irony of the orange movement's "anniversary" success was that it came at the expense of women's democratic aspirations. The "snap" 2006 election took place a year ahead of schedule, derailing preparations by many potential female candidates and forcing the others to campaign in an environment in which orange was king—but not queen. The women who ran in 2006 campaigned on issues important to women like the financial problems of divorcées and the citizenship of children of mothers married to non-Kuwaitis. Commentators usually point to the orange flood that drowned their reasonable arguments in a sea of revulsion against corruption as the reason why no woman won in the 2006 elections, but Rola Dashti, one of the unsuccessful female candidates, saw something more:

> Everyone had a perception that a woman would not get more than 200 or 300 votes. So we would lose. They put their eggs in the basket of the

candidates they thought would bring votes. . . . The election was about two things, curbing corruption OR deepening democracy. . . . The priority was not deepening democracy but fighting corruption. This corruption was already in process, vote buying and also a coalition among the corrupt.

There is always vote buying. In 2006 it was unusual. The corrupted person usually does not mind where the second vote goes—it is your choice. . . . So you always have the second vote floating. When I was running, I expected to pick up a lot of these second votes.[44]

In the 2006 election, however, many "second votes" were not "your choice." Orange allies brokered across candidates and political groups so that the second vote from one would go to another orange supporter. When the "corrupt candidates" saw this, they joined with other corrupt candidates to do the same, buying one vote for themselves and the second for a vote-buying ally pledged to return the favor. There were no floating votes from these bargains, and women were the losers. After the five-districts law was passed, this disadvantage was diminished by a provision allowing each voter to choose up to four candidates. The second election held under the new law produced four female parliamentarians.

Tribal Primaries and the Transformation of Tradition by Activism

Despite the rise of modern methods and activist strategies like establishing civil society organizations, traditional structures also provide a framework for activism. In addition to *diwaniyyas* that coordinate political action among members, unsanctioned primary elections are occasions of tribal mobilization. The tribal primary is not "traditional" in the sense of having been around for a long time; it is a contemporary manifestation of a traditional form of tribal decision-making. This innovation improves the chances of a member of a tribe winning a general election by guiding the concentration of the popular vote of the group toward one or two candidates, while the other contenders from the tribe drop out of the running.[45] The first tribal primary was held in 1976, evoking fears in many quarters about its effectiveness. Tribal primaries were made illegal in 1998, although the law forbidding them was not enforced for ten years.

Tribal social formations are often criticized as politically primitive, but the tribal primary reflects a sophisticated appreciation of the politics of representation whereby the tribe as a corporate body selects candidates in a forum much like party caucuses or primaries.[46] Other Kuwaitis also organize to "concentrate" their general election votes. What distinguished the tribal primary is that it was formal and regularized and included sanctions to enforce its decisions. Urban Kuwaitis resented the effectiveness of tribal primaries but had no convenient identity other than sect or class around which to mobilize as similar blocs. The Islamist groups come closest, but their agendas often divide co-sectarians rather than uniting them, as clan identities do.

It is unclear why the law against tribal primaries was suddenly applied for the first time in the unscheduled 2008 election campaign, but the most likely reason is that the large tribes, whose choices had the best chances of finding themselves in the parliament, had become too strong to ignore. The tribes interpreted this unanticipated action as an attack and responded with an attack of their own against a local police station where tribe members who had defied the law were incarcerated.[47] This unprecedented violence during an election campaign shook Kuwaitis. It especially shook *hadhar,* whose preferred mode of disagreement is yelling, and widened the gulf between them and Kuwaiti *badu,* one that had developed over decades of regime-directed development policies aimed at keeping the two groups separate.[48]

Prior to the unscheduled 2009 election, two outspoken tribal candidates were arrested. These arrests exacerbated the growing animosity between *hadhar* and *badu* even further. The tribes maintained that the arrests were aimed at their political culture, noting that urbanites were not similarly vulnerable. In an apparent bow to tribal pressure, security personnel responded by arresting a relation of the speaker of the parliament, an urban candidate from the second district, for an alleged offense committed more than a year earlier. The two *badu* candidates won in their districts, undoubtedly helped by their arrests, but the *hadhar* candidate lost, a reflection of the different styles of activism practiced by citizens in the outlying areas compared to those of citizens in the city. The law against tribal primaries was not enforced in 2009; it was selectively enforced in the February 2012 election (2012F), when it proved ineffective at attracting voters to support the chosen candidates. There were no tribal primaries in the December 2012 election (2012D), with most large tribes boycotting the event so that few members ran or voted. By then, other means to delegitimize the increasingly oppositional tribes were deployed to aggravate the resurgent antagonism between *hadhar* and *badu.*[49]

Opportunity Knocks with Both Hands

The Arab Spring created another opportunity for Kuwaiti activists. It catalyzed both public protests and parliamentary action and, as also occurred in Tunisia, civil action in the form of strikes. All three capitalized on existing discontent with the Kuwaiti prime minister, who was personally vulnerable to public criticism because of institutional changes in the structure of the executive.

The positions of crown prince and prime minister were "traditionally" held by the same individual, but crown prince Sa'd al-Abdullah's illness had resulted in the appointment of an acting prime minister, Shaikh Sabah al-Ahmad. He became emir after the brief reign of Sa'd al-Abdullah, who resigned shortly after the death of Shaikh Jaber al-Ahmad.[50] This complicated transition overshadowed recognition of the danger that having a prime minister who was not constitutionally protected from public criticism, as the emir and, by extension, the crown prince are, might present to the regime. Indeed, within a short time, the prime minister became a focal point of popular dissatisfaction, and allegations of corrupt dealings formed the basis of demands that he be replaced. The emir resisted these demands, reshuffling his cabinet and calling repeated unscheduled elections in a string of futile attempts to thwart parliamentary action.

The Arab Spring shifted the grounds of this confrontation in favor of the activists. Demonstrations demanding the resignation of the prime minister and another ruling family member long associated with corrupt practices brought members of parliament, representatives of professional societies, and thousands of other Kuwaitis into the streets throughout 2011. Gradually their complaints expanded from narrow calls to curb corruption to include demands that the Kuwaiti regime demonstrate that it is a "constitutional monarchy" that subscribes to the rule of law. Friday demonstrations in Kuwait were held in Safat Square, triggering memories of the two 1938–39 parliaments that had opposed the high-handed governance of the father of the serving emir. They prompted the closure of the square and the assignment of the narrow strip between the seafront and the highway in front of the National Assembly building as the only lawful site for future demonstrations.

Parliamentary action complemented the street demonstrations. In February 2011, the interior minister resigned in the face of a threat of parliamentary interpellation over the death of a citizen who, according to an investigatory report, had suffered torture in detention. His February departure postponed a street protest aimed at him by a group of youth activists calling themselves Fifth Fence, and transformed the already-planned action into a demonstration on March 8 that called for the resignation of the whole government, including the prime minister.[51]

The whole government did resign a few weeks later in the face of requests to interpellate three ministers from the ruling family. One was the deputy prime minister for the economy, who was suspected of corruption in awarding US$900 million in government contracts. The prime minister was reappointed, but his new government included only six "new faces," while scrutiny of the deputy prime minister sharpened. Citizens demonstrated against him, and when it became clear that the request to interpellate him would be approved, he resigned to escape questioning.

The unfolding of the Arab Spring was a constant backdrop to these domestic upheavals. As the year unfolded, the regime was determined to hold the line against demonstrations, which increased in number and size and spread to other groups protesting a variety of issues. Demonstrations by stateless *bidun* in the spring were quickly quashed, although the regime promised to extend citizenship to some of the *bidun* population. Citizen anger at government incompetence and malfeasance kept the initially small but persistent political demonstrations going throughout the spring and summer, reinforcing parliamentary attacks on offending ministers. Both contributed to a spectacular expression of rentier state tactics in the form of the new budget, released on June 29, which included substantial increases in salaries, housing programs, and support to religious organizations. Some recipients ridiculed the irrelevance of the regime's responses to their demands, but others saw them as an invitation to push for more.

A wave of strikes began in September with civil service workers demanding higher wages. State oil workers threatened to strike but were mollified by generous raises. Banks, factories, and Kuwait Airways also experienced strikes. In October, more than three thousand customs officers went on strike, freezing traffic in and out of ports and oil terminals, disrupting airport traffic, and blocking Kuwait's land borders with Iraq and Saudi Arabia. A week earlier, firefighters had demonstrated at the main fire department demanding workplace changes.

Meanwhile, a highly respected Kuwaiti newspaper reported that local banks were preparing to refer about fifteen members of parliament to the public prosecutor to be investigated for possible money laundering. As the investigation proceeded and more MPs were implicated, the suspicious bank deposits began to look more like bribes, and the bribes seemed to be coming from the prime minister. Protests and demonstrations intensified and spread to include people from groups that had taken to the streets only recently. On November 16, thousands of Kuwaitis, including members of the parliamentary opposition and a large number of young men from the tribes, stormed the National Assembly building, protesting corruption and the regime-conferred immunity of the prime minister to demands for his removal. Security forces expelled the protesters who had breached the building, arrested some demonstrators (including several MPs), and injured many others. But when the dust cleared, the parliament resumed its efforts to interpellate the prime minister. Finally, after five years, three snap elections, and four cabinet "reshuffles," a new prime minister, Shaikh Jabir al-Mubarak al-Hamad Al-Sabah was named in December. Nevertheless, public protests and behind-the-scenes pressures continued. Days later, the emir dismissed the 2009 parliament and called for another election, thereby touching off more than a year of conflict that included the election of not one but two parliaments, each of which was subsequently annulled after only a few months of life.

High Noon in Kuwait?

The February 2012 parliamentary election, 2012F, reflected popular rage at the extent and flagrancy of high-level corruption and sequestration of community resources against which Kuwaitis have been fighting since the 1930s. Campaign issues included calls to change the relations between government and parliament by amending the constitution. The election results demonstrated high levels of support for the opposition, particularly among tribal voters, and for Islamist candidates whose victories probably reflected popular hopes that they would be less vulnerable to corruption than their opponents.

The large majority of antigovernment representatives, most of whom were tribal and/or Islamist, changed both the complexion of the parliament and the tactics it was willing—and able—to employ. The Islamist-dominated opposition proposed to establish a "morality police" to regulate women's public behavior; Sunni Islamists wanted to amend the constitution to make sharia the sole source of Kuwaiti law, and they mobilized a large majority in support of a law calling for the possible execution of persons convicted of insulting the Prophet. The regime's response came through Kuwait's Constitutional Court, which abruptly decided in June 2012 that the 2012F election was unconstitutional. By reinstating the comparatively compliant 2009 parliament as the still-legal Majlis Al-Umma, it thrust Kuwaiti politics into uncharted territory.

December 8, 2010: Special Forces storm a gathering at the home of MP Jamaan Al-Harbash, convened to oppose any unilateral changes by the government in the election law. Attendees are beaten with wooden batons and an unknown number are hospitalized.

February 6, 2011: Sheikh Ahmed al-Hamoud steps in as the new minister of the interior, as Sheikh Jaber Khaled Al-Sabah resigns amid torture allegations.

February 19, 2011: In Jahra, security forces clash with stateless people, leaving thirty wounded, as Kuwaiti *bidun* demand citizenship, free education, and other benefits.

March 8, 2011: Anticipating planned protests to demand greater political freedoms, police block off the main square in Kuwait City.

March 31, 2011: Kuwait's cabinet resigns amid regional turmoil; some speculate that the resignations are due to three cabinet members aiming to avoid questions about why Kuwait did not send troops to Bahrain.

June 3, 2011: Five hundred antigovernment protesters gather to demand the resignation of Prime Minister Nasir al-Mohammad Al-Sabah.

August–September 2011: The public prosecutor launches a probe after local newspapers reveal that several local banks reported the deposit of millions of dollars in cash into the bank accounts of around fifteen members of parliament.

September 11, 2011: A youth group known as September 16 Youth calls for major reforms and urges the emirate to appoint a prime minister from outside the Al-Sabah ruling family.

September 21, 2011: More than five thousand protesters attend a demonstration in Kuwait City calling for radical political change and an end to government corruption.

October 10, 2011: More than three thousand customs workers go on strike demanding better working conditions.

October 20, 2011: In the largest protest to date, more than ten thousand Kuwaitis demonstrate in Kuwait City and demand the resignation of the prime minister.

November 16, 2011: Protesters and opposition MPs storm the National Assembly and call for the resignation of the prime minister. They later march to Irada Square, where they clash with riot police, leaving several injured.

November 28, 2011: After the resignation of three ministers, Prime Minister Sheikh Mohammed al-Nasir Al-Sabah holds an emergency cabinet meeting in attempt to keep his government intact.

The 2009 parliament had been known for its inability to get anything done. Given the regime's opposition to citizen demands for political restructuring, it is not surprising that the sudden end of the 2012F parliament coincided with rapid progress on parliamentary initiatives, including some that had little to do with religion. One committee was nearing completion of draft laws to reform the judiciary and require financial disclosure from public officials. Another had held its first meeting on political parties.[52] Despite widespread dissatisfaction with much of the parliament's religious agenda, there was broad support for measures to end corruption and legalize political parties.

Interest in amending the constitution was and is widespread, but what different individuals and groups mean by that varies. Indeed, the emir himself would like to amend the constitution to limit the power of parliament to check his authority to make whatever laws he likes.[53] Those hoping to move Kuwait toward a constitutional monarchy favor amendments that would change the relationship among the parliament, the prime minister, and the cabinet. As I noted above, Sunni Islamists remain wedded to a decades-old proposal to revise Article 2 of the constitution to make Islam the sole source of Kuwaiti law.

But by proceeding simultaneously with religious and political initiatives, the 2012F parliament gave the regime leverage to use against it. Those appalled by the cultural measures were encouraged to view the emir as a check on Islamist and tribal pressures to constrain civil liberties and especially women's rights. By suggesting that the 2012F body was a preview of what would happen to Kuwait under a more powerful parliament, the regime evoked popular opposition to structural reform. The regime equated street activism with lawlessness and chaos by associating the already-tainted parliamentary opposition with street protests, especially the large November 2011 march on the parliament that had ended in violence and the arrests of citizens and opposition MPs. The scene was set for the 2012D election.

After the court declared the 2012F parliament to be illegal and reinstated the 2009 body, 2012F members, including several who had been elected to both parliaments, objected. The old speaker was recalled to preside over the reconstituted body, but he could not gather a quorum, and the coexistence of two dubiously legitimate parliaments further divided the opposition with regard to how to proceed. New elections were the logical solution, but how would they be conducted? The speaker suggested that the constitutional court be asked to review the five-districts law. The new cabinet, nominated and sworn in despite the lack of a functioning parliament, agreed to this plan in early August. While Kuwaitis awaited the court's decision, opposition members threatened to boycott any election based on a new government-produced election law. When the decision came down in late September, the court declared the electoral law to be constitutional, clearing the way for new elections based on the five districts.

But the emir had other plans. On October 3, he officially dismissed the 2009 parliament and two weeks later decreed that the new elections would be held in the five districts, but each voter could select only one candidate instead of four. Seeing this both as an assault on a law approved by the parliament and the court and as a signal that the regime intended to go back to its pre-2006 strategies for manipulating election results, Kuwaitis opposed to the emiri decree geared up for a series of street protests to push for retention of the four-vote rule. Following a rally at the "legal" venue, dubbed "Irada Square," on October 15 that had been disrupted by state security forces, a "March for Dignity" was called for October 20. Irada Square filled up quickly, and a crowd variously estimated at 50,000 to 150,000 unarmed persons spilled into the street and headed for the Kuwait Towers. Waving Kuwaiti flags and singing the national anthem, they suddenly were surrounded by special forces and the National Guard, who gassed, beat, and arrested marchers, mostly as they were coming to or leaving the gathering.

A second March for Dignity was held on November 5. The organizers were prepared for attempts to prevent the march and used Twitter to move the demonstration multiple times, eventually taking it to the suburb of Mishref. Several participants I interviewed later that month were gleeful at having kept one step ahead of the vehicles intended to block their access to one public space after another in the city. Others were exhilarated but also frightened by the rapid deployment of security forces and their heavy use of tear gas, pepper gas, and stun grenades. One young woman told me that she and three friends had taken refuge in a restaurant; others reported being picked up by sympathetic motorists. Their main concern was to escape arrest and consequent physical abuse by the security forces.

The third March for Dignity was held the day before the 2012D election, when the city was full of foreign reporters. This time, the tens of thousands of marching, chanting Kuwaitis of every age and wearing a variety of costumes and banners were able to proceed unmolested. The different treatment of marchers across the preelection demonstrations was attributed to the fact that permission had been granted for the November 30 event but not for the one on October 15. Yet no permission had been required for the gathering on October 15, and the two previous dignity marches had been peaceful until the security forces attacked them.

The marches constituted half of the activist effort prior to the election. The other half was a call to boycott the election. Headed by a young activist, Mohammed Qasem, the boycott quickly gathered steam. Many liberal, Islamist, and tribal parliamentary incumbents refused to register candidacies, and citizens were soon tweeting and meeting in formal and informal debates about whether they should vote or not. The boycotters hoped to make the 2012D parliament illegitimate by holding participation down, but coverage of the opposition in the Arabic-language press was sparse, limited to a few opposition spokesmen and youth activists, and (on the whole) negative. The regime branded the boycott as a treasonous attempt to weaken Kuwait and referred to the demonstrators as rioters, a meme that was then picked up by the press. Preelection coverage featured an upsurge of activity by the emir, who spent the season meeting with citizens and foreign guests and appearing at events that garnered photographs in the daily papers. Massive efforts were made to persuade citizens to vote. Government workers were lobbied at their workplaces and until their complaints were heeded, the sleep of many citizens was disturbed by the beeps of mobile phones registering multiple text messages urging them to vote.

The absence of tribal and Sunni Islamist candidates freed regime supporters from restraint on their public criticism of groups such as the large tribes and the Muslim Brotherhood. Private criticism of individuals was extraordinarily bitter. Musallam Al-Barrak, a former MP from the largest tribe, Al Mutair, had defied the emir in public speeches, most notably on October 15 when he addressed the emir directly, saying, "We will not allow you . . . to take Kuwait into the abyss of autocracy"; Ahmad al-Sadoun was speaker of the 1986, 1992, 1996, and 2012F parliaments and had a long history of opposition to the regime.[54] Both men were accused of stirring up and then hiding behind Kuwaiti youth to create "chaos," another of the favored memes of proregime Kuwaitis.

Focus on the boycott masked two difficulties long faced by Kuwaiti activists. The first is the lack of opposition coherence and solidarity. The ability of the parliament to represent Kuwait requires reaching across the many structural and metaphorical barriers that prevent the integration of Kuwaitis and their interests into a unified vision of the nation.[55] This remained an even more distant aspiration for the 2012D parliament, whose constituency base was heavily skewed by the more than 20 percent drop in turnout attributable to the boycott. Turnout in Kuwaiti elections had fallen sharply since 2006, but 62 percent of the electorate voted in 2012F, electing a large number of regime critics. Yet, due to their energetic pursuit of two distinct and partly antagonistic legislative agendas, the goals of the 2012F parliament both lacked focus and were suspect. Similarly, citizen activism during the Arab Spring also reflected different agendas and goals, and the rhetorical fragmentation of protesters across social groups that have long histories of antagonism. The success of the regime in reinforcing those antagonisms was made sharply clear in the 2012D election. The parliament it produced not only featured many inexperienced MPs but also lacked direct representation of liberals, Sunni Islamists, and the large tribes and gave Kuwaiti Shia their largest representation ever, with seventeen elected members.

A second difficulty is the need to bridge the divide between young Kuwaitis, particularly those from the tribes who feel shut out of the economy and dismissed by society, and their navel-gazing and nervous urban elders. During the 2012F campaign, urban citizens and middle-aged candidates maneuvered gingerly around their memories of the huge 2011 protest gatherings of youth, many from the tribes, especially the occupation of the National Assembly in mid-November. This event has the same iconic status for proregime Kuwaitis as the "Harbash diwaniyya," a brutal attack by security forces sent in December 2010 to beat up 'Ubayd al-Wasmi, a professor of law, and several members of Parliament when they were rallying at the *diwaniyya* of Jamaan al-Harbash, a member of parliament, to oppose any amendment of the constitution by the regime.[56] The emir seized the opportunity presented by the 2012F parliament and the 2012D election to make regime change a terrifying proposition to many Kuwaitis, especially women, who were horrified by the initiatives of parliamentary Islamists, and both urban and tribal residents fearful of the prospect of violence by Kuwaiti youth.

Among the tragedies of Kuwait's political crisis is that it delayed addressing the aspirations of young Kuwaitis who had hoped in early 2012 to take center stage with their own proposals for reform. The youth-sponsored Kuwait Charter 2012 was endorsed by one of the winning candidates in 2012F, attorney Faisal al-Yahya, an independent young Islamist who had discontinued his affiliation with the Muslim Brotherhood ten years earlier. Faisal is credited as the first to speak in public against Nasir al-Mohammad Al-Sabah when he was prime minister, and his 2012F campaign *diwaniyya* was dubbed the "headquarters of the opposition" in recognition of his potential as a leader of the rising political generation in Kuwait.

Kuwait Charter 2012 is a general document sponsored by another group of young Kuwaitis. Khaled al-Fadhala, one of the organizers of the orange movement, is among its originators, but the group is highly diverse. It includes Kuwaitis from urban and rural backgrounds, many of whom share an activist past in human rights and in the campaign against the former prime minister. Another group is the Kuwaiti Progressive Current, a liberal-left organization of mostly young Kuwaitis working for a broad range of human rights measures to achieve social and economic equity across social groups. One of its members notes that Charter 2012 covers much of the same ground as the mission statement of his organization, although in far less detail.[57] That is because, unlike the Progressive Current, which focuses on social justice and human rights, Charter 2012 was intended to appeal to a broad constituency: "Most, if not all, of the points in the program are agreeable to all, except maybe to serious progovernment figures/forces. It seems largely non-ideological in the sense that Islamists, liberals, progressive and others can all agree on them, which is probably a deliberate move by the drafters to garner consensus. The program includes calls for combating corruption on all levels of the executive, guaranteeing the independence of the judiciary, respect for human rights within security agencies, and so on."[58]

The lack of cohesion in the opposition is a problem, but it also is a strength. Throughout the tumultuous events of 2012, which produced two parliaments nullified by the Constitutional Court, young citizen activists, despite their differences, showed themselves to be a moderating force in the movement for change. The "youth" that so many Kuwaitis have been taught to fear is a meme that signifies "tribal uprising." In reality, however, the Kuwaiti youth movement is diverse and highly eclectic. Its various segments include urban and tribal Kuwaitis, men and women, Sunna and Shia, *bidun* and nationals, and members from every social class. Their desire and ability to transcend the fault lines that divide their elders challenges the regime's strategy of divide-and-rule, just as it challenges the desire of old-line opposition figures who aspire to "lead" them for their own ends. Old-line leadership is coming to an end, however. The parliament elected on July 27, 2013, includes twenty-two members born in 1965 or later, and it chose Marzouq al-Ghanim, born in 1968, as speaker.

The demonization of youth activists is aimed at delegitimating political activism by tribal youth. It also undermines the very people who have acquired a large repertoire of nonviolent tactics and have displayed willingness and some skill at reaching not only their peers but also some of their elders across social boundaries.[59] The conscious policy of dividing Kuwaitis, such as through the manipulation of the symbol of the wall that had been built in

A Night to Remember
Marzouq al-Nusf

Marzouq al-Nusf is an economics researcher at a consultancy firm in Kuwait. He is also a freelance journalist and a member of the Kuwaiti Progressive Current.

On October 21, 2012, my friends and I marched in the largest political demonstration in Kuwait's history. We were protesting the emir's changes to the electoral system, the closing act in a series of attempts to limit parliamentary opposition.

The government had declared the march illegal and tried to stop it by violently dispersing people who managed to reach the march's starting areas. My activist group was receiving hurried calls with updates on the locations of each new security assault. You could hear stun grenades in the background. Via Twitter, the organizers suddenly announced an alternative assembly point, the road in front of the iconic Kuwait Towers. The security apparatus could not redeploy quickly enough to stop us. Within an hour, tens of thousands had assembled.

As we marched, all of us were conscious of the historic significance of our action. I ran into friends, old and new. They were smiling and proud. There were numerous chants, but the one gaining most enthusiasm and unison was: We Will Not Allow You! [i.e., allow the emir to become authoritarian—Ed.].

Our path soon ran into a wall of riot police. As the front row of the march came within meters of that wall, stun grenades and then tear gas were fired. The security forces charged the march, beating up everyone within their reach and arresting anyone who got in their way. We tried to regroup and keep marching, but they would charge again and we would fall back. I saw people crawling, suffocating from tear gas, others limping and injured from the beating. It was the first time in a generation that such violence had been used on such a scale against political opponents in Kuwait. We were shocked. As we looked at one another, we saw our shock reflected back. But we also saw something else: a newborn defiance.

1920 to protect the old city from attack and later became a metaphor for dividing *hadhar* and *badu* Kuwaitis, is recapitulated in microcosm in efforts to block the teaching of nonviolent techniques to potential demonstrators. One notable event brought security forces to break up a "conversation for change" that had convened in Irada Square. The young organizer was arrested, beaten, and accused of being a Zionist agent.[60]

Yet a clear message of the Arab Spring is that mastery of electronic media in a media-rich environment increases the cost of severe repression to authoritarian regimes. Kuwaiti youth, like young people everywhere, are the most savvy and innovative users of these tools, as the Twitter coordination of the marches for dignity and the countless posts on YouTube depicting the actual conduct of demonstrators and security personnel show very well.[61]

The formation and coordination of campaigns for change by youth disposed to reach across social and ideological divisions to achieve their common aspirations, along with the success of so many thirty- and fortysomething Kuwaitis at the ballot box in the 2013 election, are, perhaps paradoxically, the strongest indicators of a growing maturity in Kuwaiti political activism. They were preceded by the women's movement, where many of today's activists and new leaders cut their teeth. The success of that campaign depended on bridging social divisions to generate broad-based support for women's rights across usually antagonistic groups. The composition of street demonstrations against corruption and the leadership and composition of the dignity marches show similar diversity. Such movements challenge the divide-and-rule strategy of the regime and also the hardline positions of many veteran activists. Although the regime enjoyed some success at casting them as monsters during the turbulent year of the two annulled parliaments, these young Kuwaitis continue to nourish the hope that political change can come to Kuwait without violence. Formerly consigned to the periphery of the angry politics of confrontation pitting the regime against an opposition establishment seeking a fundamental alteration in the political order, they are beginning to move into the center of national politics. The new parliament, should it survive, could represent a new politics for Kuwait. Its ability to do so rests on the durability of the institutions and expectations accumulated over decades of citizen activism by Kuwaitis seeking justice and respect, not only from their rulers but also from one another.

Notes

1. Giacomo Luciani, "Allocation vs. Production States: A Theoretical Framework" and Hazem Beblawi, "The Rentier State in the Arab World," in *The Arab State*, ed. Giacomo Luciani (Berkeley: University of California Press, 1990), 65–84, 85–98.

2. Mary Ann Tétreault, Gwenn Okruhlik, and Andrzej Kapiszewski (eds.), *Political Change in the Arab Gulf States: Stuck in Transition* (Boulder, CO: Lynne Rienner, 2011).

3. Mary Ann Tétreault, *Stories of Democracy: Politics and Society in Contemporary Kuwait* (New York: Columbia University Press, 2000).

4. Mary Ann Tétreault and Mohammed al-Ghanim, "Transitions *in* Authoritarianism: Political Reform in the Arab Gulf states Reconsidered," paper prepared for the 2012 Gulf Studies Conference, Exeter, United Kingdom, July 2012.

5. See, for example, Matthew Gray, "A Theory of 'Late Rentierism' in the Arab Gulf States of the Gulf," Occasional Paper No. 7 (Doha: Center for International and Regional Studies, Georgetown University School of Foreign Service in Qatar, 2011); Michael L. Ross, "Does Oil Hinder Democracy?" *World Politics* 53(2) (2001): 325–361.

6. Doug McAdam, "Conceptual Origins, Current Problems, Future Directions," in *Comparative Perspectives on Social Movements: Political Opportunities, Mobilizing Structures, and Cultural Framings,* ed. Doug McAdam, John D. McCarthy, and Mayer N. Zald (New York: Cambridge University Press, 1996), 23–40; David S. Meyer, "Social Movements: Creating Communities of Change," in *Conscious Acts and the Politics of Social Change,* ed. Robin L. Teske and Mary Ann Tétreault (Columbia: University of South Carolina Press, 2000), 35–55.

7. John Foran, "The Comparative-Historical Sociology of Third World Social Revolutions: Why a Few Succeed, Why Most Fail," in *Theorizing Revolutions,* ed. John Foran (London: Routledge, 1997); Charles Tilly, "War Making and State Making as Organized Crime," in *Bringing the State Back In,* ed. Peter B. Evans, Dietrich Rueschemeyer, and Theda Skocpol (New York: Cambridge University Press, 1985), 169–191.

8. Ahmad Mustafa Abu-Hakima, *The Modern History of Kuwait, 1750–1965* (London: Luzac, 1983); Jill Crystal, *Oil and Politics in the Gulf: Rulers and Merchants in Kuwait and Qatar* (Cambridge, U.K.: Cambridge University Press, 1990); Zahra Freeth, *A New Look at Kuwait* (London: Allen and Unwin, 1972).

9. Alan de Lacy Rush (ed.), *Internal Affairs, 1921–1950,* Vol. 2, *Records of Kuwait, 1899–1961* (London: Archive International Group, 1989), 153–154.

10. Tétreault, *Stories of Democracy,* 62–66.

11. Crystal, *Oil and Politics in the Gulf,* 58.

12. John Daniels, *Kuwait Journey* (Luton, U.K.: White Crescent Press, 1971).

13. The limitations of the 1962 constitution include nominating the family rather than the individual as the basic political unit of the state, thereby supporting patriarchy; making Islamic law one of the foundations of positive law, thereby diluting the promise of freedom of religion also guaranteed by the document; and rendering the emir and the crown prince beyond the reach of public criticism.

14. Haya Al-Mughni and Mary Ann Tétreault, "Gender, Citizenship, and Nationalism in Kuwait," *British Journal of Middle Eastern Studies* 22(1–2) (1995): 64–80.

15. Shafeeq Ghabra, "Kuwait and the Dynamics of Socio-economic Change," *Middle East Journal* 15(3) (1997): 358–372; see also Anh Nga Longva, *Walls Built on Sand: Migration, Exclusion, and Society in Kuwait* (Boulder, CO: Westview,

1997); Anh Nga Longva, "Citizenship in the Gulf States: Conceptualization and Practice," in *Citizenship and the State in the Middle East: Approaches and Applications,* ed. Nils A. Butenschon, Uri Davis, and Manuel Hassassian (Syracuse, NY: Syracuse University Press, 2000), 179–197.

16. Nicholas Gavrielides, "Tribal Democracy: The Anatomy of Parliamentary Elections in Kuwait," in *Elections in the Middle East: Implications of Recent Trends,* ed. Linda L. Layne (Boulder, CO: Westview, 1987).

17. Tétreault, *Stories of Democracy.*

18. Mary Ann Tétreault, "Civil Society in Kuwait: Protected Spaces and Women's Rights," *Middle East Journal* 47(2) (1993): 275–291.

19. Farah Al-Nakib, "The Wall between Kuwait's Hadhar and Badu: State Policy, National Memory, and Popular Discourse," unpublished paper, 2012.

20. Interviews with the author, Kuwait, 1990, 1992.

21. Al-Nakib, "Wall between Kuwait's Hadhar and Badu."

22. Tétreault, "Civil Society in Kuwait."

23. Tétreault, *Stories of Democracy.*

24. Economist Intelligence Unit, "Kuwait Quarterly Report" (London: Economist Intelligence Unit, 1990), 7.

25. Mary Ann Tétreault and Haya Al-Mughni, "Modernization and Its Discontents: State and Gender in Kuwait," *Middle East Journal* 49(3) (1995): 403–417; Tétreault, *Stories of Democracy*; Ghanim Al-Najjar, "Human Rights in a Crisis Situation: The Case of Kuwait after Occupation," *Human Rights Quarterly* 23(1) (2001): 188–209.

26. Ibid.; Tétreault, *Stories of Democracy.*

27. Al-Najjar, "Human Rights in a Crisis Situation."

28. Tétreault, *Stories of Democracy.*

29. Al-Mughni and Tétreault, "Gender, Citizenship, and Nationalism."

30. Al-Najjar, "Human Rights in a Crisis Situation."

31. Tétreault, *Stories of Democracy.*

32. Ibid.

33. Haya Al-Mughni, *Women in Kuwait: The Politics of Gender,* 2nd ed. (London: Saqi Books, 2001).

34. Longva, *Walls Built on Sand*; Anh Nga Longva, "Neither Autocracy nor Democracy but Ethnocracy: Citizens, Expatriates and the Socio-Political System in Kuwait," in *Monarchies and Nations: Globalisation and Identity in the Arab States of the Gulf,* ed. Paul Dresch and James Piscatori (London: I.B. Tauris, 2005), 114–135.

35. Fatima Mernissi, "Democracy as Moral Disintegration: The Contradiction between Religious Belief and Citizenship as a Manifestation of the Ahistoricity of the Arab Identity," in *Women of the Arab World: The Coming Challenge,* ed. Nahid Toubia (London: Zed Books, 1988), 35–44.

36. Al-Mughni, *Women in Kuwait.*

37. Mary Ann Tétreault, Katherine Meyer, and Helen Rizzo, "Women's Rights in the Middle East: A Longitudinal Study of Kuwait," *International Political Sociology* 3(2) (2009): 218–237.

38. Doron Shultziner and Mary Ann Tétreault, "Paradoxes of Democratic Progress in Kuwait: The Case of the Kuwaiti Women's Rights Movement," *Muslim World Journal of Human Rights* 7(2) (2011): 1–25.

39. Al-Mughni, *Women in Kuwait*; Shultziner and Tétreault, "Paradoxes of Democratic Progress."

40. Interviews with the author, 2006, 2008.

41. Interviews with the author, 2004, 2006.

42. Shultziner and Tétreault, "Paradoxes of Democratic Progress."

43. Mary Ann Tétreault, "Three Emirs and a Tale of Two Transitions," *MERIP Online,* February 10, 2006, available at http://merip.org/mero/mero021006, accessed August 2, 2013.

44. Rola Dashti, interview with the author, Kuwait, December 29, 2006.

45. Gavrielides, "Tribal Democracy"; Kemal Eldin Osman Salih, "Kuwait Primary (Tribal) Elections 1975–2008: An Evaluative Study," *British Journal of Middle Eastern Studies* 38(2) (2011): 141–167.

46. Longva, "Citizenship in the Gulf States"; Khaldoun Hasan Al-Naqeeb, *Society and State in the Gulf and Arab Peninsula: A Different Perspective,* trans. L. M. Kenny (London: Routledge, 1990).

47. Interview with the author, Kuwait, 2008.

48. Al-Nakib, "Wall between Kuwait's Hadhar and Badu."

49. Anh Nga Longva, "Nationalism in Pre-modern Guise: The Discourse on Hadhar and Badu in Kuwait," *International Journal of Middle East Studies* 38(2) (2006): 171–187.

50. Tétreault, "Three Emirs."

51. The name Fifth Fence is a reference to the three walls that had been built at various times to protect the Kuwaiti settlement, plus the proposed moat with barbed wire that had been proposed as a barricade against a future Iraqi invasion.

52. Faisal al-Yahya, member of the 2012F parliament, interview with the author, Kuwait, November 27, 2012.

53. Mary Ann Tétreault, "Bottom-Up Democratization in Kuwait," in *Political Change in the Arab Gulf States,* ed. Tétreault et al., 92.

54. Catherine Cheney, "Kuwait's Opposition Crosses the Government's Red Lines," *World Politics Review,* November 1, 2012, available at www.worldpolitics review.com/trend-lines/12468/kuwaits-opposition-crosses-the-governments-red-lines, accessed August 30, 2013.

55. Al-Nakib, "Wall between Kuwait's Hadhar and Badu"; Longva, "Citizenship in the Gulf States."

56. "Kuwaiti Special Forces 'Beat' MPs and Protestors," The Gulf Blog, December 10, 2010, available at http://thegulfblog.com/2010/12/10/kuwaiti-special-forces -beat-mps-and-protestors/, accessed August 2, 2013.

57. Interviews with the author, Kuwait, 2010.

58. Marzouk Al-Nusf, interviews and email communications with author, 2012.

59. Mary Ann Tétreault and Mohammed Al-Ghanim, "The Day After 'Victory': Kuwait's 2009 Election and the Contentious Present," *MERIP Online*, July 8, 2009, available at www.merip.org/mero/mero070809, accessed August 2, 2013.

60. Interviews with the author, Kuwait, November 20, 2012.

61. See, for example, footage from the January 7, 2013 Human Dignity March, available at www.youtube.com/watch?v=FkqoJHb7c1c, accessed August 2, 2013.

CHAPTER 10

No Spring in Riyadh

Saudi Arabia's Seemingly Impossible Revolution

STÉPHANE LACROIX

M ORE THAN TWO years after a wave of uprisings started sweeping across the Arab world, Saudi Arabia seems to have survived what became known as the Arab Spring. This does not mean, however, that the regime escaped challenge completely. Political activism in 2011 and 2012 was more intense than anything the Kingdom had experienced since the early 1990s. "Islamo-liberal" intellectuals who had been active as domestic opposition figures in the years preceding 2011 were involved in the movement, but a new generation of young activists—largely independent from existing religious-political groups—also played an important role. The period witnessed an emergence of new themes of mobilization, such as the defense of political prisoners and human rights as well as a diversification of the methods of protest, with an increasing reliance on demonstrations.

This chapter starts by analyzing the structural constraints faced by those willing to challenge the Saudi regime, namely, its remarkable ability to fragment the political scene and to coopt its various components. It then shows how after the start of the Arab Spring, proreform activists strove to overcome those constraints and give birth to a broad mobilization for change. Despite their efforts, they have until now been unable to create a sustained challenge to the regime. What remains today is a Shiite-centered movement of protest based in the Eastern Province with no connection or support outside the region, which

The "State of Rights and Institutions" Petition
M.

M. is a blogger and activist from Riyadh. Born in the early 1980s, he is part of the new political generation that was once with the Sahwa but became independent (and sometimes quite critical) of it. He played an active role as coordinator for the February 2011 petition on a "state of rights and institutions."

The petition on a "state of rights and institutions" was the first step in post–Arab Spring Saudi activism—and some would say the last significant one. It was not written by a single person but by thirty or forty. Each of them drafted a part of it, and they circulated the different parts among the group. There were some big names of the Saudi reformist movement among them, including Sheikh Salman al-'Awda, Khalid al-Duwaysh, and Tawfiq al-Sayf. After that, the petition was sent to other people. I personally called tens and tens among the intellectual and religious elite to tell them about the text and convince them to sign. We also created a website on which the petition was uploaded so that people could sign through the internet. Every time a well-known name signed, I looked for his number and called him to make sure it was really him and not someone pretending to be him. I and others advertised the petition through Twitter. The result was astonishing, as we ended up gathering more than nine thousand signatures. Among the elite, there was a quasi-consensus from most patriotic and Islamist currents to support the demands—Islamists of different brands signed, Sunnis and Shiites signed, even leftists and liberals signed. Despite the fact that we were careful not to ask explicitly for a constitutional monarchy—although our demands amounted to that—the government was shocked by the number and diversity of the signatories. There were three other petitions from other groups—one from liberals, one from a small group of youth activists, and one from Sururis—that came out around the same time, but ours concentrated all the attacks. From the responses I received on Twitter from progovernment users, I could tell that we had crossed a red line. Some of us were summoned by the authorities. Up to now, nothing has been implemented—but I believe our text will remain a milestone in the history of the Saudi reformist movement.

makes its chances of effectively affecting the regime quite low in the short term.

A Fragmented Political Scene

The dominant feature of political activism in Saudi Arabia has historically been fragmentation. The first line of cleavage is sectarian. Since its beginnings in 1744, the Saudi state has been based on an alliance between princes and the *ulama*, a body in charge of upholding an official religious doctrine sometimes referred to as "Wahhabism." A rigorous heir to Hanbalism, Wahhabism is characterized by its extreme sectarianism: for the doctrine's founder Muhammad bin Abd al-Wahhab (1703–1792), Sufis and Shiites were not worthy of being called Muslims. In the wake of the Saudi conquest of lands populated by Twelver Shiites (in the East) and Ismaili Shiites (in the South), Shia believers, who today make up approximately 10 percent of the Kingdom's inhabitants, found themselves in the awkward position of living in a state whose official clergy brands them as heretics (*rafidha*).

It is true that, under the modernizing impulses of kings such as Abd al-Aziz (1902–1953) and Faisal (1964–1975), Wahhabism became slightly more inclusive, at least in practice. Acting pragmatically, the regime even developed close ties with networks of Shiite notables, who served as proxies to Saudi rule. Yet the rejection of "deviant" Muslims has remained a central feature of Wahhabi discourse.[1] Although Wahhabism has regularly been contested, its teachings have pervaded most parts of Saudi society. The consequence is that sectarianism is now strongly rooted in the Kingdom's Sunni community. The ruling family has also consciously fueled the sectarian rhetoric since the 1980s in order to insulate Sunnis from the influence of revolutionary Iran, widely seen in Riyadh as the Kingdom's main regional rival.

This explains why there have been remarkably few occurrences of trans-sectarian cooperation among the Kingdom's political activists. Even in the 1950s and 1960s, when the dominant political ideologies were secular, there was little national coordination: Just like in neighboring Iraq, activist Shiites tended to join the communist parties, whereas Sunnis were more likely to subscribe to Arab nationalism or Baathism. When political Islam gained prominence in the 1970s, each community developed its own separate Islamist movement.

In the Eastern Province, the teachings of the Movement of the Message (*al-Haraka al-Risaliyya*), founded in Iraq in 1967 by Ayatollah Shirazi, started spreading among a new milieu of young activists.[2] In the wake of the 1979 revolution in Iran, "Shirazi" activists founded the Organization of the Islamic Revolution in the Arabian Peninsula, which spearheaded the "intifada of muharram" in the Eastern Province. Huge demonstrations took place, protesting against the religious, social, and political discrimination faced by the Shiite community and advocating for the establishment of an Islamic regime inspired by revolutionary Iran. The movement was soon crushed, prompting the most prominent activists to flee abroad, where some remained in exile for years.[3]

Among Sunnis, Islamism started spreading from the late 1960s onward. The ideology of the main Sunni Islamist movement, the Sahwa (from *al-Sahwa al-Islamiyya*, the Islamic Awakening), resulted from a mix of the political ideas of the Muslim Brotherhood brought to Saudi Arabia by Egyptian and Syrian Islamist activists who had found shelter there and the religious ideas of the Wahhabis.[4] The Sahwa developed quickly inside the Kingdom's universities before transforming into a nationwide social movement in the 1980s. In 1990, King Fahd's call for American troops to come protect the Saudi Kingdom from a potential attack by the troops of Saddam Hussein, who had just invaded neighboring Kuwait, sparked outrage among Sahwa figures who considered the presence of U.S. soldiers on Saudi soil an unbearable provocation. The movement thus started directing its Islamist rhetoric at a royal family it deemed "corrupt" and "unacceptably pro-American" and calling for radical political reform. The period between 1991 and 1994, which became known as "the Sahwa's intifada" (*intifadat al-Sahwa*), witnessed unprecedented political mobilization against the regime, with petitions, fiery sermons, and even a demonstration.

Even though the Muslim Brotherhood is not generally prone to sectarianism, the Wahhabi influence—as well as the broader social climate—made the Sahwa fundamentally sectarian. Sahwi activists did not back the 1979 Shiite uprising in the Eastern Province, and the Saudi regime even enlisted them in the 1980s to demonize Iran and denounce its alleged "ambitions of using its revolution to export Shiism."[5] Consequently, in the early 1990s, there was—with a couple of minor exceptions—no effective collaboration between the Shiite opposition abroad and the Sahwi opposition on the ground.

The second line of cleavage in the Saudi political scene is between Islamists and liberals. Although the introduction of the term *liberal* in the Saudi political lexicon dates back only to the early 1990s, the phenomenon itself is older, with its origins going back to the secular activists mentioned earlier. In the 1970s, secular activism was severely weakened, and many of its former proponents were coopted by the regime, which had decided that, in addition to its traditional religious legitimacy, it needed another "modernizing" brand of legitimacy to defend itself against the attacks of its "progressive" regional foes—Egypt, Syria, and Iraq. Those who became known as "intellectuals" were offered spaces to write and discuss modern ideas, on the condition that they limit their critique to a social critique, with no clear political implications. This would eventually lead to a backlash, with liberal intellectuals becoming, with the implicit support of the regime, the targets of virulent attacks by the Islamists in the second half of the 1980s. In the early 1990s, the situation was reversed: The liberals were now instrumentalized by the state against the Sahwi opposition, which they denounced in articles in state-owned newspapers and in books sold in the Kingdom. Due to fear of the Sahwa's religious rhetoric, the liberals decided to back the regime openly.[6]

The Saudi regime has routinely relied on this pattern of "divide and rule." The game was simple: convince the liberals of the existence of an "Islamist threat" against which only the royal family could protect them while convincing the Islamists that they faced a "liberal threat" against which only the royal family could provide protection. The regime could thus pit the two sides of the opposition, the Islamists and the liberals, against each other, while sitting above as arbitrator. Issues of gender—especially the issue of women's right to drive, which remains denied to them to the present day—were systematically instrumentalized for that purpose. As a Saudi intellectual put it: "Every time political dissent grows in the Kingdom, the state media brings the issue of women's rights to the fore; then liberals and Islamists start fighting against each other again, and the political momentum gets lost."[7]

Though this has been extremely efficient as a general rule, in one case it did backfire. In November 1990, senior princes provided covert support to a demonstration by forty-seven women demanding the right to drive; this was after Islamist unrest and outcries against the regime in the wake of its decision to allow American troops into the Kingdom. For the royal family, it seems, the goal was to divert the Islamists' attention, redirecting it toward liberals. In this case, however, the Islamists' anger had already reached such a peak that the "women's incident" only fueled their rage against a regime they accused of being two-faced. Playing the liberal vs. Islamist game works in most, but not all, circumstances.

The third line of cleavage is among the Sunni Islamists themselves. First is the divide between the Sahwa, which represents the mainstream of Saudi Sunni Islamism, and the smaller and generally more radical Islamist groups, such as the jihadis and those that Thomas Hegghammer and I have dubbed the "rejectionists."[8] More important is the divide within the Sahwa itself between its two biggest organized branches, known as *jama'at islamiyya* ("Islamic groups"). One is the Saudi Muslim Brotherhood (*al-ikhwan al-sa'udiyyun*), which was founded in the 1960s, most probably by an Egyptian exile named Manna' al-Qattan, but with Saudi membership. The other is the so-called Sururis (*al-sururiyyun*), whose name derives from that of a Syrian former Muslim Brother called Muhammad Surur Zayn al-'Abidin, who lived in Saudi Arabia in the late 1960s. Since then, the two groups have been competing fiercely to increase their influence in fields such as education, NGOs, and even business.[9] More recently, in 2005, municipal elections became a nationwide struggle between the two *jama'at*, whose candidates (unofficially so, of course, as political affiliations were banned) were present in most districts and received the majority of votes. In Riyadh, the Muslim Brotherhood prevailed, while in the Sunni regions of the Eastern Province, most elected candidates were Sururis. Although these groups have no official recognition and act as clandestine organizations, the regime obviously knows about them and is probably even happy to tolerate them as long as the sterile competition for resources between them keeps them busy and turns their attention away from more threatening political issues.

The Islamic scene grew even more complex in the early 1990s when the regime decided to offer maximal support to a group of Salafi sheikhs, mostly based in Medina, who were known to be staunchly anti–Muslim Brotherhood and generally hostile to any involvement of clerics in politics. With state encouragement, they became the Sahwa's most vocal enemies and consequently key allies of the royal family. Because one of the leading figures of this group was Rabi' al-Madkhali, a professor of *hadith* at the Islamic University of Medina, they are sometimes referred to as Madkhalis (another common name for them is "Jamis"). Though the Sahwa's "rebellious moment" ended in 1994–1995, Madkhalis have remained active until today, with the same rhetoric as in their heyday.[10]

Finally, tribal and regional cleavages are also significant. Saudi Arabia is, in many of its parts, a land of tribes, which, even if they have lost most of their political relevance in the framework of the modern Saudi state, remain an extremely significant social and cultural reality. As for the regional cleavages, they separate the political center, the region of Najd, from which the royal family and its key allies originate, from the periphery. Among the peripheral regions in the Saudi geography of power are the Hijaz, where Mecca and

Medina are located and which maintains a very strong identity, and the Eastern Province, known to be the home of the Twelver Shiite minority but whose indigenous Sunni population also sees itself as culturally and religiously distinct from the Najdis. In the last few decades, these cleavages have started fueling the rise of regionalist movements, with growing calls for the recognition and protection of separate regional identities and, in rare cases, calls for secession.

The Benefits of Cooptation

Fragmentation is thus a feature of political activism in Saudi Arabia, and the royal family has been adept at manipulating the existing divisions—if not simply engineering them—in order to force the different groups to neutralize one another. In addition, the regime has been extremely successful at coopting the different groups.

The case of the Sahwa here is telling. As mentioned earlier, it resulted from an external graft, that of the Muslim Brotherhood's political conceptions, onto the local religious culture. But it also emerged from within the Saudi state itself. The Muslim Brothers who found shelter in the Kingdom were integrated to the core of some of its key institutions, in particular in the education and media sectors. It is in these sectors that their influence first took root and where their Saudi disciples started creating the structures that would constitute the backbone of the Sahwa movement. Many of those disciples became professors, deans, journalists, or employees in the Kingdom's many Islamic organizations. Although the Sahwa's discourse had an obvious political dimension, its leaders were eager to emphasize that their denunciation of the "jahiliyya of the twentieth century" (to quote the title of a book by Muhammad Qutb, the brother of radical Muslim Brotherhood ideologue Sayyid Qutb and professor at Umm al-Qura University in Mecca) applied only outside of Saudi Arabia.[11] The regime felt absolutely no threat, and it encouraged the development of the Sahwa by providing the institutions in which the Sahwa was based with significant amounts of financial resources, especially after the 1973 oil boom.

After a radical group known as *al-Jama'a al-Salafiyya al-Muhtasiba* ("The Salafi group which commands Good and forbids Wrongdoing") attacked the Grand Mosque in Mecca in 1979, the regime more than ever saw the Sahwa as the solution rather than the problem. It then provided the Sahwa with even more resources so that its influence might prevent the rise of other such radical groups. For the Sahwa, this was an awkward position. On the one hand, its rhetoric was implicitly subversive, and in closed Sahwa study circles, explicit criticism of the Saudi regime was becoming common, especially when talking about the moral practices of some of the princes or the Kingdom's alliance with the United States. On the other hand, this was a movement that benefited greatly from the continuing support of the state.[12] The Sahwis were rebels without a cause. Adding to this was the fierce internal competition between the two main *jama'at* within the Sahwa, the Saudi Muslim Brotherhood and the Sururis. At every level—from the neighborhood mosques to the ministries of education or *waqfs*—the *jama'at* were struggling to place their members in strategic positions in order to make sure the resources poured in by the state benefited the group. For the Muslim Brotherhood, the adversary was the Sururi (and vice versa), not the royal family.

As a consequence, throughout the history of the movement, the general rule was that the Sahwa implicitly or explicitly sided with the Saudi regime against the latter's enemies. The only major exception to the rule was the Sahwa's intifada when, in the wake of the 1991 Gulf War, a number of clerics and intellectuals with close ties to the Sahwa but acting independently from the *jama'at* launched a large-scale movement of protest across the Kingdom. The momentum initially gained by the movement convinced the *jama'at* that it could succeed; most of their leaders thus decided to back the protest. This meant a lot, since the *jama'at* have tens of thousands of organized members. The movement expanded.

However, in late 1992 and early 1993, when it became obvious that the royal family was firmly in control and ready to use full-scale repression, the *jama'at* suddenly decided to withdraw their support.[13] This was a strong blow to the protest, which declined steadily until most of its leaders were arrested in 1994 and 1995. Because of their early decision to back down, the *jama'at* were mostly spared by the wave of arrests. However, the government did take a number of measures to try to limit their influence. The *jama'at* learned their lesson: They would think twice before making the same mistake in the future. Since that period, the *jama'at* have thus returned to the largely quietist stance that characterized them before the Sahwa's intifada. Despite the initial official attempts to weaken them, they have managed to keep their networks mostly untouched.[14]

In the late 1990s, the clerics who had spearheaded the protest were released from jail. Many observers claim there was a deal with the regime: They would be able to regain influence, even entering new spaces such as the internet and the satellite channels, but they would have to abandon all forms of political activism.

This is exactly what happened: Sahwa sheikhs such as Salman al-'Awda, Safar al-Hawali, and Nasir al-'Umar regained their status as religious "stars" but avoided all political issues that could bring them into confrontation with the state, even going as far as to openly support the regime in times of crisis (such as during the terrorist campaign carried out by al-Qaeda in the Arabian Peninsula after 2003).

The story of the liberals is quite different, but their ties to the Saudi state were no less strong than those of the Sahwa. As we saw, many liberals worked for newspapers controlled by the government, while those who were novelists or poets were part of the official literary clubs. To avoid alienating them, the state made sure that their institutions were well funded and that their freedom of living "liberal" lifestyles in the private space was preserved—hence, the religious police was for instance kept from entering their homes. The liberals thus became largely dependent on the state, and many of them were ready to staunchly defend it in their columns in *Asharq Alawsat* or *al-Riyadh*.

Shiite Islamists initially had a much tenser relationship with the regime. As mentioned earlier, in the wake of the 1979 Islamic revolution in Iran, the Shirazi-inspired Organization of the Islamic Revolution in the Arabian Peninsula launched an insurrection in the Eastern Province. In the late 1980s, the movement started to change its strategy radically: It abandoned the revolutionary rhetoric of its beginnings and even changed its name to the "reformist movement" (*al-haraka al-islahiyya*). Later, in 1993, its exiled figures negotiated an agreement with the Saudi regime in which King Fahd pledged to improve the situation of the Kingdom's Shiite community. In return, most of the activists who had been abroad reestablished themselves in Saudi Arabia. From then on, the Shirazi movement adopted a much more accommodating rhetoric vis-à-vis the regime. Its leader, Sheikh Hasan al-Saffar, even became a prime interlocutor in the state's dealings with the Shiite community. It would be an exaggeration to say that he and his associates were coopted, but they certainly have become some form of "loyal opposition." This is extremely significant, as the Shirazis represent the vast majority of Shiite Islamist activists in Saudi Arabia. The disciples of Khomeini (known as "the line of the Imam," *khatt al-imam*) have adopted a much more confrontational approach, leading to the 1996 Khobar Towers bombing, which was allegedly carried out by an affiliated group called Hezbollah al-Hijaz.[15] But their influence has remained limited. They also are the ones with the strongest ties to Iran. In contrast, the Shirazis have only limited connections to Iran—so Iran was no major obstacle to their transformation into the "loyal opposition" they have become.[16]

The situation in the late 1990s was thus that of a fragmented and a largely coopted opposition. This has been a constant obstacle for those activists who have tried to remobilize the political scene ever since.

The "Islamo-Liberal" Experiment

There were several attempts at political remobilization, however. The first attempt took place when a group of Islamists who had been imprisoned after being associated with the Sahwa's intifada started calling for a resumption of political activism, but with new content. The demands formulated by the Sahwi opposition at the height of the Sahwa's intifada had been quite vague: On the one hand, there were demands that could be categorized as prodemocracy, including an elected parliament and a separation of powers. On the other hand, the Sahwi opposition was calling for a stricter enforcement of Islamic norms in the public sphere and for increasing the control of clerics over political affairs. Though this was far-fetched given the differences between the Saudi and Iranian contexts, Ghazi al-Qusaybi, a prominent liberal intellectual and staunch opponent of the Sahwa, compared the Sahwa opposition's project to Khomeini's conception of the Islamic republic, which blended democratic procedures with clerical supervision.[17]

In the late 1990s, rising Islamist figures such as Abdallah al-Hamid and Abd al-Aziz al-Qasim put forward a much less ambiguous project: In books and articles, sometimes taking inspiration from "liberal Islamist" scholars such as the Tunisian Rached al-Ghannouchi, they argued for the full compatibility between Islam and democratic procedures, respect of human rights, and the development of a vibrant civil society. What was needed was to interpret Islam correctly, they said. One need not even abandon the Salafi tradition to which Wahhabism belongs; the Salafi tradition, they argued, is broad enough that, if one reads Ibn Taymiyya's books with a democratic mindset, one will find in there all the references one needs.[18] This vision would soon translate into calls to transform the Saudi regime into an "Islamic constitutional monarchy."[19]

In addition, those "Islamo-liberal" thinkers understood that the fragmentation of the political sphere had been instrumental in preventing previous movements of change from succeeding. Thus they started establishing relationships with activists from all political, regional, and sectarian backgrounds. By 2003, the group had expanded significantly, now including hundreds of proponents from the intellectual elite, as well as Sunni Islamists, liberals, Shiite Islamists, and even Hijazi and Ahsa'i regionalists.

Prominent among the repertoires of contention used by the opposition in the 1990s was the public petition. The opposition saw this as a legitimate means of activism because it resembled the *nasiha* (advice to the king) traditionally provided by the *ulama*. Following in the footsteps of the Sahwa's intifada, the new reformists decided to use that tool. In January 2003, they presented their first petition, called "Vision for the Present and the Future of the Homeland" (*ru'ya li-hadir al-watan wa mustaqbalihi*); it was signed by 104 people. This would be the first petition of many—a practice that has continued to the present day. Other significant texts include "A National Call to the People and Leadership Together: Constitutional Reform First" (*nida' watani ila-l-sha'b wa-l-qiyada ma'an: al-islah al-dusturi awwalan*), published in December 2003, and "Milestones on the Way to a Constitutional Monarchy" (*ma'alim fi tariq al-malakiyya al-dusturiyya*), published in February 2007.

This group never represented a major threat to the royal family because its members, being mostly intellectuals, did not have much in the way of an authentic popular following, but the boldness of their demands led the regime to try to silence them. A wave of arrests followed the December 2003 and the February 2007 petitions. Abdallah al-Hamid, the leading ideologue of the group, has spent considerable time in jail over the past few years, while several of those arrested in February 2007, including Saud Mukhtar al-Hashimi and Sulayman al-Rashudi, have been sentenced to spend between fifteen and thirty years in prison. Ironically, the regime's repression gave great publicity to the Islamo-liberals, turning some of them into well-known and respected figures. Despite the arrests, the group has remained active and has continued to attract followers. In 2009, several of its leading figures decided to create the Saudi Civil and Political Rights Association (*jam'iyyat al-huquq al-madaniyya wa-l-siyasiyya fi-l-sa'udiyya*), partly to report on human rights violations in the Kingdom and partly to promote the fate of their jailed comrades.[20]

The Arab Spring Factor

One consequence of the "Islamo-liberal experiment" was that, when the uprisings took place in Tunisia and Egypt in December 2010 and January 2011, an active prodemocracy "Islamo-liberal" milieu already existed in Saudi Arabia, ready to seize the opportunity. And, unsurprisingly, the first moves came from the Islamo-liberals. On February 10, 2011, ten activists announced the foundation of Saudi Arabia's first political party, the Islamic Umma Party (Hizb al-Umma al-Islami).[21] A leading figure in the group was Abd al-Aziz al-Wuhaybi, an important actor of the Sahwa's intifada who had also supported the "Islamo-liberal" movement, signing the petitions in 2003 and 2007.[22] The political identity of the Islamic Umma Party was relatively distinct from the rest of the "Islamo-liberal" movement, however, because it drew inspiration from a Kuwaiti ideologue named Hakim al-Mutairi, the author of a famous book, *Liberty or Deluge (al-hurriyya aw al-tawfan)*.[23] In his writings, al-Mutairi attempted to justify democratic principles with references to Salafi authors. Al-Mutairi was also the founder of an Umma party in Kuwait that maintains close ties to its Saudi counterpart. The Saudi regime reacted to this provocation by imprisoning seven out of the party's ten founders.

Two weeks later, two major petitions were released. The first, called "National Declaration of Reform," came from liberals.[24] The second, entitled "Toward a State of Rights and Institutions," came from activists with ties to the "Islamo-liberal" milieu.[25] In that sense, the second petition was the more significant one because, like previous "Islamo-liberal" petitions, it brought together activists from diverse backgrounds on a common platform that called for a fully elected Majlis al-Shura (the Saudi parliament) and a government accountable to it. In other words, the document was advocating an "Islamic constitutional monarchy" but without using those words for tactical reasons. The momentum created by the uprisings in Tunisia and Egypt also had an impact in that the number and diversity of signatories was much larger than ever before. The petition was put online, and close to nine thousand people signed with their real names. Also, a significant number of Sahwi Islamists who had previously shunned the reform movement now agreed to back the demands. Many of the Sunni Islamist signatories came from the Saudi Muslim Brotherhood. According to activists, there was even an official decision among at least parts of the group to back the protest.[26]

One remarkable signatory was Salman al-'Awda, one of Saudi Arabia's most popular clerics and an important figure in the Sahwa's intifada. After his release from jail in 1999, he had avoided criticizing the Saudi royal family, even allegedly developing close relations with some of its members. The uprisings in Egypt and Tunisia had changed him. From January 2011 on, he started showing enthusiasm for the protests on his weekly show *Life is a Word (al-haya kalima)* on the Saudi-owned MBC1 channel. As a result, the show was cancelled in early February. He now went further by putting his name on a proreform petition—something he had not done since the 1990s. Another prominent signatory was Muhammad al-Ahmari. A former leading Sahwa intellectual and the head of the Islamic Association of North America in the 1990s, he has in the last few years emerged as one of the most influential prodemocracy Islamist activists in the Kingdom.[27]

A significant proportion of young people, generally in their twenties, signed the petition. Many of them are part of the new political generation that rose to prominence in the 2000s. They share many features with the young activists who started the uprisings in Egypt, Tunisia, Yemen, and the other "revolutionary" countries. They are generally postideological, in the sense that they do not feel bound by any group affiliation, be it Islamist or not, even though some were socialized in Sahwa circles, which was extremely common for individuals born in the 1980s and 1990s. This does not mean that they are secular, however—many of them are actually quite religious on the personal level. But what distinguishes them above all is their prodemocracy and pro–human rights commitment.[28] This is in part the result of their global socialization through the new media and social networks (Facebook, Twitter, blogs), where they have been exposed to discourses radically different from those of their elders.

A limitation of the February 2011 petition was that it did not include any major figures from the Sururi *jama'a*.[29] Sururis even presented their own separate petition a few days later, in which they mostly limited their criticism to Shiism and liberal trends in Saudi society.[30] To remedy this and to expand the support base for change, some of the activists began to emphasize a theme of mobilization deemed more attractive to Sururis: the issue of "political prisoners" and, through it, that of human rights. Despite official denials, prisoners detained on political charges without judgment are said to number in the thousands, up to thirty thousand, according to some sources.[31] There is a small number of prominent Islamo-liberal activists among them, but the majority are Sahwis—mainly Sururis—accused of harboring jihadi sympathies. By taking up this issue, the reformists were offering Sururis the opportunity to defend a large number of their jailed followers.

From February to June 2011, activism in favor of "political prisoners" gained momentum. Small protests organized in front of the Ministry of the Interior were attended by relatives and activists.[32] Prominent sheikhs close to the Sururi *jama'a* delivered fiery speeches calling for the release of (or a fair trial for) political prisoners.[33] This led to arrests: Muhammad al-Bijadi, a young activist close to the Islamo-liberals, and Yusuf al-Ahmad, a rising Islamist star close to the Sururis, were both imprisoned (they were later sentenced to four and five years in prison, respectively).

The regime's strategy of social control was being openly challenged. The groups that had until now been seen as coopted were once again active. The participation of the *jama'at* was especially significant because, as mentioned earlier, they represent the country's main mobilizing structures. After the trauma of 1994 and 1995, this support was unprecedented. In addition, the newborn protest movement had managed to bring together the different segments of the Saudi activist scene, regardless of their political, regional, and even—although this remained the most difficult divide to overcome—sectarian backgrounds.

Taking to the Streets: Failure in Riyadh and Success in the East

Feeling the momentum, a number of online young Saudi activists who had created a Facebook group called the Free Youth Coalition (*I'tilaf al-shabab al-ahrar*) decided that it was time to take to the streets in the capital. They named March 11, 2011, a "Day of Anger" in which Saudis were asked to demonstrate in Riyadh to demand radical political reform.[34] The Islamic Umma Party released an official statement supporting the call.

Since February 17, demonstrations were also taking place among the Shiites of the Eastern Province. Except for radical cleric Nimr al-Nimr, the leaders were young and independent from the major Shiite groups, including the Shirazis. They were mobilizing through a number of Facebook pages, with names such as "The Revolution of the Eastern Province" (*Thawrat al-mintaqa al-sharqiyya*). One issue first figured prominently on the activists' agenda: the demand for the release of the "forgotten prisoners" (*al-sujana' al-mansiyun*) who had been detained without trial since the 1996 Khobar Towers bombing. The protests were also largely fueled by events in neighbouring Bahrain, where a "revolution" had started on February 14. After mid-March, the rhetoric of protesters would become more radical, demanding genuine political reforms and, in some cases, the fall of the regime.

From late February 2011 onward, in order to stop the protests from spreading or even taking place, the Saudi regime made maximal use of the material and symbolic resources at its disposal. First, it mobilized the entirety of its coercive apparatus. On the planned "Day of Anger" in Riyadh, police were out in full force, making it extremely difficult for prospective protesters to reach the square where the demonstration was to take place. Well-known activists were also personally threatened with arrests should they decide to show up. In the Eastern Province, where preventive measures were not as easy to implement because protests were organized in many small villages, police did not hesitate to intervene physically. There, hundreds of arrests were made.

Saudi intelligence also played a major role, notably by hacking some of the Facebook accounts used to call for demonstrations.

In late February and mid-March 2011, King Abdullah announced a package of about US$130 billion in aid to the Saudi population. Civil servants received extra pay, jobs were created, and housing subsidies were made available. Religious institutions, such as the Committee for Commanding Good and Forbidding Wrongdoing (also known as the religious police), also received extra funding. Simultaneously, the state's official religious establishment released fatwas explaining that any form of public dissent—and even more so if it took the form of demonstrations—was *haram* (religiously forbidden). Such statements came from the mufti and the Council of Senior Ulama as well as from a number of other individual figures, some close to the Madkhalis. The official Saudi media took a similar stance.

That regime officials denounced the protest was no surprise; after all, this is what they are paid to do. The success of the regime's response was better measured by the fact that, soon, more independent voices joined the official condemnations. Liberal intellectuals wrote articles in support of the regime, while leading Sahwi sheikhs, including Nasir al-'Umar, issued fatwas warning of the risk of *fitna* (chaos).[35] Thus, just as the opposition thought it was about to undermine the regime's strategy of cooptation, the royal family was reactivating the very links that had guaranteed its resilience. The US$130 billion aid announcement also played a major role in quelling dissent. Sahwis in particular were satisfied by the extra funding provided to religious institutions, their stronghold. Here, they were confronted with the same dilemma they had faced in the early 1990s: to show loyalty to the government or to risk jeopardizing the extremely favorable position they enjoy in the Saudi system. It did not take long for them to move back to the first option; and even some of those who signed the February 2011 petition later abandoned the protest. This meant a lot: Again, the opposition was deprived of the support of the most organized part of the Islamist movement, the *jama'at* that constitute the backbone of the Sahwa.[36]

The regime also played the sectarian divide-and-rule card, as it had done many times before. The official rhetoric was that protests in the Eastern Province had been inspired and driven by Iran, the Kingdom's regional archenemy. The "Day of Anger" planned in Riyadh was associated with the events in the Eastern Province as part of the same alleged Iranian conspiracy.[37] Responding to government propaganda, Sunni opponents stressed that they had nothing to do with the Shiites and refrained from showing any support for the latter's protests. The result was the same as always: Sunni activism, centered in Riyadh and to a lesser extent Burayda and Jeddah, and Shiite activism in the Eastern Province were made absolutely separate, with no possibility of creating a trans-sectarian dynamic.[38]

The government's policies were not equally successful in Riyadh and in the Eastern Province. In Riyadh, the "Day of Anger" was a complete fiasco. Apart from a previously unknown activist, Khalid al-Jihani, who was subsequently arrested, no one showed up.[39] The protests in the Eastern Province gained much more momentum, bringing thousands of people to the streets. The peak in the number of protesters—about ten thousand—was reached on March 18 and 19, a few days after the Saudi military, under the umbrella of the Gulf Cooperation Council's "Peninsula Shield," intervened in neighboring Bahrain to quell protests there.

This contrast between Riyadh and the Eastern Province can be explained by different factors. First, as mentioned earlier, it was easier to organize protests in the many small villages of the Eastern Province than it was in the country's capital, Riyadh, where the security apparatus is concentrated. Also, because a large part of Shiite society has been kept outside of official networks, Shiites have developed their own community institutions over which the state has little control; those are the institutions that provided support bases for the protest.[40]

Second, there are differences of political culture between the Eastern Province and Najd. In Najd, of which Riyadh is the capital, demonstrations have in the past very rarely been used as a means for political expression. The only known previous occurrences happened in September 1994 when nearly two thousand people marched in Burayda against the expected arrest of the leading sheikhs of the Sahwa's intifada—a major failure for a movement of protest that in its heyday had claimed hundreds of thousands of followers—and in 1965 when conservatives demonstrated in Riyadh against the first television broadcasts in the Kingdom. In the case of the "Day of Anger" on March 11, 2011, it seems that the call for demonstrations in Riyadh actually had a back-firing effect by scaring off many of those who had supported the movement when it was limited to petitions. In the Eastern Province, in contrast, demonstrations have regularly occurred since the 1950s, when Aramco workers launched their first general strikes. Later came the 1979 "intifada of muharram," followed by several shorter episodes of mobilization, in which demonstrations were the core technique used.

Finally, although the distributive measures outlined above were meant to benefit all Saudis, regardless of their faith, they did not appease Shiites as much as they did Sunnis. The problem for Saudi Shiites is not that their situation is bad in absolute terms; they also receive a share of the country's wealth. Their problem is that, when it comes to development and the distribution of riches, they are less favored than the Sunnis, in addition to facing blatant discrimination at the religious level. This generates a feeling of relative deprivation, which explains the resilience of their hostility toward the regime.

From mid-2011 on, a number of events ended up unintentionally serving the goals of the regime. First, in May 2011, a number of women activists led by Manal al-Sharif decided to seize the political momentum in order to push for the improvement of women's rights in the Kingdom. One of their core demands was that the government lift the ban on women to drive cars, and they chose to defy the ban and put videos of themselves driving on YouTube.[41] Liberal segments of the elite largely backed their movement, while conservatives staunchly opposed it. As a result, individuals who had stood together in opposing the government and tried to create a joint political platform were now devoting their energies to fighting each other. The royal family could sit and watch, posing as the arbitrator of their disputes—without, however, making the slightest move on the women driving issue, an inertia justified because "the different segments of society disagree." A step was finally made in September 2011 when the king announced that women would have the right to vote in the municipal council elections in 2015 and that women representatives would be appointed to the Majlis al-Shura. Given that these bodies have little real power, however, this remained a largely symbolic measure—although it did add to the anger of the conservatives.

In January 2012, a young Saudi man named Hamza Kashgari tweeted an imagined address to Prophet Muhammad on the occasion of the Prophet's birthday. Some people denounced his tweets as disrespectful to the Prophet.[42] This ignited a nationwide campaign against Kashgari, with Sahwi sheikhs (mainly Sururis) asking for him to be tried and executed.[43] Some in the liberal camp, however, defended Kashgari's "freedom of expression" or else remained silent. Soon, the Sahwis started attacking the liberals, presenting Kashgari as a natural product of Saudi liberalism.[44]

The Sunni activist milieu was thus again plagued by internal disputes, while all attempts at creating a rapprochement had been forgotten. By mid-2012, it looked as if most of the national political momentum had dissipated. Young people were still active on Twitter, and sporadic gatherings demanding the release of political prisoners still occurred every now and then, but the largest share of the opposition found themselves as coopted and fragmented as ever.

January 16, 2011: A group of female Saudi activists launch *Baladi,* a campaign designated to involve women in the municipal elections.

January 21, 2011: In the southwestern town of Samitah, a man in his sixties immolates himself.

January 29, 2011: After ten die in floods, hundreds of protesters gather in Jeddah to demonstrate against the city's poor infrastructure.

February 5, 2011: Forty women gather in Riyadh to demand the release of prisoners held without trial.

February 10, 2011: Ten moderate Saudi scholars and intellectuals petition the king for recognition of the Islamic Umma Party, *Hizb al-Umma al-Islami*; it will become the kingdom's first political party.

February 16, 2011: Authorities arrest a group of people associated with the Islamic Umma Party.

February 17, 2011: Shiite protesters gather in the town of Qatif to demand the release of three prisoners. They are released three days later.

February 23, 2011: In an attempt to quell protesters' desires for a "Day of Rage" on March 11, King Abdullah preemptively announces a US$37 billion aid package.

February 25, 2011: Peaceful protests are staged in the eastern towns of Safwa and Qatif calling for the release of nine Shiite prisoners detained without

charge. In Jeddah, Jeddah Youth for Change call for a rally.

February 27, 2011: As three petitions, one of them signed by nine thousand Saudi citizens, call for political reform, King Abdullah gives permanent contracts to government workers with temporary contracts. Shiite cleric Sheikh Tawfiq al-'Amir is arrested.

March 4, 2011: More than seventeen thousand people back a Facebook group call for a protest in Qatif, Riyadh, and Hofuf. Hundreds of members of the Saudi Shiite minority groups stage a protest in the eastern part of the kingdom. Security forces detain at least three people.

March 6, 2011: Following demonstrations by Shiite minority groups, clerics reassert that protests are banned throughout the Kingdom.

March 10, 2011: Three protesters are wounded as police clash with hundreds of Shiite protesters in the eastern city of Qatif.

March 11, 2011: Saudi security forces are deployed en masse to prevent demonstrators from calling for democratic reforms on the "Day of Rage." In four cities in the Eastern Province, at least five hundred protesters call for the release of prisoners held without charges. Twenty-seven people are arrested.

March 13, 2011: More than two hundred Saudis demand the release of detainees in a protest outside the Ministry of the Interior.

March 18, 2011: In an extreme effort to appease protesters, King Abdullah offers a reform package of US$93 billion that will include pay raises, loans, low-income housing, and the creation of sixty thousand security jobs.

March 20, 2011: Nearly two thousand security forces protect the Ministry of the Interior in Riyadh as one hundred Saudi men and women protesters demand the release of detainees.

April 5, 2011: Over one hundred teachers gather outside the Ministry of Civil Services to demand full-time employment.

April 23, 2011: Women attempt to register to vote in Jeddah, Riyadh, and Dammam for the September 22 municipal elections despite a ban on their voting rights.

May 5, 2011: Hundreds of antigovernment protesters clash with security forces in Qatif.

May 14, 2011: Forty-five-year-old Najla Hariri begins driving her car around the kingdom in an effort to break the ban on women driving.

May 21, 2011: Activist Manal al-Sherif is detained for six hours after footage of her driving is released. She is released on May 30 after signing an agreement that she will not drive again.

June 17, 2011: In a sign of changing sentiments, police are ordered not to intervene as at least thirty women drive their cars in Jeddah, Riyadh, and Dammam.

August 6, 2011: Security forces outside the Ministry of the Interior kill a gunman as he opens fire on the palace.

September 25, 2011: King Abdullah announces that women will have the right to vote and run in local elections in 2015.

September 29, 2011: Saudi Arabian men vote in the country's second nationwide municipal elections. Turnout is low, since municipal councils barely have any power.

October 3, 2011: After a sixty-year-old man is arrested, clashes break out between armed men and police in the Eastern Province. Fourteen people are injured.

October 22, 2011: Crown Prince Sultan bin Abdul Aziz dies of colon cancer in the United States. Interior Minister in Charge of Internal Security Forces Prince Nayef replaces him.

November 24, 2011: In Qatif, clashes continue between police forces and Shia, leaving four dead.

December 16, 2011: One hundred women and several dozen men demonstrate in Riyadh and Burayda to call for the release of detainees. Security forces detain thirty-four women and several men.

December 23, 2011: Security forces arrest thirty men and thirty women for participating in silent protests in Riyadh to call for the release of controversial cleric Yusuf al-Ahmad.

Only the Shiites of the Eastern Province were continuing their protests. To appease the Shiite youth, the government counted on both the traditional Shiite elite that had worked with the royal family for decades and the Shirazi Islamist leaders who had struck a deal with the state in the mid-1990s. Statements were released by Shiite religious notables and Shirazi figures, including Hasan al-Saffar, calling for an end to the demonstrations. The government also made promises to free detained protesters and to improve the situation of the Kingdom's Shiites. This worked temporarily; by May 2011 protests had become rare. The truce did not last for long, however, and in October 2011, after an incident in which the fathers of two young Shiite activists were arrested, protests started happening again in an even more sustained fashion than before. The government response was brutal: Four protesters were killed by the end of 2011, and there were several other victims during the first months of 2012. On July 8, 2012, leading opposition sheikh Nimr al-Nimr was shot in the leg during his arrest by the Saudi police.

Conclusion

The Saudi regime has faced multiple political challenges since February 2011, not only from established domestic opposition figures but also from a new generation of activists in their twenties. They have revealed an increasing consensus among most political forces, Islamist and liberal, on the demand for an "Islamic constitutional monarchy" that is respectful of basic democratic principles. New issues have also been brought to the fore. The questions of human rights and fair treatment of political prisoners have, for instance, gained an unprecedented prominence in the discourse of the diverse segments of the opposition. More specific demands, such as the right for women to drive cars, have also gathered support among certain groups. Protesters continued to use public petitions, just as they had since the 1990s, but activists have increasingly advocated more radical means as well, including demonstrations—a practice that had been relatively uncommon in the Kingdom over the previous twenty years. In that sense, the events of 2011 and 2012 helped change political activism in the Kingdom.

Despite this, the Saudi government's traditional strategy of cooptation and fragmentation, in addition to repression, has allowed it to keep the opposition under control. That the regime could rely on its considerable material and symbolic resources undoubtedly contributed to the success of this strategy. The most spectacular challenge remains the continuing Shiite protests in the Eastern Province, which show the limit of the Saudi methods of social control: The

Shiites' feeling of relative deprivation has fueled their anger against the regime, and they possess both the mobilizing structures and the political culture necessary for a sustained protest. Yet, this does not represent a major risk for the government: Shiites constitute 10 percent of the population, and no united front with the Sunni opposition seems possible. Events in the Eastern Province will not turn into a countrywide revolution, but continued unrest there is likely.

However, in Najd, the "political center" of the Kingdom, the political momentum seems for the time being to be lost. In the current context of political apathy, the activists' greatest hope in the short term is that a split in the royal family could provide an opportunity for remobilization. The fact is that, after the death of Crown Prince Nayef in June 2012, only a handful of influential first-generation princes remain. A transition to the next generation of princes will eventually be necessary, which could lead to infighting and—some hope—the rise of a "reformist" wing whose figures would seek the support of civil society in order to prevail in the family, just like King Saud and Prince Faisal had done in the late 1950s.

For Saudi prodemocracy activists, the picture these days does look grim. Yet the rise of a new generation with greater political awareness and a willingness to use new and daring forms of activism should in itself offer them hope. It is true that the regime's recipes for social control have until now worked quite well, but the same recipes may not work forever, especially as the regime may not always have the same amount of resources at its disposal.

Notes

1. David Commins, *The Wahhabi Mission and Saudi Arabia* (London: I.B. Tauris, 2006).

2. Laurence Louër, *Transnational Shia Politics: Religious and Political Networks in the Gulf* (New York: Columbia University Press, 2008), 120.

3. Toby Jones, "Rebellion on the Saudi Periphery: Modernity, Marginalization, and the Shi'a Uprising of 1979," *International Journal of Middle East Studies* 38(2) (2006): 213–233.

4. Many of those Islamist activists were fleeing the persecution of secular and nationalist Arab regimes. In the context of what became known as the "Arab cold war," Saudi Arabia was the main regional rival of those regimes.

5. One prominent Sahwi book on this issue is Muhammad Surur Zayn al-'Abidin, *Wa ja' dawr al-majus* (Here come the Zoroastrians), which was published in 1984. In it, Zayn al-'Abidin explains that the Iranian Revolution is nothing but the starting point for a strategy of Shiite domination of the Middle East.

6. For an account of this, see Stéphane Lacroix, *Awakening Islam: The Politics of Religious Dissent in Contemporary Saudi Arabia* (Cambridge, MA: Harvard University Press, 2011), 129–200.

7. A Saudi intellectual, interview with the author, Riyadh, February 2005.

8. Stéphane Lacroix and Thomas Hegghammer, "Saudi Arabia Backgrounder: Who Are the Islamists?" *International Crisis Group Middle East Report* no. 31, September 21, 2004.

9. Lacroix, *Awakening Islam*, 122–129.

10. Lacroix, *Awakening Islam*, 211–221.

11. Muhammad Qutb, *Jahiliyyat al-qarn al-'ishrin* [The Jahiliyya of the twentieth century] (Cairo: Dar al-Shuruq, 1995). In Arabic, *Jahiliyya* refers to the "days of ignorance" that preceded the advent of Islam.

12. Stéphane Lacroix, "Understanding Stability and Dissent in Saudi Arabia: The Double-Edged Nature of the Jama'at in Saudi Politics," in *Complexity and Change in Saudi Arabia,* ed. Bernard Haykel, Thomas Hegghammer, and Stéphane Lacroix (Cambridge, U.K.: Cambridge University Press, forthcoming).

13. Lacroix, *Awakening Islam*, 228–229.

14. Stéphane Lacroix, "Saudi Islamists and the Potential for Protest," *Foreign Policy,* June 2, 2011, available at http://mideast.foreignpolicy.com/posts/2011/06/02/saudi_islamists_and_the_potential_for_protest, accessed August 3, 2013.

15. Toby Matthiesen, "Hizbullah al-Hijaz: A History of the Most Radical Saudi Shi'a Opposition Group," *The Middle East* 64 (2) (2010).

16. Louër, *Transnational Shia Politics,* 120. On this transformation, see also Fouad Ibrahim, *The Shi'is of Saudi Arabia* (London: Saqi Books, 2007).

17. Ghazi al-Qusaybi, *Hatta la takun fitna* [Until there is no more *fitna*] (1991).

18. The medieval scholar Ahmad Taqi al-Din Ibn Taymiyya (1263–1328) was Muhammad 'Abd al-Wahhab's main inspiration. He is considered a dominant authority in Salafism.

19. On this group, see Stéphane Lacroix, "Between Islamists and Liberals: Saudi Arabia's New Islamo-Liberal Reformists," *Middle East Journal* 58(3) (2004): 345–365.

20. The Saudi Civil and Political Rights Association's website can be found at http://acpra.me/.

21. The Islamic Umma Party's website can be found at www.islamicommaparty.com.

22. Abd al-Aziz al-Wuhaybi, interview with the author, Riyadh, November 2005.

23. Hakim al-Mutayri, *Al-hurriya aw al-tawfan* (al-mu'assasa al-'arabiyya li-l-dirasat wa-l-nashr, 2008).

24. *I'lan watani li-l-islah*, www.saudireform.com.

25. *Nahwa dawlat al-huquq wa-l-mu'assasat*, www.dawlaty.info.

26. Young activists close to the Saudi Muslim Brotherhood, online interviews with the author, Spring 2011.

27. On al-Ahmari, see Saud al-Sarhan, "The Neo-Reformists: A New Democratic Islamic Discourse," Middle East Institute, October 1, 2009, available at www.mei.edu/content/neo-reformists-new-democratic-islamic-discourse, accessed August 3, 2013.

28. Young activist interviews, Spring 2011.

29. Young activists close to the drafters of the petition, online interviews with the author, Spring 2011.

30. *Bayan da'wa li-l-islah*, available at www.islamlight.net/index.php?option=content&task=view&id=21468&Itemid=33, accessed August 3, 2013.

31. "Detainees Disappear into Black Hole of Saudi Jails," Reuters, available at www.reuters.com/article/2011/08/25/us-saudi-detainees-idUSTRE77O34O20110825, accessed August 30, 2013.

32. See, for instance, www.youtube.com/watch?v=L5Z-ybZTK-Q, accessed August 3, 2013.

33. See, for instance, Ibrahim al-Sikran's speech, available at www.youtube.com/watch?v=ni2oqCVOcUs; Yusuf al-Ahmad's speech, available at www.youtube.com/watch?v=TLPcUJn_ioc, both accessed August 3, 2013.

34. See www.facebook.com/ksa1Freedom1day.

35. For Nasir al-'Umar's speech, see www.youtube.com/watch?v=qB5I5Vo99BI, accessed August 30, 2013.

36. On these developments, see Stéphane Lacroix, "Comparing the Arab Revolts: Is Saudi Arabia Immune?" *Journal of Democracy* 22(4) (2011): 48–59.

37. On those arguments, see Madawi al-Rasheed, "Sectarianism as Counter-Revolution: Saudi Responses to the Arab Spring," *Studies in Ethnicity and Nationalism* 11(3) (2011): 520–522.

38. An exception was the petition published early December 2011 criticizing the Saudi government's heavy-handed response to protests in the Eastern Province. In addition to a majority of Shiite figures, there were a small number of Sunni signatories, all liberals; the most prominent was arguably Muhammad Sa'id Tayyib, a veteran reformist and former Nasserist from Jeddah. See http://mstayeb.com/index.php?option=com_content&view=article&id=259:bayan&catid=20:isla7&Itemid=5, accessed September 8, 2013.

39. See "Where Is Khaled? The English-Subtitled Interview," available at www.youtube.com/watch?v=mxinAxWxXo8, accessed August 3, 2013.

40. On the Shia protests, see Toby Matthiesen, "A 'Saudi Spring?': The Shi'a Protest Movement in the Eastern Province 2011–2012," *Middle East Journal* 66 (4) (2012): 628–659.

41. For a background analysis by a participant, see "Saudi Women Driving Movement," Saudiwoman's Weblog, June 29, 2011, available at http://saudiwoman

.wordpress.com/2011/06/29/saudi-women-driving-movement/, accessed August 3, 2013.

42. For instance, he wrote: "On your birthday, I shall not bow to you. I shall not kiss your hand. Rather, I shall shake it as equals do. . . . I will say that I have loved aspects of you, hated others, and could not understand many more. . . . I shall not pray for you."

43. In a recorded sermon that went viral on the internet, prominent Sahwi figure Nasir al-'Umar weeps before calling for Kashgari's execution. See www.youtube.com/watch?v=qB5I5V099BI, accessed August 3, 2013.

44. For instance, in a series of tweets and TV show appearances, Sahwi preacher Khadar bin Sanad, an associate of Safar al-Hawali, denounced the existence of what he called "an atheist cell" in Jeddah run by well-known liberal figures.

From Activism to Democracy

LARRY DIAMOND

THE TIMING OF this book is both propitious and awkward. The passage of more than two years since the eruption of the Arab Spring affords an opportunity to begin to take stock of the historic protests that have challenged regimes in at least half of the sixteen states of the Arab Middle East. We remain, however, at what will likely be seen historically as a very early point in the trajectory of political change throughout the region. By the beginning of 2013, protests had toppled four of the region's sixteen autocracies, but only in one case—Tunisia—had they given birth to a full electoral democracy (and a tentative one at that).

In the case of Egypt, which has seen the most extensive and sustained political protest over the last decade, unprecedented activist mobilization brought a swift and shocking conclusion to the twenty-nine-year reign of Hosni Mubarak and then the demise of his entire system of rule. Yet while the January 25 Revolution opened the doors of political power to a long-marginalized collective actor, the Muslim Brotherhood, that deeply contested experiment in democracy foundered on the rocks of extreme polarization and distrust between different social and political actors, violations of democratic norms and principles by both President Mohammed Morsi and his opponents, and the determination of the Egyptian military to preserve its power and privileges. The July 2013 military coup that overthrew the Morsi government confirmed as much as it engineered the failure of Egypt's democratic experiment. And the bloody crackdown that followed—as well as the militant and uncompromising stance of the Brotherhood to the coup—appear to have set back Egyptian hopes for real democracy by many years, if not a generation.

Next to Tunisia, Libya has moved the furthest toward democracy, holding reasonably free and fair elections for the transitional General National Congress. But the country's emerging pluralist politics are outpacing the task of rebuilding a shattered state. With political order still (and, it appears, increasingly) undermined by the de facto authority of a welter of armed militias outside of state control, Libya remains a long way from democracy. Through combinations of peaceful and violent resistance and domestic and international pressure, Yemen achieved the ouster of President Ali Abdullah Saleh, whose more than thirty-three years in power exceeded even Mubarak's pharaonic reign. But as this book went to press, Yemen remained a deeply divided society along political, tribal, and sectarian lines, leaving the National Dialogue Conference struggling against steep odds to identify a viable constitutional formula for a future democracy.

All of these four regimes were republics. So far, not a single contemporary Arab monarchy has fallen. But as the chapters in this volume make clear, several Arab monarchies are under serious stress, and there are strong societal aspirations in Jordan, Morocco, Bahrain, and Kuwait for a transition to constitutional monarchy—in other words, democracy. These have not yet reached the scale and coherence necessary to compel reform or impose transformation, save Bahrain, where authoritarian monarchy was preserved only by the external intervention of Saudi Arabia and the Gulf Cooperation Council. But in each of these four cases, the ongoing churning of activist dissent and protest keeps the quest of democracy on the table. None of these monarchies can be stable until that question is explicitly addressed.

As the cases in this volume demonstrate, however, it is one thing for activists to protest and quite another for protest to give birth to democracy. We cannot neatly predict the likelihood of a democratic breakthrough based on the length and intensity of prior protests, or else Egypt and not Tunisia would have been the first of the Arab Spring countries to cross the threshold into electoral democracy. Neither is there a clear correlation with economic development, or we might have seen the Gulf monarchies democratizing first, and certainly we would not expect Yemen, the poorest of the sixteen countries, to be one of the furthest along toward pluralist (if not fully democratic) politics. If the sheer amount of street mobilization were the test, again Egypt would have gone the furthest—or Bahrain, if we were to weigh the percentage of a country's citizens who had taken to street activism to demand democratic change.

Clearly, other factors weigh heavily in determining how and whether political activism translates into democratic change. The purpose of this concluding chapter is to look beyond the crucible of grassroots activism to identify what those other factors are.

Activist Movements Must Organize to Be Effective

The Arab countries that have experienced the downfall of dictators remain in a transitional period. At most, there is a window of opportunity for democratic change—still a large window (as of this writing) in Tunisia, but the window may have shut for some time to come in Egypt. The Arab Spring protest movements have been calling for lasting democratic change as opposed to merely minor adjustments or piecemeal liberalization. The well-rehearsed repertoires of recalibration, or what Daniel Brumberg has called "tactical liberalization," are not likely to be effective anymore. The demographic development in the Middle East—extremely young populations with high youth unemployment—helps to feed this impatience. But so do the experiences of decades of false promises and the growing access to information on the part of youthful Arab populations. Despite all of these developments there is still a lot of variation in what movements are demanding, what they can reasonably be expected to achieve, and how democracy might unfold in different countries.

It is important to distinguish the study of activist movements from the study of democratic change. Democratic change cannot be brought about by activism and grassroots protests alone. Protests can undermine dictatorship, but in themselves, they cannot create democracy. Democratization requires organization and strategy, but this insight stands in tension with the youth-dominated protest movements in Egypt and Morocco, which have rejected the hierarchies that come with organization. Viral videos and protests alone will not be able to confront the powerful interests of the incumbent regimes—whether the old regimes that remain in many authoritarian countries or the new authoritarian regimes that are emerging in countries like Egypt.

The Arab Spring has brought about an inspiring array of new forms of activism, but few activist movements have found ways of translating their activism into effective institutional and political change. That requires organizational capacity and the skillful aggregation of interests and national coalition building. These are the things political leaders—not least, political party leaders—build and do, but a notable feature of the Arab Spring, especially in Egypt and Libya, is the way that protests and resistance have leveled old political parties and organizational hierarchies without establishing broadly supported and effective new ones in their place. As a result, the activists who brought down the Mubarak regime found themselves outmaneuvered by better-organized—but not democratic—interests. The tables eventually turned not through democratic (and certainly not electoral) politics but only through the mobilization of massive new street demonstrations, with Egypt's military (no true friend of democracy) playing the decisive card to force the Muslim Brotherhood government out of power.

As Charles Tilly has stressed, there is an intimate relationship between mobilization and organization; mobilization for fundamental political and social change cannot be sustained without the unifying structure that comes with effective organization.[1] A Facebook network can mobilize street protests for days or weeks or months, but it cannot forge those protests into a disciplined and focused movement demanding change. Only organization—with some degree of clear leadership, authority, and command structure—can do that. The key to democratic change is the ability of protest leaders to make credible threats of mobilizing mass protests that will demand real institutional change and that can impose high (even paralyzing) costs on the regime if these expectations are not met. Protest movements need a political structure (or better, a coalition of parties and civil society organizations) that can generate such credible threats.

Unfortunately, as the chapters in this volume make clear, it is exceedingly difficult to convert a diffuse, grassroots protest movement into a coherent organization or political party or to forge a broad, effective organization out of protest in a way that is capable of sustaining anything close to the breadth of mobilization of the initial movement. Thus, the transition from social movement to institutionalized politics has been a difficult one for protest movements, especially youth-based protest movements, to negotiate. Structurally, these movements have drawn from diverse constituencies that do not want to be yoked to a single political or organizational leadership. Moreover, many of the youth who have grown accustomed to the flat, fluid, nonhierarchical world of social networks chafe at the idea of accepting the authority of new and somewhat bureaucratic formal organizations. And the moral fervor that brings committed people, especially young people, into the streets also makes them resistant to the compromises that must be made when challenging forces move from the streets into the arenas of electoral, bureaucratic, and legislative politics, or even into the more mundane work of ongoing civil society monitoring and lobbying. There is also the additional problem of the cultural gulf between urban and well-educated protest leaders, who are often secular and Western-oriented as well, and the rural and urban underclasses, many of them quite religious. The Muslim Brotherhood and its affiliates have had longstanding experience in serving and building bonds with these social groups and mobilizing them at election time. For the Facebook generation of protesters in many Arab countries, connecting with these socially conservative, lower-class constituencies requires a shift in tactics and mindset.

Democratic Change in Monarchies: Negotiated Transitions

In monarchies such as Jordan, Morocco, Bahrain, and Kuwait, the most likely path to sustainable democracy is a transition negotiated between the regime and the opposition. Such a transition would involve a bargain between the incumbent ruling elite and an organized protest movement. Such pacts are likely to be painful for both sides, as historical precedents in Latin America have shown, and will have to include contentious elements, such as amnesties for crimes committed by the incumbent regime and a tentative toleration of the continued concentration of economic power within the old elite. The activists' strategy may thus have to be to make such necessary concessions at first and then work through the newly established democratic processes to transform the remainders of the old order. The passage of time, generational changes, and continued societal pressures for reform and accountability will later help to move these countries from flawed to deeper and more authentic democracy, removing the "birth defects" that are common to negotiated transitions. But that is an agenda for down the historical road, often far down the road.

Monarchs in the countries mentioned above fear that their national protest movements could get out of control and turn them into the next Mubarak or Nicolae Ceauşescu. Hardliners would be able to play on this fear to counsel the monarchs to hold to a hard line. But one need only examine the fates of Mubarak and Ceauşescu (or the Shah of Iran, for that matter) to realize that a steadfast resistance to negotiated reform can ultimately lead to catastrophe, while if authoritarian incumbents like F. W. de Klerk in South Africa or the Francoists in Spain (and behind them, the restored King of Spain) negotiate an exit, the loss of power does not bring with it the loss of everything. Only the fear of losing everything, together with pressure from international actors, will bring ruling monarchs to the negotiating table. The nature of protests since mid-December 2010 has been fluid, leaderless, fractionalized, and anti-hierarchical. The democracy movements, however, need the above-mentioned structures of political organization and authority to be able to apply this pressure on elites in a strategic and coordinated way.

Building a System of Mutual Security to Sustain Transitions

In both Tunisia and in Egypt, deep, polarizing political divisions must be attenuated if democracy is to be viable. There is a need in these two countries and in other emerging Arab democracies (present and future) for deliberate political steps by political elites to build what Robert Dahl has termed a "system of mutual security."[2] This requires a set of understandings, a "pact" among contending political forces to give each side the confidence that the other will play by the rules of a democratic game; that if its opponents gain power, they will not entrench themselves in power undemocratically; and that no political party or leader will seek to use or abuse political power to wipe out its opponents or to attack their most fundamental interests. The complete and total lack of any semblance of such mutual restraints and understandings fostered the political polarization and undemocratic acts that consumed the possibility for a transition to democracy in Egypt. A system of mutual security requires a protracted period of confidence building and ultimately a political culture of tolerance, restraint, and respect for democratic norms among contending political elites. All of this was missing in Egypt, and no significant section of Egypt's political elites and activists, Islamist or secular, had any plan or inclination to try to cultivate it.

The pact that is needed in the Arab Spring countries is not so much, or at least not simply, between the surviving elites of the old regime and the rising elites of the opposition but also, and very often especially so, an agreement between rival opposition forces. In all of these countries, a major cleavage among opposition forces is between secular and Islamist orientations, but each of these camps is also cleaved (among Islamists, for example between the Muslim Brotherhood parties and more puritanical Salafist forces). And as previously noted, Yemen also must manage a complex and volatile mix of other cleavages based on regional, tribal, and personal (factional) divisions. Whatever the basis of the cleavages, rival groups, deeply distrustful of one another and their respective intentions, need to forge compromises that restrain the exercise of power (by the winner of the next election) and ensure that political victory will be temporary, not permanent. These compromises must then be guaranteed by a constitution that constrains the abuse of power by a ruler or ruling party bent on hegemony and that enables competing political forces to put their trust in institutions, and through them, in one another. Tunisia is still struggling to achieve a constitutional bargain that will facilitate this. Despite the formidable obstacles, Yemen does have a serious (and reasonably though not adequately representative) dialogue process to try to craft the necessary constitutional compromises, plus the assistance of a United Nations advising mission that is seeking to facilitate agreement.

Leaders Must Condemn Use of Political Violence

Under circumstances of intense uncertainty, mutual distrust, and enmity, which often prevail in situations of political transition, democracy cannot wait for incremental progress. Elites must take deliberate efforts to forge a system of mutual security. Two types of efforts are crucial. One is to reach across the deep chasm of political and social division and distrust by seeking good-faith negotiations to share and restrain political power constitutionally. The second is to personally practice and promote among their followers rhetorical and behavioral restraint so that they do not demonize their opponents and clearly, unconditionally reject political violence as a means for achieving their aims. There is no greater danger to a democratic transition, or to democracy itself, than the willingness of significant political leaders and organizations to use, condone, tolerate, or cover up acts of political violence. When violence occurs, contending political forces must unite behind the principle that it is unacceptable, out of bounds, and therefore must be vigorously investigated, prosecuted, and deterred by the transitional state.[3]

This presents a particular problem for many of the Arab transitions. While Tunisia's transition was virtually free of violence, political violence has crept into politics in the form of assassinations of some prominent secular leaders. This has introduced a new element of fear and anxiety into the political equation. Of course, the situation is far worse in Libya, where authoritarianism fell ultimately not through peaceful political activism but through violent resistance; in Egypt, where the Brotherhood's use of intimidation and targeted violence and then the military's bloody August 2013 repression of Muslim Brotherhood protest camps have probably destroyed any chance of even partial accommodation that might have existed; and even more so in Syria, which has descended into a ghastly, grinding civil war. Unless political parties and movements can be pulled back from violent rhetoric and means toward negotiation and peaceful politics, the prospects for democracy are dismal.

Agreement on Rules of the Game Is Needed

If they are to be self-enforcing, political pacts require explicit guarantees of fairness in observing and enforcing the rules of the democratic game, and these must be embedded in the constitution, as implied above. As Dankwart Rustow stressed in one of the most important articles ever written about democratic transitions, it is not necessary for contending elites to be committed democrats in order to launch and sustain democracy. They need only recognize that it is in their mutual interest to confine their pursuit of power and advantage to democratic methods. If they do so, over time the system will become routinized. It will gain broad legitimacy as it is seen to work at least passably well for all concerned. Gradually the normative roots will develop, and democracy will become consolidated.[4]

As Guillermo O'Donnell and Philippe Schmitter stress, pacts may be political, with each side committing to restraint—in other words to underutilize its distinctive power.[5] And they may have social and economic aspects—agreeing to take certain issues off the table in order to reduce the stakes in political competition and to enable the accumulation of trust. But institutional designs—and thus constitutional arrangements—are often a key matter for negotiation. How can the political game be structured in order to reduce mutual insecurity and to give each group a stake—and a feeling of confidence—in the emerging democratic order?

The design of political institutions is a tricky business. There is no one constitutional formula that is right for all national and historical circumstances. What fits a country's needs is obviously a matter of judgment and certainly of political interest. And it may change over time. But there are certainly some institutional arrangements that are wrong for circumstances of intense political polarization and insecurity in societies that have yet to establish a strong democratic culture. At the top of the list to avoid is a majoritarian political system, which deliberately empowers an electoral majority—or even a plurality—with decisive power to govern unilaterally.

The first place to start to limit extreme—and undemocratic—majoritarianism and to build mutual confidence in the rules is with electoral administration itself. Here is a cardinal principle of democratic development, particularly where mutual security is weak or nonexistent: Elections must be administered by a neutral, professional, independent body, which is insulated from political control or interference and which welcomes domestic monitoring and international election observing. The failure of a transitional ruling party or powerful contending party to embrace this principle—and to take positive steps to facilitate it—is legitimate cause for worry about its intentions. Many attempts to inaugurate democracy fail from the start or founder early on because of the inability of the country or the unwillingness of key actors to establish an independent, capable, and neutral electoral management body. In the absence of this most basic task, the most basic function of democracy—to choose a national government and legislature through free and fair elections—descends into mutual suspicion, recriminations, and even violence.

Building Institutions with Integrity

The problem, of course, is that authoritarian regimes polarize and corrupt the societies they leave behind when they fall. Thus, it may not be easy to identify untainted individuals who command the respect and confidence of all major contenders for power. But if societies look honestly and openly, they can find them in civil society, the judiciary, and even the expatriate community. The most important electoral management positions are at the top, and international organizations like the UNDP, International IDEA, and the International Foundation for Electoral Systems, among others, stand ready to help with technical assistance and best practices if the political will is there.

Neutral and fair electoral administration reduces the stakes in political conflict by giving each political party or group confidence that its competitors will not use force or fraud to obtain power and that if they do attempt to do so, their efforts will come to nothing. But truly free and fair elections also require that related institutions of the state that may play a role in refereeing political competition and ensuring a rule of law—particularly the police and the judiciary—similarly become depoliticized.

This presents a dilemma in a transitional situation. On the one hand, these institutions may have been pillars of the old authoritarian order, and if there is not some vetting and replacement, the old order may seek to sabotage democracy and reassert itself or at least favor one group or another in the politics of the new era. However, vetting or lustration must proceed very carefully through every sector of the state. Too wide a purge risks creating (as it did in Iraq) a broad class of "losers" with a stake in sabotaging the new political order and also presents a challenge of how the new positions will be filled in a way that does not bias the state politically in new ways.

What is true for electoral administration is true more broadly for the judiciary, the police, and the civil service. The goal must be to seek a neutral, professional, depoliticized state that will implement the law and government policies without systematically favoring one party or another. This is a very tall order, but a consensual political pact can devise means by which recruitment, promotion, and termination in these institutions are managed by neutral or broadly based bodies and not by actors who represent the interests of one single political party or another. Once again, in the absence of mutual security, competing political parties may have good reason to fear that if "the other side" gets ahold of these appointment and control processes, it will use this power to stack the state, control the police, bias the judiciary, and thereby entrench itself in power. Delegating these recruitment functions to nonpartisan bodies is a way of achieving one of the most crucial goals of a political pact: to get all parties to commit to underutilize their power and put their faith in new and impartial institutions.

Let us now enlarge the concept of neutral referees. A reasonably independent and neutral electoral commission, police service commission, judicial service commission, and civil service commission are all manifestations of a larger principle of horizontal accountability.[6] All of these represent agencies of restraint, bodies that are capable of checking the power of the executive branch and potentially of one another. They are among the institutional means for building a rule of law, for ensuring that the laws will be impartially and fairly enforced and that no one will be advantaged or punished purely as a result of where they stand in the relations of political power.

Fear of Losing Everything Motivates Parties to Condone Political Violence

Furthermore, when there are independent institutions to constrain executive power, the stakes in political conflict are lowered, because losing an election does not mean losing everything. Those who win control of government are constrained in what they can do—by the constitution and the law.

It has been my experience in studying a wide range of new and emerging democracies that the deepest fear that drives competing parties to lawlessness and violence is not that they will lose an election but that in losing they will lose everything and thus be permanently shut out of power. Building a system of mutual security means reducing the stakes in political competition, and that means limiting how much power is at stake in an election.

Mutual security is not the only goal of institutional design. In a deeply divided society, there is a value not only to limiting the power of the "winners" of elections but also to enhancing the power of the losers through various consensual or power-sharing arrangements. But it is important to recall that different institutional choices fit together in intricate ways, that different societies have different needs and at different historical moments, and that there is a cost to diffusing and checking power too much—namely that government may be so hamstrung that it is not able to make any effective decisions at all.

In the Arab world, democracy is seeking to take root in formidably challenging circumstances. A third of all the democracies that have existed during the third wave of democratization have broken down, and the failure rate is much higher in countries that have not had a democracy in the modern era. Seek democracy in a deeply divided country, and the failure rate rises further.[7]

The transitional period, when the rules of the game are being written and the patterns of future political conduct are being forged, represents a priceless opportunity to begin to build a system of mutual security. It is an opportunity that may not come again for a long time and one that should not be missed. Activists have an important role to play in keeping the pressure on authoritarian elites—and subsequently on putatively democratic ones—to press for genuine democratic reforms. But in the end, activism from below cannot forge the agreements and design and implement the institutions that will transform popular aspirations for freedom and accountability into workable democratic bargains. That requires leadership from the top and a willingness of activists to adapt to changed circumstances. Many of those activists will need to move into the political party arena or to forge more formal and enduring organizations in civil society. Otherwise, the transition may implode, or they will be swept aside by political actors who recognize those imperatives but who may not share the democratic intentions of the activists who made the revolution.

Is the Arab Spring Over?

As this book goes to press, a pall has fallen over the Arab Spring. The hopes for democracy in Egypt have been crushed by violence, intolerance, extremism, and authoritarian intent at many points on the political spectrum. Syria is mired in a ghastly civil war, out of which many scenarios may be possible—including quite plausibly the survival of the Assad dictatorship—but the least likely one is a transition to democracy. Yemen's transition is threatened by the deep and multiple societal cleavages noted above and by the renewed activity of one of the most tenacious al-Qaeda cells in the world. One could go on and on about how grim the picture looks in late 2013, but even with these dire examples of crisis and failure, popular protests for freedom, justice, and accountability are unlikely to cease in the Arab world. Like people everywhere, Arab publics fear chaos and instability, but they are also tired of gross oppression and injustice, and they want a better life. The underlying conditions that sent Arab publics in so many countries into the streets beginning in December 2010 remain. So do the capacities of youthful and increasingly resourceful Arab civil societies to mobilize protest. A single success story could energize and give hope to the region, even as so much of it is slipping backwards into polarization and despair. This is why so much continues to ride on the outcome of Tunisia's experiment. There are still many dominos yet to fall among the corrupt and stagnant autocracies of the Arab world. If Tunisia is able to negotiate a path to viable democracy, they will fall more quickly and more democratically.

Notes

1. Charles Tilly, *From Mobilization to Revolution* (Reading, MA: Addison-Wesley, 1978).

2. Robert A. Dahl, *Polyarchy: Participation and Opposition* (New Haven: Yale University Press, 1971).

3. This is a fundamental point of Juan Linz's seminal work, *The Breakdown of Democratic Regimes: Crisis, Breakdown, and Reequilibration* (Baltimore: Johns Hopkins University Press, 1978).

4. Dankwart A. Rustow, "Transitions to Democracy: Toward a Dynamic Model," *Comparative Politics* 2(3) (1970): 337–363.

5. Guillermo O'Donnell and Philippe C. Schmitter, *Transitions from Authoritarian Rule: Tentative Conclusions about Uncertain Democracies* (Baltimore: Johns Hopkins University Press, 1986).

6. Andreas Schedler, Larry Diamond, and Marc F. Plattner, *The Self-Restraining State: Power and Accountability in New Democracies* (Boulder, CO: Lynne Rienner Publishers, 1999).

7. I present the evidence for this in Larry Diamond, *In Search of Democracy* (New York: Routledge, forthcoming).

HICHAM BEN ABDALLAH EL ALAOUI is a consulting professor at Stanford University's Center on Democracy, Development, and the Rule of Law and the founder of the Moulay Hicham Foundation for Social Science Research on North Africa and the Middle East.

AHMED BENCHEMSI is a Moroccan journalist and analyst. In 2011–2012 he was a visiting scholar at Stanford University's Center on Democracy, Development, and the Rule of Law. Before joining Stanford, he was the founder, publisher, and editor of Morocco's two bestselling news magazines *TelQuel* (French) and *Nichane* (Arabic). Ahmed has twice been awarded "Best Investigative Journalist in the Arab World" by the European Union (Brussels in 2004, Beirut in 2007). His writings have appeared in *The Journal of Democracy, Time, Newsweek, The Los Angeles Times, The Guardian, Le Monde,* and other publications. Ahmed has an MPhil in political science from Sciences Po (Paris) and an MA in Development Economics from the Sorbonne.

LIHI BEN SHITRIT is an assistant professor at the University of Georgia, Athens. She holds a PhD in political science from Yale University. Her research focuses on the intersection of religion and political activism in the Middle East, with particular attention to women's activism in religious-political movements. She has also worked extensively with civil society organizations and with the U.S. State Department on programs supporting democracy and peace-building in the Middle East. She has taught international relations, women and politics, and Middle East politics at DePaul University.

LARYSSA CHOMIAK is the director of the Centre d'Etudes Maghrébines in Tunis. She received her PhD in political science in August 2011, which was based on eighteen months of qualitative research in Tunisia and six months of comparative field work in Ukraine. She was a Fulbright scholar in Morocco in 2001 and 2002. She is currently working on a book about the politics of dissent in Ben Ali's Tunisia; portions of her work have appeared as journal articles in *Middle East Law and Governance, The Journal of North African Studies,* and *Middle East Report.*

JANINE A. CLARK is an associate professor in political science at the University of Guelph. She is the author of *Islam, Charity, and Activism: Middle-Class Networks and Social Welfare in Egypt, Jordan, and Yemen* (University Press of Indiana, 2004) and numerous articles on Islamism and civil society. Her current research is on decentralization and municipal politics.

LARRY DIAMOND is a senior fellow at the Hoover Institution and at the Freeman Spogli Institute for International Studies at Stanford University, where he also directs the Center on Democracy, Development, and the Rule of Law. He is a professor by courtesy of political science and sociology. He is the founding coeditor of the *Journal of Democracy* and also serves as senior consultant at (and was previously codirector of) the International Forum for Democratic Studies of the National Endowment for Democracy. His latest books are *The Spirit of Democracy: The Struggle to Build Free Societies throughout the World* (Times Books, 2008), and *Squandered Victory: The American Occupation and the Bungled Effort to Bring Democracy to Iraq* (Times Books, 2005).

GAMAL GASIM earned his Ph.D. in political science from Texas Tech University and is an assistant professor of Middle East studies and political science at Grand Valley State University. Before Grand Valley, he taught at Texas Tech, University of Wisconsin-Madison during the summers of 2006 and 2007, and at the University of Illinois at Urbana-Champaign and Beloit College during the summers of 2008 and 2009, respectively. His research interests include Islamic political parties, elections, Muslim Americans, and higher education in the Middle East. He has contributed articles to *Studies in Ethnicity and Nationalism, Politics and Religion, Electoral Studies, The Journal of Political Science Education,* and other journals.

SALAM KAWAKIBI is a researcher in political and international relations. He is a deputy director and research director at the Arab Reform Initiative. His main interests are media, civil society, international relations, and human rights in Arab countries. He also has written many articles on European and Arabic media and books.. Furthermore, he is President of Initiative for a new Syria association and board member of The Day After in Syria project. Kawakibi is formally educated in economics, international relations, international humanitarian law, international human rights, and political science.

LINA KHATIB is director of the Carnegie Middle East Center in Beirut. Previously she was the co-founding head of the Program on Arab Reform and Democracy at Stanford University's Center on Democracy, Development, and the Rule of Law. She has published widely on the intersections of political and social dynamics in the Middle East. Her books include *Image Politics in the Middle East: The Role of the Visual in Political Struggle* (I. B. Tauris, 2013) and *The Hizbullah Phenomenon: Politics and Communication* (co-authored with Dina Matar and Atef Alshaer, Hurst/Oxford University Press, 2014).

STÉPHANE LACROIX is an associate professor of political science at Sciences Po in Paris and a visiting researcher at the Centre d'Etudes et de Documentation Economiques, Juridiques et Sociales (CEDEJ) in Cairo. His research focuses on Islamic politics in Saudi Arabia and Egypt. His most recent books are *Awakening Islam: The Politics of Religious Dissent in Contemporary Saudi Arabia* (Harvard University Press, 2011) and, with Thomas Hegghammer, *The Meccan Rebellion* (Amal Press, 2011).

LAURENCE LOUËR is a research fellow at Sciences Po, the Center for International Studies and Research (CERI), and the National Center for Scientific Research (CNRS), in Paris. She is the editor in chief of the peer-reviewed quarterly French journal *Critique Internationale* and served as a permanent consultant for the Policy Planning Staff of the French Ministry of Foreign Affairs between 2004 and 2009. She specializes in identity politics in the Middle East. She is the author of *To Be an Arab in Israel* (Columbia University Press, 2007), *Transnational Shia Politics: Religious and Political Networks in the Gulf* (Columbia University Press, 2008), *Shiism and Politics in the Middle East* (Columbia University Press, 2012).

ELLEN LUST is an associate professor in the Department of Political Science and founding director of the Program on Governance and Local Development at Yale University. Her research focuses on the politics of authoritarianism and the prospects for development. Her publications include *Structuring Conflict in the Arab World: Incumbents, Opponents, and Institutions* (Cambridge University Press, 2005), *Political Participation in the Middle East* (Lynne Rienner, 2008; coedited with Saloua Zerhouni),

The Middle East (CQ Press, 2010, 2013), and *Governing Africa's Changing Societies* (Lynne Rienner, 2012; coedited with Stephen Ndegwa) as well as numerous articles and book chapters. She is a founding associate editor of the journal *Middle East Law and Governance* and has lived, studied, conducted research, and led student and alumni tours in Egypt, Israel, Jordan, Morocco, Palestine, Syria, and Tunisia.

RABAB EL-MAHDI is associate professor of political science at the American University in Cairo. She is the coeditor of *Egypt: The Moment of Change* (Zed Press, 2009). Her recent publications include *Empowered Participation or Political Manipulation? State, Civil Society, and Social Funds in Egypt and Bolivia* (Brill, 2011); "Orientalizing the Egyptian Revolution," in *Jadaliyya* (April 2011); "Labor Protests in Egypt: Causes and Meanings," in *Review of African Political Economy* (September 2011); and "Women in the Revolution," (coauthored with Lila Abu Lughod), in *Feminist Studies* (January 2012).

INTISSAR K. RAJABANY holds an MA in international relations theory from the University of Warwick. She has worked with the British Council and other local and international NGOs on programs that support advocacy and raise awareness in the Greater Middle East. She is involved in community service initiatives in Libya, including the Women4Libya campaign, and the Libya Women Economic Empowerment Project, and her main interests are human rights and women empowerment in governance. She has provided assistance to the Libyan interim government on establishing human resources best practices in the public sector and centers for civilian reintegration. In addition to being an ardent linguist, Intissar runs her own consultancy business specializing in the oil and gas sector in Libya.

WAEL SAWAH is a Syrian researcher on issues of civil society in Syria, author of a number of research papers in Arabic and English, and coauthor of a number of books in Arabic. He is a member of the annual Middle East Legal Studies Seminar (MELSS, Yale University); a founding member of the Syrian Center for Media and Freedom of Expression in Damascus; a founding member of the Syrian League for Citizenship; a founding member of the Arab Rationalists League in Paris; and editor of the Al-Awan Website for Laic Studies (www.alawan.org). Sawah is coauthor of "Issues of Secularism in the Levant" and "A Tale Entitled Syria" in Arabic; coauthor of "Le Printemps arab: un premier bilan" (Centre

Tricontinental, Belgium, 2012) in French; and a regular columnist for the *al-Hayat* newspaper. Sawah has also written dozens of papers and policy briefs in English and Arabic for international and regional institutions. In addition, Sawah has worked as a political analyst at the U.S. Embassy in Damascus.

MARY ANN TÉTREAULT is the Una Chapman Cox Distinguished Professor of International Affairs Emerita at Trinity University in San Antonio, Texas. Her publications include books and articles about democratization, social movements, gender, oil markets, war crimes, international political economy, world politics, and American foreign policy. Her regional focus is the Gulf with an emphasis on Kuwait, about which she has written many articles and two books. She is presently working on higher education policy and food security in the Gulf.

MOHAMMED YAGHI is a PhD candidate in political science at the University of Guelph. His thesis is on the structure of mobilization and democratization in Egypt, Tunisia, and Jordan. He is a columnist at the Palestinian *Al-Ayyam* newspaper and, between 2006 and 2009, was a Lafer International Fellow with the Washington Institute for Near East Policy, focusing on Palestinian politics. His publications include two book chapters on the Palestinian-Israeli Conflict, and op-ed articles for *Arab Insight Magazine, Carnegie, Project Syndicate,* and other journals.

Al-Qaeda in the Arabian Peninsula
(AQAP), viii, 135, 165, 306
Al-Qaeda in the Islamic Maghreb
(AQIM), 39, 200
al-Qasim, Abd al-Aziz, 307
al-Qattan, Manna', 303
Alqdah, Ghaith, 254, 266
al-Qusaybi, Ghazi, 307, 319
Al-Rai Center for Studies, 248
al-Rashudi, Sulayman, 308
Al-Sabah (clan), ix, 270, 271, 275, 285,
286, 290; al-Ahmad, Jaber (Shaikh),
272, 273, 275, 278, 283; al-Ahmad,
Sabah (Shaikh), 279, 283; al-Jaber,
Ahmad (Shaikh), 271; Jabir al-Mubarak
al-Hamad (Shaikh), 285
Al-Sabeen Square, 127, 128
al-Saffar, Hasan, 306, 317
al-Salim, Abdullah (Shaikh), 271, 272
al-Saqqaf, Abd al-Aziz, 119
Al Saud (clan): Abd al-Aziz (King), 300,
318; Abdullah bin Abd al-Aziz (King),
312, 315, 316; Fahd bin Abd al-Aziz
(King), 301, 306; Faisal bin Abd al-Aziz
(King), 300, 318; Nayef bin Abd al-Aziz
(Prince), 316, 318; Saud bin Abd
al-Aziz (King), 318
al-Sayf, Tawfiq, 299
al-Sharif, Manal, 314
al-Thawra (newspaper), 118
al-Turk, Riad, 145
al-'Umar, Nasir, 306, 312, 320, 321
al-Wa'd (National and Democratic Action
Society), 176, 177, 184
al-Wafa', 181, 183, 185, 187
al-Wafd, 6, 57
al-Wefaq, 7, 10, 173, 175–79, 181–84,
187–89, 191–97
al-Wuhaybi, Abd al-Aziz, 308, 319
Al-Yaseen, Majdi, 249, 257
al-Zindani, Abdul Majeed, 111, 113,
127, 131
Alternative Movement for Individual
Freedoms (MALI) (activist group), 206,
233
Amari, Kamal, 200
Amazigh, 213, 234. See also Berber;
Tamazight
Amine, Abdelhamid, 234

Amnesty International, 133, 277
an-Nahda, 25, 27, 39, 42, 43, 46, 48, 148
an-Nahj ad-Dimocrati (an-Nahj) (party),
203, 204, 211, 216, 224–27, 230, 232
Anti-Globalization Egyptian Group
(AGEG), 55
anti-glorification law, 99
antiwar movement, 54
April 6 Movement, 3, 5, 6, 9
April 6 textile strikes, 5
Arab League, viii, 92, 163–66
Arab nationalism, 174, 300
Arab nationalists, 137, 273
Arab Organization for Human Rights,
277
Arab Socialist Baath Party, 242
Aramco, 313
Arsalane, Fathallah, 229
ashaab yurid isqat an-nitham, 10
Ashid, 117, 118
authoritarianism, vii, 17–19, 50, 51, 74,
260, 261, 269, 294, 328, 337; regime
under, viii, 2, 4, 6, 7, 12, 16, 22, 85, 87,
186, 324, 330
Awadallah, Basim, 249

baath, ix, 138, 139, 159, 162, 242, 260,
300
Bab al-Azizia, 80
Bahrain Center for Human Rights
(BCHR), 184, 185
baltagia (Arabic term for regime thugs),
122, 221
bandargate, 178
Bani Sakhr, Salem, 251, 263
Bani Walid, 79, 94, 101
Basic People's Congresses, 78
Basists, or Qa'idiyin (political group),
227, 235
Bayda, 88
Beaugé, Florence, 235
Benchemsi, Ahmed, 199, 231, 234, 235
Benghazi, 76, 79, 80, 84, 86–88, 90, 91,
94–96, 100, 101, 103, 107
Benkirane, Abdelilah, 201, 228–30, 235
Berber, 210, 234. See also Amazigh;
Tamazight
bidun (stateless persons), 277, 284, 286,
291
Bin Talal, Basma (Princess), 257

Ghalioun, Burhan, 156, 164
Ghamian, Marwa, 168
Gharaibeh, Rheil, 252, 253, 261
Gharyan, 102
Ghoga, Abduk Hafiz, 88
Global Voices (website), 104, 106, 209
Google, 64, 209; Google Maps, 210
government-sanctioned, 24, 25
graffiti, 23, 81, 141, 143, 161
green book, 78
Green Movement, 19
Green Square, 88, 89, 105
Gulf Cooperation Council (GCC), ix, 12, 115, 116, 128, 173, 191, 194, 313, 323
Gulf Cooperation Council Initiative, 12, 124, 128, 129, 132
Gulf War, 54, 241, 305

Habashneh, Ali, 247, 260, 263–65
hadhar/badu, 274, 282, 292, 295, 296
Haj Saleh, Yaseen, 156, 169
Hamas, 148, 214, 243, 246, 252, 256, 261
Hanbalism, 300
harbash diwaniyya, 290
hardliners, 188, 194, 195, 239, 326
Hariri, Rafic, 140
Hashid, 110, 113
Hassan II of Morocco (King), 202, 205, 218
Hay al-Tafaileh, 245, 248, 263
hegemony, ix, 67, 154, 328
Hezbollah, ix, 120, 140, 194, 252, 306
Hezbollah al-Hijaz, 306
Higher Committee for the Coordination of National Opposition Parties (HCCNOP), 244, 252
Higher National Committee for Retired Military (HNCRM), 249, 264
Hijaz, 303, 307, 319
Hizb ut-Tahrir al-Islami, 145
HOOD (National Organization for Defending Rights and Freedoms), 119, 134
horizontal accountability, 331
Houthi, viii, 116, 120, 122, 128–30, 134
Hussain, Abdulwahab, 181
Hussein, Louay, 149
Hussein of Jordan (King), 242, 265
Hussein, Saddam, 136, 275, 301

Ibn Taymiyya, 307, 319
Idris I of Libya (King), 78
informal activism, 2–4, 6, 184
institutional designs, 329
International Center for Not-for-Profit Law (ICNL), 98
International Criminal Court, 42, 86, 100, 101
International Foundation for Electoral Systems (IFES), 330
International IDEA, 330
international intervention, 10, 12, 165
interpellation, 272, 283
invasion, 8, 11, 58, 61, 140, 214, 269, 296
Irada Square, 268, 288, 292
Iran, 20, 43, 94, 120, 129, 135, 165, 175, 182, 189, 194, 195, 273, 301, 306, 307, 312, 318, 326
Irbid, 241, 243, 244, 246, 251, 254, 256, 262
Irish Republican Army (IRA), 81
Islamic Action Society, 175, 177, 192, 197
Islamic Bahrain Freedom Movement, 176, 183
Islamic Front for the Liberation of Bahrain (IFLB), 174, 175, 177, 197
Islamic Umma Party, 308, 309, 311, 315, 319
Islamist group, 7, 9, 14, 19; in Egypt, 67; in Kuwait, 282; in Morocco, 201, 215, 231; in Saudi Arabia, 302; in Syria, 146, 148
Islamo-liberals, 308, 310
Ismaili Shiites, 300
Israeli attack on Gaza, 8
Israeli occupation, 55, 241, 252
Ittihadi National Congress, or CNI (party), 232

jama'at, 303, 305, 311, 319
Jamahiriya, 78, 103
January 14, 2011, Revolution, 22, 24, 25, 31, 35, 37, 40, 41, 45, 49
January 25 Revolution, 6, 8, 9, 52, 53, 57, 59, 60, 62, 63, 65, 69, 71, 208, 260, 264, 266, 322
Jasmine Revolution, 9, 13, 35. See also Tunisian Revolution
Jeddah, 275, 276, 313, 315, 316, 320, 321
Jimenez, Trinidad, 223

Jobless graduates (militant group), 230
Joint Meeting Parties, 14, 120, 124, 129, 133
Jordan National Congress Party, 258
Jordanian Social National Party, 258
Jordan's Chamber of Deputies, 240
judiciary, 26, 45, 120, 202, 210, 217, 287, 291, 330, 331
July 2013 military coup, 322
Justice and Development Party (PJD), xi, 14, 201, 202, 227–31

Kafr Nebel, 152
Kaladeh, Khalid, 255, 264
karama Friday, 123
Karman, Tawakkol, 6, 109, 124, 125, 132
Kashgari, Hamza, 314
Katiba al-Fadil, 88, 90
Kerak (Youth Movement), 241, 243–45, 254, 260–62, 264–66
Khaddam, Abdul Halim, 145, 147
Khomeini, Ruhollah (Ayatollah), 182, 306, 307
Kifaya, 3, 6, 9, 11, 53, 55–58, 64
Kurdistan, 146
Kurds, 14, 146, 161, 162
Kuwait Charter 2012, 290
Kuwait Oil Tanker Company, 277
Kuwait Towers, 288, 292
Kuwaiti Association to Defend War Victims, 276
Kuwaiti Overseas Student Union, 279
Kuwaiti Progressive Current, 291, 292

Laasri, Jamal, 215
Laasri, Khalid, 215, 222, 223
Latin America, 15, 21, 86, 105, 326
Law 49 (Syria), 137, 145
Lawyers for Justice in Libya, 95, 99, 106
Lebanon, 61, 120, 155, 214, 241
leftists: in Egypt, 54–56, 58; in Jordan, 252, 254, 265; in Kuwait, 270; in Morocco, 214, 250; in Saudi Arabia, 299; in Syria, 176; in Tunisia, 27
Le Monde (newspaper), 235, 335
liberalization, 47, 48, 55, 56, 61, 136, 175, 180, 184, 241, 243, 324; tactical, 324
Libya Alhurra TV, 92
Libya Outreach Group, 99
Libyan Civil Rights Lobby (LCRL), 99

Libyan Islamic Fighting Group (LIFG), 80, 100, 104
Libyan Women's Platform for Peace, 102
Likud Party, 241
Local Coordination Committees, 8, 169, 204, 218
Lockerbie bombing, 81

Maan, 241, 243, 244, 266
Madaba, 238, 243, 254, 261
Madkhalis, 303, 312
Mafraq, 239, 246, 263
Mahalla (El-Mahalla), 5, 53, 58, 59, 60
Majlis al-Umma (parliament), 272, 275, 285
Majlis al-Watani (unconstitutional assembly), 275
majoritarianism, 329
Mamfakinch.com or Mamfakinch (website), 209, 210
Mansur Hadi, Abd Rabbuh, 115, 116, 128
March 24 Sit-In, 254, 255
Maroc Hebdo (magazine), 235
Marrakech, 200, 213, 214, 227, 233, 234
martial law, 275
Matar, Ghayath, 153
Mecca, 303, 304, 337
Medina, 303, 304
Meftah, Mostafa, 234
memes, 289
Menouni, Abdeltif, 234
mercenaries, 93, 183
merchants, 159, 268, 270, 271, 273, 275
MI6, 82
middle class, 37, 47, 52, 57, 64, 65, 68, 133, 136, 138, 140, 174, 175, 206, 229, 275, 336
military intervention, viii, ix, 12, 156, 252
milk petition, 153
minorities, 136, 219
Mishref, 288
Misrata, 79, 83, 88, 91, 96, 100, 101
modernization, 46, 278, 295
Mohammed VI of Morocco (King), 199–201, 208, 216–18, 221, 228, 231, 232, 235
Monday diwaniyyas, 273, 275
Moroccan Association for Human Rights (AMDH) (activist group), 7, 203–9, 211, 216, 225–27, 230, 232, 234

Moroccan Committee to Support the
Masses (activist group), 211, 216
Moroccans Converse with the King
(Facebook group), 208
Morsi, Mohammed, 322
mothers, 6, 31, 86, 104, 280
Mouatana Movement, 149, 169
Movement for Justice and Development,
146, 168
Movement of April 15, 245
Movement of the Message, 300
Muasher, Marwan, 250, 264
Mubarak, Gamal, 55, 63
Mubarak, Hosni, 53, 63, 69, 83, 199, 322
Muhammad, Ali Nasir, 117, 122
mukhabarat, 243, 244, 252, 253, 255–57,
261, 266
Muqbil, Abbad, 119
Mushaima, Hasan, 177, 183, 190, 196
Muslim Brotherhood, 14, 326, 327; in
Bahrain, 177, 178, 179, 188, 189; in
Egypt, 53, 54, 57, 66, 68, 70, 72–74,
322, 325, 328; in Jordan, 238, 239,
242, 252, 254, 255; in Kuwait, 289,
290; in Libya, 80, 85, 99, 107; in Saudi
Arabia, 301, 303–5, 309, 320; in Syria,
138, 139, 145, 147, 148, 156, 157, 166,
168; in Yemen, 117, 129

Nabad Movement, 149
Nabbous, Mohammed, 92
Naciri, Khalid, 207
Nafusa Mountains, 88, 96
Najd, 273, 303, 304, 313, 318
Nantes (town in France), 209
Nasser, Gamal Abdel, 61, 133, 245, 246,
259, 272
Nasserites, 54, 56
National Action Charter, 176, 177, 179,
183, 185
National Bloc, 138
National Coordinating Committee
Against the High Cost of Living
(activist group), 204
National Coordination Commission
(NCC), 10, 156, 157, 166, 167
National Council for Support of the
Feb20 Movement, or Support Council
(activist group), 216, 217, 221, 224,
225, 227

National Democratic Party (NDP), 63, 69,
70, 75
National Democratic Rally, 157
National Dialogue Conference, 323
National Front for Reform, 253
National Front for the Salvation of Libya
(NFSL), 80, 99, 107
National Organization for Defending
Rights and Freedoms (HOOD), 119,
134
National Progressive Front, 138, 151
National Transitional Council (NTC), 76,
88, 90, 92, 96, 99–102, 107
National Unity Gathering (NUG), 188,
189, 198
nationalism (Arab). See Arab nationalism;
Arab nationalists
NATO, 84, 90, 93, 96, 97, 100, 101
Nawaat (website), 48, 209
neoliberal, 61, 62, 75, 141
newspaper, 32, 38, 99, 118, 119, 121,
263, 164, 165, 166, 284, 286, 302, 306,
339
Nichane (magazine), 234, 235
1952 Constitution Movement (Jordan),
245
nongovernmental organizations (NGOs),
13, 34, 73
nonmovement, 5, 18, 30, 140, 168
nonviolence, 9, 130, 136, 152, 153, 155,
158
Noss Noss (internet advocacy campaign),
210
November 2011 march (Kuwait), 287

Obama, Barack, 194, 198
Obeidat, Ahmad, 239, 250, 252, 253, 264
occupation (military), 275–77, 295, 336
October 18 Collectif, 19
Omar, Jarallah, 119, 120
Open Makhzen (internet advocacy
campaign), 210
Operation Mermaid Dawn, 96, 107
opportunity structure, 3, 4, 11, 18, 20, 87,
179–81, 188, 269; political, 3, 4, 11,
18, 20
orange movement, 280
Organization of the Islamic Revolution in
the Arabian Peninsula, 301, 306
organized protest movement, 17

Osama Munajed, 146
Oslo Accords, 241
Ottoman, 239, 270

Palestine, 11, 26, 29, 49, 54, 146, 214,
  241, 242, 260, 338
Palestine Liberation Organization (PLO),
  239, 240, 242
Palestinian Intifada, 11, 61, 68
Palestinian Second Intifada, 52–54, 241,
  243
Paris, 4, 18, 209, 335, 337
parliament, x; in Bahrain, 172, 174,
  176–79, 181–83, 188, 189, 193; in
  Egypt, 59, 68, 70; in Jordan, 236, 244,
  247, 251, 255–57, 264–66; in Kuwait,
  268, 270–76, 278–80, 282–87, 289–91,
  293, 296; in Morocco, 202, 203, 208,
  211, 216, 224, 228; in Saudi Arabia,
  307, 309; in Syria, 138, 139, 141; in
  Tunisia, 26; in Yemen, 110, 112, 113,
  118–20; speaker of, 41, 110, 118, 273,
  274, 282, 287, 289, 291; 1938–39
parliament (Kuwait), 270, 283; 1985
parliament (Kuwait), 273; 1992
parliament (Kuwait), 276; 2009
parliament (Kuwait), 285, 287, 288;
  2012D parliament (Kuwait), 289; 2012F
parliament (Kuwait), 287, 289, 290, 296
patriarchy, 278, 294
Parti Communiste des Ouvriers de Tunisie
  (PCOT), 25–29, 31, 32, 41
pearl roundabout, 172, 179, 188–91
Peninsula Shield, 173, 183, 194, 313
personal status law, 244
police violence, 25, 32, 48, 51
policy secretariat, 63, 75
Polisario Front (armed group), 233
political Islam, 44, 46, 80, 148, 177, 197,
  300
political liberties, 24, 33, 37, 38, 40
political mobilization, 4, 17, 123, 174,
  301
political prisoners, 9; in Bahrain, 190; in
  Libya, 76; in Morocco, 203, 210; in
  Saudi Arabia, 298, 310, 314, 317; in
  Syria, 146, 150, 161, 162, 164; in
  Tunisia, 24, 26, 28, 32
Popular Campaign for Change (Freedom
  Now), 55

Popular Committee to Support the
  Intifada (PCSI), 54, 55
Popular Gathering for Reform, 253
Posterous (website), 209
Press and Publication Law, 243
private space, 275, 306
privatization, 61, 204, 241, 242, 247, 249,
  250, 260, 278
prodemocracy movement, 52, 53, 55, 57,
  59, 60, 73, 209, 273, 276
propaganda, 51, 58, 93, 97, 195, 312
protected space, 274, 275, 295
protest politics, 269
public self-representation, 9
public space, ix, 25, 34, 61, 83, 276, 288
public sphere, 77, 102, 126, 132, 197,
  253, 278

Qabaleen, Majdi, 246, 262
Qaddafi, Aisha, 98
Qaddafi, Saif al-Islam, 98, 101
Qaddafi era/regime, viii, 12–14, 76, 80,
  90, 94, 96–98, 107, 141
Qaddafi International Foundation for
  Charity Associations, 97
qarqoubi (drug), 234
Qasem, Isa, 174
Qasem, Mohammed, 289
qat chew circles, 10
Qatar, 90, 100, 106, 148, 167, 294
Qatif, 315, 316
Qawma (used in Al Adl Wal Ihsan's
  political rhetoric), 222
Qutb, Muhammad, 304, 319
Qutb, Sayyid, 304

Rajab, Nabil, 184
Ramadan (month), 81, 164, 207, 224,
  233, 275
Rania (Queen), 249, 257
rapprochement, 78, 82, 85, 93, 183, 314
recalibration, 324
Redeyef (town in Tunisia), 22, 27–33, 35,
  36, 38, 40, 41, 44, 45, 49–51
Redha, Jasim, 179, 182
Refai, Samir, 244
referendum, 55, 63, 67, 71, 176, 200, 201,
  210, 221, 223, 228
religion, 75, 79, 139, 148, 149, 154, 287,
  294, 335, 336

rentierism, 180, 264, 268, 269, 271, 284, 293, 294

representation, 9, 67, 78, 102, 108, 122, 132, 159, 240, 251, 272, 282, 290

Responsibility to Protect (R2P), 93

Retired Military Committee, 249

revolutionary committees, 78

revolutionary infrastructure, 2

revolutionary socialists, 54, 57

Royal Armed Forces (Morocco), 202

Rsheid, Zaki Bani, 247, 255, 263, 265

Russia, 94, 152, 165

Sa'dah, 119, 120

Safat Square, 271, 283

Sahwa, 189, 299, 301–10, 312, 313

Said, Khaled, 64, 66; Facebook group of, 6, 58, 61, 64–66, 70

Salafist, 43, 44, 145, 327

Salé (town in Morocco), 210, 233

Saleh, Ali Abdallah, 6, 7, 12

Salman, Ali, 175, 194

Samiramis Conference, 149, 169

sanctions, 81, 82, 84, 91, 98, 104, 162, 163, 165, 167, 282

Sarkozy, Nicholas, 223

satellite television, 88

Saudi Civil and Political Rights Association, 308, 319

Saudi, Elham, 95, 106

Sebha, 96

second votes, 281

sectarian movements, 13, 14, 323; in Bahrain, 172–75, 178, 184, 185, 187, 189, 191, 196; in Egypt, 7, 53; in Kuwait, 282; in Libya, 94; in Morocco, 224; in Saudi Arabia, 300, 301, 311–13, 320; in Syria, ix, 136, 141, 146, 151, 152, 154, 161

secular movements, xii, 6, 9, 14, 326–28, 338; in Bahrain, 174, 176, 184; in Egypt, 53, 67; in Kuwait, 276; in Morocco, 205, 207, 217, 229–31; in Saudi Arabia, 300, 301, 310, 318; in Syria, 139, 145, 147, 150; in Tunisia, 43, 44, 46; in Yemen, 118

Seif, Riad, 145, 160

Seif Palace, 280

Senussi, Abdullah, 86, 101

shabeeha, 152, 153, 169

Shah of Iran, 326

Shaqran, Khaled, 248, 263

Sharaf, Faris, 250

Shbeilat, Laith, 239, 252, 253, 265

Shia, viii, 4, 14, 337; in Bahrain, 173–78, 181, 183, 189–91, 192, 194–97; in Kuwait, 271, 290, 291; in Saudi Arabia, 316, 318–20; in Yemen, 134

Shiite opposition, ix, 111, 279, 298–301, 304, 306, 307, 311–14, 317, 318, 320; and Twelver Shiites, 300. See also Zaidi

Shirazi (movement), 174, 300, 301, 306, 311, 317

Shurbaji, Yahiya, 153

Sidi Bouzid, 1, 22, 38, 40–43, 48

silmiyya, 9

Sirte, 80, 94, 101

Skype, 96, 142

social media, xi, 17, 23, 34, 35, 65, 68, 73, 92, 99, 123, 208, 249. See also Facebook; Twitter

social movement, xi, 2, 5, 16–18, 20, 21, 325, 339; in Egypt, 64; in Jordan, 261; in Kuwait, 294; in Libya, 105; in Morocco, 223; in Saudi Arabia, 301; in Tunisia, 29, 46, 49

social movement theorists/theory, 9, 17, 87

social networks, viii, 4, 18, 19, 325; in Bahrain, 185; in Egypt, 52, 66, 67; in Jordan, 247; in Libya, 82, 85, 92, 93, 95, 97, 105; in Morocco, 234; in Saudi Arabia, 310; in Tunisia, 32; tools of, 2

souk juma, 89

South Africa, 32, 326

Spain, 21, 45, 326

state security forces, 71, 277, 288

street demonstrations, 152, 283, 293, 325

student activists, 26, 32, 123, 124, 134

Sub-Saharan Africa, 15

Sufi, 79, 205, 300

Sukkar, Nabil, 170

Sunni, ix, 14; in Bahrain, 173–75, 177–79, 183, 184, 188–91, 193–97; in Kuwait, 271, 279, 285, 287, 289, 290; in Saudi Arabia, 299–304, 307, 309, 312, 314, 318, 320; in Syria, 136, 148, 154, 162, 169; in Yemen, 123, 134; Islamists, 14, 285, 287, 290, 302, 307

Sunni-Shia sectarianism, 14